OHIO

WILDLIFE ENCYCLOPEDIA

— AN ILLUSTRATED GUIDE TO —
BIRDS, FISH, MAMMALS, REPTILES, AND AMPHIBIANS

SCOTT SHUPE

Skyhorse Publishing

Skyhorse Publishing books may be purchased in bulk at special discounts for sales promotion, corporate gifts, fund-raising, or educational purposes. Special editions can also be created to specifications. For details, contact the Special Sales Department, Skyhorse Publishing, 307 West 36th Street, 11th Floor, New York, NY 10018 or info@skyhorsepublishing.com.

Skyhorse® and Skyhorse Publishing® are registered trademarks of Skyhorse Publishing, Inc.®, a Delaware corporation.

Visit our website at www.skyhorsepublishing.com.

10 9 8 7 6 5 4 3 2 1

Library of Congress Cataloging-in-Publication Data is available on file.

Cover design by Rain Saukas
Cover photos courtesy of James H. Harding, Phil Myers IV, Dave Speiser, Matthew R. Thomas, and Scott Shupe

Print: 978-1-5107-2883-7
eBook: 978-1-5107-2888-2

Printed in China

ACKNOWLEDGMENTS

The author gratefully acknowledges the following individuals who contributed to the completion of this book. In no particular order those individuals are:

Rob Mottice, Senior Aquarist at the Tennessee Aquarium in Chattanooga, TN, for help in identifying freshwater fish species photographed at that facility.

David Wilkins, Curator at the South Carolina Aquarium in Charleston, SC, for his help in identifying freshwater fish species photographed at his facility.

Larry Warner, North Carolina Aquarium on Roanoke Island, NC, for his help in identifying freshwater fish species photographed at his facility.

The staff of the North Carolina Aquarium at Pine Knoll Shores, NC, for help in identifying freshwater fish species photographed at that facility.

The staff at the Georgia Fish Center, for helping identify minnow species photographed at that facility.

The staff at the Texas Freshwater Fish Center, for help in identifiying minnow species photographed at that facility.

Dave Frymire, for helping the author secure herp specimens for photography and for allowing me to photograph several snake species in his possesion.

John R. MacGregor, KDFWR, for providing a number of amphibian and mammal photographs used in this book and for providing technical information and scientific advice regarding the reptiles and amphibians of Kentucky.

Matthew R. Thomas, KDFWR, for help in identifiying several species of darters and minnows photographed by the author for this book as well as for his technical advice and icthyological expertise; and for providing a large number of fish photographs used in the book.

Amy Berry, Clay Hill Memorial Forest and Nature Center, for providing fish and amphibian specimens for photography.

Dr. Gordon Weddle, Campbellsville University, for providing fish and amphibian specimens for photography.

Dr. Ritchard Kessler, Campbellsville University, for help collecting fish specimens for photography.

Jim Harrison and Kristin Wiley, of the Kentucky Reptile Zoo, for allowing the author to trap on their property mammal and fish specimens for photography.

Clinton Cunningham, for assistance in acquiring and photographing herpetology specimens.

Kathleen Mount, for assistance in acquiring and photographing herpetology specimens.

Judy Tipton, for alerting me to the presence of and allowing me to photograph nesting birds in her yard.

Tim Johnson, for helping secure lizard specimens for photography.

Matt Wagner and John Hardy, from the Mississippi Museum of Natural History, for helping to ID fishes photographed in aquariums at that facility.

Brainard Palmer-Ball, of the Kentucky Ornithological Society, for help identifying fall warblers photographed by the author for this book.

Barbara Graham, for taking the author spelunking in the sandstone caves of eastern Kentucky, searching for bats to photograph.

Candy McNamee, for guiding the author on a search for migratory birds along the Texas coast.

Karen Finch, for guiding the author in a search for migratory birds in south Florida.

Dr. Tim Spier, Murray State University, for his help in collecting fish specimens for photography.

Jennifer Rader, of the Kansas Department of Wildlife, Parks, and Tourism, for allowing me to photograph freshwater stream fishes at the Southeast Kansas Nature Center.

John Hewlett, who accompanied the author in the field and helped locate and collect fish and reptile specimens for photography.

James Kiser, for providing several photographs of Kentucky species.

Loren Taylor, KDFWR, for help in locating contributing bird photographers.

Kate Slankard, KDFWR, for her photo contribution and her help in locating contributing bird photographers.

Don Martin, of Don Martin Bird Photography, for contributing several of the more excellent bird photos in the book.

Don Brockmeir, for his photo contribution and also for allowing the author to use his photo blinds in his home state of Nebraska many years ago.

T. Travis Brown, for several photo contributions.

David Speiser, www.lilibirds.com, for several professional-quality bird photo contributions.

Jeffrey Offereman, for his photo contribution.

David Haggard, naturalist with Tennessee Department of Conservation, for his photo contribution of a rare blue morph Green Treefrog.

Kevin Lawson, for his photo contribution.

Phil Myers, University of Michigan, for contribution of several small mammal photos.

Konrad Schmidt, of North America Native Fish Association, for contributions of several fish photos.

Kris Light, for photo contribution.

Uland Thomas, for photo contribution.

Dave Neely, for photo contribution.

Sterling Daniels, TWRA Wildlife Biologist, for his photo contribution.

Brian Zimmerman, www.ZimmermansFish.com, for several fish photo contributions.

Cheryl Tanner, for her photo contribution.

And to any others whose names I forgot to include; my thanks—and my sincere apologies for inadverdantly omitting your name!

Last but certainly not least, I would like to thank my publisher, Jason Katzman of Skyhorse Publishing.

In our negotiations Jason has not only shown patience and a willingness to compromise, but also great faith in this author. He has also exhibited extraordinary entrepreneurial courage in taking on a huge project of which this book is but a first step.

Finally, this book is dedicated to the author's three sons, Haydn, Denham, and Kyle Shupe. Though now adults, as youngsters their keen eyes, youthful enthusiasm, and unflinching companionship were responsible for the author getting many of the photographs in this book. More importantly, their presence in this world has consistently provided this author with the motivation to repeatedly bite off more than I can chew.

PHOTO CREDITS

Most of the 648 wildlife photographs that appear in this book were taken by the author. However, most of the really good photographs were contributed by several other wildlife photographers from across the USA. Those individuals were critical to the completion of this book and their remarkable photographs add much to its content. The names of those additional photographers and the number of photos each contributed appear below.

Matthew R. Thomas—23

John R MacGregor—14

Don Martin Bird Photography—12

David Spieser www.lilibirds.com—12

Konrad Schmidt—11

Brian Zimmerman—10

James Kiser—3

Phil Myers—2

Jeff Poklen—2

Nate Tessler—2

Cheryl Tanner—1

Jeffrey Offermann—1

T.Travis Brown—1

Kate Slankard—1

Don Brockmeir—1

Sterling Daniels—1

Uland Thomas—1

Dave Frymire—1

Phil Myers, IV—1

Wayne T. Helfrich—1

James H. Harding—1

Tom Murray—1

Thanks also to many other photographers who offered their help but whose photographs I was not able to use due to redundancy or timing constraints. A complete list of photo credits appears in the back of this book.

TABLE OF CONTENTS

Ohio County Map

INTRODUCTION

Ohio's wildlife has always played an important role in the history of human beings inhabiting the state. Native Americans depended on birds, mammals, and fish for sustenance. Early Europeans hunted and trapped in the region both for food and for profit.

Although the state's wildlife is still an important resource for trappers, hunters, and fishermen, wildlife is also increasingly important for its intrinsic, aesthetic value. Though the age-old practice of hunting and fishing is the most obvious example of how wildlife can enrich our lives, for many Ohioans the opportunity to simply observe wildlife and experience nature also serves to enhance our existence.

In more recent history the pursuit of wildlife has evolved to encompass more benevolent activities such as bird watching, wildlife photography, etc. In fact, the numbers of Americans who enjoy these "non-consumptive" forms of wildlife related recreation today exceed the numbers of those who hunt and fish, and the range of wildlife-related interests and activities has broadened considerably. In addition to the previously mentioned bird watching and wildlife photography can be added the activities of herpetology enthusiasts (reptiles and amphibians), freshwater aquarists, and lepidopterists (moths and butterflies), to name a few.

With interest in wildlife and nature continuing to grow throughout Ohio, the need for a single, simple reference to the state's wildlife has become evident. There are available a number of excellent books that deal specifically with Ohio's birds, reptiles, mammals, fishes, etc., but there are none that combine all the state's wildlife into a comprehensive, encyclopedic reference. This volume is intended to fill that niche. It is hoped that this book will find favor with school librarians, life science teachers, students of field biology classes, and professional naturalists as well as with the general populace.

As might be expected with such a broad-spectrum publication, intimate details about the natural history of individual species is omitted in favor of format that provides more basic information. In this sense this volume is not intended for use as a professional reference, but instead as a handy, usable, layman's guide to the state's wildlife. For those who wish to explore the information regarding the state's wildlife more deeply, a list of references for each chapter appears in the back of the book and includes both print and reliable internet references.

Embracing the old adage that a picture is worth a thousand words, color photographs are used to depict and identify each species. Below each photograph is a table that provides basic information about the biology of each animal. This table includes a state map with a shaded area showing the species' presumed range in the state, as well as general information such as size, habitat, abundance, etc. The taxonomic classification of each species is also provided, with the animal's Class, Order, and Family appearing as a heading at the top of each page.

The range maps shown in this book are not intended to be regarded as a strictly accurate representation of the range of any given species. Indeed, the phrase "Presumed range in Ohio," which accompanies each species range map, should be literally interpreted. The ranges of many species in the state are often not well documented. The range maps for some species in this book may be regarded as at best an "educated guess." Furthermore, many wide-ranging species are restricted to regions of suitable habitat. Thus a lowland species like the Beaver, while found statewide, would not be expected to occur on the top of a mountain. Additionally, other species that may have once been found throughout a large geographic area may now have disappeared from much of their former range.

The compilation of species range maps is always a challenging endeavor. That challenge is further complicated by the fact that animals like birds and bats, possessed with the ability of flight, are capable of traveling great distances. Many species of both birds and bats are migratory and regularly travel hundreds or even thousands of miles annually. It is not uncommon for these migratory species to sometimes appear in areas where they are not typically found. The mechanisms of migration and dispersal of many animals is still a bit of a mystery and the exact reason why a bird from another portion of the country (or even from another continent) should suddenly appear where it doesn't belong is often speculation. Sometimes these appearances may represent individuals that are simply wandering. Other times it can be a single bird or an entire flock that has been blown off course by a powerful storm or become otherwise lost and disoriented. Whatever the cause, there are many bird species that have been recorded in the state that are not really a part of Ohio's native bird fauna, and their occasional sightings are regarded as "accidental."

On the other hand, some species like the Gyrfalcon or the Scissor-tailed Flycatcher may appear somewhere in the state once every few years dependent upon weather conditions or availability of prey in its normal habitat. Although these types of "casual species" could be regarded as belonging among Ohio's native bird fauna, their occurance in the state is so sporadic and unpredictable that deciding which species should be included as a native becomes very subjective. The point is that the reader should be advised that while all the bird species depicted in this volume can be considered to be members of the state's indigenous fauna, *not every bird species that has been seen or recorded in Ohio is depicted in this book.* However, the reader can be assured that if a species is widespread, common, or otherwise likely to be encountered or observed, that species has been included in this book; as have *most* of the rarer and less likely to be seen species.

For readers who wish to delve into more professional and detailed information about the vertebrate zoology of Ohio, the list of references shown for each chapter in the back of this book should adequately provide that opportunity.

Scott Shupe, 2017

CHAPTER 1

THE FACE OF THE LAND

—THE NATURAL REGIONS OF OHIO—

Defining and understanding the natural regions of Ohio is the first step in understanding the natural history of the state. Man-made political boundaries such as county lines and state borders are meaningless to wildlife, whereas mountains, rivers, or lakes can be important elements in influencing the distribution of the state's wildlife.

The major considerations used in determining and delineating natural regions are such factors such as elevation, relief (topography), drainages, geology, and climate. All these are important elements that can determine the limits of distribution for living organisms. It follows then that some knowledge of these factors is essential when involved in the study of the state's natural history.

The study of natural regions is known as *Physiography*, which means "physical geography" or literally "the face of the land." While the terms geography and physiography are closely related and sometimes used interchangeably, geography is a broader term which includes such things as human culture, resource use, and man's impact on the land, while physiography deals only with elements of geography created by nature.

The term used to define a major natural region is *"physiographic division."* Physiographic divisions are subdivided into smaller units called *"physiographic provinces."* There are several major physiographic divisions across the United States and Canada, and portions of two affect the state of Ohio. The two major physiographic divisions of Ohio are the *Appalachian Highlands Division* and the *Interior Plains Division.* See Figure 1 on the following page.

The Appalachian Highlands Division occupies eastern portion of the state. Just to the west of the Appalachian Highlands Division the Interior Plains Division covers the rest of Ohio. Elevation and topography are the major defining characters of the two main provinces affecting Ohio. Generally speaking the higher elevations and most pronounced relief occurs in the Appalachian Highlands Division, but interestingly, the highest elevation in the state occurs in the relatively flat Interior Plains Division.

A unique geological feature known as "Campbell's Hill" rises to over 1500 feet above the surrounding plains. This unique feature was formed by glacial activity.

Each of Ohio's two major physiographic divisons are futher divided into smaller divisions known as *"physiographic provinces,"* which are then divided again into even smaller *"physiographic sections."*

Figure 1 on the following page is map of the eastern United States showing where the major physiographic divisions of the eastern half of the country occur. Figure 2 on the next page shows how these major divisions are divided into physiographic provinces. Figure 3 shows how those provinces are then subdivided into their respective physiographic sections.

Some appreciation of these various divisions is helpful when it comes to discussing the distribution of some of the vertebrate species of Ohio. Many species may occur in only a few of the regions defined by the maps on the following page. Some may even be found in only one (or even a portion of one) of these regions.

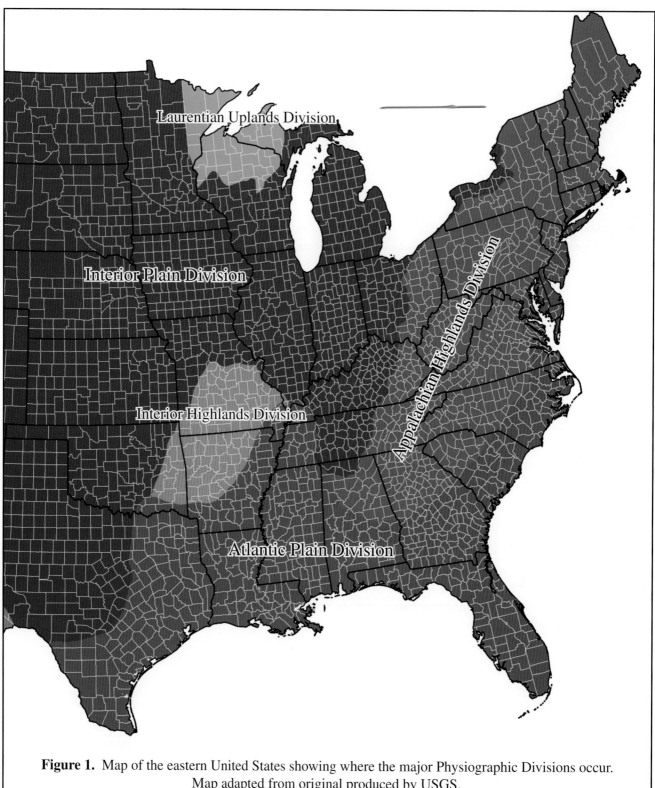

Figure 1. Map of the eastern United States showing where the major Physiographic Divisions occur. Map adapted from original produced by USGS.

Two of the major physiographic divisions shown on the map above occur within the borders of Ohio. The **Interior Plains Division** and the **Appalachian Highlands Division**.

Figure 2 on the following page shows how each of these divisions are subdivided into smaller *Physiographic Provinces*.

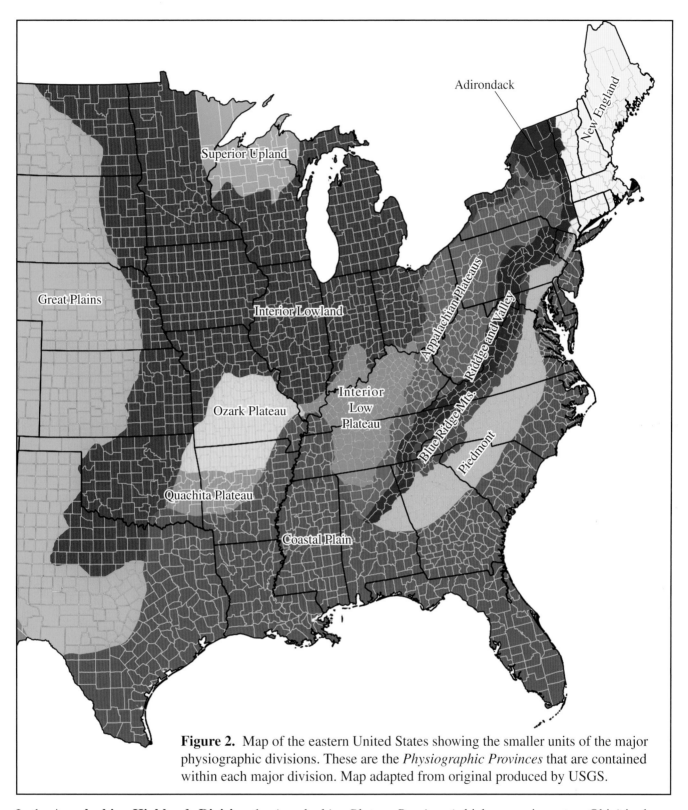

Figure 2. Map of the eastern United States showing the smaller units of the major physiographic divisions. These are the *Physiographic Provinces* that are contained within each major division. Map adapted from original produced by USGS.

In the **Appalachian Highlands Division** the *Appalachian Plateau Province (*which occurs in eastern Ohio) is shown on the map above in bright green.

In extreme southeastern Ohio the portion of the **Interior Lowlands Division** known as the *Interior Low Plateau Province* invades the state from Kentucky to south. This province is shown in purple.

The portion of the **Interior Plains Division** that occurs in Ohio is the *Interior Lowland Province* (dark purple). It constitutes most of the western half of the state.

The provinces shown in Figure 2 can be further divided into *Physiographic Sections,* which are then further divided into regions. The sections and regions affecting Ohio are shown on the map below (Figure 3).

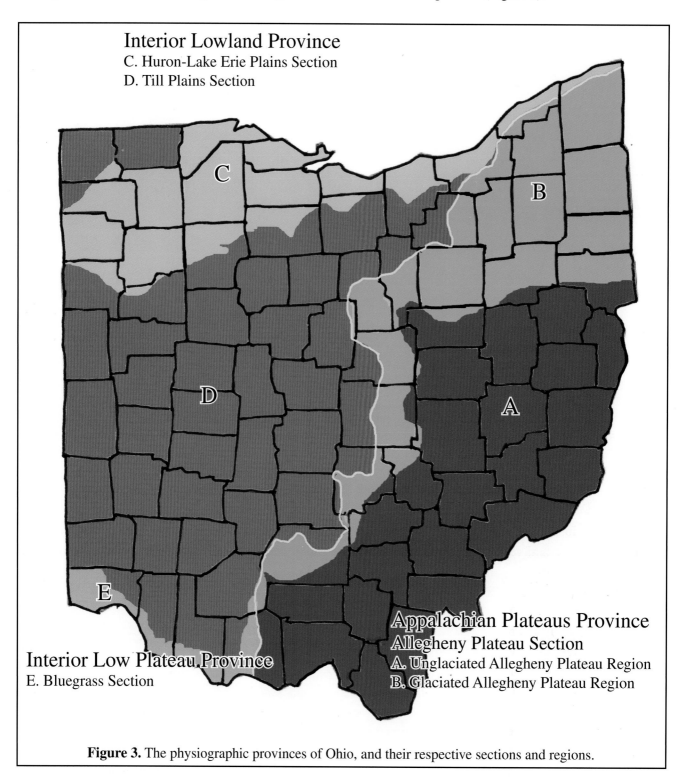

Figure 3. The physiographic provinces of Ohio, and their respective sections and regions.

The bright yellow line on the map above is the Allegheny Escarpment, which is the demarcation between the Interior Plains Division and the Appalachian Provinces Division. All of Ohio *except* the area in dark green (A. Unglaciated Allegheny Plateau) was once impacted by glaciers. These regions of the state are often referred to as "Glaciated Ohio." Likewise, the area in dark green (A.) is often called "Unglaciated Ohio."

Table 1 below provides another reference for the discussion of the physiographic divisions affecting Ohio and their respective provinces. It should be noted that most of the provinces of the major divisions can also occur outside the boundaries of the state of Ohio. Those provinces that occur in the state of Ohio are shaded. Table 2 shows how the different provinces of Ohio are subdivided into sections.

Table 1. The Provinces of the Major Physiographic Divisions of Ohio. Provinces occuring in Ohio are shaded.

Appalachian Highlands Division					
Peidmont Plateau P.	Blue Ridge P.	Valley and Ridge P.	New England P.	Adirondack P.	Appalachian Plateau P.
Interior Plains Division					
Interior Lowland Province			Great Plains Province		
Interior Highlands Division					
Central Lowland Province		Ozark Plateau Province		Quachita Plateau Province	

Each of the physiograpic provinces in Ohio can be subdivided into several smaller units, called *Physiographic Sections* (or natural regions). Table 2 below shows how physiographic provinces in Ohio are subdivided into sections.

Table 2. The Sections and Regions of the Physiographic Provinces of Ohio.

Appalachian Plateau Province	
Allegheny Plateau Section	
Glaciated Allegheny Plateau Region	Unglaciated Allegheny Plateau Region
Interior Lowland Province	
Till Plain Section	Huron—Lake Erie Plains Section
Interior Low Plateaus Province	
Bluegrass Section	

A written description of each of Ohio's physiographic provinces and the natural regions contained within those provinces is as follows:

The Appalachian Plateau Province

The Appalachian Plateau Province is a subdivision of the Appalachian Highlands Division (Figure 1). This is a region of older mountains that have been heavily eroded over time to produce a high plateau region that is moderately to highly dissected by rivers and streams. The entire region extends from northern Alabama to central New York. Elevations in Ohio are lower and relief is much less pronounced in comparison to the Appalachian Plateau in other nearby states. Historically this region was nearly completely covered in mature forests. The area is still the most heavily wooded region of Ohio and most of the state's remaining forests occur here. In Ohio the Appalachian Plateau Province is represented by a smaller subdivision (physiograpic section) known as the *Allegheny Plateau*. The Allegheny Plateau is divided into two smaller physiographic regions, the *Allegheny Plateaus region* and the *Glaciated Allegheny Plateaus region*.

A brief description of these two regions follows:

Glaciated Allegheny Plateau

This region of the Allegheny Plateau has been impacted significantly by glaciers in its geologic history.

Glaciers can act like giant bulldozers ond the land and tend to level everything in their path. Thus this region, despite being part of the Appalachian uplift, shows fewer hills and uplands and less relief than the related Unglaciated Allegheny Plateau region. Some of the hills and ridges in the region are glacial deposits of sand and gravel known as "kames."

Unglaciated Allegheny Plateau
This region is an uplifted plateau that shows considerable relief due to erosional action and it can be quite rugged in some areas of southeastern Ohio. While many people would consider this to be a mountainous region, these are not true mountains in the sense that there is no uplifted folds of the earth's crust, such as may be seen in other parts of the Appalachian Highlands or in the Rocky Mountain region. Likewise, the elevation here is not as high as would be seen in true mountains. The highest points on this plateau are typically only about 1200 feet above sea level.

The Interior Lowland Province
The Interior Lowland Province is a vast area of geologically stable bedrocks. Here the earth's crust has been little affected by the forces of plate tectonics that uplift mountains and plateaus. Most of the area is a relatively flat plain and where this province affects the midwestern US it has been subjected to the impacts of glaciation. Relief here is slight to moderate and usually associated with the actions of rivers and streams, although in Ohio glacial deposits of sand and gravel have also contributed to the region's topography. This province is subdivided into two sections. A brief description of those sections is as follows.

Huron-Lake Erie Plains
This excepitonally flat region of the Interior Lowlands was once covered by water in a massive freshwater lake (Lake Maumee) that was continuous with what is now Lake Erie. At the end of the last ice age the lake shrank to its present size and the former lake bottom became the Huron-Lake Erie Plain. Remnants of the old lake shoreline now form one of Ohio's most unique

ecological regions known as "Oak Openings." Much of the rest of the region was historically wetland, including an area known as "the Great Black Swamp." A few ecologically important wetland areas still remain in the region.

Till Plains
The Till Plains constitutes a large area of gently rolling plains in the western and central portions of Ohio. The region owes its topography to glacial activity, with long, gently sloping hills and ridges being formed from glacial moraine. The fertile soils of the region are highly suited to agriculture and today most of the rural areas in the region are farmlands. This region once contained large swaths of native tallgrass prairies with decidous woodlands dominating river valleys. Strangely, the highest point in the state (Campbell's Hill-Elevation 1,549 feet) occurs in the Till Plains near the border with Indiana.

The Interior Low Plateau Province
This area is a low, dissected plateau with lower elevations and less relief than what is seen in the much higher Appalachian Plateau Province. Most of the Interior Low Plateau is located in central Kentucky and in middle Tennessee, but the province extends from northern Alabama to southern Indiana and a tiny portion of southern Illinois and southeasternmost Ohio. Most is under 1,000 feet above sea level, and some areas are less than 500 feet in elevation. It is essentially an area of rolling landscape well dissected by numerous rivers and streams that create areas of moderate relief. The region once contained extensive forests, grasslands, and wetlands, but today is mostly agriculture or urban. The Interior Low Plateau is subdivided further into three sections, one of which, the Bluegrass Section, extends northward from Kentucky into southeastern Ohio.

The Bluegrass
In Ohio the Bluegrass region consists of rather flattened hills and uplands deeply dissected by streams. The substrate is mostly limestone, dolomite, and shale. The topography ranges from gently sloping to cliffs.

Glaciated and Unglaciated Ohio

In the state of Ohio, the history of the state's climate has played and important role in both the state's topography and in differentiating natural regions. Within the relatively recent geological history of Ohio (beginning about one and half million years ago and ending only a few tens of thousands of years ago), much of the state of Ohio (and most of the northern half of North America) was covered by immense glaciers. These glaciation events impacted so significantly upon the landscape of the region that naturalists today sometimes regard Ohio as almost being two different states, "glaciated" and "unglaciated" Ohio. The map below shows how the state of Ohio is divided into "Glaciated" and "Unglaciated" regions.

Figure 4. The regions on the map above are repeatedly referred to throughout this book. Becoming familiar with this and other maps shown in this chapter should prove useful the reader to obtain a better understanding of the distribution and natural history of many of Ohio's vertebrate wildlife species.

CHAPTER 2
ECOREGIONS AND WILDLIFE HABITATS OF OHIO

—PART 1: ECOREGIONS—

First, it should be noted that in ecology, as in the study of most other scientific disciplines, different opinions exist among experts as to the definition of a particular habitat or ecoregion (such as types of forests). Man's understanding of the earth's ecology continues to evolve and not every ecologist adopts the same model or criteria in describing habitats and ecosystems. Moreover, different models may be used by different researchers based on the needs of that research. The ecological model adopted here is derived from the Ecoregions used by the Environmental Protection Agency (www.epa.gov/wed/ecoregions).

The Environmental Protection Agency recognizes a total of fourteen "Level I Ecoregions" in the US and Canada. Each of these Level I Ecoregions consists of several progressively smaller divisions, known respectively as Level II Ecoregions, Level III Ecoregions, and Level IV Ecoregions. The entire state of Ohio falls within one of the larger of North America's fourteen Level I Ecoregions, known as **Eastern Temperate Forest** (see Figure 5 below).

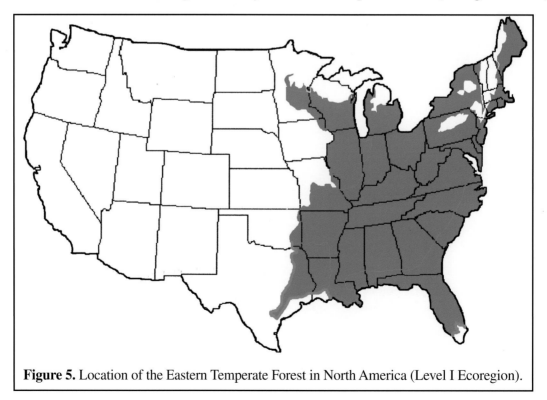

Figure 5. Location of the Eastern Temperate Forest in North America (Level I Ecoregion).

The designation of Ohio as a forest habitat is based on the state's *naturally occurring wildlife habitats,* i.e., the historical natural conditions found in Ohio prior to the changes wrought by European settlers. Obviously, today much of Ohio is not forested. In fact the natural habitats of the state have been so altered by man that today very little land area in the state remains in a pristine, natural condition. Some estimates are that prior to the European invasion of Ohio, as much as 98 percent of the state was forested. Today that percentage is closer to 30 percent, most of it in the Appalachian Plateau, and it is virtually all regrowth. West of the Appalachian Mountains, most of the state's forests have been cleared and converted to agricultural land, with only small pockets of regrowth woodlands scattered throughout.

When considering the state's wildlife habitats, it is important to remember that despite the fact that while all of the land area of Ohio is regarded as a within the eastern Temperate Forest Ecoregion, some areas of grassland, wetland, and savannah habitats also historically occured

(and still occur) in the state. Thus, although the habitat type is designated as forest, Ohio has always contained a variety of other habitats that were embedded within the boundaries of the eastern Temperate Forest Ecoregion.

The eastern Temperate Forest (Level I Ecoregion) consists of five Level II Ecoregions. The Level II Ecoregions of the eastern Temperate Forest are the **Ozark-Ouachita-Appalachian Forest,** the **Southeast US Plains**, the **Mississippi Alluvial and Southeast Coastal Plains**, **Mixed Wood Plains**, and **Central US Plains**. The location of these five Level II Ecoregions are shown in Figure 6 below.

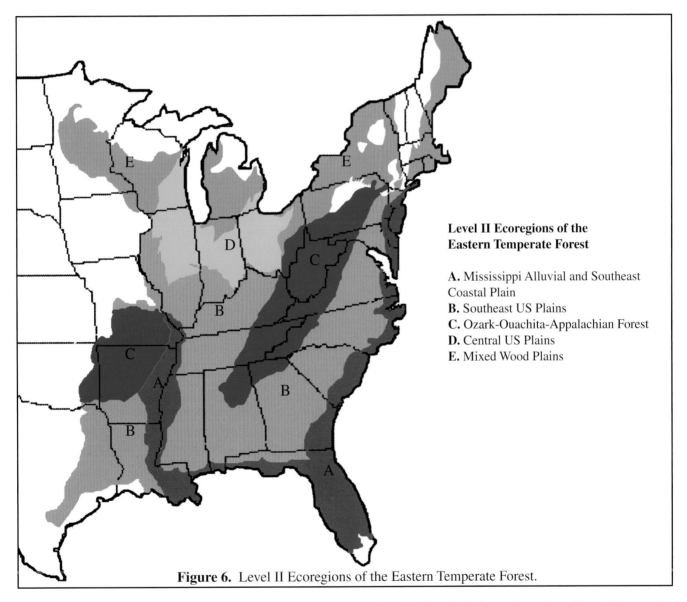

Level II Ecoregions of the Eastern Temperate Forest

A. Mississippi Alluvial and Southeast Coastal Plain
B. Southeast US Plains
C. Ozark-Ouachita-Appalachian Forest
D. Central US Plains
E. Mixed Wood Plains

Figure 6. Level II Ecoregions of the Eastern Temperate Forest.

Four of the five Level II Ecoregions shown above occur in Ohio. The Level II Ecoregions that affect Ohio are the **Ozark-Ouachita-Appalachian**, the **Mixed Woods Plains**, the **Southeast US Plains**, and the **Central US Plains.**

The Level II Ecoregions shown in Figure 4 are sometimes referred to differently by other ecological models. The portion of the Ozark-Ouachita-Appalachian Forest that occurs in Ohio is often called "*Appalachian Mixed Mesophytic Forest*." Similarly, the part of the Southeast US Plains found in Ohio may be referred to as "*Central US Hardwood Forests*."

A written descripton of the Level II Ecoregions affecting Ohio is as follows:

Ozark-Ouachita-Appalachian Forest

The portion of this ecoregion which affects Ohio is also sometimes called *Mixed Mesophytic Forests*. This region encompasses the highland regions of the western slope of the Appalachian Mountains from Pennsylvania, West Virginia, and Ohio south and west to northern Alabama. In Ohio this ecoregion corresponds closely to the Appalachian Plateau physiographic province (see Figures 1, 2, or 3 in Chapter 1). These forest boast a high diversity of species for a temperate region. They are characterized by being relatively cool and damp forests. They have a wide variety of deciduous trees (oaks, hickories, walnuts, birches, ashes, maples, elms, beech, etc.) as well as a variety of evergreen species such as pines, hemlocks, rhododendron, magnolia, and Mountain Laurel. Within this ecoregion several types of localized habitats occur including mesic (damp) woodland, xeric (dry) woodland, wetlands (seeps and bogs), and open lands (glades, barrens, and some agricultural lands in valleys). Also widespread are ecotone habitats, successional areas, and man-made habitats (see Table 3). Virtually 100 percent of this type of forest ecoregion occuring in Ohio has been altered from its original state, and no significant areas of virgin forests remain in the state.

Central US Plains

In Ohio this ecoregion roughly corresponds to the physiographic province known as the Interior Lowlands (see Figure 2). Originally this region was primarily hardwood forest with oak, hickory, maple, elm, ash, and beech as the dominent tree species. Significant but scattered areas of tall grass prairies also occurred here, along with wetland areas of marsh and swamp and scattered glacial lakes (especially in northwestern Ohio).
Today the region is dominated by agriculture.

Southeast US Plains

In Ohio this ecoregion roughly corresponds to the physiographic province known as the Interior Low Plateaus (see Figure 2). Hardwoods are dominant in this ecoregion with more drought tolerant species such as oaks and hickories being more common. Pines also occur commonly in much of the region. Grasslands were once sporadic but fairly widespread within this ecoregion, and wetland swamps and marshes dominated river valleys and lowlands. Also widespread are ecotone habitats, successional areas, and most commonly, man-made habitats (see Table 3). This ecoregion supports the highest number of herbaceous plants and shrubs in North America (over 2,500 species). Modern agriculture has drastically altered the natural habitats in this region and in fact pristine examples of the original habitats of this region in Ohio are virtually non-existent.

Mixed Wood Plains

This ecoregion includes parts of Ontario and Quebec in Canada as well as much of the New England states. The term "Mixed Wood Plains" is appropriately descriptive as the physiography is mostly flat and the endemic tree species are a mix of deciduous and coniferous evergreens. Historically the area included some wetlands and was heavily forested. Today it is mostly open agricultural land except for uban areas.

Figure 5 on the next page shows how the Level II Ecoregions discussed above are subdivided into Level III Ecoregions and where those Level III Ecoregions affecting in Ohio are found within the state.

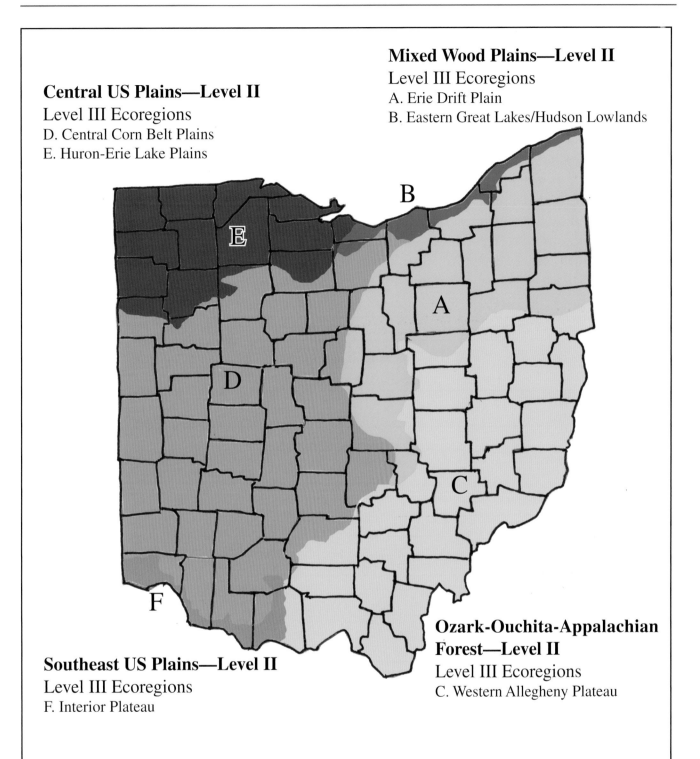

Central US Plains—Level II
Level III Ecoregions
D. Central Corn Belt Plains
E. Huron-Erie Lake Plains

Mixed Wood Plains—Level II
Level III Ecoregions
A. Erie Drift Plain
B. Eastern Great Lakes/Hudson Lowlands

Ozark-Ouchita-Appalachian Forest—Level II
Level III Ecoregions
C. Western Allegheny Plateau

Southeast US Plains—Level II
Level III Ecoregions
F. Interior Plateau

Figure 7. Level III Ecoregions of Ohio The map above shows how the Level II Ecoregions from Figure 4 are divided into Level III ecoregions in Ohio.

The Level III Ecoregions of Ohio can be divided even further into Level IV Ecoregions. Ecologist and wildlife biologists can find these finer eco-region divisions useful in the study of the natural history of organisms. Some species are dependent upon a specific habitat or eco-region for survival. Thus, an understanding of the various eco-regions and what factors are important in the designation of that ecoregion are imperative to wildlife management and conservation efforts.

—PART 2: HABITATS—

In this book, as in many discussions about the natural environments of America, the terms *habitat* and *ecoregion* are frequently used interchangeably. But strictly speaking, there are differences between the two. The term "ecoregion," as defined by the World Wildlife Fund, means "a large unit of land or water containing a geographically distinct assemblage of species, natural communities, and environmental conditions." A *habitat* meanwhile is usually defined simply as "where an organism lives." Thus, an area of mesic (moist) forest, or xeric (dry) forest, are both *habitats* that are contained within the larger forest *ecoregion*. In many publications, the word biome is sometimes used synonymously with both the term habitat and the term ecoregion.

Table 3 below shows the various natural and man-made habitats that are today found within Ohio's eastern Temperate Forest Ecoregion. The table below was created by the author for this book and may not necessarily match the habitat models of other authors, agencies, or organizations.

Level I Ecoregion			
Eastern Temperate Forests			
Level II Ecoregions			
Ozark-Ouachita-Appalachian Forest	**Southeast US Plain**	**Central US Plains**	**Mixed Woods Plains**
Ecoregion Habitats			
Woodland — Mature, Regenerative — Mesic (moist), Xeric (dry)	Woodland — Mature, Regenerative — Mesic (moist), Xeric (dry)	Woodland — Mature, Regenerative — Mesic (moist), Xeric (dry)	Woodland — Mature, Regenerative — Boreal Forest
Wetlands — Bog, Marsh, Springs/Seeps	Wetlands — Swamps, Marsh, Springs/Seeps	Wetlands — Swamps, Marsh, Bogs	Wetlands — Swamps, Marsh, Bogs
Open Lands — Glades and Barrens	Open Lands — Glades and Barrens, Grassland	Open Lands — Savanna, Grassland, Dunes/Beaches	Open Lands — Marsh, Bogs and Fens
Caves	Caves	Caves	

Universal Habitats
Occuring throughout all Ecoregions.
Ecotones
Successional Areas
Riparian Zones
Man-Made Habitats
Occuring sporadically or commonly in all Ecoregions.
Agricultural Areas
Reclaimed Lands
Urban Areas

Table 3. Ohio Ecoregions and Their *Naturally Occuring* Wildlife Habitats

Definitions of Ohio's Habitats

Ecoregion Habitats

Woodlands

Since the naturally occurring Level I ecoregion of Ohio is the eastern Temperate Forest, it comes as no surprise that woodlands are the most widespread *naturally* occurring habitat type in the state. Although professional biologists and ecologists recognize a larger number of different woodland habitat types, in this volume woodland habitats have been simplified and combined into two major types of woodland habitats that can occur *in all of Ohio's three Level II forest Ecoregions.* Nearly all of Ohio's woodland habitats are regenerative woodlands, i.e., woodlands that have been logged for timber at some time during the last 150 years.

Xeric (dry) Woodlands

These woodlands are usually found at the tops of mountains and ridges where the soil is thin and runoff is high. They can also occur on the sides of south or west south facing slopes. Drought tolerant plant species dominate these habitats. Dry woodlands are also common in areas where rocky substrate may be near the surface or gravels and sand are common elements of the soil and the topsoils are thin or very poor. Conifers like pine or cedar are usually the dominant tree in xeric woodlands but some of the tree species that occur in mesic woodlands may also be present. In the xeric woods these trees are often stunted and gnarly.

Mesic (moist) Woodlands

In upland areas mesic woods are found on north or east facing slopes, at the bottoms of deep gorges, and in protected coves and valleys where prolonged direct sunlight is limited and evaporation is low. Small streams and springs and seeps may occur in mesic woodlands. In the Appalachian Plateaus mesic woodlands can contain plant species that are of a more northern origin. Mesic woodlands are also a refuge for moisture-loving animal species, especially salamanders, which reach their highest diversity within moist forests. In the glaciated Ohio mesic woodlands are typical in low lying areas such as valleys and bottom-lands. Mesic woodland habitats can be common in river valleys but the dominant tree species may be different from those found in upland mesic woods.

Savanna

Savannah habitats are best characterized as grasslands with widely spaced trees. Only a tiny portion of land in northwestern Ohio is regarded as natural savanna.

Glades and Barrens

Glades and Barrens are openings within forests where there is no canopy allowing ample sunlight to reach the ground. The two terms are generally used synonymously. These habitats occur where rock substrates break the surface and prohibit the formation of soils, thereby limiting the growth of woody plants and trees.

Wetlands

Wetlands are one of the most productive wildlife habitats. Sadly, most of Ohio's wetlands are gone and have now been replaced by farmers fields, shopping malls, and suburbs. As much as 90 percent of Ohio's original wetland habitats are gone today, making the protection of remaining wetland areas of utmost importance.

Swamps

A swamp is best defined as a wetland area in which the dominant plants are trees. Much of Ohio's Swamplands were found in the northwest portion of the state. Generally speaking swamps are permanently flooded, but some habitat models may include seasonally flooded bottomland forest. Swamps are important areas of biodiversity and are critical to the survival of many vertebrate wildlife species. Northwest Ohio was historically home to the states largest swamp. Known as "The Great Black Swamp" it once covered an area of 120 miles by 40 miles.

Marshes

Marshes are wetlands in which the main plant species are grasses, sedges, and shrubs. Some small trees like willows may be present, but they are never dominant. Cattails, Pickerel Weed, Buttonbush, Rose Mallow, and Water Lily are common plants in marshes. Some marshes may be only seasonally flooded, while others have permanently standing water. As with swamps, marshes enjoy significant diversity and are vital habitats to many vertebrate wildlife species. As is the case with swamps, most of Ohio's marshland has been drained and converted to other land uses such as agriculture.

Bogs

Bogs are shallow depressions without an outlet for drainage. They are thus usually permanently moist and often contain standing water. The vegetation usually consists of mosses, ferns, sedges, Jewelweed, and other herbaceous plants. Organic detritus from dead plants can accumulate in bogs creating "Peat Bogs." In a peat bog the accumulation of dead plant material (peat) can sometimes be many feet deep. Bogs are widespread in the boreal forests of the far north, become scarcer in the southern regions of the continent. In some usages the terms "bog" and "fen" are synonymous.

Wet Meadows and Fens

Wet meadows are treeless areas dominated by grasses and forbs. In a wet meadow local topography and soil substrate creates poor drainage conditions leading to the soil being wet for most of the year. Fens are essentially the same as wet meadows but tend to remain wet throughout the year. Sedges and grasses are the dominant plant species in both habitats.

Vernal Pools

Vernal pools are low depressions that hold water seasonally during the wettest times of the year, typically from late winter through spring. Vernal pools typically dry up in summer and remain dry through the fall and into winter. They are important breeding sites for many amphibians.

Open Lands

The naturally occurring areas of open land in Ohio were historically limited to small patches of prairie, marshes, wet meadows, glades, etc. Today most of Ohio's open lands are agricultural or urban / suburban. These man-made habitats have replaced much of the naturally occuring forests that once dominanted the state.

Universal Habitats

These habitats occur in virtually all Ecoregions throughout North America. The term "universal habitat" is not a commonly used scientific denotation, but rather it is a term created by the author for this book as a way to designate those types of habitats that can and do occur almost everywhere. However, three types of universal habitats listed immediately below (ecotones, successional areas, and riparian zones) are scientifically recognized terms.

Ecotones

Ecotones are defined as areas of transition between two or more habitats. The term "edge area" is often used synonymously with ecotone. Classic examples of ecotone areas would be a place were a woodland meets an open field or where a swamp or bottomland abuts against a ridge of upland woods. Ecotones are universal habitats found in all regions. These are very productive areas for wildlife, as species from varying habitats can often be found together around ecotones.

Successional Areas

This is another type of habitat that can occur anywhere. Nature is never static. Grasslands are always in the process of becoming woodlands unless the successional process is altered by fire or mowing. Woodlands destroyed by fire may become grassland. A lake subject to sedimentation can become a swamp or marsh. In time a marsh can fill and become a meadow. Beavers can create a new wetland where before there was a meadow with a small stream. In Ohio, the most familiar successional habitat is the regeneration of a woodland following logging or the reversion to a weedy field of a neglected cropland. These last two types of successional areas are favored by wildlife species like the Whitetail Deer and the eastern Cottontail.

Riparian Zones

A riparian zone is a narrow band of habitat bordering a stream or river. Technically, the term is used to describe the narrow zone of lush growth that accompanies a stream coursing through an otherwise arid landscape (as in the riparian habitats of the desert southwest). In Ohio, where so much of the natural landscape has disappeared, stream courses through open farmlands with their associated ribbon of trees, shrubs, and forbs are significant zones of natural habitat which can become very important corridors for the movement and dispersal of vertebrate wildlife. Riparian habitats occur throughout the state.

Man-Made Habitats

Man-made habitats usually receive little attention in most scientific discussions regarding *natural* habitats. However, humans have so altered the natural condition of the land that much of the wildlife habitat that exists in America today has been created by human activities. Although the loss of natural habitats has contributed to the disappearance of many species and continues to be the greatest threat to wildlife worldwide, many species have been able to adapt to man-made habitats and a few actually thrive in these new habitats.

Agricultural Areas

Although some may find it difficult to envision a harvested soybean field as a wildlife habitat, in truth some wildlife species have adapted to occupy or use on a part-time basis the state's abundant agricultural areas. In Ohio the harvested soybean field in winter is one of the best places to see winter migrant birds like the Lapland Longspur. A cattle pasture in summer is home to the eastern Meadowlark and flocks of Common Grackles will use both habitats throughout the year. Some species like the White-tailed Deer and the Wild Turkey in part owe their present day abundance to the ever present food supply provided by grain farmers. In fact, most mammals and many birds found in Ohio have adapted to include agricultural areas in their habitats.

Reclaimed Lands

Strip mining for coal and minerals has destroyed many thousands of acres of naturally occurring wildlife habitat in America. Many of these lands have undergone *reclamation* and now constitute radically altered but significant wildlife habitats. Although the reclaimed habitats are quite different from the original habitats, and support a much lower species diversity, they are utilized by several vertebrate species. Sadly, the habitats lost in the mining process were many times richer in species diversity than the present day reclaimed habitats, and

those original habitats are now forever gone from the reclaimed areas.

Urban Habitats

As is the case with Agricultural lands, it is sometimes difficult to think of urban landscapes as wildlife habitat. Again however, many species adapt well to towns and cities and in fact some will thrive there. The Chimney Swift experienced a population boom in the days when every building in America had a chimney. The Common Nighthawk frequently nests on the flat rooftops of downtown buildings, and everyone is familiar with the sight of a Robin plucking worms from a well manicured suburban lawn or a Rock Dove (Pigeon) strolling the sidewalks of a large city.

Today most of America's land mass in the eastern half of the country is held in private ownership. Very little of these private lands are managed for wildlife or set aside as areas for the conservation of natural habitats. Fortunately, there are a number of agencies that hold land in public trust with the goal of providing and maintaining natural wildlife habitats. The largest single owner of public lands in America is the federal government. The US Forest Service, the National Park Service, the US Fish and Wildlife Service and the Department of Defense together own millions of acres of wildlife habitat.

To anyone with an appreciation of wilderness and nature in its pristine condition, the eastern half of North America has become an impoverished place. Many of the Ohio's wildlife species face a perilous and uncertain future. Happily, many species continue to adapt and some to thrive in the new human altered environments. Thankfully, agencies like the Ohio Department of Natural Resources and the US Fish and Wildlife Service work unceasingly to protect, manage, and enhance America's wildlife and remaining wild habitats. But there is only so much that these organizations can accomplish. That means that the real responsibility for stewardship of nature in Ohio falls to individual landowners. Unfortunately, most landowners are forced by economics to make land ownership pay, or at least to make owning land economically feasible. Protecting wildlife habitat is rarely a profitable venture, especially when compared to the economic benefits of timber harvest, row cropping, or livestock operations. Thus natural habitats are under constant assault. For those species unable to adapt to the changes created by man, loss of habitat can pose a serious threat to that species' continued existance.

We humans, to a very great degree, have succeeded in altering our natural landscapes so much that we no longer feel an intimate connection to the land. We consider ourselves to be residents of an artificially created locality. We are Ohioans rather than residents of the formerly great eastern Temperate Forest. If asked what part of the state in which your town is located you may say "Ottawa County" rather than reply that your town is located within Huron-Lake Erie Plains.

To some extent, natural boundaries have always been utilized by man when creating political boundaries. A prime example is the Ohio River that serves as the southern border of Ohio. Smaller creeks and rivers regularly serve as county lines, and much of the state's northern border is defined by the shores of Lake Erie. But we humans have a strong tendency to create regions and boundaries which ignore natural boundaries and instead serve our serve our personal, social, and political needs.

While this mindset serves our society well in many ways, it often does a disservice to our environment. If we could learn to think of ourselves more as a part of the larger ecosystems, we would perhaps show more Concern for the stewardship of those ecosystems. At this stage in human history, with our population topping seven billion people, our natural resources being pushed to the point of exhaustion, our ocean ecosystems possibly on the verge of collapse, mass extinctions just around the corner, and global climate change the immediate future, a new understanding and appreciation of the natural world by *all citizens* seems to be the only hope for a promising future.

The pages that follow are intended to introduce Ohioans to the remarkable diversity, wondrous beauty, and miraculous lives of the state's wildlife species. It is hoped that this introduction will lead to a greater awareness, concern, and appreciation for our natural heritage. It is further hoped that acquiring that awareness and appreciation will lead to a better stewardship of the living things with which we share this planet. And more importantly, the natural ecosystems upon which both they and we ultimately depend.

CHAPTER 3

THE MAMMALS OF OHIO

Table 4.
The Orders and Families of Ohio Mammals

Class—**Mammalia** (mammals)

Order—**Didelphimorphia** (opossums)

Family	**Didelphidae** (opossum)

Order—**Carnivora** (carnivores)

Family	**Ursidae** (bears)
Family	**Procyonidae** (raccoons)
Family	**Felidae** (cats)
Family	**Canidae** (canines)
Family	**Mustelidae** (weasels)
Family	**Mephitidae** (skunks)

Order—**Artiodactlya** (hoofed mammals)

Family	**Cervidae** (deer)

Order—**Lagamorpha** (rabbits and hares)

Family	**Leporidae** (rabbits)

Order—**Rodentia** (rodents)

Family	**Sciuridae** (squirrels)
Family	**Castoridae** (beavers)
Family	**Cricetidae** (rats and mice)

Order—**Insectivora** (insectivores)

Family	**Soricidae** (shrews)
Family	**Talpidae** (moles)

Order—**Chiroptera** (bats)

Family	**Vespertilionidae** (other bats)

Class—**Mammalia** (mammals)

Order—**Didelphimorphia** (opossums)	Order—**Carnivora**
Family—**Didelphidae**	Family—**Ursidae** (bears)
Virginia Opossum *Didelphis virginiana*	**Black Bear** *Ursus americanus*

Size: About 2.5 feet from nose to tail tip. Males can weigh up to 14 pounds, females are smaller.

Presumed range in Ohio

Abundance: Very common. In fact, this is one of the most common medium-sized mammals in Ohio.

Size: 4–5 feet in total length. Males can weigh up to 400 pounds, females are smaller, averaging about 200.

Presumed range in Ohio

Abundance: Rare but increasing yearly. Today's population is estimated to be between 50 and 100 bears.

Variation: Opossums are quite variable. In most the fur is grizzled gray (as in photo above). All white or all black individuals can also occur, along with a cinnamon color phase.

Variation: Despite their name Black Bears may be black, cinnamon, blond, blue gray, or even white. Ohio specimens are invariably black in color.

Habitat: Virtually all habitats within the state are utilized. Including suburban and even urban areas where there is enough vegetative cover. Opossums are more common in areas altered by humans, such as farmlands and the vicinity of small, rural communities. They are less common in areas of true wilderness.

Habitat: Throughout their range in North America Black Bears utilize a wide array of habitats. In the deep south they use swamplands and woodlands, in the far north they are found in both boreal forests and tundra. In the Ohio and neighboring states they are restricted to the Appalachian Plateau. Inhabits remote, rugged, and inaccessible wilderness.

Breeding: This is America's only member of the mammalian subclass Marsupialia. Young Opossums are born as embryos only twelve days after conception. The newborn babies are just over 1/2 inch in length. At one month they are about the size of a mouse. Litters are large (up to 13) and two litters per year is common.

Breeding: Breeds in summer but development of the embryo is delayed until fall. One to three cubs are born in January or February in the female's winter den. Twins are common. Newborn cubs will weigh only about a pound. Females will typically breed only every other year. Young stay with the female for about a year.

Natural History: Opossums are one of the most successful medium size mammals in America, which is somewhat surprising given that they are slow moving, rather dim-witted animals that rarely survive beyond two years in the wild. They are mainly nocturnal and eat most any palatable plant matter (seeds, grains, fruits, berries), and any type of meat they can catch or scavenge. They are known to kill and eat venomous snakes and have a strong resistance to pit viper venoms. They are well known for faking death (playing opossum) when stressed. They have strong nocturnal tendencies but they are sometimes active during the day, especially when breeding. When hard pressed they will climb to escape. In trees they use their prehensile tail to compensate for their somewhat clumsy climbing. Their greatest enemy today is the automobile. Thousands are killed nightly on highways across America.

Natural History: Prior to the European invasion of Ohio the Black Bear was a common large carnivore in the state. Over-hunting and deforestation led to their complete disappearance by the mid 1800s. In recent years Black Bears have begun to re-colonize the southeastern part of Ohio. There has been a natural expansion of Black Bear populations from historic strongholds in the Appalachian Mountains that began several decades ago. Young male bears will disperse for sometimes hundreds of miles, and are the first individuals to colonize a new area. A variety of plant and animal matter is eaten. In Ohio, the annual mast crop (acorns and nuts) is the most important food item in preparing for a winter hibernation that can last five months. Bears enjoy a keen sense of smell and rely more on the sense of smell and hearing than on eyesight. Black Bears have been known to live up to 30 years.

Class—**Mammalia** (mammals)

Order—**Carnivora**

Family—**Procyonidae** (raccoons)	Family—**Felidae** (cats)
Raccoon *Procyon lotor*	**Bobcat** *Lynx rufus*

Size: Up to 2.5 feet in length. Weights of 15—30 pounds Record 62 pounds. Females are smaller than males.	Presumed range in Ohio 	**Size:** Length up to 3 feet. Weighs 15—35 pounds. Maximum of about 45 pounds.	Presumed range in Ohio 
Abundance: Common to very common. Can even be found in urban and suburban environments with cover in the form of trees and shrubs.		**Abundance:** Very rare in Ohio, but recently increasing in numbers. Map shows core range but is expanding into other areas of the state.	

Variation: There is little variation in Ohio specimens. A few black indivuals occur occasionally. Most resemble the photo above. As many as 25 subspecies in the US, but only one occurs in Ohio.

Variation: Several subspecies occur in America but there is little variation in Ohio. Some specimens have more pronounced spotting to their fur and males are about 1/3 larger than females.

Habitat: Found in virtually every habitat in the state, but wetlands, stream courses, and lake shores are favorite haunts.

Habitat: Rugged, remote mountains and impenetrable swamps are preferred sanctuaries.

Breeding: Breeds in late winter with an average of four (maximum of eight) young born two months later (April or May). Young begin to accompany the mother on foraging trips at about two months. They are on their own by five months.

Breeding: Most breeding occurs in winter or spring with an average of three or four young born two months later. Young Bobcats begin to forage with the mother by late summer and may stay with her for up to a year while perfecting hunting skills.

Natural History: Raccoons are omnivores that feed on a wide variety of crustaceans, insects, amphibians, reptiles, small mammals, and eggs as well as grains, berries, fruits, acorns, weed seeds, and some vegetables. Although they are mainly nocturnal, they are often active by day, especially in morning and late afternoons. During particularly harsh weather they may den for days at a time. Summer dens are often tree hollows while old groundhog burrows may be used during the winter. In Ohio the Raccoon is an important game animal harvested for its fur and to a lesser extent as food. More often they are hunted just for sport and released unharmed after being treed by hounds. Like many other mammals, Raccoons are subject to an interesting phenomena known as "Bergman's Rule." Bergman's rule states that the body size of mammals tends to be larger the farther north the species is found. This phenonmena is the result of the fact that larger bodies are capable of retaining more heat. A really big male Raccoon from northern Ohio may top the scales at 40 pounds. Meanwhile an adult male Raccoon in Florida may weigh only 10–12 pounds.

Natural History: Strictly a meat eater, the Bobcat's food items range from mice to deer. Cottontail Rabbits are a favorite prey as are squirrels, young turkeys, and songbirds. Hunts by ambush or stalking to within close range and making an explosive attack. Although mainly nocturnal, Bobcats can be abroad at any time of day. Their home range can be from one to several square miles and males have larger ranges than females. Scent marking territory with urine and feces is common. In captivity Bobcats have lived for over 20 years, but the estimate for wild cats is 12–14 years. This species has just begun to return to Ohio after being completely extirpated over a hundred years ago. Off and on reports of occasional specimens persisted over the years but stable, breeding population have only recently begun to return to the state. The range map above shows the "core range," where Bobcats are known to have become re-established, but they have become much more widespread in Ohio in the last decade. Today they may rarely be seen almost statewide in rural regions, especially in areas where there are large tracts of woodland, swampland, or protected natural habitats.

Class—**Mammalia** (mammals)

Order—**Carnivora** (carnivores)

Family—**Canidae** (canines)

Gray Fox *Urocyon cinereoargenteus*	**Red Fox** *Vulpes vulpes*	**Coyote** *Canis latrans*

Gray Fox	Red Fox	Coyote
Size: Length 32 to 45 inches. Weight up to 15 pounds. **Abundance:** Fairly common. Presumed range in Ohio	**Size:** Length 33 to 43 inches. Weight up to 15 pounds. **Abundance:** Fairly common. Presumed range in Ohio	**Size:** Length up to 49 inches. Average about 35 pounds. **Abundance:** Fairly common. Presumed range in Ohio
Variation: As many as six subspecies range across North America. Only one race occurs in Ohio with no significant color variation.	**Variation:** Red Foxes can occur in several different color phases, the best known of which are red, silver, and cross fox. Ohio specimens are typically red.	**Variation:** Very dark individuals and reddish specimens are know to occur. Most specimens in Ohio will resemble the photo above.
Habitat: Primarily a woodland animal that is more common in the forested regions of the eastern half of the state. Tends to avoid expansive open regions like farmlands and prairies.	**Habitat:** Although habitat generalists, Red Foxes shows a preference for open and semi-open country over deep woods. They are thus most common in the western half of Ohio.	**Habitat:** Coyotes have adapted to all habitats in Ohio, but they are most common in the more open agricultural areas in the western half of the state. Occasionally adapts to urban parks.
Breeding: Dens in a burrow, hollow log, or rock cave. Four pups is usual but up to seven is known.	**Breeding:** About four to five young are born underground, often in an old groundhog burrow, but they will dig their own hole.	**Breeding:** Coyotes are able to breed before their first birthday. Litter size (two to ten) varies with availability of prey.
Natural History: The Gray Fox is the only American canine with the ability to climb trees. Insects are important food items in summer with mice and rabbits becoming more important in winter. When grapes, persimmons, and other fruits are ripe they will eat them almost exclusively and in fact this is the most omnivorous canine in America. Home range can vary from a few hundred acres to over a square mile, depending upon habitat quality. Unlike the Red Fox that can be found as far north as the arctic circle, the Gray Fox is a more southerly animal and ranges southward into South America. Gray Foxes have lived for up to 14 years in captivity, but the average lifespan in the wild is only a few years. Contrary to popular belief, Gray Foxes never interbreed with Red Foxes.	**Natural History:** The Red Fox is one of the world's most widespread mammals and is found in Europe, Asia, north Africa, and Australia (introduced) as well as throughout North America. They are adaptable, opportunistic omnivores that will eat everything from grasshoppers to grapes. Scavenging carrion is also common. Their fur is such a good insulator that they can sleep atop a snow bank without melting the snow beneath their body. These are important fur-bearing animals and are today often reared in captivity on "fur farms." Red Fox populations in Ohio have probably increased since European settlement and subsequent clearing of forests for agriculture. The short, summer coat is paler than the luxurious winter fur. All color phases have a white tail tip.	**Natural History:** The Coyote is a relative newcomer to Ohio, having begun their invasion from the west about a half century ago. Today they range all the way to the Atlantic. They are the top predator in much of the state, occupying a niche once held by the wolf and the Cougar. They are extremely intelligent, adaptable canines that quickly learn to thrive in almost any environment. In rural areas where hunters abound they are extremely wary, but in urban areas or protected lands they may become quite bold around humans. The characteristic yipping and howling of these vocal canines has become a common nighttime sound in rural Ohio. Mostly nocturnal, but also active by day. The longevity record is 18 years for a specimen in captivity.

Class—**Mammalia** (mammals)

Order—**Carnivora** (carnivores)

Family—**Mustelidae** (weasel family)

Mink *Mustela vison*	**Long-tailed Weasel** *Mustela frenata*	**Least Weasel** *Mustela nivalis*
	Summer pelage	

Size: 20 to 27 inches in length. Weighs 2—3 pounds. **Abundance:** Fairly common.	Presumed range in Ohio 	**Size:** 12 to 15 inches from snout to tail tip. Weighs 6—11 ounces. **Abundance:** Uncommon.	Presumed range in Ohio 	**Size:** 7 inches. Weighs about 1.5 ounces. **Abundance:** Uncommon to rare.	Presumed range in Ohio 

Variation: Males are twice as large as females. Pelage color varies from light brown to very dark brown. Ohio Mink resemble the specimen above.	**Variation:** Males are nearly twice the size of females. Specimens in northernmost Ohio may turn white in winter, southern Ohio weasels stay brown.	**Variation:** Specimens from farther north turn white in winter but most Ohio specimens will remain brown. Males are about 1/3 larger than females.
Habitat: Swamps and marshes are the primary habitat. Also frequents creeks, rivers, and lake shores.	**Habitat:** Occupies a wide variety of habitats but favors being near stream courses.	**Habitat:** Avoids deep woods and lives mostly in or around the edges of fields and marshes.
Breeding: Three to six young are born in an underground den that is often an old muskrat house. Young begin to hunt with mother at about two months.	**Breeding:** Mating occurs in mid-summer but embryo development is delayed until the following spring. Four to five young is typical and babies have white fur.	**Breeding:** Breeds throughout the year and can produce two litters per year of one to six young. Young develop quickly and can hunt on their own in six weeks.
Natural History: Mink are well known for their luxurious fur. Most mink fur sold in America today is from captive, farm raised mink. Mink are excellent swimmers and will catch fish in stream pools. They are strict carnivores that feed heavily on amphibians and crayfish during the summer. In winter their diet turns to mammal prey such as rabbits and rodents. Muskrats are a favorite winter food of the large males who kill their formidable prey with a bite to the back of the neck. As with other members of the Mustelidae family, mink have well developed musk glands that produce a distinct musky odor when the animal is excited, breeding, or marking territory. The range of the mink extends from the southeastern United States all the way to Alaska, including most of Canada.	**Natural History:** Weasels are known for being, on a pound per pound basis, one of the world's most ferocious predators. Although their prey includes animals as small as insects, they will also take prey the size of a grown Cottontail Rabbit. Mice, voles, and other rodents, along with shrews and small birds, make up the bulk of their non-invertebrate diet. Of these, voles are a favorite prey and may make up as much as 1/3 of the diet. They have also been known to scavenge the dead bodies of large animals such as deer. These highly active mammals have a high metabolic rate and they are active by both day and night, consuming up to 1/3 of their body weight in a day. When an animal is killed that is too large to consume at one meal, they will cache the remains and return to finish it later.	**Natural History:** This is one of the world's smallest carnivores. Their tiny, elongated bodies allow them to maneuver easily into rodent burrows, and mice and voles are their primary prey. They hunt day and night, alternating hunts with short naps. They are active year-round and their rapid metabolism means they must consume one-half of their body weight each day. When the opportunity presents they will kill more than they can eat and store the extra food for later. They are known to line their nest with mouse fur or bird feathers from their prey. Few Ohioans will ever see this tiny, secretive little predator. In Ohio they are least common in the southwestern portion of the state. A third weasel species, the **Ermine** (*M. erminaea*) is a very rare resident in the northernmost portion of Ohio.

Class—**Mammalia** (mammals)

Order—**Carnivora** (carnivores)

Family—**Mustelidae** (weasels)

River Otter	**Badger**
Lutra canadensis	*Taxidea taxus*

Family—**Mephitidae** (skunks)

Striped Skunk
Mephitis mephitis

Size: Length 35–45 inches. Up to 25 pounds.	Presumed range in Ohio 	**Size:** Up to 30 inches in length. Males up to 24 pounds, females 12 to 15 pounds.	Presumed range in Ohio 	**Size:** Length 23–31 inches. Average weight about 8—10 pounds.	Presumed range in Ohio 
Abundance: Uncommon in Ohio.		**Abundance:** Uncommon in Ohio Species of Concern.		**Abundance:** Common.	

Variation: As many as seven subspecies range across North America. There is very little variation in Ohio specimens.

Habitat: Any unpolluted aquatic habitat in the state may be suitable for River Otters. They are always in association with rivers, lakes, swamps, or creeks.

Breeding: Two or three young are born in an underground den often dug in a stream bank. Births are usually in the spring or summer.

Natural History: River Otters are semi-aquatic mammals that possess fully webbed toes and waterproof fur. They are excellent swimmers that prey on fish, frogs, crayfish, turtles, and small mammals. Their fur is highly valued, a fact that lead to their extirpation from Ohio and most of the eastern United States by the late 1800s. Restocking programs by the Ohio Division of Wildlife begun in 1986 have been highly successful and today these endearing animals can once again be found in many areas of the state. Although there are still parts of Ohio where they may not yet have colonized, by 2009 they had been recorded in 67 counties (Donofrio, 2009). It is reasonable to consider their range today as being nearly statewide in suitable habitats. Limited trapping is now allowed.

Variation: Although there are two subspecies in Ohio, the differences are minor and both are similar in appearance.

Habitat: The Badger is primarily an animal of the prairie. In ohio they will frequent open pastures and grassy areas in search of ground squirrels, voles, etc.

Breeding: Breeds in mid-summer with young born in early spring. Average number of young is two or three but can be as many as six or seven.

Natural History: The Badger is a digging machine. It possess long claws, powerful forelegs, and a specialized structure of the eye known as a "nictitating membrane" which keeps dirt from entering the eye sockets. Badgers feed mostly by digging small mammals from their underground burrows. Ground squirrels and gophers are the favorite prey, but almost any type of animal may be eaten, including carrion. In the western US Badgers have been observed hunting co-operatively with Coyotes. The Coyote guards the escape holes (and catches a few fleeing animals), while the Badger benefits from having the Coyote blocking the escape route long enough for the Badger to dig out the hapless ground squirrel or gopher. Abandoned Badger dens are utilized by a wide variety of other animals.

Variation: Varies considerably in the amount of white in the dorsal stripes. Can be nearly all white or solid black.

Habitat: Striped Skunks are found in all habitats in Ohio, but they are most common in mixed, semi-open habitats and edge areas.

Breeding: Breeding occurs in late winter. Litter size averages three or four but can be as many as ten. Weanlings follow the mother in single file while foraging.

Natural History: The Striped Skunk's distinctive black and white color is almost as well known as its primary defense, which of course is to spray an attacker with its pungent, foul smelling musk. The musk can burn the eyes and membranes and its odor is remarkably persistent. They can effectively project the musk up to about 15 feet and the odor can be detected hundreds of yards away. A direct hit to the face from the musk glands can cause debilitating nausea and temporary blindness. Striped Skunks dine mainly on invertebrates and as much as three-fourths of their diet consists of insects and grubs. They possess well developed front claws for digging and a powerful sense of smell for locating buried grubs, worms, turtle eggs, etc. Also eats baby mice, eggs, and nestlings of ground nesting birds.

Class—**Mammalia** (mammals)

Order—**Artiodactyla** (hoofed mammals)

Family—**Cervidae** (deer family)

Whitetail Deer—*Odocoileus virginianus*

Buck	Doe	Fawn

Size: Males up to 40 inches high at shoulder. Females about 20 percent smaller. Mature males can weigh over 200 pounds, females up to 150, though most are smaller. Deer from the northernmost regions of Ohio have larger body size than those in the southern parts of the state. This is due to a phenomena known as "Bergman's Rule." Larger bodies lose heat less rapidly due to the smaller ratio of body volume to surface area, thus in colder regions mammals with a larger body size tend to survive better.

Abundance: Very common.

Variation: There are as many as 13 different subspecies of Whitetail Deer recognized in mainland North America, plus several more island races. The Ohio subspecies is the Northern Woodland Whitetail Deer, *Odocoileus virginianus borealis.* Young (fawns) exhibit a pattern of white spots that fade with age. Adults have reddish brown color in the summer and grayish in the fall/winter.

Presumed range in Ohio

Habitat: Found in virtually every habitat within the state and increasingly common in urban areas. Favorite habitats are a mix of woodland, brushy areas and weedy fields, especially near farmlands. Successional areas, such as regrowth of woodlands after fires or logging is also a prime habitat. In Ohio, deer are more common where there is a mixture of agricultural land and woodlands. They are least common in mature, unbroken forests, and in areas of intensive agriculture or major urbanization.

Breeding: Breeding begins in early fall and may continue into the winter, with the peak breeding season occurring in November. One to two (rarely three or even four) young are born in the spring or early summer following a six and a half month gestation. Females (does) usually bear their first offspring at two years of age. The first pregnancy typically results in a single fawn, the second pregnancy usually is twins, and the third through fifth twins or triplets (rarely quadruplets). Young lie hidden for the first few weeks and are left alone much of the time. The female will visit the hidden fawn about once every four hours to allow nursing, then moves away to avoid attracting predators. At about one month of age the young will begin to follow the mother and stay close through the summer and into the fall.

Natural History: Bucks (males) shed their antlers each year in late winter and regrow a new set by fall. Growing deer antlers are among the fastest-growing animal tissue known. While growing, the antlers are covered in a spongy, fuzzy skin called "velvet." Antlers grow larger each year up to about six or seven years of age, when they begin a gradual decline. Whitetail Deer are browsers and they feed on a wide variety of forbs, leaves, twigs, buds, crops, and mast (especially acorns). Although they are sometimes destructive to farm crops like corn or soybeans, they are an important game animal in Ohio with as many as 188,000 harvested in 2015 for food and sport. The maximum life span is 20 years, but most are dead by age 10. State wildlife agencies like the Ohio Department of Natural Resources are charged with the responsibility of protecting and managing the state's wildlife populations. In Ohio, this means taking into consideration not only the health and well being of the state's deer herd, but also the cultural aspect of providing food and recreation for the state's hunting population. Additional considerations regarding crop depredations and deer collisions with autos are also a part of the wildlife management formula. Thus determining how many deer of what sex should be harvested annually involves taking into consideration many factors. Happily, this animal represents one of the world's great wildlife conservation stories. Nearly wiped out by the early 1900s, the Whitetail Deer is today as numerous in America as it was during the time of Daniel Boone. At present, the population in Ohio numbers nearly a three quarters of a million deer, up from a low of only a few thousand a century ago. In recent years these animals have begun to invade urban areas where deer hunting is restricted. In towns and cities they can become a nuisance.

Class—**Mammalia** (mammals)

Order—**Lagomorpha** (lagamorphs)	Order—**Rodentia** (rodents)	
Family—**Leporidae** (rabbits, hares)	Family—**Sciuridae** (squirrel family)	

Eastern Cottontail *Sylvilagus floridanus*	**Thirteen-line Ground Squirrel** *Spermophilus tridecemlineatus*	**Red Squirrel** *Tamiasciurus hudsonicus*
		 Summer pelage

Size: Adult length about 17 inches. Weight up to 2.5 pounds.

Abundance: Very common and wide-spread.

Presumed range in Ohio

Size: Maximum of about 12 inches total length. Weighs 5—8 ounces.

Abundance: Fairly common. Unglaciated Ohio only.

Presumed range in Ohio

Size: Total length 12 inches. Head and body 7 inches, tail 5. Weight 6 ounces.

Abundance: Fairly common. More common in northern OH.

Presumed range in Ohio

Variation: No variation in Ohio, but at least 12 very similar subspecies of this wide-ranging rabbit are recognized across the United States.

Variation: No variation. In fact, these animals are remarkably similar throughout their range which includes the midwest and the entire Great Plains.

Variation: Summer pelage is duller and less red and the prominent "ear tufts" are only seen in fall and winter squirrels.

Habitat: May be found in virtually any habitat within the state except for permanent wetlands. Most common in overgrown fields and edge areas. Fond of briers, honeysuckle, and tall weeds.

Habitat: Natural habitats are prairies and sandy grasslands. Today pastures, golf courses, cemeteries, lawns, and even highway right of ways are utilized. Prefers areas of short, sparse grass.

Habitat: Like most tree squirrels this is a forest species. Any type of northern forest may be inhabited, including deciduous and mixed, but conifer forests are where they are most common.

Breeding: This is the most prolific of the several rabbit species in America, producing up to seven litters per year with as many as five young per litter.

Breeding: Mating takes place soon after emerging from hibernation. The average of six to eight young are blind and naked at birth. They wean at six weeks.

Breeding: Capable of producing two broods per year. Three to five young is typical. In years of good mast crops they may produce larger litters of seven or eight.

Natural History: In the spring and summer Eastern Cottontails feed on a wide variety of grasses, legumes, and herbaceous weeds. Briers, sapling bark (especially Sumac) leaf buds, and other woody materials may make up the bulk of the diet in winter. During periods of deep snow they will spend the day burrowed under the snow and emerge at night. These rabbits are prey for many predators including foxes, coyotes, bobcats, and hawks and owls, especially the Great Horned Owl. The life expectancy for a Cottontail is not high, and only about one in four will live to see their second birthday. Populations are known to fluctuate and during years when their numbers are highest good habitat may support up to nine rabbits per acre.

Natural History: Although they often go by the nickname "Striped Gopher," the Thirteen-lined Ground Squirrel is a member of the Squirrel Family and not very closely related to the true gophers that inhabit so much of the American west. This species seems to have expanded its range in Ohio from pre-settlement days. Cutting of forests and clearing of land for agriculture and other human uses seems to have benefited this open country species. They are confirmed burrowers that may excavate several tunnels which can be six feet in length and over a foot deep. Below-ground hibernation begins in October in Ohio and lasts about six months. In addition to grasses and clovers they will eat seeds and some insects.

Natural History: Like most tree squirrels the Red Squirrel is diurnal in habits. While most people find them to be endearing little animals, others regard them as pests and there is a widespread myth among squirrel hunters that Red Squirrels will attack and castrate the males of the more desirable (from the hunter's point of view) Gray Squirrel. Red Squirrels will store huge piles of conifer cones, usually at the base of large trees. These piles are known as "middens" and they can attain an enormous size. Piles 15 feet across and three feet high have been recorded. The range of the Red Squirrel includes all of Canada except the Arctic and the Great Plains, and all the northern US and south in the Appalachians to Georgia.

Class—**Mammalia** (mammals)

Order—**Rodentia** (rodents)

Family—**Sciuridae** (squirrel family)

Eastern Chipmunk *Tamias striatus*	**Gray Squirrel** *Sciurus carolinensis*	**Fox Squirrel** *Sciurus niger*

Eastern Chipmunk
Tamias striatus

Size: About 10 inches in length and weighing about 4.5 ounces.

Abundance: Fairly common. Absent from many areas.

Presumed range in Ohio
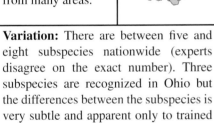

Variation: There are between five and eight subspecies nationwide (experts disagree on the exact number). Three subspecies are recognized in Ohio but the differences between the subspecies is very subtle and apparent only to trained mammologists. The specimen shown above is a good representative.

Habitat: Deciduous forests in upland areas. Avoids wetlands. Fond of rock outcrops, stone fences, etc. Can be common in urban parks and suburbs.

Breeding: May breed twice per year, first in February and again in April. Produces four to five young per litter.

Natural History: While they are excellent climbers, chipmunks are true "ground squirrels," sleeping, rearing young and wintering in an underground burrow which they dig themselves. They also will use rock crevices or hollow logs. They become less active in winter and will remain below ground living on stored nuts and seeds for long periods during harsh weather. Although Chipmunks are fairly common in much of Ohio they are usually absent from expansive open areas and areas of extensive agriculture. Like other squirrels the chipmunk is a vocal animal but its voice is less raspy, sounding at times like the chirping of a bird.

Gray Squirrel
Sciurus carolinensis

Size: 19 inches in total length. Weight about 18 ounces.

Abundance: More common than Fox Squirrel in southeast Ohio.

Presumed range in Ohio

Variation: At least six subspecies are occur in the US and some are quite variable. Melanistic (black) populations can be found in some areas of northern Ohio and albino populations occur in a few locations. Some Ohio specimens may have reddish brown tails but most resemble the specimen pictured above.

Habitat: Prefers mature deciduous forests but also found in mixed coniferous forests and second growth areas. Can be common in urban parks and lawns.

Breeding: Breeds December through February and again in June/July. Four to six young per litter.

Natural History: Feeds on nuts, seeds, fungi, tree buds and the inner bark of trees as well as bird eggs and hatchlings. May sometimes even eat carrion. Like most rodents they will gnaw bones or shed deer antlers for calcium. Well known for burying and storing nuts. Frequently calls with a raspy "bark," especially when alarmed. Builds summer nests of leaves in tree crotches. Winter dens are in tree hollows. During severe weather may be inactive for several days. Poor mast years may produce mass migrations. Gray Squirrels are extremely athletic little animals and exhibit remarkable agility in trees. They are strictly a woodland animal.

Fox Squirrel
Sciurus niger

Size: 23 inches from snout to tail tip. Weighs about 28 ounces.

Abundance: More common than Gray in northwest Ohio.

Presumed range in Ohio

Variation: There are a total of ten subspecies nationwide and they range in color from solid black to reddish to silver-gray. *S. n. rufiventer* (reddish phase) occurs in Ohio. Most are like the standing specimen shown above, but a variety of color morphs may be seen in other regions.

Habitat: Prefers open forests with trees widely spaced. Can be common in swamps. Prefers edge areas, overgrown fence rows, etc., over extensive woods.

Breeding: Produces four to six young twice annually, breeding in winter and again in summer.

Natural History: Fox Squirrels wander frequently into open areas and spend more time on the ground than Gray Squirrels. Their home range may be ten times larger. They are generally less common than the Gray, rarely reaching the population densities of their smaller cousins. In some areas of Ohio however they may be more common than the Gray Squirrel, especially in semi-open country. They feed on the same foods of nuts, seeds, buds, berries, etc. But the diet of Fox Squirrels also often includes the seeds of pine cones. Barks and chatters when disturbed but is overall less vocal than the smaller squirrel species which occur in Ohio.

Class—**Mammalia** (mammals)

Order—**Rodentia** (rodents)

Family—**Sciuridae** (squirrel family)

Southern Flying Squirrel *Glaucomys volans*	Groundhog *Marmota monax*

Size: 10 inches and 2—3 ounces.

Presumed range in Ohio

Abundance: Fairly common.

Variation: There is little variation and the sexes are alike. Some biologists recognize as many as eight subspecies nationwide but differences are very subtle.

Size: Length 16—26 inches and weighs from 6—9 pounds.

Presumed range in Ohio

Abundance: Common.

Variation: Individuals vary in color from brown to grayish, reddish, or rarely, nearly black. Most specimens in Ohio resemble the specimen shown above. 2 subspecies in Ohio.

Habitat: These little squirrels are totally dependent upon trees and make their home in woodlands. Primarily hardwoods but also in mixed pine-hardwood forests. They will live in suburbs and urban areas if sufficient mature trees are present.

Habitat: Fields and woodland edges. The main habitat requirements are some open ground within the vicinity of the burrow for foraging, as well as some higher ground that is above the floodplain for locating the burrow. They avoid swamps and permanent wetlands.

Breeding: Only one litter per year with up to six young. Nest is usually within a hollow in a tree. Bluebird boxes and other artificial nest sites are also used.

Breeding: Mating occurs in March or April with two to four young typical. Only one litter per year. Young are born below ground and remain there until weaned at about six weeks.

Natural History: Lives in tree hollows and old woodpecker holes. Ohio's only nocturnal squirrel. Leaps from tree to tree and glides using flaps of skin between front and hind legs like a parachute. Flattened tail serves as a rudder while gliding. Feeds on nuts, seeds, fruits, fungi, lichens, tree buds, insects, bird eggs, and nestling birds as well as mice. Flying Squirrels are gregarious animals and several may share a den. Southern Flying Squirrels can live up to ten years and will become quite tame in captivity, making reasonable pets. Wild squirrels in rural areas sometimes invade homes and attics where they can become a noisy nuisance as they scramble about in the wee hours. They will raid bird feeders in the middle of the night for sunflower seeds and other bird foods. A much larger version, the Northern Flying Squirrel (*G. sabrinus*), occurs in America in the far north and in the higher elevations of the Appalachian Mountains as far south as northeast Georgia. It can be twice as large as its southern cousin.

Natural History: These large ground squirrels dig extensive underground burrows where they retreat from danger, spend the night, and overwinter. They accumulate huge deposits of fat during the summer and fall, which sustains them during winter hibernation. During this time their metabolism slows dramatically with as few as four heartbeats per minute. They will sometimes climb small trees and bushes in springtime to eat swelling tree buds, but their primary diet is forbs and grasses. Except during breeding or when rearing young they are solitary animals and typically only one adult occupies a burrow. If too numerous they can become pests in rural gardens or farmers croplands and in Ohio they can be hunted year-round. They are sometimes eaten by humans and are known to be palatable table fare. Also known by the name "Woodchuck." They are members of a group known to biologists as "Marmots." Their empty burrows are used as dens by a wide variety of animals, making them an ecologically important species. As they avoid extensive forests, Groundhogs have benefited from land clearing and deforestation in Ohio.

Class—**Mammalia** (mammals)	
Order—**Rodentia** (rodents)	
Family—**Castoridae** (beaver family)	
Beaver—*Castor canadensis*	Beaver dam (top)—Beaver lodge (bottom)

Presumed range in Ohio

Size: Up to 43 inches in total length. Can weigh up to 65 pounds. 35 to 50 pounds is average.

Abundance: In Ohio the Beaver is least common in upland regions, but even there it is common in river valleys.

Variation: The American Society of Mammologists recognizes twenty-four subspecies in North America. The status of Beavers in the eastern US is difficult to determine due to re-introduction programs using transplanted Beavers.

Habitat: Beavers are thoroughly aquatic mammals that to a great extent create their own wetland habitats. To construct their ponds and waterways they require the presence of a stream or spring run with constantly or near constantly flowing water which can be dammed. Streams that are subject to fierce flooding or with exceptionally powerful flows are avoided in preference for more easily contained water flows. In addition to creating their own habitats they will use lakes, rivers, swamps, marshes, and large, deep creeks. In rivers and lakes the lodge or den is often a burrow into the bank of the lake or river. In dammed streams or swamps and marshes a stick lodge typical of the one pictured above is usual. Although they are found throughout Ohio, in the Appalachian Plateaus Province they are restricted to river valleys, bottomlands, and hollows.

Breeding: Mating takes place in mid-winter with the young being born about four months later. There is only one litter per year. Baby Beavers are quite precocious and are born with well developed fur and eyes that open immediately. Four or five young, called kits, is typical. In ideal habitats more young may be produced. Young Beavers are usually weaned in just two/three weeks, but the young Beavers will remain with the family for up to two years before striking out on their own to find new territories. Adult Beavers may mate for life.

Natural History: Beavers are primarily nocturnal in habits, but they may be active at dawn and dusk. In remote locations where human intrusion is absent, they are observed active during the day as well. They feed mostly on the inner bark of trees, with willow being a dietary mainstay. They will also consume sedges and other aquatic vegetation, but in winter live exclusively on bark. The dorsal-ventrally flattened tail is hairless and scaly and along with the webbed hind feet provide these animals with powerful swimming tools. They also possess enlarged incisors which grow continually throughout life and are used to gnaw through trunks and fell trees. Most trees cut by Beavers are small saplings which are used as food, but they will also cut large trees up to two feet in diameter to open the canopy and promote the growth of new food sources. These largest of the North American rodents are famous for their dam building abilities and they will also build elaborate living quarters known as "lodges." After many years of use these lodges may become up to 15 feet across and can house an entire extended family. They have underwater entrances for protection and a hollow "room" that is above the waterline and lined with wood chips or grasses. Other species such as Muskrats and mice may take up residence within these lodges. At one time Beaver fur was one of the most valuable natural resources in America and the pursuit of Beaver fur led to the exploration of much of the continent. Within a few decades they were nearly exterminated by trappers. They can sometimes be a pest when their dam building activities flood farmers' fields, but their wetland creating activities benefit many scores of wetland wildlife species. In fact, the Beaver is one of the most significant players in local ecosystems throughout North America and their value to the overall ecology would be hard to overstate.

Class—**Mammalia** (mammals)
Order—**Rodentia** (rodents)
Family—**Cricetidae** (rats and mice)

Muskrat *Ondatra zibethicus*	Allegheny Woodrat *Neotoma magister*	Norway Rat *Rattus norvigicus*

Muskrat
Ondatra zibethicus

Size: Adults reach 20 inches total length and weigh about 2.5 pounds.

Abundance: Common.

Presumed range in Ohio

Variation: There is no significant variation among individuals in Ohio, but there are several subspecies across the rest of North America.

Habitat: Aquatic. Prefers marshland but also inhabits swamp, ponds, and lakes. Rarely in rivers or large streams. Often sympatric with the Beaver.

Breeding: Prolific. Capable of multiple litters annually and may produce as many as six young per litter. Young are weaned in about a month.

Natural History: Primarily nocturnal but often active during daylight hours in the spring. With webbed hind feet and a laterally flattened tail muskrats are excellent swimmers. They feed on a variety of aquatic vegetation. The name comes from the presence of well developed musk glands. These rodents are an important fur-bearer and in the recent past millions were trapped annually across America for their fur. Life span is only 3—4 years in the wild. The Mink may be the most important predator on muskrats, especially of the young. Adults build lodges similar to the Beaver, but use grasses rather than sticks. The entrance to the Muskrat lodge is below water level while the chamber of the lodge itself is above the high water mark. Sometimes burrows into banks.

Allegheny Woodrat
Neotoma magister

Size: Adults reach 16 inches and about 12 ounces.

Abundance: Rare. Endangered in Ohio.

Presumed range in Ohio

Variation: There are no subspecies and no variation is known to occur in Ohio, or anywhere within its range.

Habitat: Woodrats usually associate with rocks and cliff faces where they make their dens in crevices. They will also use logs, derelict buildings, etc.

Breeding: Breeds spring through fall. Three to four litters per year is possible with two young being typical. Litter sizes of up to six young have been recorded.

Natural History: The range of this species in Ohio is poorly known, and the range map above is an approximation. ODNR reports the only recent sightings are from Adams County. Allegheny Woodrats favor rocky outcrops, talus slopes, boulder piles and cliff faces where they make their den in crevices or small caves. They are sometimes known as "packrats," a name derived from their habit of collecting shiny objects that range from aluminum cans to eating utensils. They cache food in large quantities in what are known as "middens." Ancient woodrat nests in caves can persist for centuries and are studied to gain insight into the historical natural history of a region. Dens are occupied by one adult (and young). When the current occupant dies a new rat may move in.

Norway Rat
Rattus norvigicus

Size: Length can be as much as 15 inches and weigh up to 12 ounces.

Abundance: Common.

Presumed range in Ohio

Variation: None in the wild. The well known laboratory rat is an albino form of this species. Domestic forms can be brown, gray, black, or white.

Habitat: This highly adaptable rodent can live virtually anywhere, including as a stowaway on ships, which is how it immigrated to America from Europe.

Breeding: The fecundity of the Norway Rat is legendary. From six to eight litters per year with up to a dozen young per litter.

Natural History: Also called the Brown Rat, this species has followed man to every corner of the globe. They are responsible for an almost unimaginable degree of human suffering. Throughout the history of human civilization these rodents have destroyed crops and stored foods while spreading devastating diseases, most notably Bubonic Plague. Though less of a threat to modern societies, these rats still shadow the human species. They are common in both urban and rural settings. In cities they live on human garbage, in rural areas livestock food and crops. The common laboratory rat is a domestic version of this animal that has somewhat redeemed the species for humans as an experimental animal for medical and scientific research.

Class—**Mammalia** (mammals)

Order—**Rodentia** (rodents)

Family—**Cricetidae** (rats and mice)

House Mouse *Mus musculus*	Deer Mouse White-footed Mouse *Peromyscus maniculatus Peromyscus leucopus*

White-footed Mouse

Size: Adults reach about 6.5 inches and weigh about 0.75 ounce.

Presumed range in Ohio

Abundance: Very common.

Size: 5 to 8 inches total length (head, body, and tail). Weighs about 1 ounce.

Presumed range in Ohio

Abundance: Fairly common. Species of Concern.

Size: 7 inches total length (head, body, and tail). Weighs about 1 ounce.

Presumed range in Ohio

Abundance: Very common.

Variation: Wild specimens show surprisingly little variation throughout the world, but domesticated laboratory mice come in a variety of colors and patterns. The most well known color is solid white, and most of the "white mice" seen in labs and pet stores are albinos.

Variation: These two species are so similar that most people will not be able to tell them apart. The specimen shown above is the White-footed Mouse, but the Deer Mouse is nearly identical. Both have several subspecies nationwide (over a dozen in the White-footed Mouse and over 50 in the Deer Mouse). In the Deer Mouse, short-tailed, small-eared forms are found in open fields and grasslands and a long-tailed, large-eared variant occurs in woodland habits. Both species exhibit some age related color variation, with younger mice being darker, more grayish in color.

Habitat: A highly adaptable and successful rodent that usually associates with human habitations and man-made structures, but can also live in wild environments.

Habitat: Deer Mice can be found in both woodland habitats and open fields, including agricultural land. This mouse can sometimes be found in wide-open, harvested crop fields.

Habitat: White-footed Mice prefer the woods but may also be found in overgrown fields, fence rows, etc. Unlike the previous species these mice avoid open areas.

Breeding: Broods can number from five to 12. Young females begin breeding at six weeks and produce 14 litters per year.

Breeding: Both these species are prolific breeders that can breed nearly year-round. A typical litter is four or five young, but can be more. The young mice develop rapidly and are ready to breed themselves when only two months old.

Natural History: The House Mouse has adapted to living in close proximity to humans and today they are found wherever there are people throughout the world. As their name implies they regularly enter into houses where they can become both a pest and a health hazard. They live both in cities and farmlands. Like the Norway Rat the House Mouse originated in Eurasia and traveled around the world as a stowaway on sailing ships, eventually populating the entire globe. These mice are primarily nocturnal and their food includes nearly everything eaten by humans plus insects and fungi. Domestic versions are the familiar "white mice."

Natural History: These common mice serve as prey for a variety of predators, from coyotes and bobcats to weasels, snakes, and birds of prey. Both species are primarily nocturnal. They feed on a wide array of seeds, nuts, and grain as well as berries, insects, snails, centipedes, fungi, and occasionally other mice. They will cache large stores of seeds and nuts in the fall and they remain active throughout the winter. Both can become a nuisance as they will regularly enter human dwellings, often nesting in a little-used drawer or cupboard. Several species of *Peromyscus* mice are vectors for tick-born Lyme's disease and in the southwestern United States some Deer Mice can harbor the deadly Hanta Virus. Humans who experience close contact or prolonged exposure to their feces and urine may be at risk. Both species can be arboreal and they may den or nest well above the ground, or they may live beneath a rotted log or stump. Both are adaptable and successful native rodents. The Deer Mouse is found in every habitat type in America and ranges from near sea level to the high mountains. The White-footed Mouse is nearly as adaptable. Professional mammologists use measurements of the skull, tail, and hind foot to differentiate between these two similar and sympatrically occurring species. Together they constitute much of small mammal foods for many of Ohio's predators.

Class—**Mammalia** (mammals)

Order—**Rodentia** (rodents)

Family—**Cricetidae** (rats and mice)

Eastern Harvest Mouse *Reithrodontomys humulis*	Woodland Jumping Mouse *Napaeozapus insignis*	Meadow Jumping Mouse *Zapus hudsonius*

Ohio's two jumping mice are nearly identical. Pictured here is the Meadow Jumping Mouse. Woodland species is very similar but has a white tail tip.

Size: Length 4.5 inches. Weight 0.5 ounce.	Presumed range in Ohio	**Size:** Length 9 inches (mostly tail). Weight 1 ounce.	Presumed range in Ohio	**Size:** Length 8 inches (mostly tail). Weighs 0.67 ounce.	Presumed range in Ohio
Abundance: Rare. Threatened in Ohio.		**Abundance:** Rare. A Species of Concern in Ohio.		**Abundance:** Though widespread they are uncommon.	

Variation: No sexual variation and no variation among specimens in Ohio. One other subspecies occurs west of the Mississippi River.	**Variation:** None in Ohio. Some experts recognize at least five subspecies in North America. Differences are so slight as to be unapparent to the laymen.	**Variation:** No sexual dimorphism is noted and there are no subspecies within Ohio.
Habitat: Fallow fields, especially areas dominated by broomsedge. Thickets are also inhabited but they are absent from large forests. Moist soils and lowlands are primary habitat regions.	**Habitat:** As their name implies the Woodland Jumping Mouse is a decidedly woodland animal that rarely ventures into open areas. Inhabits both spruce/fir and mixed conifer/hardwood forests.	**Habitat:** Meadows and fields that contain dense cover. Generally avoids woodlands but may occur in edge areas or tree-line fence rows and stream banks. Often found near water.
Breeding: Breeds from early spring through fall. Average litter size is small for a mouse, only two or three. Maximum of five.	**Breeding:** Unlike most small rodents, this mouse breeds only once or twice annually producing three to six young.	**Breeding:** Three to six young are born after an 18-day gestation period. Breeds about three times a year from spring to late summer.
Natural History: The Harvest Mouse is easily confused with several other mice species that are found in Ohio. Trained biologists confirm the identity of the Harvest Mouse by examining the upper incisor teeth, which have grooves. These mice are widespread across the southeastern United States but are apparently not common anywhere. Grass seeds and weed seeds are the main food item, but insects may also be eaten. In habits they are mainly nocturnal. Their nests are usually on the surface of the ground (often at the base of a tuft of grass) and consist of a ball of plant fibers and grass. This is one of Ohio's smallest mouse species. Despite the disdain most humans have for small rodents, they play an important role in nature and are food for many predators.	**Natural History:** A mainly boreal (northern) species that ranges southward through the Appalachian Plateau. These mice hibernate for up to six months in the northern parts of their range. They have very long tails and long hind legs which bestow them a remarkable jumping ability. When startled they can reportedly leap a distance of ten feet! Food is fungi, seeds, berries, and insects. They are mainly nocturnal and they sometimes use the burrows and runways of other small rodent species. Woodland Jumping Mice can be told from the very similar Meadow Jumping Mouse by habitat preference and by the white color on the tail tip. The range of this species in Ohio is difficult to determine, and the map above may not represent the exact range of this species in Ohio.	**Natural History:** This rodent, along with the preceding species, comprise the North American representatives of the family Dipodidae. This unique family also ranges into the Old World. The Meadow Jumping Mouse is distinguished from the similar Woodland Jumping Mouse by the uniformly dark tail (as opposed to a white tipped tail). As with the previous species they are mainly nocturnal and do not make runways of their own, but frequently use those made by *Microtus* or other small rodents. Food items are similar to the Woodland Jumping Mouse (fungi, insects, seeds, berries). Both species of Jumping Mice put on heavy layers of fat just prior to their long hibernation, but mortality during hibernation is high and many will not survive their winter sleep.

Class—**Mammalia** (mammals)

Order—**Rodentia** (rodents)

Family—**Cricetidae** (rats and mice)

Meadow Vole *Microtus pennslyvanicus*	**Woodland Vole** *Microtus pinetorum*	**Prairie Vole** *Microtus ochreogaster*

Meadow Vole		Woodland Vole		Prairie Vole	
Size: About 6.5 inches and 1.75 ounces. Max 6.75 inches.	Presumed range in Ohio	**Size:** Length 5 inches. Weight 1 ounce.	Presumed range in Ohio	**Size:** 6 inches and 1.5 ounces.	Presumed range in Ohio
Abundance: One of the most common and widespread voles in Ohio.		**Abundance:** Widespread but uncommon in Ohio. Species of Concern.		**Abundance:** Species of Concern in Ohio. Uncommon.	

Meadow Vole	Woodland Vole	Prairie Vole
Variation: Summer pelage is chestnut brown. Winter pelage is darker, more grayish. Juveniles very dark gray.	**Variation:** There are several subspecies of this widespread vole. Three subspecies occur in Ohio, all are very similar.	**Variation:** *M.o. ohionensis* is the subspecies that occurs in Ohio. No significant variation in this subspecies.
Habitat: Primarily fields and meadows from the northern US to the Arctic Circle. Favors moist soils.	**Habitat:** Tolerates a wide variety of habitats as long as there is sufficiant cover. Primarily deciduous woodlands.	**Habitat:** This species generally avoids the woods and prefers open, grassy habitats and overgrown fields.
Breeding: A remarkably fecund animal, young Meadow Voles can breed within four weeks after birth. Litter size is four to six.	**Breeding:** Breeds spring through fall with up to four litters per year. One to four young per litter. Young wean within three weeks and can reproduce by 12 weeks.	**Breeding:** Unlike most rodents, Prairie Voles are monogamous. Three to five young is typical. Nest is a ball of woven grasses situated within a grass tussock.
Natural History: Generally regarded as the world's most prolific mammal. Populations in many areas are cyclical and subject to "boom / bust" cycles. During years of high population density there can be as many as several hundred per acre in prime habitat. Because they can be so common, these voles are an important food source for predatory species ranging from snakes and carnivorous mammals to birds of prey. They can also impact humans by eating crops, garden produce, young trees in orchards, etc. They feed on a wide variety of grasses and plants and will eat seeds, roots, and even bark. The well maincured runways of the Meadow Vole are kept clear by constant cropping of grasses within the runway. These well used pathways are typically hidden beneath tall grass, but they are easily discernable following a grass fire.	**Natural History:** Woodland Voles create networks of tunnels just below the ground or "runways" that are near the surface but beneath the leaf litter on the forest floor. These tunnel sytems are utilized by other small mammals such as shrews. They rarely venture far from these tunnels, but do emerge to glean seeds, grasses, and mast. They also eat roots, especially roots of grasses, and root crops like potatoes are also eaten. Active both day and night. Their subterrean habits render them less vulnerable to many predators, but they are prey for a wide variety of carnivores, raptors, and especially snakes which are able to enter the burrow systems. Young exhibit a dark gray color. Adults are more chestnut. Populations of Woodland Voles are remarkably stable and they do not experience the "boom-bust" cycles of other vole species.	**Natural History:** Coarse, grizzled gray fur and shorter tail distinguish this species from the Woodland Vole. It is very similar to the Meadow Vole but lives in drier, more upland habitats. Although insects are eaten, these voles feed mostly on vegetation. Including but not limited to grasses, roots, herbaceous weeds, seeds, leaves, stems, etc. Like other voles creates a system of shallow burrows. The North American range of this species mostly approximates the occurrance of the original American prairies. It does range well into the eastern Temperate Forest Ecoregion, but is found mostly in open areas within that ecoregion. It is probably less common today than in historical times. Populations can cycle between extreme densities of up to 50 voles per acre, down to as few as two per acre during population crashes.

Class—**Mammalia** (mammals)

Order—**Rodentia** (rodents)	Order—**Insectivora** (moles and shrews)	
Family—**Cricetidae** (rats and mice)	Family—**Soricidae** (shrews)	
Southern Bog Lemming *Synaptomys cooperi*	**Least Shrew** *Cryptotis parva*	**Northern Short-tailed Shrew** *Blarina brevicaudus*

Southern Bog Lemming (*Synaptomys cooperi*)

Size: Adult is 5 inches (total length) and 1.25 ounces.

Presumed range in Ohio

Abundance: Uncommon. Species of Concern in Ohio.

Variation: Several subspecies but very little variation in Ohio specimens.

Habitat: Although they can found in bogs, they occupy nearly all habitat types. The presence of grasses seems to be the only habitat requirement.

Breeding: Breeds most of year except for mid-winter. Typical litter is three with a maximum of eight.

Natural History: Bog Lemmings often use the same burrows as other mice and vole species, as well as mole tunnels. They also make runways on the surface beneath leaf litter or grass/vegetation. Primarily nocturnal and crepuscular, they feed on green plants and berries mainly. They often occur in colonies. Bog Lemmings are mainly northern mammals that range southward into the southern Appalachians as far as east Tennessee and western North Carolina. They also occur in parts of Kentucky, Missouri, and Kansas. Though their range includes the entire state of Ohio, they may be very locally distributed. Some experts suspect that the Bog Lemming may be declining as a result of competition with the more common Meadow Vole. As with many small mammal species, the numerous subspecies of Bog Lemming can be told apart only by expert mammologists.

Least Shrew (*Cryptotis parva*)

Size: Three inches and 0.2 ounce.

Presumed range in Ohio

Abundance: Probably fairly common but rarely observed.

Variation: Summer pelage is brownish, turning to slate gray during winter.

Habitat: Grassy areas and overgrown fields primarily, but also in woodlands. Seems to avoid the wetland areas of Ohio in favor of drier habitats.

Breeding: Several litters per year is common averaging four to five young per litter. Breeds March through November.

Natural History: Possessing an extremely high metabolism, this tiny mammal can consume its own weight in food daily. Like many other shrews they are known to cache food items. Although these shrews are rarely seen due to their diminutive size and reclusive habits, they are usually a fairly common mammal throughout their very large range. Owls are a major predator and in fact the presence of these tiny shrews in a given area is often confirmed by examining owl pellets for skeleton remains. Known food items are caterpillars, beetles, other insects, snails, spiders, and earthworms. Unlike other shrews that tend to be quite solitary, the Least Shrew is much more social and sometimes several can be found together. They are very similar to the next species (Northern Short-tailed Shrew). Experts examine the teeth to differentiate between the two species.

Northern Short-tailed Shrew (*Blarina brevicaudus*)

Size: Maximum of 5.5 inches and 1 ounce.

Presumed range in Ohio

Abundance: Very common. This is Ohio's most common shrew.

Variation: Winter pelage is longer and darker and juveniles are nearly black.

Habitat: Fond damp woodlands and in fact cannot tolerate excessively dry conditions very well. Does avoid saturated soils however.

Breeding: Breeds in spring and fall. Up to four litters of four to six young per litter. Nest is shredded leaves or grasses.

Natural History: Northern Short-tail Shrews are primarily nocturnal animals and have very high metabolic rates. They are hyperactive animals that will eat as much as one-half their body weight daily! They are known to have periods of intense activity followed by periods of lethargy. Food is a variety of insects, snails, earthworms, millipedes, etc. as well as much larger prey including mice that are as large as themselves. The Northern Short-tailed Shrew is known to possess venomous saliva with which kills its prey. Like most shrews they have tiny eyes and their vision is quite poor, they are known to utilize echolocation. Except when breeding and rearing young these are solitary animals. They forage beneath the leaf litter in runways and tunnels and will dig their own tunnels or use those of other small rodents. Experts identify shrew species by examining their teeth!

Class—**Mammalia** (mammals)

Order—**Insectivora** (moles and shrews)

Family—**Soricidae** (shrews)

Masked Shrew *Sorex cinereus*	**Smokey Shrew** *Sorex fumerus*

Size: Length 3.8 inches. Weight 0.375 ounce.

Abundance: Probably fairly common but rarely seen.

Variation: Brownish in summer, grayish in winter. Young specimens tend to be browner than adults.

Size: Length 4.5 inches. Weight 0.5 ounce.

Abundance. Uncommon. A Species of Concern in Ohio.

Variation: Winter pelage dark gray, summer pelage browner. Summer pelage is April to October.

Habitat: Found in virtually all wild habitats. Primarily a northern species.

Breeding: Four to ten tiny (1/2 inch) young are born from spring to fall.

Natural History: Though mainly nocturnal, these shrews are active both day and night. They dart in and out of leaf litter on the forest floor or move rapidly along runways in overgrown fields. They will make chirping noises as they forage and some believe they echolocate. Known food items are snails/slugs, caterpillars, grubs, spiders, and ants. They will also eat carrion. Shrews do not hibernate, and must forage year-round. For an animal with such high food requirements, survival in winter would seem a daunting task. But dormant insects and other invertebrates are located and eaten in large quantities. In fact, shrews may be quite beneficial to man by consuming enormous quantities of injurious insects and grubs. Like other shrews their life span is short, believed to be only about a year and half for the Masked Shrew. Masked Shrews also frequently go by the name Cinereous Shrew. The map above is a close approximation of this species range in Ohio, but may not be exact. This is one of Ohio's smallest mammals, but not the smallest. That distinction goes to the **American Pygmy Shrew** (*S. hoyi*-not shown). The Pygmy Shrew is one of the world's smallest mammals. The average adult weighs about as much as a dime! American Pygmy Shrews often occur in the same habitats as other shrew species, with the various species dividing the habitats in accordance with their size. Smaller shrews may feed on different prey in different micro-habitats than their larger cousins.

Habitat: Moist woodlands. Especially where there is abundant ground cover.

Breeding: Litter size averages five to six. Two or three litters in warmer months.

Natural History: This is another primarily northern species that invades the southern United States as far south as northern Georgia along the Appalachian Plateau. Like other shrews it does not hibernate and will be active even in the coldest weather. Its diet is mostly insects and other invertebrates, but salamanders are also listed as prey. The Smokey Shrew, along with other shrew species, is undoubtedly a very beneficial species to man due to the large number of larvae, pupae, and adult insects consumed daily. Many of which are significant pests to forest trees. The average life span of this species is probably less than a year and half. Females will construct a nest of shredded leaves or grass in a sheltered place beneath a rock or within a rotted log or stump. Like the other small mammals in this book this animal is an important food source for a wide variety of predators, with owls being perhaps their biggest enemy. The range map shown above for this species is probably not exact. Shrews of all varieties can be difficult animals to study due to their tiny size and secretive behaviors. Unlike many more familiar animals, proper identification of shrews is exceedingly difficult and usually involves close examination of the teeth with a hand lense or low-powered microscope. Thus mammologists who study shrews can rarely rely on second-hand information obtained from non-professionals. Instead they must verify sightings personally to be sure of the exact species involved.

Class—**Mammalia** (mammals)

Order—**Insectivora** (shrews and moles)

Family—**Talpidae** (moles)

Eastern Mole *Scalopus aquaticus*	Hairy-tailed Mole *Parascalops breweri*	Star-nosed Mole *Condylura cristata*
		Close-up of snout

Size: 6 inches and 2 ounces.	Presumed range in Ohio 	**Size:** 6.33 inches and 1.8 ounces.	Presumed range in Ohio 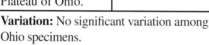	**Size:** Total length 7 inches. Weight 2 ounces.	Presumed range in Ohio 
Abundance: Very common. This is the mole that is typically the bane of gardeners in Ohio.		**Abundance:** Common. Replaces the Eastern Mole in the Appalachian Plateau of Ohio.		**Abundance.** Uncommon. ODNR lists this mole as a Species of Concern in Ohio.	

Variation: Males are slightly larger than females.	**Variation:** No significant variation among Ohio specimens.	**Variation:** No sexual dimorphism noted. Juveniles have darker pelage.
Habitat: Except for wetlands these moles can be found in any habitat where soils are suitable for burrowing.	**Habitat:** Except for wetlands these moles can be found in any habitat where soils are suitable for burrowing.	**Habitat:** Wet meadows, swamps, mesic woodlands, and near stream courses. Even inhabits muddy habitats.
Breeding: One litter per year in early spring. Two to five young.	**Breeding:** Mating takes place in the spring and four or five young is average.	**Breeding:** Breeds in late winter and litters of two to seven are born in early spring.
Natural History: The most wide-ranging mole in America. Although considered a pest in suburban lawns and rural gardens, Eastern Moles actually perform some helpful tasks. The tunnels they dig help to aerate the soil and allow rainfall to penetrate more easily. They also prey heavily upon destructive grubs such as the Japanese Beetle. The pelage of the Eastern Mole is "reversible" and will lie smoothly against the skin whether the mole is moving forward or backward in tight tunnels. The powerful forelegs allow this animal to burrow at an astonishing pace, and the webbed toes help move dirt aside. The eyes are tiny and covered with skin, and there are no external ears. This is an animal that is superbly adapted to a subterranean lifestyle and Eastern Moles will spend 99 percent of their lives below ground. Ranges from the Atlantic Coastal Plain well into the Great Plains (except for the Appalachian Highlands). The range map above is an approximation and may not be exact.	**Natural History:** Active year-round in both day and night but in winter utilizes deeper tunnel systems. More shallow tunnels are used in warm weather when it may sometimes leave tunnels at night to forage above ground. Feeding on earthworms and grubs this mole has been known to consume its own weight in food daily. The tunnels of the Hairy-tail Mole are less obvious above ground than those of the Eastern Mole. Many other small mammals such as shrews and mice are known to use the tunnels constructed by this mole. Life span of four years. The range of this species in Ohio closely includes all of the physiographic region known as the Appalachian Highlands Division. Meanwhile the previous species (Eastern Mole) fills the same ecological niche in the lower elevations of the Interior Plains Division (see Figure 1). Very similar to the preceding species from which it can be told by its hairy tail. The range map above is at best a close approximation.	**Natural History:** Morphologically speaking, this is surely one of America's most unusual animals. The tip of the snout is adorned with fleshy tentacles. At first glance it resembles a mole with a sea anemone (or perhaps a small octopus) attached to its nose! The fleshy tentacles are most likely tactile, and some experts cite evidence that they may also serve to detect electrical impulses emitted by fish and other aquatic animals (Whitaker and Hamilton 1998). In habits this mole is also unique among the Talpidae of Ohio in that they are decidedly aquatic animals. Their tunnels sometimes open directly into streams and they are excellent swimmers. Aquatic insects, worms, and even crustaceans and small fish are captured underwater. Their primary food however is earthworms and the unusual tentacled "star" on the snout undoubtedly plays an important role in locating the moles' food. The map above may not be exactly accurate for its Ohio range.

Class—**Mammalia** (mammals)

Order—**Chiroptera** (bats)

Family—**Vespertilionidae** (mouse-eared bats)

Eastern Pipistrelle *Perimyotis subflavus*	Evening Bat *Nycticeius humeralis*	Silver-haired Bat *Lasionycteris noctivagans*

Eastern Pipistrelle

Size: 3.5 inches. Weight about 0.25 ounces.

Presumed range in Ohio

Abundance: Fairly common but now an ODNR Species of Concern.

Variation: None.

Habitat: Woodlands, stream courses, and edges of fields bordering woodlands are favorite hunting areas.

Breeding: Females give birth to one or two babies (pups) in June.

Natural History: Eastern Pipistrelles are widespread and formerly very common throughout the eastern United States. Today they are in decline due to a fungal disease known as "White-nose Syndrome." They are a migratory species to some degree and in Ohio they most common during warmer months, although some will hibernate in caves in Ohio. Food is tiny airborne insects. They will leave the roost before dark and are often seen hunting at dusk. Like many bats the females form maternal colonies where young are reared, often in buildings or sheds. Unlike many other species however, these maternal colonies are usually small, numbering only one or two dozen individuals. Hibernation begins in late fall (October) and lasts until April or May. Hibernating bats may lose as much as 25–30 percent of their body weight during the winter.

Evening Bat

Size: 4 inches. Up to 0.5 ounce.

Presumed range in Ohio

Abundance: Species of Interest. Fairly common in southeast Ohio.

Variation: None.

Habitat: Swamps, stream corridors, and woodlands as well as woods openings and edge areas are used.

Breeding: One to three young are produced in late spring/early summer.

Natural History: Evening Bats in Ohio are summer residents that winter farther south where hibernation is not necessary. Most leave by early fall, but some may stay into late fall. Summer roosts include hollow trees as well as buildings, and they do not seem to utilize caves as is the habit of many bat species. A wide variety of small insects are eaten, including species that are injurious to farm crops. Though widespread across much of the southeast, these are lowland and low plateau animals that avoid the higher elevations of the Appalachian Mountains. Most of these bats found in the northern portions of their range in summer are females. The males apparently stay farther to the south. In recent years a few Evening Bats have been seen as far north as northern Ohio but they are mostly seen in the southern half of the state.

Silver-haired Bat

Size: 4 inches and 0.3 ounce.

Presumed range in Ohio

Abundance: Uncommon. ODNR Species of Concern.

Variation: None.

Habitat: The Silver-haired Bat is a forest species that hides in tree hollows or beneath peeling bark during daylight.

Breeding: Young are born in late spring. Two pups is typical.

Natural History: While this bat might be seen anywhere in the state during the spring and fall, it is a passage migrant through most of Ohio. A few will winter in southernmost Ohio but most travel farther to the south. It spends the summer in the boreal forests of North America, from just to the north of Ohio well into Canada. This is a widespread species that ranges from coast to coast in North America. Its summer range is as far north as southeastern Alaska. Unlike many bat species the Silver-haired Bat is mostly a solitary animal that roosts singly, although some colony activity is reported among females with young. Silver-haireds derive their name from the "frosted" appearance of their pelage, which is a unique and identifying characteristic among the bats of Ohio. Feeding flights mostly near water (streams, bogs, lakes, etc.).

Class—**Mammalia** (mammals)
Order—**Chiroptera** (bats)
Family—**Vespertilionidae** (mouse-eared bats)

Eastern Red Bat *Lasiurus borealis*	Hoary Bat *Lasiurus cinereus*	Big Brown Bat *Eptisicus fuscus*

Eastern Red Bat
Lasiurus borealis

Size: Maximum 5 inches. Up to 0.5 ounces. Wingspan 13 inches.

Abundance: Fairly common but regarded as a Species of Concern in Ohio.

Presumed range in Ohio

Variation: Males are red, females are chestnut or yellowish.

Habitat: Woodlands and edge areas in both rural and urban regions. Will catch insects around streetlights in towns.

Breeding: Litter size is one to four with the pups born in late May or early June.

Natural History: In summer this species usually roosts in trees by hanging from a limb. Usually solitary but sometimes more than one bat will roost together. Roosting bats resemble dead leaves. Trees chosen for roosting are often at the edge of a woodland bordering an open field. Red Bats are migratory and summer in Ohio while wintering farther to the south. The range is quite large and includes most of the United States east of the Rocky Mountains and much of southeastern Canada. Hibernation takes place in hollow trees or beneath leaf litter on the forest floor, a very unusual tactic for a bat! Though mainly nocturnal, this species often flies in daylight, especially in late afternoon or early evening.

Hoary Bat
Lasiurus cinereus

Size: Maximum 5.5 inches. Wingspan to 16 inches.

Abundance: Rare. Species of Concern in Ohio

Presumed range in Ohio

Variation: Females are on average slightly heavier than males.

Habitat: Another forest species that may be seen in both rural and urban areas.

Breeding: Averages two pups born in mid-May to mid-June.

Natural History: With a wingspan of 16 inches, this is the largest bat species in Ohio. Its name comes from the white-tipped hairs of the fur on its back. Hoary Bats have the greatest distribution of any American Bat. They summer as far north as Canada and winter in the coastal plain of the southeastern United States or in the desert southwest. Most of the Hoary Bats seen in Ohio are migrating to and from summer / winter residences. Oddly, the sexes segregate themselves following breeding and most of those seen in the eastern US in summer are females. Males summer farther west in the great plains, Rocky Mountains, or west coast. Like the Red Bat these bats are mostly solitary and roost among the foliage in trees. Moths are reported to be their primary food.

Big Brown Bat
Eptisicus fuscus

Size: 4.5 inches and nearly 1 ounces. Wingspan 14 inches maximum.

Abundance: Formerly common. Now a species of Concern in Ohio.

Presumed range in Ohio

Variation: None in Ohio.

Habitat: Open fields, vacant lots, rural and urban areas. Sometimes seen hunting insects around suburban streetlights.

Breeding: Breeds in fall. Delayed fertilization. Twins born in late spring.

Natural History: Stays year-round in Ohio. Winters in caves or derelict buildings. Summer roosts are usually associated with human structures (buildings, eaves, bridges). Also known to use hollow trees and abandoned mines. The primary food is reported to be beetles. These are the large, brown bats that are common around human habitations and they range throughout the state. These bats seem to tolerate cold fairly well and they remain active well into the fall. They can sometimes even be seen flying around on warm days in winter. Small flying beetles are its favorite food item, but a wide variety of insects are eaten. This bat is a useful consumer of insect pests and is thus a valuable friend to man. Has been hard hit by "White-nose Syndrome."

Class—**Mammalia** (mammals)
Order—**Chiroptera** (bats)
Family—**Vespertilionidae** (mouse-eared bats)
Myotis Bats—genus—*Myotis* (4 species in Ohio, 3 shown below)

Eastern Small-footed Bat *Myotis leibii*	**Northern Bat** *Myotis septentrionalis*	**Little Brown Bat** *Myotis lucifugus*

Presumed range in Ohio	Presumed range in Ohio	Presumed range in Ohio

Size: All *Myotis* are somewhat small bats, ranging in size from 3 to 3.5 inches and weighing from 0.2 to 0.33 of an ounce. The the Little Brown Bat is the largest *Myotis* in Ohio (3.5 inches), with the smallest being the Eastern Small-footed Bat (3 inches).

Abundance: The four species of *Myotis* Bats found in Ohio range in abundance from fairly common to rare. The rarest species are the Eastern Small-footed Bat (Species of Concern) and the Indiana Bat (not shown, Endangered). The Little Brown Bat is fairly common but is regarded as Species of Concern and the Northern Bat is listed as a Threatened Species.

Variation: Most bats present an identification problem for the average person, but the *Myotis* bats can be especially confusing. Confirming the exact species of these bats usually requires looking very closely and may sometimes mean having the bat in hand.

Habitat: Some *Myotis* species may hibernate in caves but will also use other places such as hollow trees or buildings for summer-time roosts. Some species are sometimes seen roosting in clumps by day beneath the shelter of roof overhangs, roofs of picnic pavilions, inside old barns, etc. A wide variety of habitats are utilized by these bats during warmer months. Forests, fields, wetlands, and especially stream courses.

Breeding: Mating occurs in the fall with fertilization delayed until early spring. Young are born in late spring or early summer and all species form "maternity colonies" of females with young which may be in caves, buildings, hollow trees, or other structures. All of Ohio's *Myotis* bats produce a single baby annually.

Natural History: Indiana Bats are known for their huge hibernating colonies that tend to concentrate in only a few select caves during winter. Species like this are thus vulnerable to human or natural disturbance of their select hibernating locales. And congregating in large colonies can lead to epidemics of pathogens like the "White-nose" fungus. Some *Myotis* bats are migratory, moving south during winter months. Most feed in flight on flying insects but one species (Northern Bat) feeds by gleaning insects from leaves while hovering. Some like to forage primarily over water above ponds, creeks, and wetland areas (Little Brown Bat). Throughout America, many bat species are in steep decline and many once-common species have been hard hit by the fungal disease known as "White-nose Syndrome." The Little Brown Bat, once perhaps the most common *Myotis* in the eastern United States, has been especially hard hit by this disease. All bats are remarkable little animals that consume untold numbers of injurious insect species, including millions of mosquitoes, and they are thus extremely useful to man. The impact of White-nose Syndrome on some of America's bat populations has been catastrophic. No one yet knows how much this disease and its subsequent decimation of North American bats will impact on the overall health of America's ecosystems.

CHAPTER 4
THE BIRDS OF OHIO

Table 5.
The Orders and Families of Ohio Birds

Class—**Aves** (birds)

Order—**Passeriformes** (songbirds)

Family	**Tyrannidae** (flycatchers)
Family	**Turdidae** (thrushes)
Family	**Lanidae** (shrikes)
Family	**Alaudidae** (larks)
Family	**Mimidae** (thrashers)
Family	**Motacillidae** (wagtails)
Family	**Bombycillidae** (waxwings)
Family	**Certhidae** (creepers)
Family	**Paridae** (chickadees)
Family	**Regulidae** (kinglets)
Family	**Sittidae** (nuthatches)
Family	**Troglodytidae** (wrens)
Family	**Polioptilidae** (gnatcatchers)
Family	**Hirundinidae** (swallows)
Family	**Corvidae** (jays and crows)
Family	**Vironidae** (vireos)
Family	**Parulidae** (warblers)
Family	**Icturidae** (blackbirds)
Family	**Thraupidae** (tanagers)
Family	**Sturnidae** (mynas)
Family	**Passeridae** (weaver finches)
Family	**Emberzidae** (sparrows)
Family	**Calcaridae** (longspurs)
Family	**Cardinalidae** (grosbeaks)
Family	**Fringillidae** (finches)

Order—**Apodiformes** (swifts and hummingbirds)

Family	**Apodidae** (swifts)
Family	**Trochylidae** (hummingbirds)

Order—**Coraciiformes**

Family	**Alcedinidae** (kingfishers)

Order—**Piciformes**

Family	**Picidae** (woodpeckers)

Order—**Cuculiformes**

Family	**Cuculidae** (cuckoos)

Order—**Columbiformes**

Family	**Columbidae** (doves)

Order—**Galliformes** (chicken-like birds)

Family	**Phasianidae** (grouse)
Family	**Odontophoridae** (quail)

Order—**Caprimulgiformes**

Family	**Caprimulgidae** (nightjars)

Order—**Strigiformes** (owls)

Family	**Tytonidae** (barn owls)
Family	**Strigidae** (typical owls)

Order—**Falconiformes** (raptors)

Family	**Accipitridae** (hawks, eagles, kites)
Family	**Cathartidae** (vultures)
Family	**Falconidae** (falcons)

Order—**Ciconiiformes** (wading birds)

Family	**Ardeidae** (herons)

Order—**Gruiformes** (rails and cranes)

Family	**Rallidae** (rails)
Family	**Gruidae** (cranes)

Order—**Chariidriformes** (shorebirds)

Family	**Charidriidae** (plovers)
Family	**Scolopacidae** (sandpipers)
Family	**Laridae** (gulls and terns)

Order—**Gaviiformes**

Family	**Gaviidae** (loons)

Order—**Pelecaniformes**

Family	**Pelecanidae** (pelicans)

Order—**Suliformes**

Family	**Phalacrocoracidae** (cormorants)

Order—**Podicipediformes**

Family	**Podicipedidae** (grebes)

Order—**Anseriformes** (waterfowl)

Family	**Anatidae** (ducks, geese, and swans)

Class—**Aves** (birds)

Order—**Passeriformes** (songbirds)

Family—**Tyrannidae** (flycatchers)

Eastern Wood Pewee *Contopus virens*	**Olive-sided Flycatcher** *Contopus cooperi*	**Eastern Phoebe** *Sayornis phoebe*

Size: 6.5 inches.

Abundance: Common migrant and nester.

Variation: None. Sexes are alike.

Presumed range in Ohio

Size: 7.5 inches.

Abundance: Uncommon to rare.

Variation: None. Sexes are alike.

Presumed range in Ohio

Size: 7 inches.

Abundance: Common.

Variation: No variation. Sexes alike.

Presumed range in Ohio

Migratory Status: Wintering in South America, the eastern Wood Pewee arrives in North America in late spring (peak arrival in Ohio mid-May). They are a summer/breeding resident across the state that stays throughout the summer. They beginning leaving in late August with a few lingering into early October.

Migratory Status: A spring and fall passage migrant in Ohio. Birds that pass through Ohio spend the summer in the boreal forests of Canada and winter from southern Mexico to South America. Spring migrants begin to arrive in Ohio in May and have moved on by mid-June. Fall migration through Ohio is mid-August through September.

Migratory Status: Eastern Phoebes begin to arrive in Ohio as early as March, perhaps a little later in the northernmost portion of the state. They are summer residents that will nest in the state. Fall migration begins late September through October and in the southernmost region of Ohio a few may occasionally linger through the winter.

Habitat: Wood Pewees are forest birds but they favor small openings in the woods or edge areas where marshes or fields border woodlands.

Habitat: The summer habitat is coniferous forests of the Rocky Mountain region and northern North America where it associates with small forest openings.

Habitat: Woodlands and woods openings. Also in rural yards or parks in wooded regions. Can be common around rural homesteads.

Breeding: Nests are usually built high in trees in a terminal fork. Nest material consists of grasses and lichens. Two to four eggs are laid.

Breeding: Nest is typically on a branch of a conifer and built of sticks, lichens, and rootlets. One clutch per year. Three to four eggs per clutch.

Breeding: Pheobes are early nesters in Ohio. Nesting can occur by early April and there will often be a second nesting later in the summer.

Natural History: These nondescript little brown birds often go unnoticed except for the distinctive call from which they derive their name. Their "pee-a-weee" song is a common summer sound in the woodlands throughout Ohio. Like other members of the flycatcher family, they hunt flying insects from high perches, swooping out to catch their food on the wing. They are typically fairly tolerant of humans and can sometimes be closely approached. They are very similar to eastern Pheobe, but note orange lower bill and pale wing bars on the eastern Wood Pewee.

Natural History: These flycatchers are quite acrobatic in the air. They feed in typical flycatcher fashion by sallying forth from a high perch to snatch flying insects. Bees and wasps are reportedly a favorite food. This species avoids deep forest in favor of openings such as bogs, meadows, or second growth and may benefit from forest fires or human activities such as logging. Paradoxically, the species has been declining in recent decades. This decline is possibly tied to changes in the winter habitat in tropical America. They are federally listed as Species of Concern by the USF and WS.

Natural History: The eastern Pheobe is most easily told from other Flycatchers by its habit of constantly wagging its tail down and up. Its nests are also distinctive, being constructed of mud and lined with mosses. Nests are placed beneath some form of overhang, most often the eaves of buildings. The cup-shaped nest is plastered to the surface in the manner of many swallows. These are normally tame little birds that will allow humans to approach to within a few yards before flying off only a short distance. Similar to the Wood Pewee but has a dark bill and lacks wing bars.

Class—**Aves** (birds)

Order—**Passeriformes** (songbirds)

Family—**Tyrannidae** (flycatchers)

Empid Flycatchers
genus—*Empidonax* (5 nearly identical species in Ohio)

Acadian Flycatcher *Empidonax virescens*	**Willow Flycatcher** *Empidonax traillii*	**Least Flycatcher** *Empidonax minimus*

Alder Flycatcher *Empidonax alnorum*	**Yellow-bellied Flycatcher** *Empidonax flaviventris*	Presumed range of *Empidonax* Flycatchers in Ohio. All five species may be seen throughout the state.

Size: Range in size from 5.25 to 5.75 inches.

Abundance: Least Flycatcher is fairly common throughout its broader range but has declined in Ohio and is regarded as a Species of Special Interest by the ODNR. Alder Flycatcher may be the least common of the group. Acadian is probably the most common. Willow and Yellow-bellied are probably fairly common.

Variation: Five species of *Empidonax* flycatchers may be seen in Ohio. All five species are so similar in appearance that even expert bird watchers have trouble identifying individual species. Most people must content themselves with calling them all "Empid Flycatchers."

Migratory Status: The Yellow-bellied Flycatcher is a spring and fall migrant that merely passes through the state. All other *Empidonax* flycatchers in Ohio will breed in the state. All winter far to south, some as far as South America. *Empidonax* species return to Ohio from early or mid-May to mid-June. All begin to leave in August and are gone by mid-September.

Habitat: All are woodland species. Acadian and Willow Flycatchers are fond of streamside habitats, swamps, and marshes. Least Flycatchers prefer regenerative woodlands and edge areas. Yellow-bellied Flycatchers summer in the boreal forests of the far north. Both the Alder Flycatcher and the Least Flycatcher also range well to the north of Ohio in summer. All five species may be seen throughout Ohio during migration. All but the Yellow-bellied are known to nest in the state.

Breeding: The Acadian Flycatcher weaves a flimsy nest of grass on a low branch and lays two to four eggs. Willow Flycatchers build their nest in the fork of a low branch or bush and lay two to four eggs. Least Flycatcher breeds mostly to the north of Ohio but a few will breed in the northern part of the state. They usually lay four eggs in a nest woven of grasses and fibers and placed in a fork of a tree branch. Alder Flycatcher nests are coarsely woven cups typically placed in low bushes with four eggs.

Natural History: Some species, like the Acadian Flycatcher, may be less numerous in Ohio today due to the decline in forested habitats. The Willow Flycatcher on the other hand may be helped by the regeneration of successional forests. Serious birdwatchers find that the most reliable way to identify these small flycatchers is to learn their songs. In fact, Willow and Alder Flycatchers are so similar in appearance that visual identification alone is unreliable.

Class—**Aves** (birds)

Order—**Passeriformes** (songbirds)

Family—**Tyrannidae** (flycatchers)

Eastern Kingbird *Tyrannus tyrannus*	**Great Crested Flycatcher** *Myiarchus crinitus*

Size: 8.5 inches

Abundance: Fairly common.

Variation: None. Sexes alike.

Migratory Status: A summertime resident of Ohio that nests in the state. Winters in South America. Seen in Ohio from late April to September.

Presumed range in Ohio

Size: 8.75 inches.

Abundance: Fairly common.

Variation: None. Sexes alike.

Migratory Status: A summertime resident of Ohio. Arrives in Ohio in early May. Winters in Central America, Mexico, or southern Florida.

Presumed range in Ohio

Habitat: Prefers open fields and pastures in rural areas. In urban settings it likes open parks and large empty lots. Commonly seen perched on fences.

Habitat: Openings in deciduous and mixed woodlands. Edge areas and open woodlands are also used in Ohio. Winter habitat is tropical forests of many types.

Breeding: The nest is built of twigs and grass high in trees. The average clutch size is three to five eggs. One clutch per year. Sturdy nest is placed on limb near the top of large tree.

Breeding: Unlike most flycatchers this bird is a cavity nester, often using old woodpecker holes. Three to five eggs, laid in mid-May, is typical.

Natural History: The name "Kingbird" is derived from this species' aggressive defense of territory against other birds, including even large hawks! They hunt flying insects from an open perch, which is frequently a fence or power line. When flying insect prey is spotted they will launch themselves into an attack that often results in an aerial "dogfight" between bird and insect. They will also hunt flying insects by hovering. Berries are an important food item, especially mulberrys. Serviceberries, blackberries, and Elderberrys are also eaten. These are conspicuous birds. Their charcoal gray upper parts contrast strongly with a whitish breast and belly. The bright reddish-orange blaze on the top of the head is usually not visible to the casual observer. Winters in South America, as far south as Argentina. Some populations in the eastern United States have shown declines in the last few decades, but this remains a common species.

Natural History: The name comes from the "crested" look of the head, which may not be readily apparent. Reddish underside of the tail and wing primaries along with the distinctly yellowish belly contrasting with gray breast is unique among Ohio flycatchers. These features plus large size make it one of the more recognizable members of the flycatcher family. However, they are a rather unobtrusive species that can be easily overlooked. Food is large insects captured in flight from its perch, which is often high in the canopy. Returns to Ohio in late April from wintering grounds in Central America. Forages for insects in treetops and catches flying insects on the wing. Also consumes some berries. More common in the southeastern United States than in Ohio and the midwest. Breeding success may be tied to woodpecker populations since old woodpecker holes are a favorite nesting site.

Class—**Aves** (birds)

Order—**Passeriformes** (songbirds)

Family—**Turdidae** (thrush family)

Robin *Turdus migratorius*	**Eastern Bluebird** *Siala sialis*	**Wood Thrush** *Hylocichla mustela*
	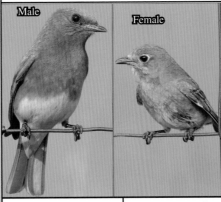  Male / Female	 

Size: 10 inches.	**Size:** 7 inches.	**Size:** 7.75 inches.
Abundance: Very common.	**Abundance:** Common.	**Abundance:** Fairly common.
Variation: Sexes similar but females are paler.	**Variation:** Male is more vividly colored (see above).	**Variation:** No variation. Sexes alike.

Presumed range in Ohio (for each species)

Migratory Status: Robins are most common in spring, summer, and fall months but they can be seen year-round in southern Ohio.

Migratory Status: Farther to the north the Bluebird is a summer-only resident, but in Ohio they are often present year-round. Will migrate in harsh weather.

Migratory Status: A summer resident that winters in Central America and even as far as south as northern South America. April to Sept. in Ohio.

Habitat: Virtually all habitats in the state may be utilized. Most common in areas of human disturbance, especially older suburbs. They are fond of hunting earthworms in suburban lawns.

Habitat: Field edges, woods openings, and open fields, marshes, and pastures. Savanna-like habitats, i.e., open spaces interspersed with large trees, are a favorite habitat.

Habitat: Woodlands. May be found in both mature forests and successional areas. In both it likes thick undergrowth. The Appalachian Plateau Province offers the most habitat in Ohio today.

Breeding: The three to four "sky blue" eggs are laid in a nest constructed of mud and grass, often in the crotch of a tree in an urban yard.

Breeding: Bluebirds are cavity nesters that readily take to man-made nest boxes. Two broods per summer is common. Three to six eggs per clutch.

Breeding: Nest is mud, twigs, and grass similar to that of the Robin. Nest may be in under-story or at mid-level. Lays two to five blue-green eggs.

Natural History: Despite the fact that the Robin is a migratory species, individuals are seen in Ohio year-round. It is likely that the state's summer residents retreat south during winter and are replaced by southward-moving individuals that have summered much farther to the north. In winter they are sometimes seen in large migratory flocks numbering over 100 birds. Perhaps the best known of America's bird species, Robins are commonly seen on both urban and rural lawns throughout the state. They may also been seen in remote wilderness areas. The Latin name *migratorius* is appropriate for this species and its summer range extends all the way to the Arctic. Feeds heavily on earthworms.

Natural History: The eastern Bluebirds habit of readily adapting to artificial nest boxes has helped bring them back from alarmingly low numbers decades ago, when rampant logging of eastern forests depleted nest cavities. They are primarily insect eaters and are vulnerable to exceptionally harsh winters. Harsh winter weather will prompt a mass movement south and prolonged periods of very cold weather can literally wipe out entire populations that are caught too far north. In winter Bluebirds eat many types of berries and will readily eat raisins from feeders. Their popularity among humans has lead to the establishment of The North American Bluebird Society, dedicated to Bluebird conservation.

Natural History: The Wood Thrush feeds on insects, spiders, earthworms, and other invertebrates found by foraging beneath leaf mold on the forest floor. They will also feed on berries which can be an important food during fall migration. Like many songbirds this species is threatened by the fragmentation of forest habitats throughout North America. Smaller forest tracts make it easier for Cowbirds to find Wood Thrush nests. Consequently nest predation by Cowbirds is increasing and may be one reason for recent population declines. The exceptional song of the Wood Thrush is usually described as "flute-like," or "ethereal" and is heard mostly at dawn and dusk.

Class—**Aves** (birds)
Order—**Passeriformes** (songbirds)
Family—**Turdidae** (thrush family)

Hermit Thrush *Catharus guttatus*	**Veery** *Catharus fuscescens*	**Swainson's Thrush** *Catharus ustulatus*

Size: 7 inches.	**Size:** 7 inches.	**Size:** 7 inches.
Abundance: Fairly common.	**Abundance:** Uncommon.	**Abundance:** Fairly common.
Variation: Varies slightly from reddish brown to grayish brown.	**Variation:** Ohio birds are reddish, those from farther west are duller.	**Variation:** No significant variation in Ohio specimens. A dozen subspecies.

Presumed range in Ohio	Presumed range in Ohio	Presumed range in Ohio

Migratory Status: Mostly a spring-fall migrant. May be seen throughout the summer in parts of northern Ohio and is a winter resident in southern Ohio.

Habitat: Damp woodlands, thickets, and successional areas with heavy undergrowth.

Breeding: Three to five blueish-green eggs are laid in a nest built just above ground level. Most will nest in the boreal forests of Canada. Some nest in northeast Ohio.

Natural History: Any Thrush seen in Ohio during the winter will be this species. They are rather shy but less so than other *Catharus* and they will sometimes visit feeders for suet or raisins. They feed mainly on insects found on the forest floor and beneath leaf mold, but berries are also an important element in the diet, especially in winter. The song of the Hermit Thrush is regarded by many as one of the more beautiful summer sounds in the northern forests. Although secretive, their presence during winter makes them more conspicuous. Unlike most other thrush species, populations of the Hermit Thrush appear stable. As with other thrush species the Hermit Thrush is known for the quality of its song.

Migratory Status: Spring and fall migrant throughout most of the state. A few will summer in northern Ohio. Mostly in the northeast portion.

Habitat: Under-story of deciduous woodlands. Most common in second growth forest with thick undergrowth.

Breeding: Breeds mostly to the north of Ohio. Some nesting in north Ohio. Nest is hidden in thickets on or near the ground. From three to five eggs are laid.

Natural History: Although the Veery is widespread during migration, they are hard to observe in Ohio since most are usually just passing through and they migrate mostly at night. One of the more secretive of the thrushes, they stay mostly in thick undergrowth where they feed on a variety of insects, earthworms, spiders, and berries. Bird watchers often confirm this bird's presence by recognizing its distinctive call, which has been described as "hauntingly beautiful." This species has shown a downward population trend in many regions of its range in North America. Factors cited as possibly contributing to this trend are loss of wintering habitat in South America and fragmentation of breeding habitats in North America.

Migratory Status: Spring and fall migrant. Winters in South America and summers quite far to the north in Canada and even Alaska.

Habitat: Moist to wet woodlands and swamps with heavy underbrush and cool, heavily shaded woods.

Breeding: Builds its moss-lined nest in a coniferous tree in boreal forest well to the north of Ohio. Lays three to five eggs that are blue with brown spots.

Natural History: Another secretive, difficult to observe thrush that in migration flies by night and spends its days resting and feeding in heavy undergrowth. As with many of the thrushes, positive identification can be difficult. This species and the Gray-cheeked Thrush are easily confused. The buff colored cheeks are a good identification character. Like others of its kind the Swainson's Thrush feeds on insects and invertebrates as well as berries. Unlike others of its genus, however, this thrush is known to feed higher in trees (most other thrushes feed mostly on the ground). Spring migration in Ohio begins in late April and runs through mid-May. Fall migration peaks in September.

Class—**Aves** (birds)

Order—**Passeriformes** (songbirds)

Family—**Turdidae** (thrush family)	Family—**Lanidae** (shrikes)	Family—**Alaudidae** (larks)
Gray-cheeked Thrush *Catharus minimus*	**Northern Shrike** *Lanius excubitor*	**Horned Lark** *Eremophila alpestris*

Size: 7.25 inches.

Abundance: Fairly common.

Variation: Overall coloration varies from grayish to slightly brownish.

Presumed range in Ohio

Size: 10 inches.

Abundance: Rare in Ohio.

Variation: Sexes alike. Juveniles have stronger barring on breast.

Presumed range in Ohio

Size: 7.5 inches.

Abundance: Common in west Ohio.

Variation: Sexes similar. Males more vividly colored, immatures duller.

Presumed range in Ohio

Migratory Status: A secretive spring and fall night-time migrant that is easily missed, but does travel through the entire state of Ohio.

Habitat: Summer habitats are boreal forests. Winters in South America. May be seen in woodlands throughout the state during migration.

Breeding: Breeds in remote tundra and taiga in northern Canada and Alaska. Lays three to six eggs.

Natural History: Secretive and uncommon, the biology of the Gray-cheeked Thrush is poorly known. Its summer habitats are dense spruce forests and willow-alder thickets in the far north. Breeding range extends well into the Arctic Circle and winter range is at least as far south as northern South America. Differentiating between the various thrush species can be challenging. The Gray-cheeked Thrush is easily confused with both the Swainson's Thrush and the Hermit Thrush but can be told by the gray color of the cheek. This is one of America's newest bird species, having only recently been differentiated from the Bicknell's Thrush. Some data suggests that the Gray-cheeked is outnumbered by other Ohio thrushes by a ratio of as much five to one.

Migratory Status: A winter resident only. Summers as far north as Northern Canada and Alaska. A few can be seen in northernmost Ohio in winter.

Habitat: Summer habitat is the taiga-tundra ecoregion of the far north. In Ohio frequents edge areas and semi-open regions near woodlands or brush.

Breeding: Nest is proportionately large Built of twigs and rootlets lined with feathers, hair, or fur. Lays four to six eggs.

Natural History: These fierce little birds are much like a miniature raptor. They hunt mostly insects, but will also attack and kill lizards, mice, small snakes, and birds as large as themselves. Sometimes called "Butcher Bird," they kill with a powerful beak and have the unusual habit of caching food items by impaling the bodies of prey onto a thorn or fence barb. They will form permanent territories which they defend from other shrikes. Northern Shrikes range across the northern portions of North America south to the central Rocky Mountains in the west, the Great Lakes region of the Midwest and all of New England. It is also found across Eurasia. Sadly, this unique species is declining throughout its range. They are endangered in Ohio.

Migratory Status: Year-round, but much more common during spring and fall as resident birds are supplemented by birds from farther north.

Habitat: This is a prairie species that is seen only in expansive, open fields. Large, harvested crop fields are the primary habitat for this bird in winter.

Breeding: Nests on barren ground. Lays three to five eggs. Breeds throughout most of western and northern Ohio.

Natural History: This prairie species needs open ground and has probably benefited from human activity in Ohio as a result of land clearing and agricultural operations. Closely cropped pastures or tilled lands are used almost exclusively in Ohio. Except during nesting, these are gregarious birds that are nearly always seen in flocks. They feed on small seeds and tiny arthropods gleaned from what may appear to be nearly barren ground. Harvested agricultural fields, gravel bars, and other open lands are utilized, especially in winter. Like the American Pipit, with which it sometimes associates, the Horned Lark is a species that is often overlooked by the average Ohioan. During outbreaks of severe winter weather flocks may move farther south.

Class—**Aves** (birds)

Order—**Passeriformes** (songbirds)

Family—**Mimidae** (thrasher family)

Mockingbird *Mimus polyglottos*	**Gray Catbird** *Dumetella carolinensis*	**Brown Thrasher** *Toxostoma rufum*

Size: 10.5 inches.

Abundance: Common.

Variation: No variation. Sexes alike.

Presumed range in Ohio

Migratory Status: Summer-only resident in northwestern Ohio, but is a year-round resident in most of the rest of the state.

Habitat: Prefers semi-open habitats with some cover in the form of bushes and shrubs. Found in both rural and urban environments. During colder months they are usually found in the vicinity of berry-producing plants.

Breeding: The nest is made of sticks and is usually in a thick bush or small tree. Three to four eggs are laid and more than one nesting per season is usual.

Natural History: The name "Mocking Bird" is derived from this birds' habit of mimicking the calls of other birds, and they have a huge repertoire of songs. They are known to mimic the calls of everything from warblers to blue jays and even large hawks. New songs are learned throughout their life and the number of different songs recorded by this species is up to 150. They feed largely on insects, but in the winter will switch to berries and fruits. Mockingbirds have a reputation among rural folk as a useful bird that will chase away other pesky birds such as blackbirds and other species that can be garden pests. Appears to be expanding its range northward into southern Canada.

Size: 8.5 inches.

Abundance: Common.

Variation: No variation. Sexes alike.

Presumed range in Ohio

Migratory Status: Spring, summer, and fall only. A few reach the shores of Lake Erie by late April, most arrive later in early May. Departs in August and Sept.

Habitat: Edge areas, thickets, and overgrown fence rows are this birds preferred habitat. In urban areas it is often found in older neighborhoods containing landscapes overgrown with large bushes and shrubs.

Breeding: The loosely constructed nest is made of sticks, vines, and leaves placed in dense bushes. Three to four eggs is common.

Natural History: The Gray Catbird is much more secretive than its relative the Mockingbird. Food includes all manner of insects, spiders, larvae, and berries. Feeds both in the trees and on the ground. When feeding on the ground will use the bill to flip over dead leaves. Named for their call which sounds remarkably like a meowing cat, these shy birds are often heard but unseen as they "meow" from beneath a dense shrub. Like their cousins the Mockingbirds, Gray Catbirds have a large repertoire of songs and they are accomplished mimics of other bird species. They winter along the lower coastal plain of the US, Florida, the Caribbean, Mexico, and Central America.

Size: 11.5 inches.

Abundance: Fairly common.

Variation: No variation. Sexes alike.

Presumed range in Ohio

Migratory Status: Seen in Ohio from late March (south) and early April (north) to mid-August (north) and mid-September to early October in southern Ohio.

Habitat: Edges of woods, thickets, fence rows, overgrown fields, and successional areas. Suburban lawns that have adequate cover in the form of bushes and shrubs may also be used. Avoids deep woods.

Breeding: Builds a stick nest in the heart of a dense shrub, usually within a few feet of the ground. Lays two to five eggs in late spring.

Natural History: During warm weather the Brown Thrasher feeds on insects and small invertebrates of all types. It uses its long bill to overturn leaves and debris beneath trees and shrubs and also actively hunts in the grass of urban lawns. In winter they will eat berries and sometimes come to feeders for raisins or suet. During the breeding season males perch atop bushes or small trees and serenade all within earshot with their song. Though the Brown Thrasher lacks the repertoire of its cousin the Mockingbird, it does possess one of the most varied song collections of any bird in America. Migrates at night. A few will remain in Ohio throughout the winter, especially in southern Ohio.

Class—**Aves** (birds)		
Order—**Passeriformes** (songbirds)		
Family—**Motacillidae** (wagtails)	Family—**Bombycillidae** (waxwings)	Family—**Certhiidae** (creepers)
American Pipit *Anthus rubescens*	**Cedar Waxwing** *Bombycilla cedrorum*	**Brown Creeper** *Certhia americana*

Size: 6.5 inches. **Abundance:** Uncommon. **Variation:** Significant seasonal plumage changes. Winter birds are as above.	Presumed range in Ohio 	**Size:** 7 inches. **Abundance:** Fairly common. **Variation:** No variation. Sexes alike.	Presumed range in Ohio	**Size:** 5.25 inches. **Abundance:** Uncommon. **Variation:** No variation. Sexes alike.	Presumed range in Ohio

Migratory Status: Mostly a migrant seen during spring (late March to early May) and fall (late Sept. to November).

Habitat: In migration the American Pipit is usually seen in expansive open areas such as harvested croplands or mud flats.

Breeding: Breeds in tundra areas and southward into the higher altitudes of the Rocky Mountains. Lays three to seven eggs in a nest on the ground.

Natural History: The American Pipit is a hardy species that nests in America's coldest climates. They move south in the winter where they are easily overlooked. Their mottled brown winter plumage is highly cryptic, especially where they usually reside in expansive, open fields or mud flats. During migration and in winter they may be seen in the company of flocks of Horned Larks or rarely with Lapland Longspurs (another winter migrant from the far north). Characteristically wags its tail up and down. American Pipits are found throughout North America and in parts of eastern Asia. Several other related species of Pipit are found on every continent except for Antarctica. Despite being widespread they are relatively unknown birds to many.

Migratory Status: Year-round resident but usually more common in Ohio in winter or during spring-fall migration.

Habitat: Found both in forests and semi-open country including overgrown fields, orchards, etc. May be seen in both rural and urban settings.

Breeding: Builds a nest of grasses. Nest site is typically high on a tree branch. Nesting in Ohio occurs in June. Lays three to five eggs.

Natural History: Waxwings are named for the peculiar red-colored waxy feathers on their wings. The name "Cedar" Waxwing comes from their propensity for eastern Red Cedar trees where they consume large quantities of cedar berries. These birds are highly social and are usually seen in large flocks. They feed mostly on berries and wander relentlessly in search of this favored food item. In summer, insects, mulberries, and serviceberries are important food items. Crabapples and other fruiting trees are also favored. They are highly irregular in occurrence but are frequently seen across the state as they rove around in search of food sources. Large flocks are known to descend on a fruiting bush and consume every berry. Rarely seen singly or in pairs.

Migratory Status: Mainly a winter resident, but there are year-round residents in the northern part of the state.

Habitat: This is a forest species that prefers mature woodlands with large trees for breeding. In winter they are seen in a variety of wooded habitats.

Breeding: The nest is nearly always built behind a piece of loose bark on the trunk of a large dead tree. Five or six eggs is typical.

Natural History: Brown Creepers feed on small insects, spiders, etc., found in tree-trunk bark crevices. They have the peculiar foraging habit of landing on the trunk at the base of the tree and "creeping" upward, spiraling around the tree as they go. When they reach a certain height, they fly down to the base of another nearby tree and begin again. In Ohio, the Brown Creeper is a bit of a loner, and it is rare to see more than one or two in any one area. This is the only representative of the creeper family (Certhidae) found in North America. Several other species occur in Eurasia and Africa. Population declines in regions where mature forests have been reduced suggest a dependence upon that habitat type. This is an ODNR Species of Special Interest.

Class—**Aves** (birds)

Order—**Passeriformes** (songbirds)

Family—**Paridae** (chickadee family)

Carolina Chickadee *Poecile carolinensis*	**Black-capped Chickadee** *Poecile atricapillus*	**Tufted Titmouse** *Baeolophus bicolor*

Carolina Chickadee	Black-capped Chickadee	Tufted Titmouse
Size: 4.75 inches. **Abundance:** Very common. **Variation:** None. Sexes alike.	**Size:** 5.25 inches. **Abundance:** Common. **Variation:** None. Sexes alike.	**Size:** 6 inches. **Abundance:** Very common. **Variation:** None. Sexes alike.

Presumed range in Ohio (shown for each species).

Migratory Status: Carolina Chickadee is year-round resident in the southern two-thirds of the state. Replaced by Black-capped Chickadees in the northern third of Ohio. Both are much more conspicuous in winter when they visit bird feeders.

Migratory Status: A year-round resident. Like Chickadees this species is common at seed feeders during winter.

Habitat: Carolina Chickadee is primarily a deciduous woodland species but may be found anywhere so long as at least a few trees are present. Black-capped Chickadee adds coniferous woodlands to its habitat types. Both may be found in urban and rural areas, and both show a preference for edge areas.

Habitat: Small woodlots and successional areas. Favors edge habitats. Common in both rural and urban habitats.

Breeding: Both species are cavity nesters that will use hollows in limbs, rotted fence posts, etc. or very often, old woodpecker holes. Man-made nest boxes may also be used but are natural cavities are preferred. Carolina Chickadee lays four to six eggs in April or May. Black-capped lays six to seven eggs from late April to early June.

Breeding: This species is a cavity nester that will utilize natural cavities as well as old woodpecker holes. Average of five eggs.

Natural History: Among Ohio's smallest songbirds, the Chickadees are a familiar bird at feeders throughout the state. They will become quite acclimated to people and with some patient coaxing they may be induced to land upon an outstretch hand containing sunflower seeds. An acrobatic little bird when searching for insect prey, they can dangle upside down from tiny branches. Their whistling song and their "chick-a-dee-dee-dee" call is distinctive and they can be quite noisy at times. In winter they will form mixed flocks with other small birds. They are hyper-active, tiny birds that have high energy requirements. Winter mortality can be high. The ranges of these two very similar species are generally mutually exclusive, with the Black-capped occupying the more northerly regions and the higher altitudes of the Appalachians. In fact, the Black-capped ranges as far north as northern Canada and Alaska. The Carolina on the other hand is a southern bird that ranges across the southeastern United States (except for the highest elevations in the Appalachian Mountains). In harsh winter weather Black-cappeds may move a little farther south into the range of the Carolina Chickadee and hybrids between these two species are known to occur where the ranges meet in the eastern United States. Of the two, the Black-capped is slightly larger and has more of a white "frosting" on the wings. The range maps above are at best close approximations of the ranges of these two species rather than exact depictions of where they might occur in the state.

Natural History: Primarily a seed eater in winter, the Tufted Titmouse is one of the first birds to find a new bird feeder. sunflower seeds are favored, but they also love peanuts. Like Chickadees they are sometimes quite bold around humans servicing feeders. In warm months they forage for small insects and spiders among the foliage of trees. They can sometimes be seen hanging upside down on a small branch or leaf as they search for prey. Their familiar song is a melodic "birdy-birdy-birdy." In winter they mix readily with Chickadees and other small birds. Their range corresponds closely to the eastern Temperate Forest Level I Ecoregion. Recently this species appears to be expanding its range farther to the north.

Class—**Aves** (birds)

Order—**Passeriformes** (songbirds)

Family—**Regulidae** (kinglets)

Ruby-crowned Kinglet *Regulus calendula*	Golden-crowned Kinglet *Regulus satrapa*

Size: 4.25 inches.

Presumed range in Ohio

Abundance: Fairly common. During periods of peak migration they can be quite common, especially during fall cold fronts.

Variation: Male has red stripe on head that is most visible when the male is excited. Females lack this red stripe on the crown. Otherwise sexes are very similar. Spring birds and juveniles are grayer above and less yellowish below.

Migratory Status: Spring and fall migrant that passes through the state. They summer well to the north and the bulk of the populations will winter south of Ohio. A few may spend the winter in the southernmost parts of the state, but will move south if the weather gets too harsh.

Habitat: Summer habitat is undisturbed boreal forest across all of Canada from the Atlantic to the Pacific and well into Alaska. Also summers in the higher elevations of the Rocky Mountains. Winter habitats much more generalized to include deciduous and mixed woodlands as well as swamps and lowlands.

Breeding: Breeds in old growth conifers in the far north. Produces enormous clutches of up to 12 eggs. Nest is built near the tops of spruce trees or fir trees. Nest is constructed of a wide variety of materials including mosses, lichens, blades of grass, and conifer needles. Fur, feathers, or animal hair are used to line the nest.

Natural History: This is one of America's smallest songbird species, smaller even than the Chickadee. The bright red blaze on the top of the head of the male is usually not visible unless the feathers of the crown are erected. Males most often display the red feathers on the crown when issuing a challenge to other males, displaying to females, or singing their territorial song. Otherwise their bright red crown feathers will remain hidden from view. In summer they prey on arthropods and their eggs. In winter they will also feed on berries and some seeds. They are hyper-active little birds that forage throughout the canopy as well as along lower branches. Clumps of dead leaves hanging from a tree limb are like magnets to these tiny hunters who will find small spiders, insects, and other diminutive arthropods hiding within the clumps. Flicks wings open and shut while in near constant motion. Hunts mostly along the tips of smaller branches. Some studies suggest this species may be declining in the eastern United States. Some suggest this decline may be due to logging and forest fragmentation in the breeding range. Birds that pass through Ohio are true latitudinal (north-south) migrants. Populations in the living in the Rocky Mountains of the western United States migrate from high elevations to lower elevations (altitudinal migration).

Size: 4 inches.

Presumed range in Ohio

Abundance: Fairly common.

Variation: Males have orange crown, females (shown) have yellow crown.

Migratory Status: Another winter resident in Ohio that usually arrives from up north in Sept. / Oct. May move on farther south if winter is harsh.

Habitat: This is a forest species that prefers mature woodlands with large trees for breeding. In winter they are seen in a variety of wooded habitats.

Breeding: Builds its nest in the top of a spruce or fir in northern woodlands. Lays a large clutch of up to 11 eggs and may produce two broods per year.

Natural History: Even smaller than its cousin the Ruby-crowned Kinglet, the Golden-crowned is a hardier bird that can tolerate colder winter weather. However severe winter conditions can lead to near 100 percent mortality in localized areas. Amazingly, this little carnivore manages to find arthropod prey throughout the winter and does not switch to seeds and berries in colder weather. Hyperactive and always in motion. They often feed by "leaf hawking" (hovering while picking tiny insects from beneath a leaves). In winter they are often seen in small groups or mixed flocks. There are a few records of Golden-crowned Kinglets breeding in Ohio, but it is very rare in summer in the state.

Class—**Aves** (birds)
Order—**Passeriformes** (songbirds)
Family—**Sittidae** (nuthatches)

White-breasted Nuthatch *Sitta carolinensis*	Red-breasted Nuthatch *Sitta canadensis*

Size: 5.75 inches.

Abundance: Fairly common.

Variation: None. Sexes alike.

Migratory Status: A year-round resident in Ohio.

Habitat: This is a bird of deciduous and mixed woodlands. Mature forests are preferred, but they also occupy regrowth.

Presumed range in Ohio

Size: 4.5 inches.

Abundance: Fairly common.

Variation: None. Sexes alike.

Migratory Status: Mostly a fall and winter resident in Ohio.

Habitat: Summers in the spruce-fir forests of the north and west. Occupies deciduous woodlands in Ohio.

Presumed range in Ohio

Breeding: Nests in natural tree cavities or woodpecker holes. Averages six eggs per clutch.

Breeding: Cavity nesters that excavate their own nest holes in the manner of woodpeckers. Average of six eggs.

Natural History: Nuthatches are famous for foraging tree trunks in an upside down position. This behavior gives them the opportunity to occupy a different feeding niche from woodpeckers and other bark hunting birds that hunt from an upright position. By creeping down the trunk in an upside down position the nuthatches may see tiny prey hidden in crevices visible only from an above perspective and therefore missed by woodpeckers and creepers. In this regard the nuthatches provide an example of how different species can use the same habitat and avoid competition by exhibiting different foraging behaviors. In addition to insects they also eat seeds and are regulars at most bird feeders in the state. They will cache seeds in bark crevices and they tend to be quite territorial. Pairs will stake out a territory and typically live within that area throughout the year. One of four species of nuthatch found in North America and the only one that is a full-time inhabitant of deciduous woodlands. Other species occupy boreal forests, southern pine forests, and western pine forests.

Natural History: These birds have a tendency to make "irruptive" migrations far to the south in winter every few years and the exact mechanism of their irruptive movements remains something of a mystery. It is believed to be related to cone production in northern coniferous forests where this species usually lives. During the spring and summer the Red-breasted Nuthatch feeds entirely on small arthropods. Seeds are the staple food during winter and sunflower seeds are a favorite item at bird feeders. They will wedge seeds into bark crevices to hold them fast while using the beak to hammer open the shell in characteristic "nuthatch" fashion. They will glean insects from bark in the same upside down manner as their larger cousin the White-breasted Nuthatch. Unlike many cavity nesters the Red-breasted Nuthatch seems to avoid using man-made nest boxes. It may take over two weeks to excavate their nest hole. They will reportedly line the entrance of the nest cavity with resin from conifers, possibly to deter other cavity nesters or potential predators.

Class—**Aves** (birds)

Order—**Passeriformes** (songbirds)

Family—**Troglodytidae** (wrens)

Carolina Wren *Thryothorus ludovicianus*	**Marsh Wren** *Cistothorus palustris*	**Sedge Wren** *Cistothorus platensis*

Size: 5.5 inches. Presumed range in Ohio	**Size: 5** inches. Presumed range in Ohio	**Size:** 4.25 inches. Presumed range in Ohio
Abundance: Common.	**Abundance:** Rare in Ohio.	**Abundance:** Rare in Ohio.
Migratory Status: Carolina Wrens are a year-round resident in Ohio.	**Migratory Status:** Summer resident in northeastern Ohio. Migrant elsewhere.	**Migratory Status:** Summer resident in glaciated Ohio. Migrant elsewhere.
Variation: No variation. Sexes alike.	**Variation:** No variation, sexes alike.	**Variation:** No variation, sexes alike.
Habitat: Carolina Wrens are very flexible in habitat choices. They can be seen in remote wilderness or in suburban back yards.	**Habitat:** Pastures, marshes, and lowland meadows as well as open, grassy edges of wetlands or ponds. Coastal salt marshes are widely used in winter.	**Habitat:** This is a wetland species that enjoys marshes and wet meadows. Unlike the Marsh Wren it does not occupy cattail marsh but prefers grassy areas.
Breeding: A nest of fine twigs and grass is built in a sheltered place, often provided by man. Eggs number three to six. Will produce at least two clutches per year.	**Breeding:** Nest is low in grasses or small bush. Nest is built of grasses woven into a ball with an entrance hole in the side. Several unused "decoy" nests are built. Seven eggs is typical.	**Breeding:** Nest is built low to the ground, often in a clump of sedges or a small bush. Six or seven eggs is typical and some may produce two broods per year. Some nesting occurs in Ohio.
Natural History: Along with the House Wren, this is one of the most common wrens in Ohio. The Carolina Wren adepts well to human-influenced habitats and is well known for building its nest in an old pair of shoes or in a vase of flowers left on the back porch for a few days. They will become quite tame around yards and porches and frequently endear themselves to their human neighbors. They are voracious consumers of insects, spiders, and caterpillars and help control insect pests around the home. They are also incessant singers whose musical song serves as a dawn alarm for many residents throughout the state. They are most common in Ohio in the southern half of the state. Although vulnerable to harsh winters, Carolina Wrens are expanding their range northward, perhaps in response to climate change.	**Natural History:** Marsh Wrens winter to the south of Ohio and summer mostly of north of the state. But they are an uncommon summer resident in the northeastern part of Ohio. They may be seen anywhere in the state where suitable habitat exists during migration periods. These are secretive birds that can be very difficult to observe, even in areas where they are common. They spend most of their time hidden in thick stands of cattails or other vegetation deep in the marsh. Like most wrens they will sing continuously in the breeding season and most birdwatchers confirm their presence by learning to recognize their song. They will build one or more "decoy" nests that are never used and they are also known to destroy the eggs of other birds that may be nesting in the vicinity of their own nests. They are an ODNR Species of Concern.	**Natural History:** This is another secretive species that is difficult to observe. Like the Marsh Wren it winters well to the south of Ohio but it is a rare summer resident in glaciated Ohio. The natural history of this species is poorly known, but it is known that nesting dates vary considerably from one region of the country to another. Nesting can occur from May to as late as September. Some birds may produce two broods per year in two different regions. The diet is spiders and insects. Sedge Wrens winter in coastal plain of the southeastern United States from the Carolinas all the way to northwestern Mexico. Fall migration begins in September and most birds are usually gone from the northern portions of their range by late October. Spring migration in the midwest begins in April and continues into early May. ODNR Species of Concern.

Class—**Aves** (birds)

Order—**Passeriformes** (songbirds)

Family—**Troglodytidae** (wrens)		Family—**Polioptilidae** (gnatcatchers)

House Wren
Troglodytes aedon

Size: 4.75 inches.

Abundance: Very common.

Variation: No variation. Sexes alike. 31 subspecies known.

Presumed range in Ohio

Migratory Status: A spring-summer resident that begins to arrive in Ohio in April and departs in the fall.

Habitat: Prefers open and semi-open habitats. These wrens readily associate with humans and are most common in small towns and suburbs. They can also be common in more natural habitats.

Breeding: A cavity nester, the House Wren readily takes to artificial nest boxes. In fact, this species may owe its increase in population to man-made "bird houses." Lays up to eight eggs.

Natural History: Although the House Wren may be seen anywhere in Ohio, it is more common in the northern portions of the state during the breeding season. It is least common in the higher elevations in the southeastern corner of the state, but it does breed statewide. They are more common today than in historical times, as they favor open and semi-open habitats over dense forests. They also have a strong affinity for human altered habitats and settlements. They feed on a wide variety of insects, spiders, snails, caterpillars, etc. When feeding large broods of young they catch huge quantities daily. House Wrens range from coast to coast across America and northward into the prairie provinces of Canada.

Winter Wren
Troglodytes troglodytes

Size: 4 inches.

Abundance: Uncommon.

Variation: No variation, sexes alike.

Presumed range in Ohio

Migratory Status: Mostly a winter resident and migrant. Lingers then moves farther south in harsh winter weather.

Habitat: Mature, old growth forests are the primary summer habitat, often near a stream or bog. Deciduous and mixed woodlands are utilized in winter, but conifers are preferred.

Breeding: Breeds mostly to the north of Ohio, mainly in the boreal forests of Canada. Nest is often constructed in the root wad of an upturned tree. A few breed in northeast Ohio. Lays five to nine eggs.

Natural History: Much shyer and more secretive than other wrens, the Winter Wren skulks about under dense bushes and shrubs where it tends to stay close to the ground. This species has likely declined since presettlement times due to the destruction of ancient forests. Like other wrens, these birds are strictly carnivorous and feed on a wide variety of small insects, larvae, arachnids, amphipoda, etc. As with many other invertivorous birds, they are vulnerable to exceptionally harsh winters. Their stubby, upturned tail makes identification easy, but they are more often heard than seen as they are persistent, loud singers. Winter Wrens are holarctic in distribution, being found in Europe and northern Asia as well as North America.

Blue-gray Gnatcatcher
Polioptila caerulea

Size: 4.25 inches.

Abundance: Common.

Variation: No significant variation, sexes very similar.

Presumed range in Ohio

Migratory Status: One of the earliest returning summer migrants, arriving in Ohio as early as late March.

Habitat: Occupies a wide variety of forested or successional habitats. Most common along wooded streams and bottoms. Shows a definite preference for deciduous woodlands.

Breeding: Nest is a cup-like structure built with lichens and plant fibers glued together with spider web. Nest usually placed at mid-level near the terminus of a branch. Four to five eggs is average.

Natural History: As their name implies gnatcatchers feed on tiny prey. Any type of small arthropod is a probable food item. They hunt the tips of tree branches and sometimes pick off prey while hovering. Despite their small size they will chase away larger birds and will mob predators such as hawks, snakes, or house cats. The gnatcatchers are a unique family that is probably most closely related to the wrens. Like many small songbird species the Blue-gray Gnatcatcher is often the victim of nest parasitism by the Brown-headed Cowbird, which lays its eggs in other birds nests. Despite cowbirds, they seem to be a thriving species and their range has been expanding northward in recent times.

Class—**Aves** (birds)

Order—**Passeriformes** (songbirds)

Family—**Hirundinidae** (Swallows)

Barn Swallow *Hirundo rustica*	**Cliff Swallow** *Petrochelidon pyrrhonota*	**Bank Swallow** *Riparia riparia*

Barn Swallow	Cliff Swallow	Bank Swallow
Size: 7 inches.	**Size:** 5.5 inches.	**Size:** 5.25 inches.
Abundance: Very common throughout most of the state.	**Abundance:** Uncommon in most of Ohio.	**Abundance:** Uncommmon; rare in southeast Ohio.
Variation: The color of males is slightly more vivid.	**Variation:** No variation. Sexes alike.	**Variation:** No variation. Sexes alike.

Presumed range in Ohio    Presumed range in Ohio   Presumed range in Ohio

Barn Swallow	Cliff Swallow	Bank Swallow
Migratory Status: Summer resident that returns to the state in April.	**Migratory Status:** Summer resident. Seen in Ohio from April to September.	**Migratory Status:** Summer resident. Seen in Ohio from April to September.
Habitat: Open and semi-open habitats. Most common in agricultural areas but found virtually everywhere in the state. Least common in the mountains.	**Habitat:** Open areas near large bodies of water are the preferred habitat for this species. Breeding habitat was historically limited to regions with cliff faces.	**Habitat:** Open country near large rivers. In migration may be seen in a wide variety of habitats but most often observed in valleys, near lakes, etc.
Breeding: Nest is bowl shaped and made of mud and grasses plastered to roof joists of a barn or eaves of buildings, beneath concrete bridges, etc.	**Breeding:** Conical mud nests are plastered beneath sheltered overhangs of concrete structures such as bridges or dams. Four eggs is typical.	**Breeding:** Historically nested in high steep banks along major rivers. Nest hole is dug by the parents and may be as much as two to three feet deep. Four to six eggs.
Natural History: A familiar bird to all who grew up on rural farmsteads. Barn Swallows are common throughout most of North America in summer, and birds that summer in the US winter in Central and South America. European breeders winter in the Mediterranean, Africa, and the Middle East while Asian breeding birds winter throughout southeast Asia to Australia. Thus this is one of the most widespread bird species in the world. its long association with humans throughout the world has led to the invention of many legends. Barn Swallows nesting in your barn was considered by pioneers as good luck, while destroying a nest in the barn would cause the milk cow to go dry. Flying insects are the main food including pesky flies and even wasps. This is the world's most common swallow species.	**Natural History:** The Cliff Swallow is primarily a western species that nested historically on cliff faces in the Rocky Mountains. They are more numerous in Ohio today than even a few decades ago. Man-made structures such as dams and bridges have likely helped this species expand its range in the eastern United States and into Ohio. These birds are colony animals that seem to always nest in groups. In the east there seems to be a preference for nesting near water and colony size varies from a few dozen to a few hundred nests. Farther west, where the species is more common and widespread, colonies consisting of several thousand nests are known. Like other swallows they feed almost entirely upon airborne insects, and they are adept at locating swarms of airborne prey.	**Natural History:** Although widespread across America during migration, this species is rather rare in Ohio. Like many swallows the Bank Swallow nests in large communities. Nest colonies are usually associated with large river systems. Despite being somewhat rare in Ohio, these birds are found throughout the world, in fact they are one of the most widespread bird species on earth. The natural nesting habitat has always been riverbanks and bluffs, but today this species utilizes the banks created by man-made quarries or road cuts through hillsides. During migration Bank Swallows can be seen in the company of other species of migrating swallows. Food is exclusively flying insects caught on the wing. Mostly flies, flying ants, small beetles, and mayflies.

Class—**Aves** (birds)

Order—**Passeriformes** (songbirds)

Family—**Hirundinidae** (Swallows)

Northern Rough-winged Swallow *Stelgidopteryx serripennis*	Tree Swallow *Tachycineta bicolor*	Purple Martin *Progne subis*

Size: 5.5 inches.

Abundance: Fairly common.

Variation: No variation, sexes alike.

Presumed range in Ohio

Migratory Status: Summer resident. Winters in south Florida and in Central America. In Ohio from April to Oct.

Habitat: Mainly open and semi-open areas, but can be found in forested regions along rivers or cliffs.

Breeding: Nests in crevices in rock faces, cliffs, etc. Today often uses man-made situations such as road cuts, quarries, etc. Not a colony nester. Lays four to eight eggs.

Natural History: As with other swallows the Rough-winged Swallow feeds by catching flying insects in mid-air. All swallows in America are diurnal hunters whose predatory role is replaced at dusk by the bats. Although this swallow is found from coast to coast across America it is not extremely common anywhere. Unlike the similar Bank Swallow, Rough-winged Swallows are not known to dig their own burrow and availability of nest burrows may be one reason why these swallows tend to be solitary nesters. They will use burrows dug by other species of birds or small mammals as well as natural cavities in cliff faces. They are also known to use man-made structures. In mountainous regions this species is usually associated with river valleys.

Size: 5.75 inches.

Abundance: Fairly common.

Variation: Sexes alike. Immatures are glossy gray.

Presumed range in Ohio

Migratory Status: A warm-weather bird that arrives in Ohio as early as March after wintering well to the south.

Habitat: Open and semi-open habitats. Fond of being near water, including small farm ponds and Beaver swamps.

Breeding: Cavity nesters, Tree Swallows will use old woodpecker holes or tree hollows. They also use artificial nest boxes and sometimes nest in close proximity to Purple Martins.

Natural History: Tree Swallows are more numerous in Ohio today than in historical times and are increasing in numbers in the state. Human activities have benefited this species by creating more open lands and also by creating more ponds and lakes throughout the landscape. The proliferation of artificial nest boxes has also helped (they take readily to Bluebird Boxes) and the resurgence of Beaver populations is also credited with helping this species. Flying insects are the primary food items, but the species also eats bayberries during the winter. They are also known to eat snails during the breeding season to obtain calcium for eggshell production. The Tree Swallow winters along the southeastern coastline of the US, Florida, Mexico, and the Caribbean.

Size: 8 inches.

Abundance: Fairly common.

Variation: Females are gray-brown and have whitish bellies.

Presumed range in Ohio

Migratory Status: Summer resident. The first arriving birds are males and they may arrive as early as late March.

Habitat: Inhabits both rural areas and suburbs. Artificial nest boxes near water in open areas are attractants.

Breeding: Originally nested in natural cavities but today nearly all use artificial nest sites. Three to six eggs is typical but may lay as many as seven or eight. Purple Martins are colony nesters.

Natural History: Our largest swallow and perhaps the most beloved bird in America. Many people anxiously await the return of Purple Martins each spring to nest boxes erected in their yard. This bird's relationship with humans extends at least as far back as the 18th century and today there are at least two national organizations dedicated to Purple Martin enthusiasts. House Sparrows and Starlings sometimes take over "martin houses" unless the landowner is vigilant. Mainly a warm weather species that is dependent upon flying insect prey, Purple Martins are vulnerable to spring cold fronts in the more northern reaches of the summer range. This species is so adapted to nesting in man-made nest boxes that today it is rare to find one nesting in natural cavities.

Class—**Mammalia** (mammals)
Order—**Passeriformes** (songbirds)
Family—**Corvidae** (jays and crows)

Blue Jay *Cyanocitta cristata*	**American Crow** *Corvus brachyrhynchos*

Size: 11 inches.	Presumed range in Ohio	**Size:** 19 inches.	Presumed range in Ohio
Abundance: Common.		**Abundance:** Common.	
Variation: None.		**Variation:** None.	
Migratory Status: Although Blue Jays in some populations may migrate, Blue Jays can be seen in Ohio year-round.		**Migratory Status:** This is one of Ohio's year-round birds, but migrant crows from Canada increase Ohio's population in winter.	

Habitat: State-wide from dense woodlands to semi-open farmlands. They can also be common in suburban and urban neighborhoods. The presence of at least some trees seems to be a requirement and they are least common in western Ohio.	**Habitat:** Occurs in virtually all habitats including urban areas. Favors regions where there is a patchwork of woods and open spaces. Also common in agricultural areas where waste grain is an important food source.
Breeding: Builds a stick nest fairly high up on a tree branch, often in a fork. Lays an average of four eggs usually in April. Blue Jays in the southern United States may produce more than on clutch per year. Probably only one per year in Ohio.	**Breeding:** Crows build a bulky stick nest high in the fork of a tree, well hidden by thick foliage. The nest is quite large and may be two feet across. Ohio crows show a decided preference for oak trees as nesting sites. Four eggs is typical.
Natural History: The Blue Jay's handsome blue, black, and white feathers and distinctive crest make it one of the most recognizable birds in the state. They mainly eat insects, acorns, and grains, but also eat eggs and young of other songbirds. They will aggressively mob much larger birds like hawks and owls, as well as snakes and house cats. Members of this family are relatively long-lived. The record life span for a wild Blue Jay is 18 years, but a captive specimen was reported to have lived for 26 years. An endemic American bird, Blue Jays are found throughout the eastern half of the United States from about the Rocky Mountains eastward. They also range northward into Canada but well below the Arctic Circle. Although they are common and widespread across the eastern half of North America, they never seem to be exceedingly plentiful. Small flocks of a few to a dozen is most common. They may be very common in suburban areas with large trees.	**Natural History:** Crows are omnivores that will eat virtually anything, including the young and eggs of other birds. They are among the most intelligent and resourceful of birds. They may be seen in pairs, small groups, or large flocks numbering in the hundreds. Highly adaptable, crows have fared well in human altered habitats and the species is more common today than prior to European settlement. It is almost certain to remain a common species. As a testament to the crow's intelligence, in rural areas where hunting is commonplace, they are extremely wary of humans; while in protected parks and urban regions they will become quite accepting of the presence of humans. In such environments they will raid suburban yards for pet food and garbage, and often haunt the parking lots of fast food restaurants in search of a dropped french fry. Longevity record for a wild bird is 17.5 years. Normally travels in small flocks, but very large flocks can occur.

Class—**Aves** (birds)

Order—**Passeriformes** (songbirds)

Family—**Vironidae** (vireos)

Yellow-throated Vireo *Vireo flavifrons*	White-eyed Vireo *Vireo griseus*	Blue-headed Vireo *Vireo solitarius*

Size: 5.5 inches.	Presumed range in Ohio	**Size:** 5 inches.	Presumed range in Ohio	**Size:** 5.5 inches.	Presumed range in Ohio
Abundance: Mostly uncommon.		**Abundance:** Common.		**Abundance:** Uncommon in Ohio.	
Variation: No variation, sexes alike.		**Variation:** No variation, sexes alike.		**Variation:** No variation, sexes alike.	

Yellow-throated Vireo	White-eyed Vireo	Blue-headed Vireo
Migratory Status: A long-range migrant that winters as far away as northern South America. Returns to Ohio in April. Departs in September.	**Migratory Status:** Winters from the lower coastal plain into Mexico, Cuba, and Bahamas. Returns to Ohio in April (south) or early May (north).	**Migratory Status:** Another spring-fall migrant that passes through Ohio in April and in September A few will summer and nest in eastern Ohio.
Habitat: A woodland bird that will inhabit a wide variety of forest types excluding stands of pure conifers. In Ohio more common in the Appalachian Plateau Province. Prefers edge areas.	**Habitat:** Dense thickets and early successional hardwoods are favored. May also be seen in later stage successional deciduous woodlands and in overgrown fields with small saplings and thickets.	**Habitat:** This vireo likes expanses of mature forests, and is also partial to conifers for its summer habitat. It thus summers mostly well to the north of Ohio in the boreal forests of Canada.
Breeding: The nest is a woven basket usually suspended from the fork of a small branch at the mid-story level. Four eggs is typical.	**Breeding:** Nest is a woven, hanging basket held together with silk from caterpillars or spiders placed in a fork very low to the ground. Three to five eggs.	**Breeding:** Nest construction is similar to other vireos. A tightly woven cup is suspended from a horizontal fork. Four eggs is typical.
Natural History: The nest is usually located in a branch overhanging a forest opening such as a lane or a stream. Feeds on a wide variety of arthropods with caterpillars being a mainstay. Also eats small amount of berries and seeds in the fall. The biology of this species is not as well understood as with many other vireos, but it is known that it has decreased in numbers in areas of deforestation. As with many small woodland songbirds, the nest of the Yellow-throated Vireo is subject to parasitism by cowbirds. The summer range of this species coincides closely with the eastern Temperate Forest Level I ecoregion. The winter range is from southern Mexico to northern South America. Migrants regularly cross the Gulf of Mexico.	**Natural History:** This is the only vireo with a white iris, making identification easy. Nest parasitism by Brown-headed Cowbirds is estimated to be as high as 50 percent, with no young surviving in parasitized nests. Highly insectivorous. Caterpillars are a favorite food item. Will also eat fruit. White-eyed Vireos winter along the lower coastal plain of the US, the Caribbean, and the Yucatan Peninsula. Like the previous species, nest parasitism by Brown-headed Cowbirds posses a potential threat. Deforestation contributes to the problem. Brown-headed Cowbirds tend to avoid deep woods in favor of more open habitats. Loss of large tracts of woodland makes life easier for the cowbirds and more difficult for the species which they parasitize.	**Natural History:** Also known as the Solitary Vireo. Most Blue-headed Vireos summer to the north of Ohio in New England and in Canada. They winter from the lower coastal plain of the southeastern US all the way to Central America. They are quite common in peninsular Florida throughout the winter. Food is mostly insects, with moths and butterflies and their larvae being a major portion of the diet. Most foraging is done in trees well above the forest floor. As is the case with many of America's migrant songbirds, the Blue-headed Vireo is highly dependent upon large tracts of forest. Deforestation negatively impacts local populations; but forest regeneration in many areas of its summer range has helped this species in recent years.

Class—**Aves** (birds)

Order—**Passeriformes** (songbirds)

Family—**Vironidae** (vireos)

Red-eyed Vireo *Vireo olivaceus*	Warbling Vireo *Vireo gilvus*	Philadelphia Vireo *Vireo philadelphia*

Size: 6 inches. **Abundance:** Very common. **Variation:** Sexes alike but males are slightly larger.	**Size:** 5.5 inches. **Abundance:** Fairly common. **Variation:** No variation between sexes or annual molts.	**Size:** 5.5 inches. **Abundance:** Uncommon in Ohio. **Variation:** Sexes alike. Juveniles brownish above.

Presumed range in Ohio  Presumed range in Ohio  Presumed range in Ohio

Migratory Status: A summer resident that winters in the Amazon Basin. Arrives in Ohio from early to late April.

Migratory Status: Appears in Ohio in late April (south) to early May (north). Winters in Mexico and Central America.

Migratory Status: Migrant. Passes through Ohio in late spring or very early summer. Winters in Central America.

Habitat: Although a woodland species, the Red-eyed Vireo is very generalized in its habitat requirements. Mature forests, regenerating woodlands, and forest fragments are all occupied.

Habitat: Although this species likes mature trees in its habitat, it avoids dense forest in favor of areas with a mosaic of small woodlands. Riparian woodlands are also utilized.

Habitat: Philadelphia Vireo can be found in large tracts of forest, but it seems to favor successional woodlands over mature Uses mixed conifer and deciduous woodlands.

Breeding: Two to four eggs are laid in May. May have two broods per summer with second brood fledging in late August.

Breeding: Nesting in Ohio takes place in mid-summer. Nests are placed high in trees. Four eggs is typical.

Breeding: The breeding range of the Philadelphia Vireo is contained mostly in Canada.

Natural History: This is one of the most common summer songbirds in Ohio forests and woodlots, but it is not readily observed due to its habit of staying high in the forest canopy. It is however regularly heard, as it sings incessantly throughout the spring. While on their breeding grounds they are primarily insectivorous feeders, they do consume some fruits while wintering in the tropics. The population health of the Red-eyed Vireo may be due to its less stringent dependence upon large tracts of forest. This species can subsist happily in small woodlands and regenerative areas. However, in these habitats it is more susceptible to the parasitic nesting of the Brown-headed Cowbird. Most Red-eyed Vireos nesting in Ohio will depart in September. Red eye color is unique among vireos.

Natural History: The Warbling Vireo is least common in Ohio in the mountainous southeastern portion of the state. They are widespread however in most of the rest of Ohio. Like the similar Red-eyed Vireo, they are persistent singers that are more often heard than seen. They feed by gleaning small insects and other arthropods from canopy foliage. A few seeds and berries are also sometimes eaten. This is one of the most widely distributed members of the North American Vironidae family. Their breeding range extends from coast to coast across the northern two-thirds of the United States as well as much of Canada. By contrast, the winter range is much smaller and restricted to the western half of Mexico and western Central America from northern Costa Rica northward.

Natural History: The Philadelphia Vireo migrates through most of Ohio each spring but it does not nest in the state. They are a somewhat rarely observed bird and are difficult to distinguish from the more common Warbling Vireo, but they usually have more yellowish wash below. They are also very similar to the Red-eyed Vireo and their song also closely resembles that species. Their food is mostly caterpillars. As with many other neotropical migrant songbirds that can be seen in Ohio, this species is a trans-gulf migrant that makes epic non-stop flights across the Gulf of Mexico during migration. The **Bell's Vireo** (*V. belli*) is another species of *Vireo* that very rarely occurs in Ohio and has been known to breed in the eastern half of the state.

Class—**Aves** (birds)		
Order—**Passeriformes** (songbirds)		
Family—**Parulidae** (warblers)		

Canada Warbler *Cardellina canadensis*	**Wilson's Warbler** *Cardellina pusilla*	**Yellow-breasted Chat** *Icteria virens*
	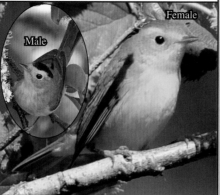	

Canada Warbler
Cardellina canadensis

Size: 5.25 inches.

Presumed range in Ohio

Abundance: Uncommon.

Variation: Females have less black on face and chest.

Migratory Status: Winters in South America. A few nest in Ohio in but most are just passing through in route to breeding grounds in Canada. Spring migration through Ohio is in May.

Habitat: Favors moist northern forests with thick under-story shrubs. In Ohio this species is known to associated most frequently with eastern Hemlock.

Breeding: Nest is on the ground and hidden amid dense vegetation. In Canada nest is often placed amid carpet of moss. Four or five eggs is typical.

Natural History: A few will nest in hemlock woodlands in Ohio along the western edge of the Appalachian Plateaus Province, but most (over 80 percent) will nest in Canada. Although they do migrate through most of the state, they do so mostly at night and pass through quickly en route to breeding grounds farther to the north. Listed as a Species of Special Interest by the ODNR, the Canada Warbler has been in decline for several decades. Loss of breeding habitat in North America as well as wintering habitat in South America is probably to blame. Future threats include the Woolly Adelgid, an alien insect that is decimating hemlock forests throughout the Appalachians. Formerly this species was placed in the genus *Wilsonia.*

Wilson's Warbler
Cardellina pusilla

Size: 4.75 inches.

Presumed range in Ohio

Abundance: Fairly common.

Variation: Black "cap" is more prominent in males.

Migratory Status: A passage migrant in Ohio. Most spring migrating birds will have passed through the state by the end of May. Fall migration peaks in early to mid-September.

Habitat: Summer breeding habitat is in the boreal forests of Canada, pacific northwest, northern Rockies, and Alaska. Winter habitat is tropical forests.

Breeding: Nest is on the ground. Uniquely, the nest of this warbler is usually placed in a small depression. From two to seven eggs may be laid.

Natural History: Wilson's Warbler is a not a common species in Ohio. Although they may migrate through any part of the state, the bulk of this species population occurs and migrates to the west of Ohio. But some will travel though the state. They are probably more numerous in the pacific states than they are in the eastern United States. However some studies indicate that they are declining in the west. Most blame the loss of riparian habitat for decline in western populations. They range as far north as the Arctic Ocean in summer and as far south as Panama in winter. The species name *"wilsonia"* is for early naturalist and ornithologist Alexander Wilson.

Yellow-breasted Chat
Icteria virens

Size: 7.5 inches.

Presumed range in Ohio

Abundance: Fairly common.

Variation: None. Sexes alike.

Migratory Status: Summer resident. Winters in southern Mexico and throughout Central America. Arrives in Ohio for breeding in late April (southern Ohio) to early/mid-May (northern Ohio).

Habitat: This warbler likes overgrown fields, second growth areas, and early successional regenerating woodlands. It avoids the deep woods.

Breeding: Nests low to the ground in brier thickets or a dense shrub such as a multiflora rose. Nest is cup-like. Lays two to five eggs.

Natural History: The Yellow-breasted Chat is America's largest wood warbler and some question its status in the family Parulidae. They are fairly common in suitable habitats in Ohio in summer months but are not easily observed due to their secretive nature and preference for dense vegetation. Foods are a wide variety of arthropods with a preference for crickets, grasshoppers, caterpillars, and spiders. They are also known to eat some fruits and berries. These birds are probably more numerous today than prior to deforestation. Their breeding range in eastern North America corresponds closely to the eastern Temperate Forest level I ecoregion. In Ohio they are more common in the southern portion of the state.

Class—**Aves** (birds)

Order—**Passeriformes** (songbirds)

Family—**Parulidae** (warblers)

Kirtland's Warbler *Setophaga kirtlandii*	Hooded Warbler *Setophaga citrina*	Northern Parula *Setophaga americana*

Male

Male

Female

Size: 5.25 inches.

Abundance: Very rare.

Variation: Females and juveniles similar to male, but duller.

Presumed range in Ohio

Size: 5.25 inches.

Abundance: Fairly common.

Variation: Black "hood" on head and face is much reduced in females.

Presumed range in Ohio

Size: 4.5 inches.

Abundance: Uncommon in Ohio.

Variation: Females lack black on breast but otherwise sexes are similar.

Presumed range in Ohio

Migratory Status: Spring and fall migrant. Passes through Ohio very quickly en route from wintering grounds in the Bahamas to breeding areas in northern Michigan and Wisconsin. Fall migration mostly in September.

Habitat: Summer habitat is mainly restricted to semi-open, successional forests of Jack Pine occurring in north-central Michigan. This specialized habitat is now artificially maintained by wildlife agencies.

Breeding: Nest is built on the ground and well concealed by grasses or shrubs. Four to six eggs are laid in late May or early June. Nest parasitism by Brown-headed Cowbirds is a threat.

Natural History: This is one of America's rarest bird species. They were among the first species to be listed on the Endangered Species list nearly 50 years ago and they remain one of our rarest birds. Concerted efforts to save this species have included habitat restoration, control of Brown-headed Cowbirds in the nesting areas, and continued monitoring of populations. Today there are an estimated 4,000 individuals of this species (up from a low of about 400). The survival of the species today depends upon the continued efforts of wildlife agencies to maintain habitat.

Migratory Status: After wintering in Central America and parts of the Caribbean, the Hooded Warbler returns to Ohio in late April (south) or as late as mid-May (northern Ohio). Leaves for wintering grounds by September.

Habitat: A forest species. Most common in the Appalachian Plateau Province in the eastern portion of the state. But may be found anywhere in Ohio that there is significant woodlands with dense under-story.

Breeding: Cup-shaped nest of grasses, bark, and dead leaves is woven into two or more upright limbs of a small bush near the ground. Nest sites are usually associated with dense shrubs. Four eggs.

Natural History: Like many small, woodland birds the Hooded Warbler is more likely to be heard than seen. On their breeding grounds in the eastern US they require large tracts of woodlands, and they have declined in areas where intensive agriculture or development has resulted in the loss of this habitat. This handsome little warbler is a good example of why the protection of extensive tracts of forest can be so important in the conservation of neotropical migrant songbirds. With the largest eyes of any warbler, this species is adapted to a life spent in heavy shade.

Migratory Status: Summer resident. Winters from south Florida to Central America. Arrives in Ohio in April and begins to leave in August or September. All are gone by early October. Migrates at night.

Habitat: Habitat is forest. Mostly bottom-land woods or swamps or along streams and rivers. Also moist ravines in the mountains. In Ohio this species is seen mostly in the southern half of the state. It is rare in northwest Ohio.

Breeding: Nests high in trees. In Kentucky Sycamores, Baldcypress, and Hemlocks are reported as favorite nest trees. In the deep south nests are often built in Spanish moss. Four or five eggs.

Natural History: The Northern Parula feeds by gleaning tiny arthropods from tree branches. They tend to feed and spend much time in the middle an upper story of the forest. This habit couple with their small size make them difficult to observe. These handsome little warblers are most common in Ohio in the deep forests of the Interior Low Plateau Province and in the Unglaciated Allegheny Plateau Region. They are also common breeding birds north of Ohio in Canada, but they seem to avoid most of the northern half of the state for nesting. They are one of Ohio's smallest birds.

Class—**Aves** (birds)

Order—**Passeriformes** (songbirds)

Family—**Parulidae** (warblers)

Yellow Warbler *Setophaga petechia*	Black-throated Blue Warbler *Setophaga caerulescens*	Cerulean Warbler *Setophaga cerulea*

Yellow Warbler	Black-throated Blue Warbler	Cerulean Warbler
Size: 5 inches.	**Size:** 5.25 inches.	**Size:** 4.75 inches.
Abundance: Common.	**Abundance:** Rare in Ohio.	**Abundance:** Uncommon in Ohio.
Variation: Male has bright chestnut streaks on breast. Lacking or much reduced on the female.	**Variation:** Strongly sexually dimorphic. Female is olive brown above, drab olive-yellow below.	**Variation:** Male is as shown above, female is blueish green with faded gray streaks.

Presumed range in Ohio (for all three species)

Migratory Status: Summer resident. Winters in Mexico and Central America. Birds nesting in Ohio arrive in late April and early May.

Habitat: Thickets of willow or buttonbush in wet lowlands are the classic habitat for this species. Riparian woodlands and mesic upland woods are also used.

Breeding: Nest is built in the upright fork of a sapling and averages four or five eggs. Nest is a cup-like structure made mostly from grasses. Breeds throughout the state.

Natural History: This is one of North America's most wide ranging of the warblers. Their summer breeding range encompasses the entire northern two thirds of North America, from the Atlantic to the Pacific and extends as far north as the Arctic Circle. Although they may be seen statewide in Ohio, this species is more common in the northern half of the state. Feeds on a variety of insects and other arthropods and uses a variety of foraging techniques including gleaning of leaves and branches, flying from perch to seize airborne prey, and picking insects from leaves and branches while hovering. Caterpillars are an important food item during breeding.

Migratory Status: Mostly a migrant in Ohio, but there are a few indications of breeding in the northeastern corner of the state. Winters in the Caribbean.

Habitat: Summer habitat consists of large, contiguous tracts of mature forests. Both hardwood and mixed forest are used, but only northern forests types are inhabited in summer.

Breeding: Nest is strips of bark lined with finer materials such as moss. Usually placed in an upright fork of dense shrub. Clutch size typically four. Breeding in Ohio is extremely rare.

Natural History: Most of this warblers summer / breeding habitat is to the north and east of Ohio. Summers mostly in the northeastern US and eastern Canada. In Ohio it is seen only as a migrant but a few may spend the summer in the northeastern corner of the state. This species forages mostly in shrubs and branches at the mid-story level for caterpillars and other small arthropod prey. Deforestation and forest fragmentation in both summer and winter habitats are the greatest threats. These threats may be compounded by habitat degradation from alien species like the Woolly Adelgid. A ODNR Species of Special Interest.

Migratory Status: Winters in the Andes Mountains. Flies across the gulf to southeast US coast then northward into interior, arriving in Ohio by mid-April.

Habitat: Summer habitat is primarily deciduous forests. Both bottom-land forest and moist mountain slopes. In Ohio this species is most common in the Appalachian Plateau Province.

Breeding: Nest is a tight cup woven around forked branches in the mid to upper canopy level. Average clutch size is three or four to as many as five. Breeding habitat includes thick under-story.

Natural History: The Cerulean Warbler hunts high in the canopy, gleaning tiny invertebrates from small branches and leaves. Searches both upper and lower surface of leaves for food. Like many species dependent upon forests, this warbler experienced significant population declines following the European settlement of America. In Ohio today the species is more common in the eastern portion of the state, as that is where most of Ohio's forests are found. Listed as a Species of Concern by ODNR, Cerulean Warbler populations have declined significantly. It is believed that as much as 13 percent of the remaining birds nest in Ohio.

Class—**Aves** (birds)
Order—**Passeriformes** (songbirds)
Family—**Parulidae** (warblers)

Magnolia Warbler *Setophaga magnolia*	**Yellow-rumped Warbler** *Setophaga coronata*	**Blackpoll Warbler** *Setophaga striata*

Female / Male

Male / Female

Female / Male

Size: 5 inches.

Abundance: Fairly common.

Variation: Female has dark gray mask (male black); immature has plain gray head.

Presumed range in Ohio

Migratory Status: Mostly a transient species in Ohio, passing through on migration in spring and fall. A few will summer in the Appalachian Plateau.

Habitat: Summer habitat for most is in spruce forests in Canada. In Ohio can be seen statewide during migration. Winters in Mexico, Central America, and the Caribbean.

Breeding: Nests in evergreen trees. The nest is usually well concealed amid dense vegetation. Four eggs laid. The few individuals that nest in Ohio will use stands of eastern Hemlock exclusively.

Natural History: Feeds on insects (including large numbers of caterpillars) that are caught near the ends of branches in dense conifer trees. Known to feed on the Spruce Budworm and may enjoy greater survival of offspring during years of budworm outbreaks. This is an abundant species that appears to be stable in population numbers. Leaves Central American wintering grounds in February and arrives in Ohio from mid-April to mid-May. They are fairly common migrants throughout the state in spring. Fall migration begins in September and may last into October. Fall migration routes generally more easterly than spring.

Size: 5.5 inches.

Abundance: Common.

Variation: Winter males, females, and immatures similar. Spring males more vividly colored.

Presumed range in Ohio

Migratory Status: Mostly a spring-fall migrant in Ohio but some may be seen in the southern part of the state in winter if the weather is mild.

Habitat: Outside its breeding range this warbler is a habitat generalist. It can be seen virtually anywhere in the state from during spring or fall migrations.

Breeding: Breeds in the boreal forest of Canada and Alaska. Nest is built on the branch of a conifer. Clutch size is usually four or five eggs. One clutch per year. Vulnerable to cowbirds.

Natural History: There are two morphologically distinct forms of this common warbler, one in the eastern US and one in the western US. The form seen in Ohio is sometimes called the "Myrtle Warbler." In summer feeds mainly on insects, but if bad weather necessitates it is capable of surviving on berries during the winter. Unlike most warblers that will winter in the tropics, the Yellow-rumped is a hardy species and in mild winters can be seen as far north as southern IL, IN, and OH in the Midwest and NJ on the east coast. Populations of this bird seem fairly stable and it is probably in less jeopardy than many other warbler species.

Size: 5.5 inches.

Abundance: Uncommon in Ohio.

Variation: Sexual, ontogenic, and seasonal variation. Fall male resembles female.

Presumed range in Ohio

Migratory Status: This is a springtime migrant that passes through Ohio in April and May enroute to breeding grounds in northern Canada.

Habitat: Summer breeding habitat is taiga and tundra-taiga transition zones; often well above the arctic circle. Winter habitat is South American forests.

Breeding: Nest is an open cup built on a branch near the tree trunk, usually in a spruce and often only a few feet off the ground. Eggs number three to five. Young fledge as early as within eight to 10 days.

Natural History: This is one of the great long distance migrants among America's songbird species. In fall migration some may travel non-stop over the Atlantic Ocean from Newfoundland (Canada) all the way to South America. Considering that this is a bird that weighs less than 0.5 ounce, that is a remarkable feat of endurance. Although some individuals will pass through Ohio during the spring, they tend to stay hidden high in the forest canopy. The fall migration is mostly along the east coast. Thus this is a rarely seen bird in the state except by those who train themselves to look for it during spring migration.

Class—**Aves** (birds)		
Order—**Passeriformes** (songbirds)		
Family—**Parulidae** (warblers)		

Bay-breasted Warbler *Setophaga castenea*	Pine Warbler *Setophaga pinus*	Black-throated Green Warbler *Setophaga virens*
Spring Male / Fall Male		Female / Male

Size: 5.5 inches.	Presumed range in Ohio	**Size:** 5.5 inches.	Presumed range in Ohio	**Size:** 5 inches.	Presumed range in Ohio
Abundance: Uncommon.		**Abundance:** Rare in Ohio.		**Abundance:** Fairly common.	
Variation: Seasonal and sexual plumage variations. See photos above. Female resembles fall male.		**Variation:** Males are brighter greenish-yellow. Females and immatures are drabber.		**Variation:** Sexes similar, but females have less black and more yellow on the throat.	

Migratory Status: Spring migrant. Passes through Ohio in May en route to breeding sites in Canada. Fall migration is mostly east of the Appalachians.	**Migratory Status:** Mainly a warm weather resident in Ohio from March through October. However a few may linger into late fall or winter.	**Migratory Status:** A spring and fall migrant throughout much of Ohio. Nests in and can be seen all summer in the highlands of the eastern half of the state.
Habitat: Summer habitat is spruce / fir woodlands of Canada. During migration through Ohio it is found in a variety of habitats. Winter habitats are tropical forests of Central and South America.	**Habitat:** Pine forests are the primary habitat, but they are also seen in deciduous and mixed woodlands, especially during migration. In Ohio they occur mostly in the southern part of the state.	**Habitat:** This warbler requires significant tracts of unbroken forests. Except for migration, it is an inhabitant of conifer and mixed conifer/deciduous forests, especially those containing hemlock.
Breeding: Nests in dense conifer trees on horizontal limb. Nest is cup shaped and made of woven twigs, pine needles, and grasses. Average clutch size is five or six eggs.	**Breeding:** Builds its nest high in pine trees. This is one of the earliest nesting warblers in Ohio, with three or four eggs laid as early as mid-April. Breeding range is limited to regions where pines occur.	**Breeding:** Rare breeding populations in Ohio are restricted to the Appalachian Plateau region. Most nests are in conifers such as hemlock or pine. Only the female incubates the four or five eggs.
Natural History: This long distance migrant is not commonly seen by residents of Ohio, as they pass through rather quickly. They migrate later than most other warblers and don't appear in northern Ohio until mid to late May. Their primary food in summer is the Spruce Budworm caterpillar, and their populations may rise and fall with the availability of this insect. Populations have declined possibly due to spraying of Canadian forests to control spruce budworms. These birds are less common today than decades ago. They winter from southern Central America to northwestern South America. In winter they will eat fruit.	**Natural History:** As its name implies, this species is always found in association with pine trees. This is the only warbler whose range is contained entirely within the United States and Canada. It is also the only one of its kind to regularly change its diet from insects to seeds in the winter, thus it is one of the few warblers seen at bird feeders. These birds can reach high densities in winter in the southern pine forests, when resident populations are supplemented by northern migrants. Pine Warblers are much more tolerant of cold weather than other warblers, perhaps because they are able to switch from insects to seeds as a food source.	**Natural History:** Like others of its kind, this small, handsome warbler faces many threats. Red Squirrels are reportedly an important nest predator in the boreal forests of Canada and New England. In Ohio the major threat may come from other birds like the Blue Jay, and from the common and widespread Midland Rat Snake. Sharp-shinned Hawks are always a threat to the adults, while Brown-headed Cowbirds parasitize the nest. Human activities such as forest fragmentation threaten populations as a whole. Add to that the impact of Woolly Adelgid insects on hemlock trees and you have an uncertain future for this and many other warbler species.

Class—**Aves** (birds)

Order—**Passeriformes** (songbirds)

Family—**Parulidae** (warblers)

Blackburnian Warbler *Setophaga fusca*	Palm Warbler *Setophaga palmarum*	Yellow-throated Warbler *Setophaga dominca*

Size: 5 inches.	**Size:** 5.5 inches.	**Size:** 5.5 inches.
Abundance: Fairly common migrant.	**Abundance:** Fairly common migrant.	**Abundance:** Fairly common.
Variation: Bright orange of males reduced to yellowish wash on females and immatures.	**Variation:** Does exhibit seasonal variation, but winter plumaged birds are not seen in Ohio.	**Variation:** Sexes similar. No significant variation between adults and juveniles.

Presumed range in Ohio (for all three)

Migratory Status: Mostly a spring/fall migrant in Ohio. It may be a very rare summer resident in eastern Ohio.

Habitat: Summers mostly in mature coniferous and mixed forests. Migration habitat is highly variable. Birds that breed in the Appalachians favor groves of eastern Hemlock.

Breeding: Nesting in Ohio is very rare. Elsewhere nest is usually in a conifer and well concealed amid foliage. Average of four to five eggs.

Natural History: The beautiful blaze orange coloration on the head, throat, and breast of the Blackburnian Warbler is unmistakable. However, this is a difficult species to observe due to the fact that it is primarily a treetop dweller. It feeds mostly on caterpillars. Most of these birds seen in Ohio are merely passing through en route to boreal forests far to the north. Some will nest in the southern Appalachians as far south as Alabama. In Ohio nesting has been recorded in the Appalachian Plateau Province. Insects (especially caterpillars) are primary food. Forest fragmentation on wintering grounds in South America may pose a threat. This is an ODNR Species of Special Interest.

Migratory Status: A spring and fall migrant in Ohio. Migrates early in the spring and late in the fall.

Habitat: Summer habitat consists of bogs and woods openings in boreal forests. Transient in a variety of habitats during migration. Winter habitat is open woodlands, mangroves, and thickets.

Breeding: Nests of moss is on the ground in a northern bog, usually at the base of a conifer tree. Clutch size is four or five. Many nest in remote wilderness.

Natural History: This species nests in the boreal forests of Canada and winters along the southeastern US coast (including all of Florida) and throughout the Caribbean. Unlike most warblers that spend most of their time high in the canopy, the Palm Warbler is a decidedly terrestrial species that hunts primarily on the ground or in low shrubs. It is one of the most northerly wintering of the warblers, with many staying in the southeast US or Florida (thus the name Palm Warbler). Their summer habitats are very far to the north, well into northern Canada. Food is mainly insects, mostly caught on the ground. Includes grasshoppers, beetles, lepidopterans, flies, and bee larvae. Some berries and nectar may be consumed in winter.

Migratory Status: A summer-time resident throughout the southern half of Ohio. Arrives in April, leaves in Sept.

Habitat: In Ohio found mostly along wooded stream corridors. Also uses bottom-land forest and mature woodlands with open under-story. Known to often associate with Sycamore trees.

Breeding: Nest is placed high in a tree, often a Sycamore. Nest is made of grasses and spider web and lined with soft materials. Four eggs is typical.

Natural History: This warbler species can be seen all summer in southern Ohio and few begin arriving in early to mid-April. It winters in south Florida and the Caribbean. This is another "treetop" species that spends most of its time high in the canopy. It feeds on diminutive arthropods gleaned in a very deliberate fashion from branches, bark, leaves, and petioles. This species retreated from the northern portions of its breeding range several decades ago, but is now showing a resurgence back into those areas. The cause of this population fluctuation is unknown, but possibly relates to habitat alterations by man, and a subsequent recovery of those habitats. They are a very rare species in northern Ohio in summer.

Class—**Aves** (birds)

Order—**Passeriformes** (songbirds)

Family—**Parulidae** (warblers)

Prairie Warbler *Setophaga discolor*	**Chestnut-sided Warbler** *Setophaga penslyvanica*	**American Redstart** *Setophaga ruticilla*

Prairie Warbler

Size: 4.75 inches.

Abundance: Fairly common in southeast Ohio.

Variation: Sexes similar, females less vividly marked, immatures paler.

Presumed range in Ohio

Migratory Status: Summer resident. Occurs rarely throughout Ohio north of area shown on map above.

Habitat: Semi-open habitats. Old, overgrown fields, shrubby successional areas, second growth woodlands, and cedar glades. Absent to very rare in intensive agricultural areas of glaciated Ohio. Uses coastal dunes during winter.

Breeding: Breeds throughout the southern and southeastern part of the state. An average of four eggs (three to five) are laid May to June.

Natural History: Insects, spiders, slugs, and other soft-bodied arthropods are listed as food items. Feeds from the ground all the way up to tree-tops, but mainly gleans lower bushes and shrubs. Tail-bobbing is a common behavior in this species. The Prairie Warbler winters farther north than many warbler species. While some fly as far as the Yucatan Peninsula, others stay in the northern Caribbean or Florida. They can be fairly common in the Florida Everglades during winter. Despite having benefited from clearing of forests the last century, there are unexplained declines in some populations in recent years. Historical records indicate this species did not occur in Ohio prior to the 1900s.

Chestnut-sided Warbler

Size: 5 inches.

Abundance: Fairly common migrant.

Variation: Yellow crown and chestnut flanks reduced on female and juveniles.

Presumed range in Ohio

Migratory Status: Mostly a spring/fall migrant in southern Ohio. Rare all summer in north Ohio. Arrives in early May.

Habitat: The Chestnut-sided Warbler is a bird of successional areas and shrubby, second growth. Forest edges, early regenerative timber harvest areas, and forest clearings are favored for nesting. In migration also seen in mature woods.

Breeding: Nests fairly low to the ground in thick cover of dense sapling growth. Three or four eggs are laid in late spring or early summer.

Natural History: This is one of the few warbler species that has benefited from deforestation. They are probably more common now than they were in the days prior to the European settlement of America. Despite their overall increase in population, they are negatively impacted by modern agricultural practices. The clearing of fence rows and overgrown field corners, and conversion of successional habitats into cropland eliminates their preferred habitat. They are thus absent from most of glaciated Ohio except as a migrant. As with many other warbler species that travel through Ohio, the Chestnut-sided warbler breeds mostly far to the north in the boreal forests of Canada and New England. Winter range is in Central America.

American Redstart

Size: 5.75 inches.

Abundance: Fairly common.

Variation: Sexually dimorphic (see photos above). Juvenile like female.

Presumed range in Ohio

Migratory Status: Summer resident. Mostly in eastern Ohio. Sporadic elsewhere. Arrives in April, departs in Sept.

Habitat: Prefers deciduous woodlands over conifers. More common in second growth areas and riparian thickets. Larger woodlands are preferred over small woodlots. In winter range uses mangroves and tropical forests.

Breeding: The nest woven of thin fibers of grass or bark strips and placed in the crotch of an upright branch or trunk. Usually four eggs.

Natural History: The striking bright orange-on-black colors of the male flash like neon in the heavily shaded forests where this species makes its home. They are active little birds that display their bright colors by regularly spreading their tail feathers and drooping their wings. They hunt tiny insects among the foliage and often catch flying insects in mid-air. In Ohio this species is much more common in the Appalachian Plateau Province in the eastern half of the state. Also fairly common along the Lake Erie shoreline. Small numbers winter in coastal Louisiana, the lower Rio Grande valley, and the everglades region of south Florida. Most winter from northwest Mexico to northern South America. Clearing of tropical forests is a threat.

Class—**Aves** (birds)

Order—**Passeriformes** (songbirds)

Family—**Parulidae** (warblers)

Cape May Warbler *Setophaga tigrina*	Orange-crowned Warbler *Oreothlypis celata*	Nashville Warbler *Oreothlypis ruficapilla*

Cape May Warbler — *Setophaga tigrina*

Size: 5 inches.

Abundance: Uncommon.

Variation: Females and immatures lack chestnut cheek patch and have less yellow on the belly.

Presumed range in Ohio

Migratory Status: Transient spring/fall migrant. Spring migration may be statewide while fall migration is generally through and east of the Appalachians.

Habitat: This is another species that summers in boreal forests, primarily in the vicinity of spruce bogs and other forest openings. Winter habitat is mostly in the West Indies.

Breeding: Nest is near the trunk in the top of a spruce or fir. Five or six eggs are laid in early to mid June. One clutch per year.

Natural History: On summer breeding grounds far to the north the Cape May Warbler spends its time high in the trees. Feeds heavily on Spruce Budworm caterpillars. Their breeding cycle corresponds to the timing of maximum availability of budworm caterpillars and the population density of this species is known to be closely tied to the presence of this food source. In years of heavy budworm infestations they will rear large broods. On wintering grounds they are known to feed heavily upon nectar and fruits and they have a specialized tubular tongue for extracting nectar from flowers and juices from fruit.

Orange-crowned Warbler — *Oreothlypis celata*

Size: 5 inches.

Abundance: Rare in Ohio.

Variation: Sexes similar. Female slightly duller, less yellow below. Varies regionally.

Presumed range in Ohio

Migratory Status: A spring/fall migrant. Most migrate to the west of Ohio in spring, but migration routes are presumed to include all of Ohio. Spring migration late April/early May.

Habitat: Summers in northern woodlands (Canada and Rocky Mts.) where it prefers habitats with significant understory. Also found old weedy fields, brier thickets, etc. during migration.

Breeding: Breeds in northern Canada and as far north as Alaska and well into the Arctic Circle. Western subspecies breeds along west coast. Lays four to five eggs.

Natural History: Like most warblers, this species is highly insectivorous, but in winter it also eats some fruit and is known to feed at the sap wells created by sapsucker woodpeckers. Feeds deliberately in the lower branches of trees and in bushes. These can be very common birds on their northern breeding grounds, but are seen in Ohio only briefly during migrations. They have been seen very rarely in the state in winter. Orange streak on crown from which it derives its name is not typically visible in the field. Winters across the southern US from the Carolinas to California, and south to northernmost Central America.

Nashville Warbler — *Oreothlypis ruficapilla*

Size: 4.75 inches.

Abundance: Common migrant.

Variation: Little variation. Sexes and immatures are all quite similar.

Presumed range in Ohio

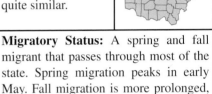

Migratory Status: A spring and fall migrant that passes through most of the state. Spring migration peaks in early May. Fall migration is more prolonged, from late August through October.

Habitat: Summer habitat includes tamarack bogs and boreal forests. Prefers second growth and open woodlands with shrubby undergrowth. Avoids the deep woods.

Breeding: Nests on the ground under bushes or in hummocks of grasses or sphagnum moss. Clutch size ranges from three to six.

Natural History: This warbler species has benefited from human alterations to the American landscape (they prefer logged over, second growth habitats). However, some human alterations have also had a very negative effect. As with many other migrant songbirds, they are vulnerable to towers, power lines, and antennas. No one knows exactly how many birds are killed during migration each year by flying into these obstacles, but some estimate the number to be in the millions. Insects are eaten almost exclusively by this warbler. Summers in northern US and Canada, winters in Mexico. This species has been recorded breeding *very rarely* in northeastern Ohio.

Class—**Aves** (birds)

Order—**Passeriformes** (songbirds)

Family—**Parulidae** (warblers)

Tennessee Warbler *Oreothlypis peregrina*	Blue-winged Warbler *Vermivora cyanoptera*	Golden-winged Warbler *Vermivora chrysoptera*
		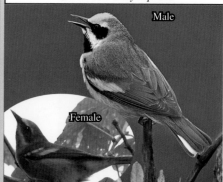

Tennessee Warbler — Male—spring, Fall

Blue-winged Warbler

Golden-winged Warbler — Male, Female

Tennessee Warbler	Blue-winged Warbler	Golden-winged Warbler
Size: 4.75 inches.	**Size:** 4.75 inches.	**Size:** 4.75 inches.
Abundance: Common migrant.	**Abundance:** Uncommon.	**Abundance:** Rare migrant.
Variation: Females more greenish overall. Fall plumage similar to females.	**Variation:** Little variation. Females and juveniles are less vividly colored.	**Variation:** Sexual and ontogenic variation. Juveniles similar to female.
Presumed range in Ohio	Presumed range in Ohio	Presumed range in Ohio
Migratory Status: Another spring/fall migrant that passes through the state rather late in the spring (mid to late May).	**Migratory Status:** Winters in southern Mexico and Central America. Breeds and summers in much of eastern Ohio, as well as farther to the north.	**Migratory Status:** A rare spring and fall migrant through most of the state. Spring migrants appear in southern Ohio in late April, early May in northern Ohio.
Habitat: Summer habitat is the boreal forest of Canada. Winter habitat in Central America is semi-open forest and forest edges. In migration may be seen anywhere.	**Habitat:** Overgrown weed fields with ample brushy undergrowth and early successional woodlands constitute this birds primary habitat. Least common in areas of intensive agriculture.	**Habitat:** Second growth woodlands and overgrown fields. Summer range is in the boreal forest of Canada and in the higher elevations of the Appalachian Mountains.
Breeding: Nest is on the ground at the base of a tree or among upturned roots. Clutch size ranges from three to eight.	**Breeding:** Nest is near the ground in or under a low bush. From four to six eggs are laid in May.	**Breeding:** Nests on the ground near the ground at the base of a bush, hidden in thick grass and weeds. four to five eggs.
Natural History: The numbers of this species passing through Ohio each spring and fall fluctuates depending upon the previous years abundance of its primary summer food, the Spruce Budworm. In the northern forests of Canada in good budworm years, this is one of the most common bird species. In years of diminished budworm populations, the population of these birds also crashes. This relationship provides a valuable insight into the intricate interdependencies of unrelated organisms. This is an inconspicuous bird as it feeds high in trees and migrates later in the spring after trees are fully leaved. Thus it is difficult to detect despite being common. The name comes from the fact that first scientifically collected specimen was from Tennessee.	**Natural History:** A shrub land specialist, the Blue-winged Warbler has experienced an upswing in populations as a result of deforestation by pioneering European settlers of eastern North America. In recent years there has been a decline in their numbers in the northeastern US as forests have begun recovering from the rampant logging of the last century. In Ohio they are most common in the Appalachian Plateau Province and rare in the agricultural regions of the Interior Lowlands Province in western Ohio. These birds sometimes hybridize with the similar Golden-winged Warbler and produce at least two additional forms of difficult to identify hybrid birds. Populations of this species have declined in Ohio in recent years, due to loss of habitat.	**Natural History:** A few individuals once nested very rarely in the state but they are now regarded as extirpated as a breeding bird in Ohio. Actual sightings of migrant birds are also rare, but they are presumed to pass through most of the state. Loss of winter habitat and nest parasitism by the Brown-headed Cowbird are possible reasons for a recent population decline. But hybridization with Blue-winged Warblers which are now expanding their range northward may be the main reason for the increasing rarity of the Golden-winged. They winter in a variety of forest habitats in Mexico, Central America, and northern South America from sea level to 7,000 feet. Like many other warblers, this species migrates across the Gulf of Mexico in spring.

Class—**Aves** (birds)

Order—**Passeriformes** (songbirds)

Family—**Parulidae** (warblers)

Ovenbird *Seiurus aurocapilla*	Louisiana Waterthrush *Parkesia motacilla*	Worm-eating Warbler *Helmitheros vermivorus*

Size: 6 inches.	Presumed range in Ohio 	**Size:** 6 inches.	Presumed range in Ohio 	**Size:** 5.5 inches.	Presumed range in Ohio 
Abundance: Fairly common.		**Abundance:** Fairly common.		**Abundance:** Uncommon in Ohio.	
Variation: No variation. Sexes alike.		**Variation:** None. Sexes alike.		**Variation:** No variation, sexes alike.	

Ovenbird	Louisiana Waterthrush	Worm-eating Warbler
Migratory Status: Winters from south Florida to southern Central America. Summers as far north as northern Canada. Arrives in Ohio in April and May. Leaves in September or October.	**Migratory Status:** A summertime resident that arrives very early (mid to late March), and also departs quite early (July). Winters from Mexico and the Caribbean to northernmost South America.	**Migratory Status:** Summer resident of the southern Appalachian Plateau in southeast Ohio. Winters in the Caribbean and in Central America. They are seen in Ohio from April through August.
Habitat: Mature, contiguous forests. Seems to prefer upland woods. A substrate of abundant leaf litter is an important element to this birds habitat.	**Habitat:** Forested streams are the preferred habitat. In migration they may also be seen along the edges of swamps or small woodland ponds.	**Habitat:** This is a woodland species, but it seems to avoid lowland forests. More common in rugged regions with steep slopes.
Breeding: Nests is on the ground and is constructed of leaves and grass. Nest is unique in that it has a domed roof with an opening in front. Three to six eggs.	**Breeding:** Nesting can occur as early as May in Ohio. Four to six eggs are laid in a nest placed in tree roots along a the banks of a stream.	**Breeding:** Nests are built on the ground in deep woods and are often hidden beneath overhanging vegetation. Four to five eggs is typical.
Natural History: This large warbler is a ground dweller, and is usually observed on the ground or in low foliage. Food is a wide variety of insects and arthropods taken mostly on the ground among the leaf litter. The song of the Ovenbird is distinctive and has been variously described as "emphatic" and "effervescent." Often two nearby birds will sing at once, with their overlapping songs sounding like a single bird. This species has experienced a decline in the last few decades. Forest fragmentation and Brown-headed Cowbird nest parasitism may be to blame. The name "Ovenbird" is derived from the fact that the nest is shaped rather like the old fashioned brick ovens that had a domed roof and opened to the front.	**Natural History:** This species is famous for its incessant "tail bobbing" behavior. The entire rear half of the body constantly wags up and down when foraging in stream side habitats. Requires ecologically healthy stream habitats and this species may be a barometer of overall stream health. *Similar Species:* The **Northern Waterthrush** (*P. noveboracensis*) is so similar to the Louisiana Waterthrush that most casual observers will not be able to tell them apart. The Northern typically passes through Ohio, while the Louisiana breeds in much of the state. Northern breeds in bogs and beaver ponds in boreal forests (some breeding has been recorded in northeastern Ohio). Both associate with wetland habitats.	**Natural History:** Although the Worm-eating Warbler may occur throughout Ohio, it is much more common in the southeastern part of the state. They are quite rare in northern Ohio and especially rare in the northeastern portion of the state. This is a species that specializes in feeding amid low bushes, searching the dead leaf clusters and low hanging foliage for insects, spiders, and primarily, caterpillars. Like many of America's neotropical migrant songbirds, the Worm-eating Warbler is highly dependent upon deciduous forests for breeding habitat. They need large tracts of woodland. They winter in Mexico, Central America, and the West Indies. Despite their name, earthworms are not an important item in their diet.

Class—**Aves** (birds)

Order—**Passeriformes** (songbirds)

Family—**Parulidae** (warblers)

Prothonotary Warbler *Protonotaria citrea*	Common Yellowthroat *Geothlypis trichas*	Kentucky Warbler *Geothlypis formosus*

Size: 5.5 inches. **Abundance:** Uncommon in Ohio. **Variation:** Females are slightly less vivid in their colors.	**Size:** 5 inches. **Abundance:** Common. **Variation:** Female lacks the prominent black mask.	**Size:** 5.5 inches. **Abundance:** Fairly common. **Variation:** Sexes very similar.

Presumed range in Ohio  Presumed range in Ohio Presumed range in Ohio

Migratory Status: A neatropical migrant warbler that winters in mangrove swamps in Central and South America. Summers in Ohio from April to August.

Migratory Status: Summer resident. Seen in Ohio from late April through late summer/early fall. Winters from south Florida to Central America.

Migratory Status: Arrives in Ohio by late April or early May. Nests and rears its young before leaving for the tropics in August or early September.

Habitat: Prothonotary Warblers always nest near water. They are most common in swamps and marshes but can also be seen along lake shores, riparian areas, and in the vicinity of small ponds.

Habitat: Likes thick vegetation in wetland areas. Cattails and sedges in marshes and swamp edges are especially favored. Avoids deep woods but may be seen around edges of woods, especially near streams.

Habitat: Throughout its summer range the Kentucky Warbler enjoys deciduous bottom-land forests and wooded riparian habitats. Within this macro-habitat it requires a micro-habitat of dense undergrowth.

Breeding: Unlike other warblers that build a nest, the Prothonotary Warbler nests in tree cavities. They will also use artificial nest boxes. Lays four or five eggs.

Breeding: The nest is woven from wetland grasses among cattails or sedges. Four to six eggs are laid in late May or early June. Cowbird parasitism occurs.

Breeding: A ground nester. The nest is constructed of dead leaves and grasses and is usually well hidden. Four to five eggs are laid by mid-May.

Natural History: The dredging and draining of swamplands throughout the eastern United States significantly reduced breeding habitat for this warbler in the first half of the 20th century. Loss of wetlands in the US has stabilized somewhat in the last few decades, but the species now faces threats from habitat loss on its wintering grounds in northern South America. Most of the swampland habitats in Ohio disappeared with European settlement. In Ohio today this warbler occurs sporadically throughout the state where suitable habitat still exists and has recently benefited from the placement of artificial nest boxes. Feeds on aquatic insects, snails, and tiny crustaceans. In winter they will also eat fruits and nectar.

Natural History: The Common Yellowthroat is one of the more abundant warblers in America and their summer range includes most of North America south of the Arctic. They do avoid the desert southwest and dry southern plains. Not surprising since they are mainly a wetland loving species. They feed low to the ground on almost any type of tiny invertebrate. Their behavior when foraging is rather "wren-like" as they negotiate dense stands of cattails, reeds, and tall grasses. They tend to stick to heavy cover and when flushed make short flights into deep cover. Nearly all of Ohio's Common Yellowthroats move south in the fall, but a few have been recorded in the state as late as December.

Natural History: Kentucky Warblers are an abundant and widespread bird in suitable habitats throughout the southern and especially the southeastern portion of Ohio in summer. They become increasingly scarce northward in the state and they are quite rare in northwestern Ohio. Like other small warblers they are easily overlooked. The Cornell Laboratory of Ornithology (birds online) website reports that this species appears to be in decline. Destruction of mature tropical forests may be to blame. It is also possible that fragmentation of large forests tracts in North America could be a threat. A handsome warbler, it feeds low to the ground on a wide variety of invertebrates.

Class—**Aves** (birds)

Order—**Passeriformes** (songbirds)

Family—**Parulidae** (warblers)

Mourning Warbler *Geothlypis philadelphia*	**Connecticut Warbler** *Oporonis agilis*	**Black-and-white Warbler** *Mniotilta varia*

Size: 5.25 inches.

Presumed range in Ohio

Abundance:
Rare in Ohio.

Variation: Sexes similar. Female has less contrasting head color.

Size: 5.75 inches.

Presumed range in Ohio

Abundance:
Very rare.

Variation: Females are duller without gray head of male.

Size: 5.25 inches.

Presumed range in Ohio

Abundance:
Uncommon in Ohio.

Variation: Sexes-very similar but female has more white on face and breast.

Migratory Status: Mostly a migrant that passes through Ohio, but a few will spend the summer in northernmost Ohio. Spring arrival in Ohio is late for a warbler, peaking in late May. Most will depart the state in early September.

Migratory Status: Moves quickly through the state on spring migration. Migrates very late in spring (from mid-May to as late as early June). Fall migration through Ohio is in September. Fall migration south follows Atlantic coast.

Migratory Status: Summer resident in southern Ohio. Winters from the southern US to South America and Caribbean. Returns to Ohio in early/mid-April. Most birds in the western and northern parts of the state are transient migrants.

Habitat: The Mourning Warblers summer/breeding habitat is mostly in the boreal forests and bogs of Canada. In Ohio they are most likely to be seen in dense regenerative woodlands. Usually seen on or near the ground.

Habitat: Summer / breeding habitat is boreal forest. There it prefers edges of coniferous woodlands bordering wetland habitats like tamarack bogs and muskeg. Winter habitat is forests in Central and South America.

Habitat: Found in a wide variety of forest types, but mature and second growth deciduous forests are the primary habitat. Mixed conifer-hardwood forests are also used. Likes woodlands with dense under-story.

Breeding: Nests on the ground in dense vegetation or a clump of grass. Lays an average four eggs. There are only few recent breeding records from Ohio, all in the northern portion.

Breeding: Nest is hidden in thick undergrowth on or near the ground. Three to five eggs are laid in late June. Young birds fledge in late July or early August. Does not breed in Ohio.

Breeding: Nest is constructed of dry leaves, dead grasses, and the bark of grapevines. Placed in a depression on the ground at the base of tree or stump. Lays three to five eggs.

Natural History: This warbler likes second growth areas with lush undergrowth. It prefers these conditions both in its summer breeding grounds in boreal forests as well as its wintering grounds in tropical forests. Thus it is one of the few neotropical migrant warblers that has actually benefited from man's insatiable appetite for wood products. This is a secretive bird that "skulks" in dense thickets. Unlike many neotropical migrant songbirds that make long distance flights across the Gulf of Mexico, this warbler follows the coastline north.

Natural History: This shy warbler is rarely observed. In part due to its secretive nature (migrating birds are typically observed low to the ground in dense undergrowth). In addition, it occurs in Ohio only briefly during migration. Finally, this is one of the rarest of America's warblers. Despite its name, this species is quite rare in Connecticut, where it may only occasionally be seen during fall migration. Due to its secretive nature and relative rarity, this is one of the least understood and least commonly observed of America's warbler species.

Natural History: Feeds by plucking tiny creatures from tree bark and branches. Its feeding habits are more similar to that of woodpeckers, nuthatches, and creepers than to most warblers. This species is dependent upon deciduous and mixed conifer forests, and it can be sensitive to deforestation in Ohio. But overall it does not appear to have been significantly impacted throughout its wider range. While this species can be seen throughout the state during migration, it nests mostly in the mountainous Unglaciated Allegheny Plateau Region of southeastern Ohio.

Class—**Aves** (birds)

Order—**Passeriformes** (songbirds)

Family—**Icturidae** (blackbirds)

Brown-headed Cowbird	Red-winged Blackbird	Common Grackle
Molothrus ater	*Agelaius phoeniceus*	*Quiscalus quiscula*

Brown-headed Cowbird	Red-winged Blackbird	Common Grackle
Size: 7.5 inches.	**Size:** 9 inches.	**Size:** 12.5 inches.
Abundance: Common.	**Abundance:** Common.	**Abundance:** Very common.
Variation: Female drab brownish gray. Male shiny black with brown head. See photos above.	**Variation:** Pronounced sexual dimorphism and some seasonal variation among males.	**Variation:** Females slightly smaller and less iridescent. 2 color morphs, "bronze" and "purple."

Presumed range in Ohio (for all three columns)

Migratory Status: The cowbird can be seen in most of the state year-round, but they are more numerous in spring and summer. Birds that move south for the winter return early in the spring.

Migratory Status: These birds are seen throughout the year in Ohio, but many summer birds may move south in winter to be replaced by birds that have summered farther north.

Migratory Status: Grackles are seen year-round in Ohio, but many do migrate. Some nesting birds may move south in winter, and some that nested farther north may winter in the state.

Habitat: Open fields and agricultural areas primarily, but can also be common in towns and suburbs. Inhabits edge areas and woods openings but avoids deep forest.

Habitat: The Red-wing Blackbirds favorite habitat is marsh or wet meadows. They are also found along roadside ditches and the edges of ponds in open areas.

Habitat: Grackles favor agricultural areas and open fields/croplands. They are also common in urban areas where they inhabit lawns, parks, etc. In winter roosts in large flocks in small woodlots.

Breeding: Female cowbirds lay their eggs in the nest of other bird species, a unique nesting strategy known as "brood parasitism" (see below). As many as 40 eggs may be laid in dozens of songbird nests.

Breeding: The nest of the Red-winged Blackbird is a woven basket usually suspended from two or three cattail blades and is most often positioned over water. Two to four eggs are laid. Young are fed enormous quantities of insects.

Breeding: Grackles often nest in groups that may consist of a dozen or more pairs. The nest is built in the upper branches of medium-size trees and several nests can be in the same tree, or in adjacent trees.

Natural History: This species is unique among Ohio birds in that the adults play no role in rearing their young. Instead the female lays an egg in another species' nest and the adoptive parents rear the young cowbird, usually to the detriment of their own offspring. The disappearance of extensive forest tracts has allowed the cowbird to parasitize many more woodland songbirds than was possible prior to settlement. As a result, this species now poses a real threat to many smaller songbird species, especially the warblers.

Natural History: In winter Red-winged Blackbirds often join large mixed flocks that can include all the birds shown on this page. Males sing conspicuously in spring. Like the other blackbirds on this page, the Red-winged has benefited from human alterations to Ohio's natural habitats, thriving in open land and agricultural areas. Food is almost entirely insects and the along with the Common Grackle this species plays an important role in insect control. The bright red and yellow "epaulets" on the wing of the male are greatly reduced in winter.

Natural History: Grackles are known for forming large flocks during the winter that will roost communally and can number in the thousands. When these large congregations move into a town or neighborhood they can become a messy nuisance, but their reputation for spreading disease is exaggerated. Throughout most of the year they are busy consuming millions of insect pests. In harsh winter weather they may descend on backyard bird feeders in large flocks that overwhelm the regular residents, creating consternation among back-yard birdwatchers.

Class—**Aves** (birds)

Order—**Passeriformes** (songbirds)

Family—**Icturidae** (blackbirds)

Bobolink *Dolichonyx oryzivorus*	**Rusty Blackbird** *Euphagus carolinus*	**Brewer's Blackbird** *Euphagus cyanocephalus*

Size: 7 inches.

Abundance: Uncommon.

Variation: Females and winter males are brownish and sparrow-like in color.

Presumed range in Ohio

Migratory Status: Both a spring/fall migrant and a summer resident in northern and central Ohio. Most begin to arrive in Ohio in mid-May.

Habitat: Bobolinks are open country birds and they are usually seen in pastures and hayfields. Their original habitats in the state were probably tallgrass prairies, which no longer exist in any significant amount.

Breeding: Females breed with a number of males and a clutch of five eggs may have several fathers. Nest is woven of grasses and placed on the ground.

Natural History: Bobolinks are one of the greatest migrators of any bird seen in Ohio. They will nest in the northern US and Canada and winter in southern South America in the open grasslands of the Pampas region of Uruguay and Argentina. That's a round trip of nearly 20,000 miles! In Ohio they are more common in the northern half of the state and uncommon to rare as a nesting bird in the southern portions of the state. This species has experienced population declines in the last half century, but has recently benefited from CRP programs. Food items include seeds, grains, and many invertebrates during breeding. Many people are surprised to learn that these birds are in the blackbird family.

Size: 9 inches.

Abundance: Uncommon.

Variation: Significant seasonal plumage variations. See photos above.

Presumed range in Ohio

Migratory Status: Both a seasonal migrant and a winter resident. Most will winter to the south of Ohio but some may linger if weather is not too harsh.

Habitat: Wintering Rusty Blackbirds favor wetland habitats. Floodplain forests, edges of swamps and woods bordering marshes make up the bulk of this birds winter habitat. Summers in wet boreal woodlands and tundra edges.

Breeding: Breeding occurs far to the north (as far as the arctic). An average of four eggs are laid in a bulky nest of twigs, lichens, and grass.

Natural History: In the last few years Rusty Blackbirds have garnered the attention of birdwatchers and conservationists concerned about an apparently significant decline in the population of this species. The loss of wet woodlands to agriculture throughout much of their wintering grounds in the southern US may be partly to blame. Unlike many blackbirds that regularly intermingle with other species, the Rusty Blackbird seems to remain mostly segregated from the large winter flocks of grackles, cowbirds, starlings, and Red-wingeds. These birds summer far to the north and are seen in Ohio mostly in winter (or during migration periods). Food is insects, seeds, grains, etc.

Size: 9.5 inches.

Abundance: Rare in Ohio.

Variation: Females are drab brown. Males are iridescent blue-black.

Presumed range in Ohio

Migratory Status: A winter/spring migrant visitor from the western United States. May be seen northeastern Ohio and a few will breed nearby in southern Michigan.

Habitat: Favors open country. In Ohio it is usually seen in harvested or plowed agricultural fields, pastures, etc. It may also frequent feedlots where it feeds on waste grain. In the bulk of its range out west it inhabits grasslands.

Breeding: As many as eight eggs may be laid, but five or six is probably average. Nests on the ground. No nesting has been recorded in Ohio.

Natural History: The Brewer's Blackbird is a western species that historically inhabited the Great Plains and Rocky Mountain Regions all the way to the Pacific Ocean. With the clearing of land brought on by human activities, the Brewer's Blackbird began to invade the eastern Temperate Forest Level I Ecoregion in the early 1900s. Although they are still rare in Ohio, birdwatchers now report sightings nearly every winter. Feeds mostly on grains and seeds of grasses or weeds in winter. Summer diet is largely insects. The stomach of one bird reportedly contain over 50 tiny grasshoppers! Despite being rare in Ohio, this is a very common blackbird in the western half of North America.

Class—Aves (birds)

Order—Passeriformes (songbirds)

Family—Icturidae (blackbirds)

Yellow-headed Blackbird *Xanthocephalus xanthocephalus*	Eastern Meadowlark *Sturnella magna*	Western Meadowlark *Sturnella neglecta*

Size: 9.5 inches.	**Size:** 9.5 inches.	**Size:** 9.5 inches.
Abundance: Very rare in Ohio.	**Abundance:** Common.	**Abundance:** Very rare in Ohio.
Variation: Females are brownish with much reduced yellow on head and breast.	**Variation:** No significant sexual variation. Breeding adult slightly brighter.	**Variation:** No significant sexual variation. Breeding adult slightly brighter.

Presumed range in Ohio (for each species)

Migratory Status: A very rare summer resident in the vicinity of Lake Erie and in extreme northeast Ohio.

Habitat: A marsh specialist. Throughout most of their range in the western US they are common around "prairie potholes" lake-shores, marshes, beaver ponds, and creeks where cattails and sedges dominate.

Breeding: A cup-like nest is woven around several upright stalks of cattail or sedge. Averages three to five eggs and produces only one clutch per season.

Natural History: Feeds heavily on aquatic insects during the breeding season and feeds them to the young exclusively. In fall and winter switches to weed seeds and grains. When engaged in territorial displays and singing the males are quite conspicuous. Females are more discreet and sometimes difficult to observe. Ohio populations are migratory. Adult males migrate separately from females and juveniles. They are seemingly less tolerant of cold than most other blackbirds as they will arrive on northern breeding grounds later and depart earlier than other blackbirds. Winters in the southwestern United States and most of Mexico. Greatest abundance in summer is in the Dakotas.

Migratory Status: Eastern Meadowlarks are year-round resident birds throughout the state of Ohio.

Habitat: Open, treeless pastures and fields that are kept closely grazed or mowed. They like short grasses and avoid overgrown areas. In winter they are often seen in harvested croplands or emerging wheat fields.

Breeding: Nest is on the ground and well hidden beneath overhanging grasses or under the edge of a grass tussock. Three to five eggs.

Natural History: As might be expected of a bird that loves open spaces, the eastern Meadowlark is least common in Ohio in the forested regions of the southeastern portion of the state. Even in the mountains however, this bird can be found in areas of open habitat. They feed mostly on insects in warmer months, with grasshoppers and crickets being a dietary mainstay in the summer. During winter they will eat seeds and grain. They tend to occur in small flocks during the winter, but pair off and scatter in the breeding season. The following species (Western Meadowlark) is nearly identical. Expert birders rely on listening to the birds songs to make a positive identification.

Migratory Status: Western Meadowlarks are very rare summer residents in the northeastern edge of Ohio.

Habitat: Open, treeless pastures and fields that are kept closely grazed or mowed. They like short grasses and avoid overgrown areas. In winter they are often seen in harvested croplands or emerging wheat fields.

Breeding: Nest is on the ground. Woven from grass stems and may be open or domed, with or without tunnel-like entrance. Lays five or six eggs.

Natural History: In appearance (and most other respects) the Western Meadowlark is very similar to the eastern species. Visually, the yellow on the throat of the Western extends farther beneath the lower jaw (malar). One might reasonably wonder how two so similar species can co-exist without interbreeding. The answer is likely in the fact that their songs are decidedly different. Thus breeders respond only to the songs of their own species. Northeastern Ohio represents the extreme eastern edge of this species range. The bulk of the population resides in the Great Plains region. They also range westward through the Rocky Mountains all the way to the Pacific Ocean.

Class—**Aves** (birds)

Order—**Passeriformes** (songbirds)

Family—**Icturidae** (blackbirds)

Baltimore Oriole *Icturus galbula*	**Orchard Oriole** *Icturus spurius*

Presumed range in Ohio

Presumed range in Ohio

Size: 8.75 inches.

Abundance: Common. Most common in northern Ohio.

Migratory Status: A summer resident that begins to return to southern Ohio in late April with migrants arriving through late May in northern Ohio. Winters in Florida, Cuba, Jamiaca, and southern Mexico south to northern South America.

Variation: Significant sexual and age related dimorphism (see photos above). Immature male less vividly colored.

Habitat: Savanna-like habitats are preferred. Pastures with scattered large trees, parks, and lawns in urban areas, or farms and ranches in rural areas. During migration may be seen in a variety of habitats.

Breeding: The nest is an easily recognizable "hanging basket" woven from grasses and suspended from a tree limb. Four to six eggs is typical.

Natural History: These handsome orange and black birds are a favorite with backyard birdwatchers. They will come to nectar feeders and fruits such as oranges, and they relish grape jelly. In addition to nectar and fruit they feed heavily on insects. In some areas of their range they have adapted well to human activities. Small town neighborhoods and city parks are among their habitats today. Although they are fond of semi-open habitats and avoid dense forests, they do like the presence of some mature trees in their habitat. Thus, they may decline from areas where intensive agriculture reduces the presence of woodland patches and large trees.

Size: 7 inches.

Abundance: Fairly common statewide.

Migratory Status: Summer resident that breeds throughout Ohio. Returns to Ohio in late April through mid-May. Departs from northern portions of breeding range early as late July. Winters from southern Mexico to northern South America.

Variation: Significant sexual and ontogenic plumage variation. Immature males resemble female (see photos).

Habitat: This species shows a preference for semi-open habitats and narrow strips of woodland bordering rivers and streams. Their name comes from the fact that they are fond of orchards and they will often nest in fruit trees.

Breeding: The nest is a rounded basket woven from grasses and suspended from a forked tree branch. Four eggs is typical, but can be as many as six.

Natural History: Like the larger Baltimore Oriole, Orchard Orioles will eat fruit. They also feed on a wide variety of arthropods gleaned from tree branches and leaves, as well as from weedy fields. Immature males resemble females but have a large black throat patch. These birds are somewhat gregarious and they often occur in flocks on tropical wintering grounds. They are also known to nest in small colonies where ideal habitat exists. Spraying for insects in orchards can be dangerous for these insect and fruit eaters as it can be for other bird species, many of which are highly susceptible to insecticides.

Class—**Aves** (birds)

Order—**Passeriformes** (songbirds)

Family—**Thraupidae** (tanagers)

Scarlet Tanager *Piranga ludoviciana*	Summer Tanager *Piranga rubra*

Size: 7 inches.	Presumed range in Ohio	**Size:** 7.75 inches.	Presumed range in Ohio
Abundance: Common in southeast Ohio, uncommon in northwest Ohio.		**Abundance:** Uncommon. Most are seen in southern Ohio.	
Migratory Status: A summer resident that breeds in Ohio and winters in tropical America. Begins to arrive in Ohio in mid to late April. Leaves for wintering grounds in September.		**Migratory Status:** Well named, this bird is seen in Ohio only during summer. It winters in the tropics. Spring arrival is usually late April to early May. Fall migration begins in September.	

Variation: Sexual and ontogenic plumage variations. Juvenile males resemble females for the first year of their lives. See photos above.	**Variation:** Sexual and ontogenic dimorphism. See photos above. The mottled yellow-green and bright red of the juvenile male entering its second year can be seen in early spring.
Habitat: The summer habitat for the Scarlet Tanager closely coincides with the Eastern Temperate Forest Level I ecoregion. It prefers large tracts of unbroken woodlands.	**Habitat:** Like their cousins Scarlet Tanagers, Summer Tanagers are birds of the eastern forests. However, this species is more likely to occupy fragmented forests and edge areas.
Breeding: The thin, saucer-like nest of the Scarlet Tanager is placed on the fork of an outer branch. Four eggs is typical. Only one brood is produced.	**Breeding:** The rather flimsy nest is on a terminal fork of a branch that is usually low over an opening such as a creek bed. The typical clutch size is three to four.
Natural History: The Scarlet Tanager is one of the most strikingly colored birds in Ohio. Unfortunately, this species dependence upon larger tracts of forested land means that its future is uncertain. Forest fragmentation leads to vulnerability to cowbird nest parasitism. Throughout much of the Midwest, where deforestation and fragmentation of forests has been rampant, this species is in decline. In Ohio it is still common in the southeastern Appalachian Plateau where large amounts of woodland remain. Food in summer is mostly insects (including wasps and hornets). Winters from Panama to northwestern South America. In Ohio these birds are most common in the Appalachian Plateau Province and least common in the Huron-Lake Erie Plains and the Till Plains Sections of the Interior Lowland Province.	**Natural History:** Summer Tanagers feed on a variety of woodland insects and larvae, but they also eat some berries and fruits. One of their primary food items however is bees and wasps, a fact that makes them an attractive species to have around the rural homestead. Immature males resemble females their first summer. By the following spring they begin transformation into the bright red plumage of the adult male. During this transformation they are one of the most colorful birds in Ohio woodlands (see photos above). Breeding bird surveys in recent years have detected a slight decline in populations of this species. Landscape changes in their wintering grounds may be the reason. They will winter from southern Mexico to northern South America. Like many migratory songbirds they often migrate at night.

Class—**Aves** (birds)	
Order—**Passeriformes** (songbirds)	

Family—**Sturnidae** (mynas)	Family—**Passeridae** (weaver finches)
European Starling *Sturnis vulgaris*	**House Sparrow** *Passer domesticus*

Size: 8.75 inches.

Abundance: Very common.

Migratory Status: A non-migratory year-round resident throughout the state.

Variation: Breeding plumage iridescent dark purple, non-breeding has white speckles. Immatures are drab brown.

Presumed range in Ohio

Habitat: Urban and suburban areas as well as farms and ranches. Starlings are closely tied to human activity and are rarely seen in true wilderness. By contrast, they can be quite common in large cities and small towns.

Breeding: Nest is made of grass, leaves, etc., stuffed into a cavity. Often uses cracks or holes in man-made structures. Also old woodpecker holes. Clutch size is typically five eggs.

Natural History: The Starling is one of the most familiar birds in America, but ironically it is a non-native species. All the Starlings in America are descendant from a handful of birds released in New York City in the 1890s. Contrary to popular belief, the Starling is not related to the blackbirds. Instead they belong to the same family as the old world mynas. These birds have enjoyed remarkable success since being introduced to North America and they are now found throughout the continent. They represent a real threat to many of our native species, especially those that nest in cavities. In winter they often join grackles and blackbirds in large mixed flocks that can become messy nuisance in urban and suburban areas. Along with the blackbirds, these birds are sometimes regarded as a threat to humans due to the avian-borne disease Histoplasmosis. In truth, this threat is exaggerated. The statewide population in Ohio is estimated to be over 6 million birds.

Size: 6.25 inches.

Abundance: Very common.

Migratory Status: Non-migratory, the House Sparrow is a year-round resident of Ohio.

Variation: Males have distinctive gray crown with black face mask. Females are a plain drab brown. See photos.

Presumed range in Ohio

Habitat: The House Sparrow's name comes from its affinity for human habitations. These are mostly urban birds and when they do occur in rural areas it is always near farms and homesteads.

Breeding: House Sparrow build bulky nests of grass, feathers, paper strips, etc. placed in hollows or crevices of barns, outbuildings or even occupied homes. Five to six eggs on average.

Natural History: A European immigrant, the House Sparrow was released into the United States about 150 years ago. They have spread across the continent and they are now perhaps the most familiar bird species in America. They roost communally in dense vegetation. Roosting sites are often in yards or foundation plantings next to houses. They are common scavengers around outdoor restaurants and fast food parking lots. They are often considered to be a nuisance bird, but their tame demeanor endears them to many. Despite being extremely common in urban areas, they are quite rare in wilderness. These highly successful birds may nest up to four times in a season. Despite their common name, House "Sparrow," they are not closely related to sparrows. They belong to an old world family known as the Weaver Finches. Along with the European Starling this is one of the most abundant birds in Ohio.

Class—**Aves** (birds)
Order—**Passeriformes** (songbirds)
Family—**Emberzidae** (sparrows)

Swamp Sparrow *Melospiza georgiana*	**Song Sparrow** *Melospiza melodia*	**Lincoln's Sparrow** *Melospiza lincolnii*

Swamp Sparrow — *Melospiza georgiana*

Size: 5.75 inches.

Abundance: Fairly common.

Variation: Breeding males are richer in color with a reddish crown.

Presumed range in Ohio

Migratory Status: Year-round resident in northern Ohio. Winter resident in the southern portions of the state. Common migrant throughout Ohio.

Habitat: Summers in wetlands. Swamps, marshes (including salt marsh) and wet meadows. More diverse habitats may be used in winter, including upland fields.

Breeding: Nest is made of grasses and placed in cattails, grasses, or low bush. Three to six eggs, four on average.

Natural History: Secretive and elusive, the Swamp Sparrow is less familiar to Ohioans than most of its kin. They will visit feeders during the winter, but they are rarely a commonly seen bird at feeders. These birds are highly dependent upon wetlands for breeding, and they may be negatively impacted by loss of wetlands. At this time however populations appear stable. Although they can be quite common in summer habitats and in the bayous of the deep south in winter, they do not flock and are nearly always seen singly. There are three distinct subspecies of Swamp Sparrow recognized by professional orinithologists. The nominant subspecies (*M. g. georgiana*) is seen in Ohio.

Song Sparrow — *Melospiza melodia*

Size: 5.5 inches.

Abundance: Very common in Ohio.

Variation: Many subspecies nationwide with light and dark color morphs.

Presumed range in Ohio

Migratory Status: Many are year-round residents whose numbers may be bolstered in winter by migrants that have summered farther north in Canada.

Habitat: Overgrown fields, dense underbrush, and rank weeds are the preferred habitat of the Song Sparrow throughout their range. They are especially common in edge habitats.

Breeding: Nests are built low to the ground in weeds or shrubs. Four eggs is typical.

Natural History: Both the common and scientific names of the Song Sparrow are references to its distinct and melodic song. Primarily seed eaters, these sparrows migrate in response to heavy snow cover, and they are common at bird feeders throughout the southern United States each winter. Sharp-shinned and Cooper's Hawks are major predators of adults, and the young and eggs are vulnerable to a variety of snake predators. However, they remain a thriving species. There are dozens of subspecies nationwide with light and dark color morphs. Most Ohio specimens resemble the photo above. One of the earliest and most comphrehensive studies of bird biology was conducted on this species by an Ohioan.

Lincoln's Sparrow — *Melospiza lincolnii*

Size: 5.5 inches.

Abundance: Rare in Ohio.

Variation: No significant variation between sexes or adults and juveniles.

Presumed range in Ohio

Migratory Status: Spring and fall migrant. Exact routes of migration through Ohio poorly known but presumably can be seen statewide during migration.

Habitat: Summer habitat is boreal regions of Canada and northern Rockies where it occupies damp woodlands with dense brush such as willow. Spruce bogs and wetlands are favored.

Breeding: Nests on the ground amid sedges or at the base of willow in boreal wetlands. Lays three to five eggs.

Natural History: Lincoln's Sparrows are more common west of the Mississippi and are rather rare in Ohio. In addition it is shy and secretive and tends to stick to heavy cover. Add to this the fact that it is a transient species in Ohio and sightings are uncommon. During migration they are believed to be fairly widespread across the state. When excited they will raise the feathers on the back of the head giving them a "crested" look. Due to their secretive habits the biology of these sparrows is not well understood. Feeds on insects in summer and seeds in winter. Unlike many sparrows they rarely visit feeders except during periods of harsh winter weather. Very similar to the Song Sparrow, but has finer streaking on the breast.

Class—**Aves** (birds)

Order—**Passeriformes** (songbirds)

Family—**Emberzidae** (sparrows)

Chipping Sparrow *Spizella passerina*	**Clay-colored Sparrow** *Spizella pallida*	**Field Sparrow** *Spizella pusilla*

Chipping Sparrow	Clay-colored Sparrow	Field Sparrow
Size: 5.5 inches.	**Size:** 5.5 inches.	**Size:** 5.75 inches.
 Presumed range in Ohio	 Presumed range in Ohio	 Presumed range in Ohio
Abundance: Very common.	**Abundance:** Very rare in Ohio.	**Abundance:** Common.
Migratory Status: A summer resident that returns in April.	**Migratory Status:** Summer migrant and rare summer breeder.	**Migratory Status:** Year-round but uncommon in winter.
Variation: No sexual dimorphism, but winter plumage is much more subdued and head markings are greatly reduced.	**Variation:** No significant variation among sexes. Non-breeding birds paler with less prominent head markings.	**Variation:** Sexes alike. No seasonal plumage changes but immature birds have dark streaks on the breast.
Habitat: Edge areas and woods openings. Thrives in human altered habitats including farmsteads, suburban yards, and parks.	**Habitat:** This is an open country species that prefers grasslands. In Ohio uses abandoned fields taken over by weeds, grass, and brush.	**Habitat:** Open and semi-open areas with good cover in the form of weeds and taller grasses. Also shrubby, early regenerative woodland areas.
Breeding: Breeds earlier than most other Ohio songbirds. Nests may be complete and eggs can being laid as early as mid-April in Ohio.	**Breeding:** Only a handful of nests have been found in Ohio. Typically nest is close to the ground in grassy or brushy environments. Four eggs is typical.	**Breeding:** Nest is on the ground usually at the base of a clump of grass or in a low bush. Two broods per year is common. Two to five eggs.
Natural History: Chipping Sparrow move to the deep south in winter. Nesting has been recorded throughout the state, but they are more common as breeding birds in the central, western, and northern parts of the state and least common in the Allegheny Plateau in the southeast. They adapt well to the human disturbance of natural habitats and they are undoubtedly more common today than prior to settlement. They can be quite common in Ohio in areas of intensive agriculture and also in urban / suburban environments. In fact, this is one of the most common sparrows in the state during summer months. The Chipping Sparrow feeds mostly on the seeds of grasses and forbs, and does most of its foraging on the ground. Insects are eaten during the breeding season and are fed to the young. They can also be a common bird at feeders.	**Natural History:** This species is a newcomer to Ohio, with the first observations occuring in the 1940s and the first confirmed nesting in 1994. The core range for this species is in the Great Plains region. Range expansion eastward into the Great Lakes region apparently began in the 1920s. The few nesting records from Ohio have all been in the northern portion of the state. Despite the fact that the Great Plains ecosystem is one of the most damaged of all America's natural habitats, this species continues to maintain healthy population numbers and it is one of the more common birds in the northern plains of Canada and North Dakota in summer. Winter range includes south Texas and Mexico. They sometimes flock with other sparrows and they have been known to hybridize with the Field Sparrow.	**Natural History:** Another species that has adapted well to man-made changes in natural landscapes, the Field Sparrow is probably more numerous today than in historical times. Unlike many sparrows however, the Field Sparrow is a "country" sparrow that prefers rural regions over towns and suburbs. Although they are seen year-round in Ohio, some southerly movement occurs in northern populations in winter that may result in a shuffling of individual birds in Ohio. Food is mostly grass seeds. Insects are also eaten, especially during the breeding season. Very similar to the American Tree Sparrow, but has all pink bill instead of dark upper mandible. Although still a common species the Field Sparrow has experienced population declines in recent years. Perhaps due to habitat changes in much of its range.

Class—**Aves** (birds)
Order—**Passeriformes** (songbirds)
Family—**Emberzidae** (sparrows)

American Tree Sparrow *Spizelloides arborea*	Lark Sparrow *Chondestes grammacus*	Savannah Sparrow *Passerculus sandwichensis*

American Tree Sparrow

Size: 6.25 inches.

Presumed range in Ohio

Abundance: Common in winter.

Migratory Status: Winter resident and seasonal migrant.

Variation: Adults show no variation and the sexes are alike. Immatures have dusky streaks on the sides and breast.

Habitat: In winter they use overgrown fields, edge areas, brushy patches with weeds, and grasses. Summer habitat is open tundra and taiga.

Breeding: Nest is on the ground. Four to six eggs. These hardy sparrows will nest as far north as the Arctic Circle and well above the tree line.

Natural History: The American Tree Sparrow is a northern species that is only seen in Ohio in winter when heavy snow cover in the northern regions pushes migrating flocks southward. Like most sparrows, seeds are the staple food in winter. Seeds are also eaten in summer months but insects are more important, especially when rearing young. Seeds of a wide variety of grasses and weeds are consumed, and this species is regularly seen at bird feeders in northern states. Despite its name this species can be found in summer on treeless, arctic tundra. Winter migrants begin to arrive in the northern US by late October and may reach southernmost Ohio by November. Degree of southerly movement can be dictated by weather conditions.

Lark Sparrow

Size: 6.25 inches.

Presumed range in Ohio

Abundance: Rare in Ohio.

Migratory Status: Summer migrant that breeds rarely in state.

Variation: No sexual variation. Immatures have dark streaks on the breast and browner facial markings.

Habitat: The Lark Sparrow is restricted to open habitats and is most common in dry grasslands of the southwestern US. Favors open field / brushy ecotones.

Breeding: Nest is usually on the ground but may be in a low bush. Three to six eggs is typical. Known to sometimes use the abondoned nest of another bird.

Natural History: A western species that ranges into Ohio very rarely and sporadically, mostly occuring in the northwestern corner of the state. There are a few scattered reports from central and southwestern Ohio as well. It is a very rare and an endangered species in Ohio, but within the core of its range in the Great Plains region it is common. Males are reported to perform a courtship "dance" that resembles that of a turkey's strutting behavior. The Lark Sparrow's facial pattern of vivid black and white stripes with chestnut cheek patch is distinctive. As with most sparrows, seeds are the primary food in winter. During warmer months both seeds and insects are eaten. Grasshoppers are reported to be a major food item for both young birds and summer adults.

Savannah Sparrow

Size: 5.5 inches.

Presumed range in Ohio

Abundance: Fairly common.

Migratory Status: Common in summer but rare in winter.

Variation: Highly variable with as many as 28 subspecies. Most birds seen in Ohio resemble photo above.

Habitat: Pastures, grasslands, mowed areas in vacant lots, and cultivated fields are used in Ohio. Elsewhere salt marsh, tundra, and bogs are habitats.

Breeding: Nests on the ground beneath overhanging vegetation. Four to five eggs is typical. Nesting in Ohio is mostly in glaciated regions of the state.

Natural History: This is one of the most widespread sparrow species in America. Between breeding range, winter range, and migration routes the Savannah Sparrow may be seen anywhere on the continent. In Ohio they are least common in the Allegheny Plateau and in the Bluegrass Section of the Interior Low Plateau along the Ohio River. They feed on arthropods in summer and seeds in winter. The name comes from the Georgia town of Savannah (where the first specimen was described) rather than from the habitat type. As with many grassland animals the Savannah Sparrow has experienced population declines in areas of intensive agriculture or urbanization. Delaying cutting of hayfields has shown to benefit by allowing young time to fledge.

Class—**Aves** (birds)

Order—**Passeriformes** (songbirds)

Family—**Emberzidae** (sparrows)

Henslow's Sparrow *Ammodramus henslowii*	**Grasshopper Sparrow** *Ammodramus savannarum*	**Vesper Sparrow** *Pooecetes gramineus*

Size: 5 inches.

Abundance: Uncommon to rare.

Variation: No sexual dimorphism. No significant variation among adults.

Presumed range in Ohio

Migratory Status: Summer resident of Ohio that winters in the lower coastal plain of the southeast US. Spring arrival in Ohio is in late April or early May.

Habitat: Undisturbed, overgrown grassy / weedy fields in open areas. Unmowed hayfields and re-claimed strip mines are used in Ohio.

Breeding: Nest is on the ground in thick grass and well concealed. Two to five eggs are laid in May. Double-broods are known.

Natural History: Henslow's Sparrow is nowhere a common species and in Ohio its relative scarcity and secretive nature make it one of the least familiar birds in the state. This is a species in decline throughout its range. Not surprising since the tallgrass prairies that once provided ample nesting habitat are all but gone. Insects, especially grasshopper and crickets, are important food items in the summer. In winter eats mostly seeds, especially small grass seeds. Snakes are reported to be a major predator on nests, along with a variety of carnivorous mammals. Breeds sparingly across much of Ohio but presumably can be seen throughout the state. ODNR Species of Concern.

Size: 5 inches.

Abundance: Fairly common.

Variation: No sexual dimorphism. No significant variation among adults.

Presumed range in Ohio

Migratory Status: Summer resident. Arrives in late April and departs in late August through September. The winter range is in the southeast US, Mexico, and California.

Habitat: A grassland species, the Grasshopper sparrow likes short and mid-grass prairie. In Ohio it uses heavily grazed pastures and hayfields.

Breeding: Nest is on the ground and well hidden beneath overhanging grass. Two broods per summer is usual with four to five eggs per clutch.

Natural History: In many ways similar to the preceding species, but much more common. Its name is derived from the sound of its song which mimics the buzzing sound made by some types of orthopteran insects. Throughout its range (which includes most of the US east of the Rocky Mountains) it is a rather inconspicuous bird. Though unfamiliar to most Ohioans, in the high plains region of the north-central US it is commonly seen (and heard). Feeds entirely on the ground. Food is mostly grasshoppers and other insects in summer. In winter eats both insects and seeds, especially tiny grass seeds. Most range maps show the entire state within Grasshopper Sparrow's summer range.

Size: 6.25 inches.

Abundance: Fairly common.

Variation: No sexual differences. Immatures are similar but drabber.

Presumed range in Ohio

Migratory Status: Summer resident in northwest and north central Ohio. Spring/fall migrant throughout much of the rest of the state.

Habitat: This is a bird of open country. Its natural habitats are grasslands and today it also uses agricultural fields. Prefers dry areas.

Breeding: Nest is on the ground in open fields, sometimes concealed by grass tussock. Three to five eggs. May to produce two broods per year.

Natural History: The Vesper Sparrow is more common in the western region of North America, but they are a fairly common breeding bird in the northwestern portion of Ohio. They are declining in the eastern portions of their range which includes much of the Midwest and great lakes region. They winter across the southern US and southward to northern Central America. In Ohio this species may nest in crop fields. Thus it may be fairly common in agricultural regions of the state. By contrast, it is uncommon, rare, or absent in much of the more heavily wooded regions in the Allegheny Plateau, although it may occur there in re-clamed strip mine areas.

Class—**Aves** (birds)

Order—**Passeriformes** (songbirds)

Family—**Emberizidae** (sparrows)

White-throated Sparrow *Zonotrichia albicollis*	White-crowned Sparrow *Zonotrichia leucophrys*

White-striped morph—adult

White-striped morph—juvenile

Adult

Juvenile

Size: 6.75 inches.	**Size:** 7.75 inches.

Abundance: Common during migration season.

Migratory Status: A winter resident and seasonal migrant throughout the state. Arrives from northern breeding grounds in November and stays through early to mid-May. Movements may be dictated by weather.

Presumed range in Ohio

Abundance: Fairly common to common in winter.

Migratory Status: A winter resident throughout most of the state except for northeastern Ohio where it can be seen as migrant in fall and spring. Seen in Ohio from October through early May.

Presumed range in Ohio

Variation: Two adult morphs. One has bright white eye stripe, other has tan. Immatures have striped breasts.

Variation: First year birds have chestnut and beige head stripe as opposed to black and white (see photos above). Sexes alike.

Habitat: Brushy thickets, fence rows, weedy fields, edges areas, and regenerative woodlands. Both in upland and lowland areas. Can be seen in both rural and urban areas but always in the vicinity of bushes, shrubs, tall weeds, or other cover.

Habitat: In Ohio they may be seen in any area where there are weeds, grasses, or brush in sufficient amount to provide good cover for roosting and escape from predators. Woodland edges and overgrown fence rows are best.

Breeding: Breeds in a broad band across Canada and the northeastern US, as well as northern great lakes states (MI, WI, MN). Nest is on the ground in open areas, forest edges, etc. Four eggs is typical. As many as seven recorded.

Breeding: Breeds in boreal regions, tundra, and mountain meadows. Nest is in a low bush with about four eggs. Breeds very far to the north in northern Canada and Alaska. Will summer well into the Arctic Circle beyond the tree line.

Natural History: This is one of Ohio's more common sparrows during winter. In early spring just before flying north to summer breeding grounds, the White-throated Sparrow serenades the fields and woodlands with its distinctive whistling song. As these birds are ground foragers, snow cover is one of the most important conditions that influence migratory patterns. Feeds mostly on insects in summer and switches to seeds in winter. When feeding uses both feet with a backwards thrusting motion to clear away leaf litter. They are well represented at bird feeders throughout the state in winter. A short-distance migrator, this species winters mostly within the United States.

Natural History: Similar in many respects to the White-throated Sparrow to which it is closely related. Ranges farther west (all the way to the Pacific) and farther north. The White-crowned Sparrow produces multiple broods (as many as four per season in some western populations). Most will have at least two broods annually. Some summer well into the Arctic Tundra and make annual migrations of over 4,000 miles up and down the continent. Eats insects and seeds in summer, mostly seeds in winter. Forages on the ground near cover. Less common than the White-Throated Sparrow, but still a familiar bird at winter feeders. This is one of the most highly studied songbirds in America.

Class—**Aves** (birds)

Order—**Passeriformes** (songbirds)

Family—**Emberizidae** (sparrows)

Dark-eyed Junco *Junco hyemalis*	**Eastern Towhee** *Pipilo erythrophthalmus*

Typical

Pink-sided morph

Male

Female

Size: 6 inches.

Abundance: Very common in winter.

Migratory Status: A common winter resident throughout the state and an uncommon year-round resident in the northeastern corner of Ohio. Northern migrants have typically all arrived by early December.

Presumed range in Ohio

Variation: Highly variable. Several different color morphs nationwide Most birds seen in Ohio are the typical "Slate-colored" morph shown in top photo.

Habitat: Occupies a wide variety of habitats in winter, but is most fond of semi-open areas or woods openings. Summer habitat is boreal forests.

Breeding: Nesting in Ohio occurs regularly only in a handful of counties in extreme northeastern Ohio where they nest in Hemlock woodlands or mixed conifer/hardwood forests. Nest is on the ground, often concealed in a clump of ferns. Four eggs is usual.

Natural History: Juncos are a familiar winter-time bird at feeders throughout Ohio. They arrive with the colder weather fronts and are often associated with snowstorms. In fact a common nickname in much of America is "Snowbird." Northern migrants arrive in Ohio in Oct./Nov. and most are gone by mid March. Those that summer in the southern United States do so only at the highest elevations in the Appalachian Mountains (above 3,500 feet). The combined summer, winter, and migratory ranges of the Dark-eyed Junco includes nearly all of the North American continent except Florida.

Size: 8 inches.

Abundance: Common. Less common in northwest Ohio.

Migratory Status: A year-round resident in the southern half of Ohio and a summer resident in the northern half of the state. All northern Ohio birds and some southern Ohio birds migrate south in winter.

Presumed range in Ohio

Variation: Sexually dimorphic. Males are black on back, head, and wings whereas females are reddish brown. No seasonal variation.

Habitat: Succesional woodlands, overgrown fields / fence rows, edges of stream courses, and woodlots where honeysuckle, briers, weeds, and saplings are predominate.

Breeding: Nests are low to the ground or even on the ground. Usually four eggs. Nesting in Ohio can occur throughout the state but is quite uncommon in the northwestern corner. By contrast this is a very common nesting species in southern and eastern Ohio.

Natural History: Our largest member of the sparrow family. Sometimes called "Rufous-sided Towhee." Its "tow-wheee" song is a familiar sound beginning as early as March. The widespread range of the eastern Towhee corresponds closely to the eastern Temperate Forest ecoregion, but they normally do not occur in dense populations. Most bird feeders in rural Ohio will have a pair for the winter, but rarely more than two pairs. The similar Spotted Towhee (*P. maculatus*) replaces the eastern Towhee in the western half of America.

Class—**Aves** (birds)

Order—**Passeriformes** (songbirds)

Family—**Calcaridae** (longspurs)

Snow Bunting *Plectrophenax nivalis*	Fox Sparrow *Passerella iliaca*	Lapland Longspur *Calcarius lapponicus*

Size: 6.75 inches.

Abundance: Fairly common in winter.

Migratory Status: Winter migrant / resident that arrives from late November to early December.

Presumed range in Ohio

Variation: Breeders are strikingly black and white. Winter plumage is off-white with dark brown wings and tail and rusty brown highlights on face.

Habitat: Winter habitat in Ohio is mostly harvested crop fields. Also weedy patches around field edges, roadsides, farmsteads, etc. Summer habitat is rocky areas in tundra.

Breeding: One of the most northerly breeding songbirds in the America. Builds its nest in rock crevices in the high arctic. Lays four to six eggs.

Natural History: After summering as far north as the shores of the Arctic Ocean, Snow Buntings will move south to winter, as far south as northern half of Ohio. In years of exceptional snowfall or extreme cold they may be seen as far south as Kentucky. They are obviously very cold-hardy birds, but they can be succeptible to winter die-offs if deep snows conceal their food source of seeds and grain. In Ohio they can be seen in mixed flocks with Lapland Longspurs and Horned Larks. Circumpolar in distribution, there are some indications are that this species is recently experiencing a sharp drop in North American populations.

Size: 7 inches.

Abundance: Uncommon.

Migratory Status: A fall/winter migrant in northern Ohio. Winter resident in southern Ohio.

Presumed range in Ohio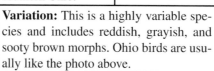

Variation: This is a highly variable species and includes reddish, grayish, and sooty brown morphs. Ohio birds are usually like the photo above.

Habitat: The Fox Sparrow is a lover of dense cover and thickets. Thick weeds and shrubs bordering woodlands or thickets. A mixture of brier, saplings, weeds, regenerating timberlands, etc.

Breeding: Nests are low to the ground or even on the ground. Breeding is in the boreal forests of Canada and in the northern Rockies. Usually four eggs.

Natural History: The Fox Sparrow is widespread across the North American Continent, summering in the far north (Canada, Alaska, and the northern Rockies) and wintering across much of the southern United States. Several distinct subspecies are recognized. They feed on a variety of insects and other arthropods in summer and subsist mainly on seeds in winter. They can be an occasional to regular visitor at bird feeders in Ohio during winter, especially during periods of snowy weather. Unlike many other sparrows, the Fox Sparrow is never seen in large flocks and it is rare to have more than one or two (rarely three) at a time visiting feeders.

Size: 6.25 inches.

Abundance: Fairly common in winter.

Migratory Status: A winter migrant from the far north that is only seen in winter.

Presumed range in Ohio

Variation: Seasonal and sexual plumage differences. Birds seen in Ohio are always in winter plumage (see above). Winter females are less vivid.

Habitat: Winter migrants in Ohio use very open areas with nearly bare ground. Large acreage harvested crop fields of are the primary habitat for flocks wintering in Ohio.

Breeding: Nests on the ground in Arctic Tundra. In places it may be the only nesting songbird. Eggs (three to seven) are not laid until early June.

Natural History: This hardy bird breeds and summers in Arctic Tundra and is circumpolar in its distribution. It is very common on its breeding grounds where it is sometimes the only songbird present. In winter they move far to the south, but are not very abundant east of the Mississippi River. Changes wrought on the landscape by modern agriculture has made for more hospitable habitat for this species in Ohio. On breeding grounds they eat dipterous insects (flies, mosquitoes) and seeds. Winter diet is mostly seeds and waste grain. In Ohio they are often seen together with mixed flocks of Snow Buntings and Horned Larks.

Class—**Aves** (birds)

Order—**Passeriformes** (songbirds)

Family—**Cardinalidae** (grosbeaks)

Dickcissel *Spiza americana*	**Northern Cardinal** *Cardinalis cardinalis*	**Rose-breasted Grosbeak** *Pheucticus ludovicianus*

Dickcissel	Northern Cardinal	Rose-breasted Grosbeak
Size: 6.25 inches.	**Size:** 8.75 inches.	**Size:** 8 inches.
Abundance: Fairly common.	**Abundance:** Very common.	**Abundance:** Fairly common.
Migratory Status: Summer resident. Winters from southern Mexico to northern South America.	**Migratory Status:** A year-round resident throughout the state.	**Migratory Status:** A summer resident that winters from the Yucatan to northern South America.
Presumed range in Ohio	Presumed range in Ohio	Presumed range in Ohio
Variation: Males are slightly larger. Females similar to males but are duller and lack the black "bib" of the male.	**Variation:** Pronounced sexual dimorphism. Male bright red, female buff-tan with reddish wings, crest, and tail.	**Variation:** Sexually dimorphic. Female drab brown, males striking black and white with rose-colored breast.
Habitat: Fallow lands with weeds, saplings, and grasses. Weedy fields in open areas are the preferred habitat.	**Habitat:** From undisturbed natural areas to suburbs, the Northern Cardinal favors edge areas with shrubs and brush.	**Habitat:** A forest species primarily, but enjoys edge areas and regenerative woodlands with thick shrubby cover.
Breeding: Breeds across the western half of Ohio, which represents the northernmost and easternmost extension of their breeding range.	**Breeding:** Nest is usually in a thick shrub or bush. About four eggs on average. Most nesting is from mid-April to August. Two broods per year.	**Breeding:** Three to five eggs are laid in a nest of twigs, grass, and plant fibers. Nesting begins in late May. May rarely produce two broods per year.
Natural History: The bulk of the Dickcissel's summer range is in the central Great Plains. Its presence in Ohio today is likely a result of range expansion into suitable habitats created by deforestation and subsequent conversion of woodlands to cropland and pasture. Outside their core breeding range they are distributed sporadically and they are also known to wander well outside their core range. Flocks numbering in the thousands have been recorded during migration. Eats seeds almost exclusively during migration and on winter range. During breeding is more omnivorous, consume insects and seeds. An open country bird, the Dickcissel avoids the more heavily forested regions of eastern and southern Ohio.	**Natural History:** Conspicuous and highly recognizable, the Northern Cardinal enjoys the distinction of being the state bird for a total of seven states (including Ohio). They are mainly seed and berry / fruit eaters, but they will eat insects and feed insects to the young. They are common birds at feeders throughout their range, especially during winter, and they are equally abundant in rural and urban regions. In the last century they have expanded their range farther to the north into the Great Lakes region and New England. Today they are seen throughout much of the United States east of the Rockies. The southern extent of their range is northern Central America. Throughout their range they are often known by the name "Redbird."	**Natural History:** Many Rose-breasted Grosbeaks seen in Ohio are passage migrants. But nesting is widespread in northern and eastern Ohio where they will reside throughout the summer. Many will nest well to the north of Ohio and pass through again in the fall enroute to wintering habitats in Central and South America. Food in summer about 50 / 50 insects and plant material such as seeds, fruits, flowers, and buds. During migration they are readily attracted to bird feeders where sunflower seeds are a favorite food. Birdwatchers throughout the state enthusiastically await the return of migrant songbirds each spring, and the Rose-breasted Grosbeak is a favorite.

Class—**Aves** (birds)

Order—**Passeriformes** (songbirds)

Family—**Cardinalidae** (grosbeaks)

Blue Grosbeak	**Indigo Bunting**
Passerina caerulea	*Passerina cyanea*

Family—**Fringillidae** (finches)

Pine Siskin
Spinus pinus

Size: 6 inches.

Presumed range in Ohio

Abundance: Uncommon.

Migratory Status: Summer resident in southern Ohio. Winters in Mexico and Central America.

Variation: Females are uniformly brown with a blueish wash that is apparent only on close examination. Juvenile males resemble females.

Habitat: On summer range the Blue Grosbeak enjoys overgrown fields dominated by forbs and saplings. Also uses fencerows, thickets, brambles, etc.

Breeding: Nest is a tightly woven cup placed in a low bush or tangle of vines, brush. About four eggs. Double brooding is known in the southern part of range.

Natural History: Although the Blue Grosbeak can probably be found throughout the much of the state in spring and summer, it is most common in the southernmost portion of the state. However, recent breeding bird surveys suggest that this species is expanding its range northward and they may soon become more common in Ohio. During summer they feed mostly on crickets, grasshoppers, and other insects, but eat mostly seeds in the early spring and fall. They often will visit bird feeders at these times. These birds are more common in the eastern United States today than they were in historic times, but they are still uncommon birds in Ohio.

Size: 5.5 inches.

Presumed range in Ohio

Abundance: Very common.

Migratory Status: A summer resident that arrives in late April and leaves in early fall.

Variation: Pronounced sexual dimorphism (see photos above). Immature males resemble females but with varying amounts of blue mottling.

Habitat: Edge areas, fence rows, rural roadsides with substantial brushy / weedy cover, and overgrown fields or early successional woodlands.

Breeding: Two broods are common. Lays two to four eggs in a nest of woven grasses that is usually placed in thick cover only a few feet above the ground.

Natural History: Indigo Buntings are common in summer throughout Ohio. Probably more so today than in historical times when forests dominated the state's habitats. The neon blue color of the male is makes it one of the most striking of North American birds. These birds are found throughout the eastern United States in summer, generally ranging from the short grass plains eastward to the Atlantic and as far north as southern Canada. They are most common in the southeastern US. Their annual migration may encompass up to 2,500 miles and many make the long flight across the Gulf of Mexico. Seeds and berries are the primary food with insects eaten during the breeding season.

Size: 5 inches.

Presumed range in Ohio

Abundance: Fairly common.

Migratory Status: Winter resident / migrant that exhibits erratic north / south movement in winter.

Variation: Males have a yellowish wash, females are heavily streaked with brown. See photos above. Juveniles resemble females.

Habitat: Pine Siskins prefer coniferous woodlands but in winter they are often seen in mixed or even pure hardwood forests.

Breeding: Nest is woven of grasses, twigs, rootlets, etc. and lined with mosses or fur. Three to four eggs is typical. May nest in loose colonies.

Natural History: The Pine Siskin is a coniferous forest species. Though it is also found in mixed deciduous/coniferous woodlands and in pure deciduous woods during winter irruptions. It is mostly a bird of the far north and the Rocky Mountains. They sometimes range as far south as the gulf coast in winter. In Ohio they can be seen throughout the state in winter, but their erratic movement means they may be common in one area and rare in another. Feeds on seeds of coniferous trees, grass seeds, and weed seeds and will regularly visit feeders in winter and where thistle seeds are favored. Insects are also eaten during breeding. They are often seen in the company of Goldfinches.

Class—**Aves** (birds)

Order—**Passeriformes** (songbirds)

Family—**Fringillidae** (finches)

Goldfinch *Spinus tristis*	**Purple Finch** *Haemorhous purpureus*	**House Finch** *Haemorhous mexicanus*

Goldfinch

Summer Male / Winter Male

Size: 5 inches.

Abundance: Common.

Migratory Status: A year-round resident throughout the state of Ohio.

Presumed range in Ohio

Variation: Exhibits sexual and seasonal plumage variations. See above. Female resembles winter male.

Habitat: Edge areas and successional habitats, fence rows, overgrown fields, and floodplains in open and semi-open areas.

Breeding: Four to six uniformly white eggs are laid. Nest is a tightly woven cup of grasses usually wrapped around a triad of upright branches.

Natural History: This well known species is widespread across North America. The transition of the male Goldfinch into its strikingly yellow breeding plumage in spring is a profound example of what is known as a prealternate (or spring-time) molt. The Goldfinch is a common visitor to bird feeders and is especially attracted to thistle seeds. Unlike many other species that eat seeds in winter and insects in summer, the Goldfinch is mainly a seed eater. Weed seeds, grass seeds, and especially seeds from forbs like thistles, sunflowers, and coneflowers are consumed. This species is apparently immune to parasitism by the Brown-headed Cowbird, as young cowbirds cannot develop on a diet that contains no insects.

Purple Finch

Male / Female

Size: 6 inches.

Abundance: Uncommon.

Migratory Status: Both year-round (in northern Ohio) and a winter resident.

Presumed range in Ohio

Variation: Significant plumage differences between the sexes. See photos above.

Habitat: Summer habitat is moist coniferous forests. In winter they are seen in almost all habitats across the eastern half of the United States.

Breeding: Nest of twigs, roots, and grasses is built in a fork on the outer portion of a branch of a conifer. Three to six eggs per clutch. Two broods per year.

Natural History: The Purple Finch seems to a be declining species in the eastern United States. Competition with the House Finch may be to blame. Although Purple Finches are seen in Ohio every winter, they may move well south in some years, all the way to the gulf coast in years of poor cone production. Seeds are the major food item, including seeds of trees (elm, maples, ash) and seeds of fruits. Buds are also eaten. Insects are also consumed. As with most other seed eaters, the Purple Finch will frequent bird feeders in winter. Easily confused with the House Finch, but is larger headed and has a heavier bill. Northeast Ohio represents the southeastern limit of the breeding range for the Purple Finch. It is regarded as a Species of Special Interest by ODNR.

House Finch

Male / Female

Size: 6 inches.

Abundance: Very common.

Migratory Status: A year-round resident throughout the state of Ohio.

Presumed range in Ohio

Variation: Plumage differences between males and females make sexes easily recognizable. See photos above.

Habitat: As implied by the name, House Finches are usually associated with human habitation. Found both in cities and rural areas.

Breeding: Typical woven nest of grasses is usually placed in dense evergreen shrub, cedar, or conifer tree. Lays three to five eggs and multiple broods are common.

Natural History: House Finches have extended their range into the eastern United States over the last few decades. Originally native to the southwestern United States, the first House Finches appeared in Ohio in the 1960s. Today they are found throughout the United States including all of Ohio. Primarily a seed eater, these birds can be very common at urban feeders. Weed seeds, fruit, buds, and flowers are also reported to be eaten. Birds seen at feeders sometimes exhibit signs of a disease (mycoplasmal conjuctivitis) that causes swelling of the eyes with occasional blindness or death. Similar to and easily confused with the less common Purple Finch, which has a larger head and lacks dark streaking on the belly of the males.

Class—**Aves** (birds)

Order—**Passeriformes** (songbirds)

Family—**Fringillidae** (finches)

Common Redpoll *Acanthis flammea*	**Evening Grosbeak** *Coccothraustes vespertinus*	**Red Crossbill** *Loxia curvirostra*

Common Redpoll		**Evening Grosbeak**		**Red Crossbill**	
Size: 5 inches.	Presumed range in Ohio	**Size:** 8 inches.	Presumed range in Ohio	**Size:** 6.5 inches.	Presumed range in Ohio
Abundance: Rare in Ohio.		**Abundance:** Very rare in Ohio.		**Abundance:** Very rare in Ohio.	
Migratory Status: Winter migrant. Irregular eruptions occur in late winter.		**Migratory Status:** Winter migrant and very rare winter resident.		**Migratory Status:** Winter migrant. A few may appear in north OH in winter.	

Variation: Shows varying amounts of reddish or pinkish on breast and throat. Females are darker. Juveniles have brown streaks.

Variation: Female is gray-brown with yellowish wash on nape, sides, and belly. Male has bright yellow throughout and bright yellow stripe on forehead.

Variation: Males show a decidedly reddish color. Females are more yellowish. Juveniles are heavily streaked with dark brown.

Habitat: Summer habitat is in the far north where they occupy edge areas of coniferous forests, open subarctic tundra, arctic tundra, and taiga.

Habitat: Boreal type forests of conifer and mixed conifer/deciduous. Summer habitat includes the forested regions of Canada and the Rocky Mountains.

Habitat: Birds seen in Ohio in winter use taiga forests in Canada as their summer habitat. Western populations exist in the conifer forests of the Rockies.

Breeding: Nest is on a branch (forest) or in low vegetation (tundra). Lays five eggs. May double brood in good years.

Breeding: Saucer-like nest of twigs and rootlets is placed high in a tree at or near the trunk. Lays three to four eggs.

Breeding: Nest is made of twigs and lined with lichens, grass, or conifer needles. Three eggs are usual.

Natural History: Circumpolar in distribution (northern hemisphere), this is one of the world's most northerly songbirds and some will stay through the winter in the far north. Many will move south, some as far northern Ohio. Very rarely they may be seen as far south as Arkansas or Tennessee. Though some Common Redpolls can be seen every winter in northern Ohio, they only approach being a fairly common bird in years of major eruptions. These eruptions are thought to be associated with poor cone production in boreal forests, which is the major winter food source for this species in boreal regions. In addition to conifer seeds they also eat small seeds produced by other trees and shrubs such as birch, willow, and alder. Grass seeds are also eaten along with arthropods which are fed to the young.

Natural History: The Evening Grosbeak is a northern species. The main food in winter is the seeds of trees like maples, Box Elder, etc. as well as conifer seeds and weed seeds. In a year of exceptionally poor seed production they will migrate southward great distances in a phenomena know to birdwatchers as an "irruption." In irruption years they may rarely be been seen as far south as the southern US. During these rare "irruption events" they might be seen anywhere in the state of Ohio. However, in typical winters northernmost Ohio represents the southern edge of their winter range. Thus sightings of this bird in the state are rare and usually elicit excitement from the state's birdwatching community. The map above is an average winter range for Ohio.

Natural History: The unique scissor-like beak of the crossbills is an adaptation for feeding on the seeds of conifers. The curved, crossed beak is used to pry open cones enough to allow the tongue to scoop out the seed. Seeds of pine, hemlock, spruce, and fir are the primary foods, but a variety of other seeds are also eaten and they will visit feeders for sunflower seeds. Their foraging habits are nomadic and small flocks wander through the forests searching for cone bearing trees. Like the other boreal species on this page they are prone to nomadic "irruptions." In years of poor cone production they may show up well south of their normal range. In a typical year northern MN, northern WI, and northern MI represents the southernmost edge of their range in the midwestern US.

Class—**Aves** (birds)

Order—**Apodiformes** (swifts and hummingbirds)		Order—**Coraciiformes** (kingfishers)
Family—**Apodidae** (swifts)	Family—**Trochylidae** (hummingbirds)	Family—**Alcedinidae** (kingfisher)

Chimney Swift	Ruby-throated Hummingbird	Belted Kingfisher
Chaetura pelagica	*Archilochus colubris*	*Megaceryle alcyon*

Size: 5.5 inches.

Presumed range in Ohio

Abundance:
Fairly common.

Migratory Status:
Summer resident that winters in the Amazon basin.

Variation: No sexual dimorphism. Immatures slightly lighter.

Habitat: Mainly seen in open and semi-open country and in urban / suburban areas.

Breeding: Nest is a flimsy cup plastered to the inside of a chimney. Two to five eggs are laid.

Natural History: This is a species that has benefited from human population expansion. Historically, the Chimney Swift nested mainly in hollow trees. These birds require a vertical surface within a sheltered place for nesting. When people began to build houses and large structures like schools, churches, and factories equipped with chimneys, their populations exploded. Today they are perhaps less common than a few decades ago when most dwellings and other buildings had chimneys. Some nesting in natural hollows still occurs. Swifts have long, narrow, pointed wings that allow for extreme maneuverability and these birds feed entirely on the wing. Small flying insects are their prey. During migration they are sometimes seen in large flocks that can contain over 1,000 birds. In Ohio, the greatest population densities occur in the vicinity of major cities.

Size: 3.75 inches.

Presumed range in Ohio

Abundance:
Common.

Migratory Status:
A summer resident that winters mostly in Central America.

Variation: Female lacks ruby throat patch. See photos above.

Habitat: Woodlands. Both deciduous and mixed forests are utilized. Edge areas and open fields are used for feeding.

Breeding: Nest is a tiny cup of fine plant fibers and lichens glued together with spider webs. Two eggs is typical.

Natural History: The tiny hummingbirds are ounce for ounce one of the world's greatest travelers. Many fly across the Gulf of Mexico each year during migration! Considering that they weigh barely more than 1/10 of an ounce that is a remarkable feat of endurance. The range of the Ruby-throated Hummingbird includes all of the Eastern Deciduous Forest Level 1 Ecoregion, as well as portions of the Boreal Forest and Great Plains Ecoregions. Nectar is the major food item for hummingbirds and they show a preference for red, tubular flowers. They possess a highly specialized beak and tongue for reaching nectar deep within flowers. They will also eat some small, flying insects caught on the wing, and are known to pluck tiny invertebrates from foliage or small spiders from their webs. These birds will readily use artificial nectar feeders containing a one to four mix of sugar water.

Size: 13 inches.

Presumed range in Ohio

Abundance:
Uncommon.

Migratory Status:
Year-round resident. Some may move south in winter.

Variation: Female has a rust colored band across belly (see inset above).

Habitat: Kingfishers require water and in Ohio they haunt creeks, rivers, lakes, swamps, and farm ponds.

Breeding: Kingfishers nest in burrows they excavate into vertical banks of dirt or sand that are at least eight feet high.

Natural History: The Belted Kingfisher is one of the most widely distributed birds in North America. In fact they range throughout the continent from Alaska and northern Canada south to Panama. Although widespread (breeding records exists from every county in the state) they are widely dispersed. In Ohio they are least common in the intensive agricultural regions of western Ohio. The presence of suitable nesting habitat in the form of vertical earthen cliffs may be a limiting factor in their abundance. Human activities such as digging of quarries and road cuts through hills and mountains may have helped this species in modern times by providing the requisite vertical banks for nest sites. Small fish are the primary food item. They are known for diving headfirst into the water from either a perch or while hovering to catch fish near the surface.

Class—**Aves** (birds)

Order—**Piciformes** (woodpeckers)

Family—**Picidae** (woodpeckers)

Pileated Woodpecker *Dryocopus pileatus*	Northern Flicker *Colaptes auratus*	Red-headed Woodpecker *Melanerpes erythrocephalus*

Pileated Woodpecker
Dryocopus pileatus

Northern Flicker
Colaptes auratus

Red-headed Woodpecker
Melanerpes erythrocephalus

Size: 16.5 inches.

Presumed range in Ohio

Abundance: Uncommon.

Migratory Status: Year-round resident.

Variation: Male has a red cheek patch.

Habitat: A forest species, the Pileated Woodpecker prefers mature woodlands. It is also seen in semi-open areas where large tracts of woods occur nearby. Floodplain forests are a favorite habitat.

Breeding: Nest is a hollow cavity excavated into the trunk of a tree (usually a dead tree, but sometimes living). Nests are usually fairly high up. Four eggs.

Natural History: By far Ohio's largest woodpecker, Pileated Woodpeckers play an important role in the mature forest ecosytem. Their large nest cavities are utilized as a refuge by many other woodland species including small owls, Wood Ducks, bluebirds, and squirrels. In the boreal forests of Canada the Pine Marten is reported to use their holes. Using their powerful, chisel-like beaks to break apart dead snags and logs they also help accelerate decomposition of large dead trees. In addition to mast and fruit such as wild cherries, they eat insects, mainly Carpenter Ants and beetle larvae. In Ohio this species is most common in the heavily forested Allegheny Plateau in eastern Ohio and in the Interior Low Plateau in the southern part of the state. They are least common in the Interior Lowlands.

Size: 12.5 inches.

Presumed range in Ohio

Abundance: Fairly common.

Migratory Status: Year-round but less common in winter.

Variation: Male has black "mustache."

Habitat: Semi-open areas and open lands with at least a few large trees. Farmlands, older urban neighborhoods, and parks are also used. Least common in dense, mature woodlands.

Breeding: Nest is usually excavated in a fairly large diameter dead tree. Also known to use natural hollows. Averages six to eight eggs.

Natural History: In addition to feeding on insects (mainly ants) usually caught on the ground, the Flicker also eats berries and in winter, grains (including corn). Two distinct subspecies of Northern Flicker occur in North America. The "Yellow-shafted Flicker" is native to Ohio and the rest of the eastern US. In the Rocky Mountain west the "Red-shafted Flicker" occurs. The two are distinguished by the dominant color on the underneath side of the wing, which is visible only in flight. As with Ohio's other large woodpecker (Pileated), the Northern Flicker is regarded as a "keystone" species that is important to other species which use its excavations for shelter and nesting. Thus recent declines in the population of this species is cause for Concern.

Size: 9.25 inches.

Presumed range in Ohio

Abundance: Uncommon.

Migratory Status: Year-round resident.

Variation: No sexual variation.

Habitat: Savanna-like habitats with widely spaced, large trees are the preferred habitat of the Red-headed Woodpecker. They seem to show a preference for areas near lake or rivers.

Breeding: Nest hole is usually in a dead tree but it is also fond of using utility poles. Five eggs is typical and some may produce two broods per summer.

Natural History: Once regarded as very common, this handsome woodpecker has declined significantly in the last century. It eats large amounts of acorns and other mast, especially in fall and winter, and may move about in fall and winter in search of areas with good mast crops. Insects are regularly eaten in warmer months and some may be caught on the wing, but they also commonly forage on the ground. In Ohio this woodpecker is probably more common in the western half of the state and is uncommon in much of the heavily forested Allegheny Plateau in the east. Overall this species has experienced a nationwide population decline. The Red-headed Woodpecker was apparently well known to many native Americans, and was a war symbol of the Cherokee.

Class—**Aves** (birds)

Order—**Piciformes** (woodpeckers)

Family—**Picidae** (woodpeckers)

Red-bellied Wood Pecker *Melanerpes carolinus*	**Downy Woodpecker** *Picoides pubescens*	**Hairy Woodpecker** *Picoides pubescens*

Red-bellied Wood Pecker	**Downy Woodpecker**	**Hairy Woodpecker**
Size: 9.75 inches. **Abundance:** Common. **Migratory Status:** Year-round resident. Presumed range in Ohio	**Size:** 6.75 inches. **Abundance:** Very common. **Migratory Status:** Year-round resident. Presumed range in Ohio	**Size:** 9.25 inches. **Abundance:** Fairly common. **Migratory Status:** Year-round resident. Presumed range in Ohio
Variation: Female has gray crown.	**Variation:** Male has red spot on nape.	**Variation:** Male has red spot on nape.
Habitat: A woodland species that inhabits all forest types in the eastern US. Semi-open and open woods are favored.	**Habitat:** Occupies a wide variety of habitats throughout the state. From wilderness to farms and urban areas.	**Habitat:** A forest species that likes woodlands with larger, more mature trees. Also in parks and neighborhoods.
Breeding: Nests in holes excavated by the adults. Four to five eggs are laid in mid-April to early June.	**Breeding:** Nests is usually excavated in a dead limb. Eggs range from three to as many as eight. Eggs hatch in 12 days.	**Breeding:** Nest hole may be in dead snags or living trees with heart rot. Four eggs is typical.

Natural History: Feeds on all types of tree-dwelling arthropods as well as seeds, nuts, fruit, and berries. Widespread and common throughout Ohio but perhaps least common in the northeastern corner of the state. These woodpeckers are known to take over the nest holes of the endangered Red-cockaded Woodpecker where their ranges overlap in the southern United States. Conversely, the introduced Starling sometimes takes over the nest hole of the Red-bellied Woodpecker. Due to its fairly large size and its tendency to be quite vocal year-round, the Red-bellied Woodpecker is a fairly conspicuous bird in both rural and urban areas in much of Ohio. Because both males and females have a significant amount of red on the head they are often misidentified as the much rarer Red-headed Woodpecker. Like other woodpeckers in Ohio they will come to bird feeders for suet or sunflower seeds.

Natural History: Ranging across all of North America except the far north and the desert southwest, the Downy is one of the most widespread woodpeckers in American and is the most common woodpecker in Ohio. These appealing little woodpeckers are well known and frequent visitors to bird feeders where they eat suet and seeds. Arthropods are the most important food item making up as much as 75 percent of the diet. Fruit and sap is also eaten. Like other woodpeckers, the Downy's nest holes in dead limbs and trunks may be utilized by a wide array of other species as a home and shelter. Many small cavity nesting birds may use old woodpecker holes, and mice, lizards, snakes, treefrogs, spiders, and insects can often be found using their abandoned nests. Very similar to the Hairy Woodpecker but is smaller and has a thinner beak.

Natural History: The range of the Hairy Woodpecker closely coincides with that of the smaller Downy Woodpecker. The two are often confused but the Hairy is a much larger bird and has a heavier, longer bill. Like the Downy, this woodpecker excavates nest holes that may be used by a variety of other species, making it an important species in forest ecosystems. A wide variety of insects and other arthropods are eaten along with seeds and fruits. This species can be seen at feeders throughout Ohio, and although it is less common than its smaller cousin it can often be seen in the company of the smaller Downy Woodpecker. When both are seen together, size differences become more apparent. The Hairy Woodpecker varies somewhat geographically in both size and coloration. Specimens shown above are typical for the eastern United States.

Class—**Aves** (birds)

Order—**Piciformes** (woodpeckers)	Order—**Cuculiformes** (cuckoos, anis, and roadrunner)	
Family—**Picidae** (woodpeckers)	Family—**Cuculidae** (cuckoos)	
Yellow-bellied Sapsucker *Sphyrapicus varius*	**Black-billed Cuckoo** *Coccyzus erythropthalmus*	**Yellow-billed Cuckoo** *Coccyzus americanus*

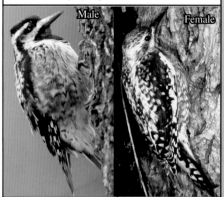
Male Female

Size: 8.5 inches.	**Size:** 12 inches.	**Size:** 12 inches.
Abundance: Uncommon.	**Abundance:** Uncommon.	**Abundance:** Fairly common.
Variation: Male has red patch on throat.	**Variation:** Sexes alike. No significant variation.	**Variation:** Sexes alike. No significant variation.

Presumed range in Ohio

Migratory Status: Mostly a winter (Sept. to April) resident that summers in the northern US and Canada. Year-round breeding populations occur in extreme northeastern Ohio.

Migratory Status: A sumer resident throughout the state. Winters in South America. Migrates later than most songbirds and peak migration arrives in Ohio from early May to early June.

Migratory Status: A summer resident that winters in South America. Migrates later in the year than many other songbirds. Typically seen in Ohio from May through September.

Habitat: In winter this woodpecker occupies a wide variety of woodland habitats. Birds that summer in Ohio use both decidous and mixed woodlands.

Habitat: Successional areas, thickets, and mature woodlands with some open areas. Shows a preference for being near water (riparian areas, lakes, etc.).

Habitat: Open woodlands, edge areas, regenerative woodlands near open fields, overgrown fence rows, etc. Uses similar habitats on winter range.

Breeding: Nest is an excavated hole in dead tree or a living tree with heart rot. Clutch size ranges from two to seven eggs.

Breeding: Breeds sparingly throughout Ohio but rare in the west-central part of Ohio. Clutch size averages two to four eggs.

Breeding: Breeds from early June through the summer. Nest is flimsy and placed in thick vegetation. Two to four eggs.

Natural History: The Yellow-bellied Sapsucker is unique among Ohio woodpeckers in that it creates feeding opportunities by drilling small holes into the bark of trees. These holes, called "sap wells," fill with sap which the sapsucker then drinks. Sapsuckers regularly visit the "sap wells" to maintain them and defend them from other sapsuckers. Many other birds species benefit from the sapsuckers activities, especially the Ruby-throated Hummingbird which will also drink sap from the woodpeckers holes. The sap also attracts insects which in turn feed many species of insectivorous birds. In addition, the nest holes excavated by the sapsucker may be used other birds, flying squirrels, etc. Though widespread across Ohio in winter months, they are not a common bird anywhere in the state.

Natural History: Although once common, the Black-billed Cuckoo has declined in abundance over the past several decades. Widespread use of pesticides may be to blame. Caterpillars are a primary food and pesticide-depleted caterpillar numbers result in a scarce food source for the birds. Ironically, large flocks of these handsome birds once acted as a natural control of caterpillars and historical observers reported seeing flocks of Black-billed Cuckoos descend on a tree full of caterpillars and eat every caterpillar on the tree! Today it is rare to see more than one or two of these birds at a time. Cicadas are another important insect food, and in years of cicada outbreaks cuckoos (and many other birds species) will produce larger clutches and successfully rear more young.

Natural History: The Yellow-billed Cuckoo is one of the latest arriving of Ohio's neotropical migrant songbirds. They often go by the nickname "Raincrow" and folklore states that they call right before a rain. Although much more common than the Black-billed Cuckoo, Yellow-billed Cuckoos are not abundant birds today. Like our other cuckoo, their numbers have diminished significantly in modern times. Caterpillars are an important food and widespread pesticide use is likely the major contributing factor in their decline. These are secretive birds that are heard more often than seen. Their call is quite distinctive and is heard most frequently during the "dog days" of mid to late summer. The young of this species develop rapidly and may leave the nest within 17 days of hatching.

Class—**Aves** (birds)

Order—**Columbiformes** (doves)

Family—**Columbidae** (doves)

Rock Pigeon *Columba livia*	**Mourning Dove** *Zenaida macroura*	**Eurasian Collared-Dove** *Zenaida decaocto*
		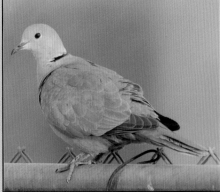

| **Size:** 13 inches.

Abundance: Very common.

Migratory Status: Year-round resident. | Presumed range in Ohio
 | **Size:** 12 inches.

Abundance: Very common.

Migratory Status: Year-round resident. | Presumed range in Ohio
 | **Size:** 13 inches.

Abundance: Rare but increasing.

Migratory Status: Year-round resident. | Presumed range in Ohio
 |

Variation: Highly variable.	**Variation:** No variation among adults.	**Variation:** No variation among adults.
Habitat: Farms and ranches in rural areas and parks and downtown streets in urban environments.	**Habitat:** Agricultural areas and open lands with short grass or areas of bare ground. Open to semi-open areas.	**Habitat:** Open and semi-open lands. Agricultural areas and small towns are favored over wilderness.
Breeding: Nests on man-made ledges and beneath overhangs in cities. Bridges and barns are used in rural areas. Multiple nesting with two eggs per clutch.	**Breeding:** Builds a flimsy nest of small sticks in sapling or low branch usually from six to 15 feet above ground. Two eggs is usual with multiple broods per year.	**Breeding:** Usually nests in trees or bushes near human habitation. Lays two eggs per clutch but can nest several times per year.
Natural History: Although the Rock Pigeon is about the same overall length as the Mourning Dove and Collard Dove, the pigeon is a much stockier, heavier bird that weighs over twice as much as the Mourning Dove. Despite the fact that this familiar bird ranges from coast to coast across North America, the Rock Pigeon is not a native species. It was introduced into North America by the earliest European settlers in the 1600s. Pigeons followed the first settlers into the west (including Ohio) colonizing towns and settlements and living in close proximity to rural farms and livestock. Today they are one of the most familiar urban birds in America and are also common around farms and ranches. Young pigeons known as "Squab" are eaten in many places throughout the world. Rock Pigeons are incredibly variable and can exhibit almost any color or pattern.	**Natural History:** Although these birds are found year-round in Ohio their numbers swell each fall with migrants from farther to the north. Mourning Doves are regarded as a game species throughout much of the United States, including Ohio. The US Fish and Wildlife Service estimates that as many as 20 million are killed each fall during America's dove season. While that seems an appallingly high number, the Mourning Dove is actually one of the most numerous bird species in America and the total population is estimated at around 350 million birds! Seeds are the chief food item. They will eat everything from the tiniest grass seeds to every type of seed crop produced by man, including corn, wheat, sorghum, millet, and sunflower as well as peanuts and soybeans. This abundant species may face competition from the invasive Eurasian Collard Dove, which occupies a similar ecological niche.	**Natural History:** Originally native to Eurasia, the Collared-Dove has colonized much of the southern United States since its release in the Bahamas in the 1970s. Since then they have rapidly expanded their range north and west. The earliest record for this species in Ohio was as recent as 2001. Today they are found mostly in the western half of Ohio but they may soon colonize the entire state. In food habits and other aspects of its biology the Collard-Dove is similar to the Mourning Dove. Young Collard-Doves disperse widely and this species continues to increase across North America. Cold weather does not seem to be a limiting factor but food availability may limit range expansion. How far this species will extend its range in North America is still unknown. As with all other members of the Columbidae family, young birds are feed a semi-liquid "crop milk" regurgitated from the adults crop.

Class—**Aves** (birds)

Order—**Galliformes** (chicken-like birds)

Family—**Phasianidae** (grouse)

Ruffed Grouse *Bonasa umbellus*	Wild Turkey *Meleagris gallopavo*	Ring-necked Pheasant *Phasianus colchicus*

Ruffed Grouse	Wild Turkey	Ring-necked Pheasant
Size: 17.5 inches. / Presumed range in Ohio	**Size:** Up to 47 inches. / Presumed range in Ohio	**Size:** Up to 35 inches. / Presumed range in Ohio
Abundance: Uncommon.	**Abundance:** Fairly common.	**Abundance:** Uncommon.
Migratory Status: Non-migratory bird that is a year-round resident.	**Migratory Status:** Non-migratory bird that is a year-round resident.	**Migratory Status:** . Non-migratory bird that is a year-round resident.
Variation: Two color morphs. Red and Gray. Male has larger "ruff" on neck.	**Variation:** Females are smaller, duller, have less red on head and neck and lack the "beard" present on the males breast.	**Variation:** Females are smaller and cryptic mottled brown. Males are strikingly colored. See photos above.
Habitat: Forests. Mainly successional forests, forest clearings, and disturbed woodlands.	**Habitat:** Inhabits all major habitats in the state except for urban areas. Most common in mixture of woods and farms.	**Habitat:** Prefers a mosaic of crop lands interlaced with cover such as wetlands, grassy patches, overgrown fence rows.
Breeding: Nest is on the ground in woodland. Usually placed near the base of a tree, stump, or beneath downed tree. Nine to 14 eggs.	**Breeding:** Nests on the ground in thick cover such as thickets, honeysuckle, Multiflora Rose, or tall grasses. Lays up to 14 eggs.	**Breeding:** Nests on the ground in thick cover such as tall grasses, cattails, etc. Lays up to 15 eggs. Rarely, two females will use the same nest.

Natural History: Mainly a bird of the northern forests, the Ruffed Grouse ranges southward in the Appalachian chain as far as northern Georgia. In Ohio they are restricted mainly to the Appalachian Plateaus Province in the eastern half of the state. The name comes from the "ruff" of feathers around the neck which are erected by the males during courtship displays. At this time the male also produces a deep, resonate sound similar to that produced by blowing across the top of a soda bottle. Known as "drumming," the sound carries quite a distance in the spring forest. This species has declined extensively since the European settlement of Ohio. The decline in populations of this species seems widespread in other states in the southern Appalachians, but numbers seem stable farther north.

Natural History: The courtship of the male Wild Turkey includes a "strutting" display that involves spreading the tail feathers, drooping the wings, and producing a low frequency "drumming" sound. When attempting to attract females in the spring breeding season males become quite vocal and regularly emit a loud "gobble" that can be heard for a mile. The saga of the disappearance and resurgence of the Wild Turkey in America is one of wildlife managements greatest success stories. In pioneer days turkeys were found throughout Ohio but by the early 1900s they had disappeared from the state. Re-stocking efforts by the ODNR aided by sportsmen groups has been highly successful and Wild Turkeys are now found in suitable habitats throughout Ohio.

Natural History: Ring-necked Pheasants are an alien species from Asia that were introduced into America in the late 1800s. The species has thrived in the Great Plains region where adequate natural habitats still exist. It was once a common bird in Ohio, but began to decline as more land was cleared for row crops. Despite annual stocking efforts of the ODNR, recovery to the numbers seen prior to modern agriculture has not occurred. More recent conservation efforts aimed at restoring patches of natural grasslands should help this and many other wildlife species. This is a popular game bird throughout its range in America and sportsmen are actively involved in attempts to restore this bird in Ohio. The conservation organization "Pheasants Forever" raises money for habitat restoration.

Class—**Aves** (birds)

Order—**Galliformes**

Family—**Odontophoridae** (quail)

Northern Bobwhite
Colinus virginianus

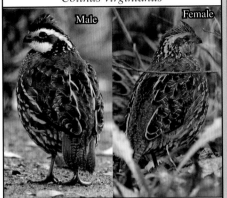

Size: 10 inches.

Presumed range in Ohio

Abundance: Uncommon.

Variation: Female has tan eye stripe and throat patch. Male's is white.

Migratory Status: A non-migratory species that is a year-round resident of Ohio.

Habitat: Small woodlands, edge areas, and overgrown fields bordering agricultural land are the favorite habitats. Requires tall clumped grasses or shrubs/vines which provide overhead cover as a protection against Cooper's Hawks.

Breeding: Ground nester. Clutch size averages about 15 eggs but nest failure due to predation is high. Multiple nestings are common.

Natural History: Bobwhite have always been an important game bird in the United States. In recent decades however the species has experienced significant population declines, especially in the northern portions of its range (including Ohio). Modern agricultural practices that have eliminated fence rows and created expansive crop fields are the main factor contributing to the decline of the Bobwhite. Through fall and winter they will stick together in family groups known as a "covey." In spring adults pair off for breeding with the resultant offspring and their parents producing the next falls covey. Mortality through the winter is high and survivors from more than one covey will often join together as winter wanes.

Order—**Caprimulgiformes**

Family—**Caprimulgidae** (nightjars)

Common Nighthawk
Chordeiles minor

Size: 9.5 inches.

Presumed range in Ohio

Abundance: Fairly common.

Variation: Sexes alike. No significant variation.

Migratory Status: Summer resident that winters in South America as far south as Brazil and Paraguay. Peak spring migration is in May. Peak fall migration begins in late August and lasts through early September.

Habitat: Open and semi-open areas. Can be common around cities and towns but also in rural areas.

Breeding: No nest is constructed and two eggs are laid on bare gravel. Most nests are on flat, gravel-covered rooftops.

Natural History: These birds sometimes go by the nickname "Bullbat." They are most common in urban areas but they are also seen in open and semi-open rural areas. Like our other nightjars the Common Nighthawk feeds on the wing, but unlike the others this bird is active both at night and at dawn and dusk, or sometimes on cloudy days. Around towns and cities they chase airborne insects attracted to streetlights at night. This is one of the great travelers of the bird world. Nighthawks are usually seen in flight, but they will occasionally be spotted resting atop a fence post in open country. They often migrate in large flocks. Most summer residents stay to the west of the Appalachian Plateau.

Whip-poor-will
Antrostomus. vociferus

Roosting

Size: 12 inches.

Presumed range in Ohio

Abundance: Uncommon

Variation: Sexes alike. No significant variation.

Migratory Status: A late spring through summer resident that winters in Florida, the Caribbean, and Central America. Arrives in Ohio in April early May. Typically leaves for wintering grounds in September. A few may linger into Oct.

Habitat: Forest edge, power-line cuts through wooded areas and xeric woods. Favors thickets for daytime roosting.

Breeding: Nests on the ground amid leaf litter. No nest is built and the eggs (usually two) are laid on the ground.

Natural History: Few animals exhibit a more cryptic color and pattern than this species. When resting on the forest floor during the day they are nearly invisible. A very similar species, the **Chuck-will's-widow** (*A. carolinensis*) is a rare summer resident in extreme southern Ohio. It is smaller (9.75 inches) and grayer than the Whip-poor-will. The two are easily differentiated by the their songs, usually described as *whip,prrr-weel* for the Whip-poor-will and as *chuk-wills wee-dow* for the Chuck-will's-widow. Both calls are usually repeated rapidly and at times incessantly. Equipped with a very large mouths for feeding on moths and other large flying insects, they are nocturnal and catch most of their food in mid-air.

Class—**Aves** (birds)

Strigiformes (owls)	Order—**Strigiformes** (owls)
Family—**Tytonidae** (barn owl)	Family—**Strigidae** (typical owls)

Barn Owl *Tyto alba*	**Eastern Screech Owl** *Megascops asio*	**Snowy Owl** *Bubo sciandiacus*
	Gray morph	Female

| **Size:** 16 inches.
Abundance: Uncommon.
Migratory Status: Year-round resident of Ohio. | Presumed range in Ohio
 | **Size:** 8.5 inches.
Abundance: Common.
Migratory Status: Year-round resident of Ohio. | Presumed range in Ohio | **Size:** 24 inches.
Abundance: Very rare in Ohio.
Migratory Status: Winter migrant. | Presumed range in Ohio
 |

Variation: Very little variation. Females have more buff on breast and sides. Also more buff spotting on breast and belly. Males appear nearly pure white below, but do have a few spots.

Variation: Two distinct color morphs occur in Ohio. Gray phase (inset), is more common in northwestern Ohio while the both gray and red phases occur throughout southern Ohio.

Variation: Females and juveniles have extensive black barring on white background. Adult males are nearly pure white below with reduced dark bars and spots dorsally.

Habitat: Prefers open and semi-open habitats. Short grass pastures are a favorite hunting ground. Probably more common around farms and small towns.

Habitat: All types of habitats within the state may be used, including suburban areas and in the vicinity of farms. Favors edge areas, fence rows, etc.

Habitat: Summer habitat is the high Arctic and open tundra. Birds that wander south in winter to Ohio favor expansive open fields.

Breeding: Nested in hollow in trees or in caves historically. Now uses old buildings or barns. As many as 11 eggs.

Breeding: Nest is in tree hollows and old woodpecker holes. Four to six eggs are laid and young fledge by mid-June.

Breeding: Nest is on the ground in open tundra. Often built atop small mounds or ridges. Lays five to 15 eggs.

Natural History: The Barn Owl is one of the most widespread owl species in the world, being found throughout most of North America south of Canada, all of Central and South America, most of Europe and sub-saharan Africa, parts of southern Asia, and all of Australia. In spite of its wide range they are usually not common anywhere. Small rodents are the primary prey, especially mice and voles. When feeding a large brood of young a pair of Barn Owls may catch over two dozen mice in a single night. Like other owls their hearing is so acute they can catch mice unseen beneath leaves by homing in rustling sounds. Ironically, man's attempts to control rodents with poisoned baits may be in part responsible for the demise of rodent-eating species like the Barn Owl. Threatened in Ohio.

Natural History: The eerie call of the Screech Owl is often described as "haunting and tremulous." Despite being at times vocal birds, these small owls often go unnoticed. They may even live in suburban yards and small towns, especially if older, large trees with hollow limbs and trunks are present. They feed on insects such as crickets and grasshoppers and on a wide variety of small vertebrate prey including mice, voles, and songbirds that are plucked from their roosts at night. These wide-ranging birds are found throughout the eastern United States as from the Altlantic to the Rocky Mountains and from southern Canada to Florida and Mexico. Birds in the northern portions of their range (including Ohio) can be negatively impacted by severe winters with deep snow.

Natural History: A true icon of northern wilderness, the sight of a Snowy Owl in Ohio is often met with excitement. Winter migrants appear fairly regularly in the northernmost portion of the state and in rare winters they can be seen as far south as the Ohio River. Every now and then large numbers of these giant owls appear in winter in the northern United States in a phenonmena known as an "irruption." The exact cause of these irruptions are not completely understood, but they may relate to food availability in the far north. One of this birds primary food items is lemmings. Populations of these rodents vary considerably from year to year in what amounts to a boom-bust cycle. In years of abundant lemmings many more young owls are produced than in years of poor lemming numbers.

Class—**Aves** (birds)

Order—**Strigiformes** (owls)

Family—**Strigidae** (typical owls)

Barred Owl *Strix varia*	**Great Horned Owl** *Bubo virginianus*

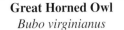

Size: 21 inches.

Abundance: Uncommon.

Variation: No sexual variation. Three subspecies are known in America with a fourth in central Mexico, only one (Northern Barred Owl-*S. v. varia)* occurs in Ohio.

Presumed range in Ohio

Migratory Status: Year-round resident.

Habitat: Woodlands primarily. Especially in bottomlands, swampy areas, and riparian corridors, but also upland woods.

Breeding: Nest is usually in tree cavities but known to nest tree crotches or old hawk nests. Usually two (rarely three or four) eggs are laid.

Natural History: The Barred Owl ranges throughout the eastern half of the United States from the eastern edge of the great plains eastward. The eight-noted call of the Barred Owl is described as "Hoo-hoo-hoo-hoo, hoo-hoo-hooaahh." In addition the species is capable of a wide array of hoots, screeches, and coarse whistles. Small vertebrates are the main prey, especially rodents like voles, mice, and flying squirrels. Birds, lizards, small snakes, and amphibians are also eaten. In the eastern United States the range of the Barred Owl closely coincides with that of the Red-shouldered Hawk and the two predators are often regarded as ecological counterparts occupying the same niche at different times. In Ohio this species is least common in the western and northwestern portions of the state and most common in the south and southeast. Not surprising since this is primarily a forest bird.

Size: 23 inches.

Abundance: Fairly common.

Variation: Males are slightly smaller and have a larger white patch on throat. There are 10 subspecies in North America. The eastern Great Horned Owl (*B. v. virginianus*) is found in Ohio.

Presumed range in Ohio

Migratory Status: Year-round resident.

Habitat: Woodlands, semi-open, and open habitats are all utilized, but most common in mosiac of upland woods and fields.

Breeding: One of the earliest nesting birds in Ohio. Horned Owls may be sitting on eggs by late January. Nest is often an old hawk nest. Two eggs is usual.

Natural History: This widespread species occurs throughout the Americas from Alaska to southern South America. In the US specimens from the western portions of the country are much paler than those seen in Ohio. In the eastern United States Red Cedars and other evergreen trees are a favorite roosting site. The Great Horned Owl is the ecological counterpart of the Red-tailed Hawk, hunting much the same prey in the same regions, with the hawk hunting by day and the owl at night. These powerful predators eat a wide variety of small animals. Rabbits are a favorite food item. They are also known to eat larger mammals like muskrats, groundhogs, and even skunks or rarely, domestic cats! They can be a problem at times for those who raise chickens and leave them out in the open at night. But they also consume many rodents. Once regarded as a varmint, they are now federally protected.

Class—**Aves** (birds)

Order—**Strigiformes** (owls)

Family—**Strigidae** (typical owls)

Short-eared Owl *Asio flammeus*	**Long-eared Owl** *Asio otus*	**Northern Saw-whet Owl** *Aegolius acadicus*

Size: 15 inches.	Presumed range in Ohio	**Size:** 15 inches.	Presumed range in Ohio	**Size:** 8 inches.	Presumed range in Ohio
Abundance: Uncommon in Ohio. **Variation:** Females tend to be slightly darker.		**Abundance:** Rare in Ohio. **Variation:** Female is darker with more rusty facial disk, and is slightly larger.		**Abundance:** Rare in Ohio. **Variation:** Immature has buff belly, dark facial disk with white eyebrow.	

Migratory Status: Mostly a winter-time resident or winter migrant, but some breeding has been recorded in OH.

Habitat: These are open country birds and the primary habitat is prairie, marsh, and tundra. In forested regions they haunt fields, pastures, meadows, etc.

Breeding: Nest is on the ground. A slight depression is scraped out by the owl and lined with grasses. Five or six eggs is typical.

Natural History: In Ohio the Short-eared Owl is most likely to be seen in open regions during winter, but a few have nested in the state in large areas of reclaimed strip mines. The food is mostly small rodents. Voles are the most significant item in their diet. Rodent prey is located mostly by sound while flying low and slow over open, grassy fields. Most hunting is done at night or dusk and dawn, but these owls are more diurnal than most and may hunt during the day. The erectile feathers on the face that form the "ears" are not usually visible unless the owl is agitated or defensive. This species appears to be in decline in much of America and is a Species of Concern in Ohio.

Migratory Status: Mostly a winter-time migrant, or less commonly a winter resident. A very few have nested in Ohio.

Habitat: Prefers open and semi-open woodlands and riparian habitats in open regions. Breeds and summers in boreal regions and mountains.

Breeding: Usually nests in trees in abandoned stick nests built by hawks, crows, or other large bird species. Five or six eggs is typical.

Natural History: Although this rare owl could possibly be seen anywhere in the state, most sightings in Ohio are in the northern portions of the state. They are most likely to be seen in winter, but there are a very few records of breeding in the state. They are considered a Species of Special Interest by ODNR. Their name comes from the well developed feather tufts on the head which are erected when resting. These "ear tufts" are folded against the head and not visible on owls in flight. Long-eared Owls during winter can sometimes be seen in small flocks that roost in close proximity to each other. Their food is almost exclusively small mammals, mostly voles and mice of the *Peromyscus* genus.

Migratory Status: Occurs mainly as a fall and winter migrant but also as a winter resident. Very rare as a breeding bird.

Habitat: Spruce-fir-pine dominated forests in the north and in the Rocky Mountain west. In the east uses mostly mixed deciduous/conifer forests.

Breeding: Uses old woodpecker holes almost exclusively for nesting. Five or six eggs is typical with a survival rate to fledging of about 50 percent.

Natural History: Small mammals (mice, voles, and shrews) make up the bulk of this little owls diet. Mice of the genus *Peromyscus* make up as much as three-fourths of the food consumed. Insects are oddly not listed as a major food item, but songbirds are known to be eaten. Small and secretive, the Saw-whet Owl roosts in thick evergreens and is typically silent except during the breeding season. Thus these birds are difficult to observe in the wild. Within its range in the Rockies and Appalachians, seasonal migration is mostly vertical, with the owls moving to lower elevations in winter. These are rare birds in Ohio, but some nesting has apparently recently occurred in the northeastern part of the state. Listed as a Species of Special Interest by ODNR.

Class—**Aves** (birds)
Order—**Falconiformes** (raptors)
Family—**Accipitridae** (hawks, eagles, kites)
Red-tailed Hawk—*Buteo jamiacensis*

Typical adult

Light morph

Dark morph

Typical juvenile

Juvenile eating Gray Squirrel

Presumed range in Ohio

Size: 19 inches.

Abundance: Common throughout the state. Perhaps slightly more common in glaciated regions.

Migratory Status: Year-round resident. Numbers are supplemented in winter with migrants from farther north.

Variation: Highly variable. Can vary from nearly solid dark brown to very pale (almost white). Most adult Ohio birds are like the typical adult specimen pictured on top left above. Light and dark morphs are mostly winter migrants in Ohio. Females are about 20 percent larger than males. Juveniles have brownish tails with dark crossbars. Some experts recognize as many as 16 subspecies throughout North America.

Habitat: Found in virtually all habitats within the state. Likes open and semi-open areas and is least common in continuous forest, although they do occur there. Favors a mosiac of woodlands, farmland, fencerows, overgrown fields, etc.

Breeding: In Ohio the large stick nest is built high in trees. Nest is usually situated in place that is remote from human activities. Lays two to four eggs. Young fledge at six weeks.

Natural History: This is the most common and widespread large *Buteo* hawk in America. Their range includes all of North America south of the Arctic and much of the Caribbean and Central America. The Red-tailed Hawk is generally regarded as the daytime counterpart of the Great Horned Owl, hunting by day many of the same species in the same habitats utilized by the owl at night. "Red-tails" prey mostly on rodents (mice, voles, and ground squirrels). Much larger prey like rabbits may also be taken on occasion. In some areas ground-dwelling birds like pheasants and quail are taken, and they have been known to attack large flocks of blackbirds. In summer they also take large snakes such as the Woodland Rat Snake (*Pantherophis*). Large examples of these snakes (which are strong constrictors) have been known to turn the tables and end up killing a hungry hawk. During winter these large hawks sometimes resort to eating carrion and can sometimes be seen feeding on road kills. In Ohio (and in much of the eastern US), the Red-tailed Hawk is often known by the nickname "Chicken Hawk" in the mistaken belief that they prey on chickens. Although they may certainly catch a few chickens occasionally, their main food is rats, mice, and other rodents, making them an overall useful species to man. Their habit of perching conspicuously in dead trees, snags, and power poles along highways makes them one of the more easily observed of Ohio's hawk species. Historically, the Red-tailed Hawk and other raptors were regarded as varmints and for many decades they were shot on sight by uninformed individuals. By the 1950s many birds of prey were becoming scarce in America. Since the passage of the migratory bird treaty act in the early 1970s providing federal protection to all of America's raptor species, Red-tailed Hawks have become common.

Class—**Aves** (birds)		
Order—**Falconiformes** (raptors)		
Family—**Accipitridae** (hawks, eagles, kites)		

Broad-winged Hawk *Buteo platypterus*	**Rough-legged Hawk** *Buteo lagopus*	**Red-shouldered Hawk** *Buteo lineatus*
	Light morph	Adult Juvenile

Size: 16 inches.	Presumed range in Ohio	**Size:** 21 inches.	Presumed range in Ohio	**Size:** 17 inches.	Presumed range in Ohio
Abundance: Uncommon in Ohio.		**Abundance:** Uncommon in Ohio.		**Abundance:** Fairly common.	
Migratory Status: Summer resident and spring-fall migrant.		**Migratory Status:** Winter only. Late November to April.		**Migratory Status:** Year-round resident.	

Variation: First year plumage is mottled brown (similar to juvenile Red-shouldered Hawk on this page).

Variation: Two distinct color morphs, a dark (nearly black) phase and a lighter morph with paler head and shoulders.

Variation: Four subspecies. Ours is the eastern race (*B. l. lineatus*). Female is larger. Ontogenic variation (see above).

Habitat: Favors large tracts of unbroken deciduous woodlands in upland areas. More common in Ohio in the eastern and southern parts of the state.

Habitat: This is a northern species that summers as far north as the Arctic. Favors tundra in summer and farmlands and prairies in winter.

Habitat: Woodlands of all kinds, but especially likes woods bordering swamps or rivers, or along wooded creek-sides. Less common in uplands.

Breeding: Stick nest is in a tree crotch, usually in deep woods. Lays two to three eggs on average.

Breeding: Nests well to north in Arctic or subarctic regions of tundra and tiaga. Clutch size (three to seven) is prey dependent.

Breeding: Bulky stick nest is in the fork of a tree about 20–40 feet high and often near water. Two to four eggs in April.

Natural History: A decidedly woodland raptor whose breeding range in North America closely mimics the Eastern Temperate Forests Level I ecoregion. In Ohio this species is much more common in the Appalachian Plateau and Interior Low Plateau regions which are more heavily forested. They may be seen as a migrant throughout the Central Lowland Province of Ohio but the lack of large tracts of forest in this region precludes nesting. They are less conspicuous than most hawks except during the migration when they band together in large flocks known as "kettles." Extremely large flocks that may contain 200 birds are usually seen during fall migrations. Hunts by scanning for prey from a perch. Food includes insects, but consists mostly of small vertebrates like rodents as well as a large amount of reptile and amphibian prey, including lizards and small snakes.

Natural History: The Rough-legged Hawk is an arctic species that moves south in winter, often as far south as northern Kentucky in the east as as far as Texas in the west. Their migrations are sporadic depending upon weather, snow cover, and prey availability, but every winter at least a few can be seen in Ohio. They prey primarily on small mammals and lemmings are an important food on the breeding grounds. During years of high lemming populations more eggs will be laid and more young fledged. In winter they take mice, voles, and shrews mostly. Hunts by soaring and hovering over open country. They can face into the wind and remain in a stationary hover for over a minute. While these are fairly large hawks, they have relatively small feet and small beaks, and are thus unable to take the larger prey taken by hawks like the Red-tailed Hawk.

Natural History: The Red-shouldered Hawk is the daytime counterpart of the Barred Owl, and the two species often occur in the same territory. These are vocal birds. Their call, described as "kee-ah, kee-ah, kee-ah," is rapidly repeated about a dozen times. They can be fairly tame if unmolested and their raucous calling will not go unnoticed when the nest is nearby. They feed on a wide variety of small vertebrates but mostly eat reptiles, amphibians, and rodents. The range of the Red-shouldered Hawk coincides closely with the level 1 ecoregion known as the Eastern Temperate Forest. However, a disjunct population (subspecies *elegans*) is found on the west coast of North America in the Mediterranean California Ecoregion. In Ohio this hawk is most common in the eastern and southern portions of the state, a reflection of its habitat preference for more extensive forest.

Class—**Aves** (birds)

Order—**Falconiformes** (raptors)

Family—**Accipitridae** (hawks, eagles, kites)

Golden Eagle *Aquila chrysaetos*	**Bald Eagle** *Haliaeetus leucophalus*	**Osprey** *Pandion haliaetus*

Size: 30 inches.	Presumed range in Ohio	**Size:** 31 inches.	Presumed range in Ohio	**Size:** 30 inches.	Presumed range in Ohio
Abundance: Very rare in Ohio.		**Abundance:** Rare in Ohio.		**Abundance:** Uncommon.	
Migratory Status: Winter migrant. In Ohio from October to April.		**Migratory Status:** Both a year-round resident and winter migrant.		**Migratory Status:** Spring through fall resident that winters in the southern US.	

Variation: Sexes are alike in appearance but female is about 20 percent larger. Juvenile birds have white in tail.

Habitat: Rugged mountains, deserts, and open plains of the western US and rugged regions of Canadian tundra.

Breeding: A large stick nest up to six feet across is usually built on the face of a steep cliff. Usually lays two eggs.

Natural History: Although they are slightly smaller than the Bald Eagle, Golden Eagles are probably the most fearsome hunting bird in America. Ground squirrels and other small mammals make up to bulk of their prey, with larger species like jackrabbits and the young of wild sheep, goats, and Pronghorn also being taken. They are sometimes persecuted by sheep ranchers in western North America, who blame them for killing young lambs in the spring. Indigenous to the entire northern hemisphere, in America the Golden Eagle is found mostly in the west. Like many large raptors they are capable of significant seasonal movements. Although very rare east of the Great Plains, they may sometimes show up almost anywhere in North America, including Ohio, especially during winter months.

Variation: May not acquire the characteristic white head and tail until their fourth annual molt at five years of age.

Habitat: In Ohio Bald Eagles are associated with large rivers and lakes, especially Lake Erie.

Breeding: Extremely bulky stick nest is re-used and gets larger each year. Usually only two eggs per clutch.

Natural History: One of the great conservation success stories, Bald Eagles were highly endangered just a few decades ago. Strigent protection, banning of the pesticide DDT, and a widespread education campaign has lead to a remarkable recovery. They first began to recover as a breeding species in Ohio in the mid 1980s following extreme conservation efforts by ODNR and the USFandWS. By 2011 there were 194 nests in Ohio. Bald Eagles feed largely on fish and carrion but are also capable hunters. Some birds specialize in hunting migratory waterfowl in winter, picking off birds wounded by hunters. Bald Eagles wander widely in the winter and may be seen virtually anywhere in the state, but they are nowhere numerous. Most nesting in Ohio is around Lake Erie. Adopted as the national emblem of the United States by congress in 1782.

Variation: No variation in plumage of adults and immatures. Females are slightly larger than males.

Habitat: Typically seen in the vicinity of Ohio's large lakes and rivers. Increasing in numbers throughout Ohio.

Breeding: Bulky stick nest is often built on man-made structures like bridges and power line towers. Two to four eggs.

Natural History: Subsists mainly on fish. Hunting tactics consist of a steep dive that ends with the Osprey plunging feet first into the water, allowing them to catch fish up three feet below the surface. Most fish caught in freshwater are non-game species, thus they have little to no impact on sport fisheries. Like the Bald Eagle, Osprey populations in the mid-United States plummeted dramatically in the first half of the 20th century. The same types of conservation efforts that restored the Bald Eagle (including re-introduction programs) have brought Osprey numbers back to respectable levels. Once regarded as an endangered species, the Osprey has recovered enough to have recently been de-listed. Ohio now boasts healthy populations of nesting Ospreys and they continue to increase across the state.

Class—**Aves** (birds)

Order—**Falconiformes** (raptors)

Family—**Accipitridae** (hawks, eagles, kites)

Northern Goshawk *Accipiter gentilis*	Sharp-shinned Hawk *Accipiter striatus*	Cooper's Hawk *Accipiter cooperi*

Size: 24 inches.

Presumed range in Ohio

Abundance: Rare in Ohio.

Migratory Status: A rare winter migrant and a very rare winter resident. Northern Ohio only.

Variation: Females are larger. Juveniles are heavily streaked with dark brown as with other *Accipiter* hawks.

Habitat: A bird of coniferous and boreal forests. In winter sometimes uses in mixed deciduous/conifer woodlands.

Breeding: Large stick nest can be three feet across, usually built in the largest tree in the area. Two to four eggs on average.

Natural History: This is a bird of wilderness. It inhabits most of Canada and the Rocky Mountains. Their primary food consists several species of grouse, but they also take smaller birds as well as squirrels, rabbits, and animals as large as the Snowshoe Hare. Known for fearlessness, the Goshawk has been known to attack humans who venture to close to its nest. It is equally couragous on the hunt and will crash headlong into thickets in pursuit of fleeing prey. This characteristic coupled with its speed and large size have made the Goshawk a favorite bird among those who practice the ancient art of Falconry. Although this species is widespread across the northern half of North America, they are an uncommon bird even within their core range. In Ohio they are seen only very rarely in the northernmost section of the state.

Size: 9–13 inches.

Presumed range in Ohio

Abundance: Uncommon.

Migratory Status: Both a winter and a year-round resident, but many move north in summer.

Variation: Ontogenic plumage variation (see photos). Females are as much twice the size of males.

Habitat: Forests and thickets. Found in both rural and urban areas where vegetative cover is present.

Breeding: Pine trees are a favored locale for placing the nest. Lays as many as eight eggs, with five to six being the average.

Natural History: A relentless hunter of small songbirds, the Sharp-shinned Hawk is sometimes seen raiding backyard bird feeders, and they are known to pluck baby songbirds from nests. These small raptors are capable of rapid, twisting flight while pursuing their small songbird prey through woodlands and thickets. In Ohio they are more common during migration periods when birds that summer farther north move southward. Although some birds are breeding residents in the state, most nest far to north, some as far north as Alaska and the Yukon Territory. The Sharp-shinned Hawk is a widely distributed species that ranges across all of North America south of the arctic region and southward all the way to southern Central America. In Ohio they are not a common bird and they are regarded as a Species of Concern by the ODNR.

Size: 14–19 inches.

Presumed range in Ohio

Abundance: Fairly common.

Migratory Status: Year-round resident, but some winter birds may be migrants that nested farther north.

Variation: First year birds are brown with streaked breast. Females are about 30 percent larger than males.

Habitat: Woodlands, regenerative areas, and edge habitats are favored. Can also be seen in tree-lined urban yards.

Breeding: Stick nest is built high in tree and eggs are laid in April or May. Clutch size averages four to six.

Natural History: Feeds almost exclusively on birds and is known to haunt backyard bird feeders. These hawks are a major predator to the Bobwhite, an important game species that is in decline throughout most of its range. Cooper's Hawks are fierce hunters that will fearlessly attack birds as large or larger than themselves, including grouse, waterfowl, and domestic chickens. Although quite widespread and fairly common, they are not as observable as the Buteo hawks. Cooper's Hawks tend to stay in wooded areas and thickets with heavier cover than their bulkier cousins. These birds are fast fliers and capable of great maneuverability, an adaptation to hunting in forest and thickets. They have adapted well to human activities and they sometimes exist in urban areas, especially in parks and heavily wooded neighborhoods.

Class—**Aves** (birds)

Order—**Falconiformes** (raptors)

Family—**Accipitridae** (hawks, eagles, kites)	Family—**Cathartidae** (vultures)	
Northern Harrier *Circus cyaneus*	**Turkey Vulture** *Cathartes aura*	**Black Vulture** *Coragyps atratus*

Size: 18 inches.	**Size:** 26 inches.	**Size:** 25 inches.
Abundance: Fairly common.	**Abundance:** Common.	**Abundance:** Fairly common.
Migratory Status: May rarely breed in the state, but most birds in Ohio are winter residents.	**Migratory Status:** Year-round resident in the southern half of the state. Summer resident in the north.	**Migratory Status:** Year-round resident, but some birds go south in harsh winters.

Presumed range in Ohio    Presumed range in Ohio    Presumed range in Ohio

Variation: Females are mottled brown above and below. Males are gray-brown above and pale gray below.	**Variation:** Essentially no variation. Skin on face is pinkish gray on immature birds, bright pink on adult.	**Variation:** No variation among adults. Older birds have lighter gray heads with more wrinkles on skin than immatures.
Habitat: Open country. Pastures, marshes, agricultural fields, wet prairies, and grasslands.	**Habitat:** Seen in all habitats throughout the state. Less common in urban areas and regions of intensive agriculture.	**Habitat:** Found in a wide variety of habitats within its range. Mainly restricted to the southern half of Ohio.
Breeding: Nests on the ground in thick grass. Builds a nest of grasses and weed stems. Lays four to six eggs.	**Breeding:** Nests on cliff faces, in large tree hollows, or on the ground in hollow logs. Almost always lays two eggs.	**Breeding:** No nest is built and the two eggs are laid on a bare surface. The nest site is often in a derelict building.

Natural History: The range of the Northern Harrier is holarctic and includes Europe and northern Asia as well as North America. Unlike most diurnal raptors that hunt entirely by sight, the Northern Harrier mimics the technique used by owls and hunts largely by sound. A special "parabola" of feathers surround the face and direct sound waves to the ears. It hunts by flying low to the ground with a slow, buoyant flight that resembles a giant butterfly. Food is mostly small mammals and birds but reptiles and amphibians are also listed as food items. Roosting and nesting on the ground and hunting as much by sound as by sight, the Northern Harrier is unique among America's diurnal raptors. In historical times before the draining of Ohio's marshes, this was a more common species.

Natural History: The absence of feathers on the head and neck of vultures is an adaptation for feeding on carrion. Vultures may stick the head deep inside a rotting carcass and feathers would become matted with filth. The bare skin on the neck and face on the other hand is constantly exposed to the sterilizing effects of sunlight. Turkey Vultures are one of the few birds with a well developed sense of smell, and food is often located by detecting the odor of rotting flesh. Sight is also important and they are quick to notice a fresh carcass on a roadway. Newly mowed fields and other disturbed areas within their range are closely scanned for small animal victims. Highly social, they roost communally, sometimes with Black Vultures. Vultures have benefited from a constant supply of road-killed animals.

Natural History: America's vultures are named for the color of the skin on the face. Turkey Vultures have reddish skin (like a turkey), Black Vulture has dark gray or black facial skin. Black Vultures also have shorter tails and lesser wing span, giving them a much "stubbier" look than the Turkey Vulture. Vultures were once regarded as a threat to livestock by spreading disease. In fact, the powerful digestive juices of the gut of vultures destroys bacteria. Both the Turkey Vulture and the Black Vulture have the unappealing habit of defecating on the legs and feet as a way of disinfecting the feet (which can become quite nasty and the birds feed on rotted carcasses). Black Vultures lack the well developed sense of smell of Turkey Vultures, but they do have keen eyesight.

Class—**Aves** (birds)

Order—**Falconiformes** (raptors)

Family—**Falconidae** (falcons)

American Kestrel *Falco sparverius*	**Merlin** *Falco columbarius*	**Peregrine Falcon** *Falco peregrinus*

American Kestrel

Size: 10 inches.

Presumed range in Ohio

Abundance: Fairly common.

Variation: Sexually dimorphic. Male has gray wings, female brown.

Migratory Status: A year-round resident that breeds in Ohio. Winter migrants increase the population in winter.

Habitat: Throughout Ohio the Kestrel is seen in open country. Least common in the mountains regions of the east.

Breeding: Usually nests in tree cavities or old woodpecker holes within trees situated in open fields. May also nest in man-made structures. Four to five eggs.

Natural History: While the Kestrel is a fairly common bird in open regions throughout Ohio, there has been some decline in populations in the eastern United States in recent years. Sometimes called "Sparrow Hawk," the Kestrel is widespread throughout North and Central America and as many as 17 subspecies are recognized. They are often seen perched on power lines and poles along roadways in rural farmlands throughout the state, but they are uncommon in the heavily forested mountains of eastern Ohio. Insects are the major food in summer (especially grasshoppers). In winter they eat small mammals and rarely, small birds. Hunts both from a perch and by hovering over open fields.

Merlin

Size: 11 inches.

Presumed range in Ohio

Abundance: Very rare.

Variation: Male has blue-gray back, female and immatures have brown.

Migratory Status: A rare spring-fall migrant, rare winter migrant, and a very rare summer resident and breeder.

Habitat: Habitat is open regions. Most likely to be seen along major river valleys, especially the Ohio River valley.

Breeding: Breeds far to the north in Canada, Alaska, and parts of the north-central Rockies and plains. Uses old crow or hawk nests as well as cliffs.

Natural History: The Merlin is seen in Ohio mostly during migration (or as very rare summer resident/breeder). These small falcons are only slightly larger than the Kestrel and they are easily confused with that species. The facial markings of the Merlin are less distinct than the Kestrels. Summering mostly far to the north and wintering along coastlines, their migration routes are mostly to the west of Ohio or to the east along the Atlantic coast. Like most falcons however, these birds are prone to wander widely. Although they may occur almost anywhere in Ohio they are quite rare in the state, and most sightings in Ohio are west of the Appalachian Plateau Province. Food is mostly small birds.

Peregrine Falcon

Size: 17 inches.

Presumed range in Ohio

Abundance: Rare.

Variation: Some geographical variation. Specimen above is typical.

Migratory Status: A few nest and live Year-round in parts of the state, but most birds seen in Ohio are migrants.

Habitat: Prefers cliffs in remote wilderness areas but has adapted to living among skyscrapers in many cities.

Breeding: Nests on ledges of cliff faces and on man-made structures like skyscrapers and bridges. Four eggs is typical, sometimes up to six.

Natural History: Falcons are fast flying birds and the Peregrine is among the fastest. Hunts pigeons, waterfowl, grouse, etc. Hunting technique usually involves soaring high above and diving in on birds in flight, or diving towards resting birds and panicking them into flight. Once airborne, no other bird can match the Peregrines speed. Diving Peregrines may reach speeds approaching 200 mph, making them perhaps the fastest animal on earth. In Ohio this species currently breeds mostly on bridges over the Ohio River or on skyscraper ledges in major cities. However, the name "peregrine" means "wanderer," and these birds may be seen almost anywhere in the state, albeit quite rarely.

Class—**Aves** (birds)

Order—**Ciconiiformes** (wading birds)

Family—**Ardeidae** (herons)

Great Blue Heron *Ardea herodias*	**Great Egret** *Ardea alba*	**Snowy Egret** *Egretta thula*

Size: 47 inches.

Presumed range in Ohio

Abundance: Fairly common.

Migratory Status: A year-round resident. Northern Ohio birds may migrate south in winter.

Variation: See Natural History below.

Habitat: Along rivers and streams, swamps, marshes, ponds, and wet meadows and floodplains.

Breeding: Nests in colonies. Most nesting in Ohio is in the glaciated regions of the state. Nest is a platform of sticks in tree or bush above water. Three to four eggs is typical.

Natural History: The largest heron in North America, the Great Blue Heron will eat almost anything it can swallow. Fish and frogs are major foods, but it also eats snakes, salamanders, small mammals, and even small turtles. Birds are sometimes eaten, including other, smaller heron species. All food items are swallowed whole. Large prey is killed by stabbing repeatedly with the beak or by bashing against a hard object. Smaller prey is often swallowed alive. Hunts both day and night and reportedly has good night vision. Great Blue Herons are found throughout most of the United States and much of Canada, including in riparian habitats in desert regions. Sexes are alike but juveniles will have streaked breast and neck and are duskier overall than adults. A solid white subspecies is found in parts of southern Florida.

Size: 39 inches.

Presumed range in Ohio

Abundance: Uncommon in Ohio.

Migratory Status: Spring through fall migrant. Rare breeder in glaciated regions and Lake Erie.

Variation: Breeders acquire plumes.

Habitat: Along major streams, lakes, swamps, and marshes. Also low lying areas subject to flooding.

Breeding: Most nesting in Ohio is along the Lake Erie shore. Sporadic nesting occurs elsewhere in Ohio. Nest is a platform of sticks in tree or bush above water. Lays three or four eggs.

Natural History: This heron species (along with the Snowy Egret and several other herons) was nearly hunted to extinction during the last half of the 19th century. The long, wispy feathers (known as "plumes") were once used to adorn the hats of fashionable ladies. The plumes are most pronounced during the breeding season. Thus the catastrophic impact of the plume hunters was magnified as hunters killed birds at their nesting colonies. Killing of parent birds doomed nestlings as well. Efforts to save this and other plume bird species lead to some of Americas earliest laws to protect wildlife. Today this species is still a symbol of conservation efforts and is the logo of the National Audubon Society. It is also known by the names Common Egret or Great White Egret. As with many other herons, it often nests in colonies.

Size: 24 inches.

Presumed range in Ohio

Breeding

Abundance: Rare in Ohio.

Migratory Status: Mostly a summer migrant, but a few dozen pair nest on islands in Lake Erie.

Variation: Breeders acquire plumes.

Habitat: Along major streams, lakes, swamps, and marshes. Also low lying areas subject to flooding.

Breeding: Nesting in Ohio occurs only on two or three islands in Lake Erie. They will nest in colonies with other heron species. Nest is made of sticks and twigs. Three to five eggs is average.

Natural History: As with several other heron species, the Snowy Egret during breeding season sports long "plume" feathers on the back. As with other plume bird species the Snowy Egret was nearly wiped out by the feather trade of the late 1800s. Today the species has recovered to healthy numbers but remains under threat due to its dependence upon coastal wetlands. This species feeds on smaller prey such as worms, insects, crustaceans, amphibians, and small fish. It is an active feeder that often chases prey through the shallows rather than using the stealth method employed by its larger cousins. It also often feeds by swishing its feet in the mud to disturb benthic organisms. The range map above shows the approximate range of summer migrants in the state. In addition, a few dozen will nest on islands in Lake Erie.

Class—**Aves** (birds)

Order—**Ciconiiformes** (wading birds)

Family—**Ardeidae** (herons)

Little Blue Heron *Egretta cearulea*	**Cattle Egret** *Bulbulcus ibis*	**Green Heron** *Butorides virescens*

Little Blue Heron
Egretta cearulea

Juvenile

Size: 24 inches.

Abundance: Rare in Ohio.

Migratory Status: Summer migrant. Very rare breeder on island in Lake Erie.

Presumed range in Ohio — Breeding

Variation: First year birds have white plumage (see inset photo).

Habitat: Wetlands. In Ohio seen mostly along the Ohio River valley in the southwestern part of the state.

Breeding: Builds a stick nest platform in bushes and low trees in wetlands. Lays two to five eggs.

Natural History: Even within the heart of its range along the lower coastal plains of the southeastern US, the Little Blue Heron is generally less common that other heron species. In Ohio it is a rather rare bird. In addition, the dark plumage of adults and its rather secretive nature make it one of the least observable of Ohio's herons. Like most herons, it is an opportunistic feeder that eats almost anything it can swallow. Food is mostly frogs, fish, crustaceans, and insects. It is a daytime hunter that hunts by stalking slowly through wetland habitats. The transitional plumage of the juvenile Little Blue Heron is unique, and produces for a brief time a white bird with blue splotches. Blue increases throughout the molt ending in a solid blue adult. The range map approximates the range of summer migrants. In addition, a few pairs nest on islands in Lake Erie.

Cattle Egret
Bulbulcus ibis

Size: 19 inches.

Abundance: Rare in Ohio.

Migratory Status: A rare summer migrant. Very rare breeder in Lake Erie.

Presumed range in Ohio — Breeding

Variation: Orange on crown and throat more pronounced during breeding.

Habitat: Unlike other herons, these birds are usually seen in open pastures and fields in association with cattle.

Breeding: Stick nest built in trees or bushes. Nests in large colonies. Three or four eggs is average.

Natural History: The Cattle Egret is one of our most interesting heron species. Originally native to Africa, Cattle Egrets began an inexplicable range expansion in the early 1800s. They first migrated across the Atlantic to South America and then appeared in North America around 1950. The first sighting in Ohio was in 1958. The species continues to expand its range and is today a rare summer migrant in western Ohio. Their name is derived from their habit of associating with cattle herds in pastures. Before expanding their range out of Africa they associated with herds of Cape Buffalo, Hippopotamus, and wild ungulates. They feed mostly on insects that are disturbed by the large grazers they follow through pastures and grasslands. The map above shows the approximate range of summer migrants in Ohio. In addition, a few pairs will nest on islands in Lake Erie.

Green Heron
Butorides virescens

Size: 19 inches.

Abundance: Fairly common.

Migratory Status: A summer resident that breeds widely across the state.

Presumed range in Ohio

Variation: Juvenile birds are browner above and have streaked throat.

Habitat: Usually seen in the vicinity of wetlands or rivers and streams. Also common around lakes and small ponds.

Breeding: Usually nests singly rather than in colonies. Nest is a stick platform in a tree fork. Lays three to five eggs.

Natural History: In many areas the Green Heron often goes by the name "Shy-poke." This is one of Ohio's most familiar herons and its range encompasses all of the eastern United States as well as the west coast. It also ranges southward throughout Central America. When flushed it nearly always emits a loud "squawking" alarm call. Feeds mostly in shallow water and often feeds from a perch on a floating log or a limb just above the waters surface. Hunts by stealth and may remain frozen for long periods as it watches and waits for prey. Fish is the primary food item with small frogs probably being the next most common prey. Amazingly, this species has been reported to catch insects and worms to use as bait for luring in fish. While the Green Heron is one of our most common wading birds, it is dependant upon wetlands. Sadly, 90 percent of Ohio's original wetland habitat is gone.

Class—**Aves** (birds)

Order—**Ciconiiformes** (wading birds)

Family—**Ardeidae** (herons)

Yellow-crowned Night Heron *Nyctanassa violacea*	**Black-crowned Night Heron** *Nycticorax nycticorax*	**Least Bittern** *Ixobrychus exilis*

Size: 25 inches.

Abundance: Very rare in Ohio.

Migratory Status: Summer resident. April through Aug.

Presumed range in Ohio

Size: 25 inches.

Abundance: Uncommon in Ohio.

Migratory Status: Mostly summer, but also rare year-round.

Presumed range in Ohio

Size: 13 inches.

Abundance: Uncommon.

Migratory Status: A summer resident from May to Sept.

Presumed range in Ohio

Variation: Juveniles are heavily streaked with brown and white.

Habitat: Swamps and marshes. Favors heavier cover than many herons.

Breeding: Breeds very sporadically across Ohio, mostly in glaciated regions. Flimsy stick nest is fairly high in tree, usually over water. Three to five eggs.

Natural History: These birds are often active at night, hence the name "night heron." Food is mostly crustaceans. Crabs are important foods in coastal regions, while crayfish are eaten in freshwater areas. A classical ambush predator, the Yellow-crowned Night Heron does most foraging from a stationery position, sitting like a statue and waiting for prey to wander into striking range. They will also stalk slowly and methodically with slow, deliberate movements that are largely undetectable to prey. Diet may be supplemented with fish and invertebrates, but this heron is mainly a crustacean specialist. Has recovered nicely from low numbers decades ago and now seems to be expanding its range farther to the north. The range map above is an approximation an may not be accurate. They are so rare in Ohio that their exact range in the state is difficult to determine. Regarded as a Species of Special Interest by ODNR.

Variation: Juvenile birds are heavily streaked with brown (see inset).

Habitat: Wetlands, river valleys, and in the vicinity of large impoundments.

Breeding: Nests in colonies that are usually situated over swamps or on an island. Colonies may contain hundreds of birds, with three or four eggs per nest.

Natural History: Although the Black-crowned Night Heron may be locally common near breeding colonies, it is a rarely seen bird in most of Ohio. Surprisingly, this is a widespread species that is found not only in much of the US, but in fact throughout most of the world. They can be found on every continent except Australia and Antarctica. As its name implies this species is often active at night. The food is primarily fish. However, the list of known foods is quite long and includes, insects, leeches, earthworms, crustaceans, gastropods, amphibians, snakes, small turtles, small mammals, and even birds! Prefers to feed in shallow water along the margins of weedy ponds, marshes, and swamps. Most breeding in Ohio occurs along the western Lake Erie shoreline and on nearby islands. A few breed in widely scattered locales across glaciated Ohio as well. Regarded as a Threatened Species in Ohio.

Variation: Male has black cap and black back. See both sexes above.

Habitat: Favors marshes with dense growths of tall grasses and sedges.

Breeding: Nest is a well concealed platform built amid dense growth of cattails or other sedges/grasses. Up to six eggs are laid.

Natural History: This smallest of American herons is also a secretive bird that often stays hidden in dense marsh grasses and sedges. When alarmed they point their bill skyward and freeze, mimicking the vertical vegetation of their habitat. These small herons move with ease through thick stands of marsh vegetation. When flushed they fly only a short distance just above the vegetation before dropping back down. Despite their seemingly weak flying abilities, they migrate great distances from wintering areas in south Florida and the Carribean to summer breeding grounds that may be as far north as northern Minnesota. They have very long toes for grasping stems of grass and sedge. Feeds on small fish, insects, crayfish, and amphibians. This species has declined significantly in Ohio over the last century. Today most use the western Lake Erie marshes. Classified as a Threatened Species by ODNR.

Class—**Aves** (birds)

Order—**Ciconiiformes** (wading birds)	Order—**Gruiformes** (rails and cranes)
Family—**Ardeidae** (herons)	Family—**Rallidae** (rails)

American Bittern *Botaurus lentiginosus*	**King Rail** *Rallus elegans*	**Virginia Rail** *Rallus limicola*

Size: 26 inches.	Presumed range in Ohio	**Size:** 16 inches.	Presumed range in Ohio	**Size:** 9.5 inches.	Presumed range in Ohio
Abundance: Rare in Ohio.		**Abundance:** Rare in Ohio.		**Abundance:** Uncommon.	
Migratory Status: Both a spring/fall migrant and a rare summer resident.		**Migratory Status:** Transient spring and fall migrant and rare summer resident.		**Migratory Status:** Transient spring and fall migrant and summer resident.	

Variation: None. Sexes alike. | **Variation:** None. Sexes alike. | **Variation:** None. Sexes alike.

Habitat: Large freshwater marshes are used in summer, coastal marshlands in winter. | **Habitat:** Marshes. Found mostly along southeastern coasts but a few move inland in summer. | **Habitat:** Primarily a marsh dweller. In migration may visit ponds, swamps, or wet meadows.

Breeding: Nest is in dense emergent vegetation of the marsh and is well hidden. Three to five eggs is typical. Densest breeding occurs in Lake Erie region. | **Breeding:** Builds a loosely woven cup from marsh vegetation. Breeds sporadically in glaciated Ohio, mostly in the region of western Lake Erie. | **Breeding:** Builds a nest platform of aquatic vegetation a few inches above water level. Nest is usually well hidden among vegetation. Lays eight or nine eggs.

Natural History: The biology of this species is not well known. Presumably they may be seen anywhere in Ohio during migration, but they are probably most likely to be seen in Ohio in the marshes bordering Lake Erie. Few Ohioans will ever see one, as they are usually quite secretive. Hunts by stealth and may remain motionless for long periods of time. The eyes of this heron are situated with a downward slant, better facilitating the birds ability to see into the water. When startled they will throw the head back and point the beak straight up. The streaked brown pattern of the neck and breast is remarkably cryptic amid the vertical stalks of marsh grasses and sedges. Like most herons, an opportunistic feeder. Eats fish, amphibians, crayfish, small mammals, and some insects. During migration they will sometimes stop at very small ponds that are heavily vegetated with cattails. | **Natural History:** Rails are well adapted to life in the marsh. They move with ease through thick grasses and rarely fly except when migrating. They can run quite fast through the grass and rarely offer more than a glimpse. They can also swim and dive beneath the surface, using the wings to swim underwater. Despite the fact that rails are listed as a game bird by most state wildlife agencies, almost no one hunts them, due probably to their scarcity and secretiveness. They feed mostly on aquatic insects and their larvae, spiders, and other invertebrates. Some plant material is also eaten. Although they may occur across much of Ohio during migration, they are never common and are rarely observed. While breeding has been recorded in a few regions of glaciated Ohio, most breeding occurs in the western Lake Erie marshes. This is one of the rarest breeding birds in the state. | **Natural History:** The Virginia Rail is more common in Ohio than the larger King Rail, both as a migrant and as a breeding bird. Nesting has been recorded in all of Ohio's major physiographic provinces, but most nesting occurs in the Huron-Lake Erie Plains and the Glaciated Allegheny Plateau. Still, this is not a common bird in Ohio and this fact coupled with its secretive nature means that it is a species that remains unfamiliar to most Ohioans. Historically, this species was much more common in the state. But today only about 10 percent of the wetland habitats that once occurred in Ohio remain. As a result, this species along with its larger cousin the King Rail are both monitored by the ODNR. The King Rail is an Endangered Species in Ohio, while the Virginia Rail is a Species of Concern. Both species will benefit from wetland conservation and restoration efforts.

Class—**Aves** (birds)

Order—**Gruiformes** (rails and cranes)

Family—**Rallidae** (rails)

American Coot *Fulica americana*	**Common Gallinule** *Gallinula chloropus*	**Sora** *Porzana carolina*

Size: 15 inches.	**Size:** 14 inches.	**Size:** 9 inches.
Abundance: Fairly common.	**Abundance:** Rare in Ohio.	**Abundance:** Uncommon.
Migratory Status: Year-round resident but more common in spring and fall. Presumed range in Ohio	**Migratory Status:** Summer resident. Arrives mid-April. Leaves in Sept.  Presumed range in Ohio	**Migratory Status:** Summer resident. Seen in Ohio April through October.  Presumed range in Ohio
Variation: Sexes alike. Juvenile paler gray with yellowish beak.	**Variation:** Sexes alike. Juvenile is paler gray without red bill and forehead.	**Variation:** Juvenile lacks black on face and throat. Sexes are alike.
Habitat: Rivers, lakes, large ponds, marshes, and wetlands in Ohio.	**Habitat:** Wetlands and lake shores with abundant vegetation.	**Habitat:** Primarily a marsh dweller. Favors heavily vegetated wetlands.
Breeding: Breeds mostly to the north and to the west of Ohio, but does nest sporadically across glaciated Ohio. Nest is a platform built amid emergent vegetation. About six eggs are laid.	**Breeding:** Nest is a platform of vegetation slightly above the water line and usually well concealed. Most nesting in Ohio is in the western Lake Erie marshes. Will lay as many as 10 eggs.	**Breeding:** Builds a nest platform of aquatic vegetation a few inches above water level. Nest is well hidden in dense upright plants. Breeds mostly in glaciated Ohio. Lays eight to 11 eggs.
Natural History: During migration and in winter American Coots gather in large flocks on open water and behave more like ducks than rails. During the breeding season they act more like rails and live among cattails and reeds in freshwater marshes. But they are not as elusive as the rails and are usually easily observed even in summer. They are considered a game species, but rarely hunted as most waterfowl hunters regard them as a "trash" species. They sometimes go by the nickname "Mud Hen." Although the feet are not webbed as with ducks and geese, their long toes are equipped with lateral lobes which flare out when swimming and create an ample surface for pushing against the water. Thus they are good swimmers. They feed both on land (on grasses) and in the water (aquatic plants, algae, and aquatic invertebrates). Small fish and small amphibians are also taken.	**Natural History:** Sometimes known as the Common Moorhen, but that name is properly reserved for a very similar bird that lives in Europe. Although these birds may be seen in suitable habitat throughout much the glaciated regions of the state, they are rare in Ohio. Farther south in places like Louisiana and Florida they can be quite common. They feed largely on seeds of aquatic plants but also eats animal matter including most predominately snails and insects. Although similar to the American Coot in size and appearance, the Common Gallinule is rarely seen in the open and prefers to stay close to heavy cover. Additionally, they don't form large flocks as do American Coots. However, they are sometimes quite tame and approachable, especially within the heart of their range in Florida and the lower Coastal Plain.	**Natural History:** The Sora is one of the more observable of America's rails. Still, it is fairly secretive, especially during fall migration. They are usually observable on both breeding and wintering grounds, but catching a glimpse of this species in Ohio is difficult. They are vocal birds however, and their whinnying call can be heard for a long distance. They feed on a variety of aquatic invertebrates but also eat seeds of aquatic plants, particularly wild rice. Soras have exceptionally long toes, an adaptation that allows for walking across floating vegetation. Another small rail species, the **Yellow Rail** (*Coturnicops noveboracensis*), also migrates through parts of Ohio. But that species is so scarce and secretive that even serious bird watchers may go their entire lives and never see it! A third rail species, the **Black Rail** (*Laterallus jamaicensis*) is even rarer!

Class—**Aves** (birds)

Order—**Gruiformes** (rails and cranes)	Order—**Chariidriformes** (shorebirds)	
Family—**Gruidae** (cranes)	Family—**Charadriidae** (plovers)	
Sandhill Crane *Grus canadensis*	**Killdeer** *Charadrius vociferus*	**Semipalmated Plover** *Charadrius semipalmatus*

Juvenile

Young

Size: 42 inches.	Presumed range in Ohio	**Size:** 10.5 inches.	Presumed range in Ohio	**Size:** 7.25 inches.	Presumed range in Ohio
Abundance: Rare in Ohio. **Migratory Status:** Rare summer resident in northern Ohio and spring/fall migrant elswhere.		**Abundance:** Common. **Migratory Status:** Most common March through November but may be seen year-round.		**Abundance:** Fairly common. **Migratory Status:** Spring/fall migrant. Fall migration protracted (late July through October).	

Variation: Juveniles are splotched with large amounts of rusty brown. See photos above.

Habitat: Open lands, farm fields, mudflats, marshes, and shallow water areas. In migration uses harvested crop fields.

Breeding: Most breeding in Ohio occurs in the Glaciated Allegheny Plateau and the Huron-Lake Erie Plains. Typically lays two eggs on a platform nest built of vegetation.

Natural History: Standing over three feet tall, the Sandhill Crane is one of the largest birds seen in Ohio. Populations were seriously depleted by the beginning of the 20th century, but the species has recovered dramatically in the last few decades. The largest populations are seen west of the Mississippi River and number tens of thousands. Eastern populations have been slower to recover but are now reasonably healthy. Several states including nearby Kentucky treat them as a game species and have regulated hunting seasons. Some conservationists question the wisdom of hunting seasons on this species. They often form into large flocks that can be vulnerable to natural disasters. Hunted in several states.

Variation: None. Sexes are alike and there is no significant seasonal or ontogenic plumage variations.

Habitat: Open lands. Mudflats, agricultural fields, lake shores, sandbars, and even gravel parking lots.

Breeding: Lays four eggs directly on the ground. Nest is often in gravelly or sandy situations in wide-open spaces. Young are very precocial and they will run about within hours of hatching.

Natural History: Although the Killdeer is found state-wide, they are much more common in the western two-thirds of the state where open habitats are more widespread. This is a species that has likely benefited significantly from human alterations of natural habitats. The creation of open spaces where there was once grassland or forest has resulted in a habitat boom for the Killdeer. They are found all over North America south of the Arctic Circle. They were once hunted for food and their populations suffered a serious decline in the days of "market hunting." They feed on the ground and earthworms are a major food source along with grasshoppers, beetles, and snails. A few seeds are also consumed.

Variation: See photos above. Both winter and summer plumages may be seen in Ohio.

Habitat: Winter habitat is along coastlines. Summer habitat is open tundra. Migrants favor mud flats and shorelines.

Breeding: Nests on the ground, usually near water. Nesting grounds are in northern Canada and Alaska. Four eggs. Chicks are precocious and able to feed themselves immediately.

Natural History: Most Semipalmated Plovers migrate along the coasts of North America, but a few travel overland and they are occasionally seen in Ohio Most sightings will likely be along the Lake Erie shoreline as they tend to favor shorelines and other open spaces. The food of the Semipalmated Plover is mostly invertebrate animals plucked from the mud. They hunt these "benthic" organisms along the edges of marshes, lakes, seashores, etc. Aquatic food items include insect larvae (especially fly larvae), polychaete worms, crustaceans, and small bivalves. On dry land these plovers will eat spiders, flies, and beetles. Most foraging is done along waters edge or in very shallow water or on exposed mudflats.

Class—**Aves** (birds)

Order—**Chariidriformes** (shorebirds)

Family—**Charadriidae** (plovers)

Black-bellied Plover *Pluvialis squatarola*	**Golden Plover** *Pluvialis dominica*

Size: 11.5 inches.

Abundance: Uncommon in Ohio.

Migratory Status: Spring and fall migrant. Spring migration in Ohio is mainly in May. Fall migration is more protracted, from September through early November. Most commonly seen along the western Lake Erie shore.

Presumed range in Ohio

Variation: Seasonal plumage variations (see above). Both plumages may be seen in Ohio.

Habitat: Beaches are the preferred winter habitat. Inland migrants will use shorelines, mudflats, and bare fields.

Breeding: Nest is a shallow cup scraped into the Arctic tundra and lined with lichens. Four eggs are laid.

Natural History: Black-bellied Plovers occur in both the new and old worlds and in fact they are one of the most widespread shorebirds in the world. They occur throughout much of the old world as well as most of the western hemisphere. North American birds winter along both coastlines from just south of Canada to South America, including the Caribbean. Summers are spent within the Arctic Circle of Alaska and Canada. During migration they are seen mostly along America's coastlines and in the great plains region, but a some will pass through Ohio. Unlike many shorebirds, the Black-bellied Plover exhibits nocturnal tendencies and will often feed at night. Food items are marine worms and small clams and mussels plucked from the mud at low tide. On the breeding grounds in the far north they will eat insects, small freshwater crustaceans, and berries. Climate change may be a threat if tundra nesting habitat undergoes transformation.

Size: 10.5 inches.

Abundance: Fairly common in spring, uncommon in fall.

Migratory Status: Spring and fall migrant. Spring migration in Ohio peaks in late April and early May. Fall migration peaks in September and early October. Golden Plovers are more common in Ohio in spring than fall. Usually seen in western Ohio.

Presumed range in Ohio

Variation: Sexes similar with seasonal plumage variations (see above). Both plumages may be seen in Ohio.

Habitat: Beaches are the preferred winter habitat. Inland migrants will use shorelines, mudflats, and bare fields.

Breeding: Nest is a scrape on tundra soil. Four eggs are laid and young are highly precocial, able to walk immediately.

Natural History: Like the similar Black-bellied Plover, the American Golden Plover is a long distance traveller that nests in the Arctic and spends its winters in southeastern South America. Its epic migrations sometimes include extensive flights over vast expanses of open ocean. Many migrate through inland regions and they are known for their propensity to appear almost anywhere during migrations. Food items include some plant material (berries, seeds, foliage) as well as a wide variety of invertebrate prey. Like many shorebirds the American Golden Plover was hunted relentlessly during the days "market hunting" throughout the 1800s. Tens to perhaps hundreds of thousands were killed annually. Today they are still legally hunted in some South American countries. Habitat loss remains an ever present threat and some scientists have expressed Concern about potential changes on tundra breeding grounds due to climate change.

Class—**Aves** (birds)

Order—**Chariidriformes** (shorebirds)

Family—**Scolopacidae** (sandpipers)

Sanderling *Calidris alba*	Pectoral Sandpiper *Calidris melanotus*	Dunlin *Calidris alpina*

Sanderling	Pectoral Sandpiper	Dunlin
Size: 8 inches. **Abundance:** Fairly common. **Migratory Status:** Spring/fall migrant. Most common in Ohio from late July to mid-September. Presumed range in Ohio	**Size:** 8.5 inches. **Abundance:** Common. Migratory Status: Spring-fall migrant. Most common in Ohio from late July through October. Presumed range in Ohio	**Size:** 8.5 inches. **Abundance:** Fairly common. **Migratory Status:** Spring/fall migrant. Seen in Ohio in April and May and in September / October. Presumed range in Ohio
Variation: Significant seasonal variation (see photos above).	**Variation:** Male breeding plumage is darker brown and more vivid.	**Variation:** Significant seasonal plumage changes (see photos above).
Habitat: Shorelines. In winter lives on the beach. During migration frequents lake shores and river bars.	**Habitat:** Migrants use wet meadows, flooded fields, marshes, and lake or pond shorelines, as well as mudflats.	**Habitat:** During migration uses flooded agricultural fields, mud flats, and seasonally flooded lowland pastures.
Breeding: Nests on arctic tundra on bare ground. Lays four eggs.	**Breeding:** Nests on the ground in the arctic coastal plain. Four eggs.	**Breeding:** Another high arctic breeder. Lays four eggs on ground in open tundra.
Natural History: Unlike most members of the sandpiper family, which are more likely to be found on mudflats, the Sanderling is commonly found on seashores. Except during migration or when breeding, these birds inhabit sandy beaches throughout the Americas. Any person who has been to the seashore has probably been amused by watching this species running back and forth in front of the waves. On beaches it feeds by running just in front of an oncoming wave and chasing right behind a receding wave, picking up tiny marine crustaceans, bivalves, and polychaetes. On the breeding ground it will eat both terrestrial and aquatic invertebrates and insects. Most Sanderlings migrate along the coastlines of America or through the great plains. Some will be seen in Ohio however, especially along the shores of Lake Erie.	**Natural History:** Breeding males of this species perform displays in which they erect the feathers of the breast, droop the wings, raise the tail feathers, and emit soft "hooting" sounds. They are the only member of the sandpiper family that vocalizes in this manner. They also perform flight displays above the heads of grounded females. These birds are remarkable travelers that breed in the high arctic and winter in the "Pampas" region of southern South America. Some individuals will cross the Arctic Ocean to breed in Siberia, then migrate back to South America, a round-trip journey of over 18,000 miles each year! The food is mostly small mud-dwelling invertebrates. In Ohio this species is most likely to be seen during migration in flooded crop fields in agricultural regions or open areas where receding waters leave mud flats.	**Natural History:** The Dunlin winters along both coasts of North America where it haunts estuaries and inter-tidal regions. In southern Louisiana and gulf coastal Texas it often uses rice fields in winter. Various clams, insects, worms, and amphipods are picked from the mud or plucked from vegetation with its moderately long, probing bill. Like other shorebird species it is usually seen in flocks, sometimes numbering in the thousands or even tens of thousands. In the early 1800s market hunters killed these birds in enormous numbers. Using cannon-like shotguns known as "punt guns" that were loaded with bird shot, a single blast could kill scores of shorebirds in a closely packed flock. Todays threats include pesticides and other contaminants and loss of wintering habitat. Widespread across Ohio during migration.

Class—**Aves** (birds)
Order—**Chariidriformes** (shorebirds)
Family—**Scolopacidae** (sandpipers)

The "Peep" Sandpipers
Genus—*Calidris* (5 species in Ohio pictured below)

Least Sandpiper *Calidris minutilla*	**White-rumped Sandpiper** *Calidris fuscicollis*	**Semipalmated Sandpiper** *Calidris pusilla*

Baird's Sandpiper *Calidris bairdi*	**Western Sandpiper** *Calidris mauri*	Presumed combined range of the "peep" sandpipers in Ohio

Size: Least Sandpiper 6 inches. Semipalmated Sandpiper 6.25 inches. Western Sandpiper 6.5 inches. White-rumped and Baird's Sandpipers both reach 7.5 inches.

Abundance: The Least Sandpiper and the Semipalmated are the most commonly seen of the "Peep" Sandpipers in Ohio. White-rumped and Baird's are both uncommon in the state, while the Western is a rare species in Ohio.

Migratory Status: Semipalmated Sandpiper, Least Sandpiper, and White-rumped Sandpiper are all spring-fall migrants in Ohio. Both the Western Sandpiper and the Baird's Sandpiper are seen in Ohio only during fall migrations.

Variation: All five of these species exhibit seasonal plumage changes. All are comparably paler in winter than in summer.

Habitat: The name "Mudpiper" would be a more appropriate name for these birds as they favor mud flats and flooded fields over sandy beaches. All can be seen along the coastlines but many migrate through the interior of North America.

Breeding: All "peep" sandpipers nest on the ground in the barren arctic tundra. Four eggs is typical.

Natural History: These five species are all similar in their natural history and are confusingly alike in appearance. While serious birders and professional ornithologists take pride in being able to correctly identify any species, most casual observers are satisfied with calling these homogeneous birds simply "peeps." Food habits and feeding methods are also similar in these sandpipers, with mud-dwelling benthic invertebrates making up the bulk of the diet in winter and during migration. Aquatic insect larvae and some terrestrial insects are eaten on the breeding grounds. The hordes of mosquitoes for which the arctic tundra is famous in summer make up a high protein smorgasboard for both the adult birds and the newly hatched young. All the sandpipers are known for their epic migrations. Some species travel non-stop for a thousand miles or more over open ocean. Flights lasting as long as five days have been reported. Quite a feat of endurance for birds that can weigh as little as 0.75 to 1.5 ounces! Recent population declines have been reported for the Least Sandpiper and the Semipalmated Sandpiper. By contrast, the Western Sandpiper (despite being rare in Ohio) is one of the most abundant shorebirds in America with a total population estimate of 3.5 million birds.

Class—**Aves** (birds)
Order—**Chariidriformes** (shorebirds)
Family—**Scolopacidae** (sandpipers)

Stilt Sandpiper *Calidris himantopus*	**Red Knot** *Calidris canutus*	**Upland Sandpiper** *Bartramia longicauda*

Summer

Summer

Size: 8.5 inches.

Presumed range in Ohio

Abundance: Uncommon in Ohio.

Migratory Status: Migrant. Seen mostly in August and September but also rarely in May.

Variation: Winter birds are much paler, more grayish.

Habitat: Ponds, marshes, flooded fields, and lake shorelines. Uses salt marsh and brackish marshes in winter.

Breeding: Nests in lowland areas near the Arctic Ocean. Lays four eggs.

Natural History: The Stilt Sandpiper gets its name from its long legs. The long legs are an adaptation that allow it to feed in deeper water than most other *Calidris* sandpipers. Its body shape and habit of feeding in deeper water rather than on mud flats is unusual for its genus and mimics the yellowlegs sandpipers (genus *Tringa*, next page). The migratory routes for this sandpiper are mainly west of the Mississippi River, but wanderers have be seen in many areas of Ohio on rare occasions. They nest along the northernmost coast of North America and will spend the winter in the interior of the South American continent. As with many other sandpiper species, the Stilt Sandpiper shows a remarkable fidelity to the nest site. After migrating thousands of miles from South America they often return to the same exact spot on the arctic coastline to lay their eggs.

Size: 10.5 inches.

Presumed range in Ohio

Abundance: Rare in Ohio.

Migratory Status: Mid-May through early June and again from late July to early October.

Variation: Winter birds are drab gray brown with off white breast and belly.

Habitat: Summer habitat is arctic tundra. Winter and migration habitat is intertidal areas and beaches/coastlines.

Breeding: Nest on tundra all the way to the Arctic Ocean. Four eggs is typical.

Natural History: This is North America's largest member of the *Calidris* genus. Like many other Sandpiper species, the Red Knot is a remarkable traveller, covering nearly ten thousand miles in its round-trip journey from southern South America to the Arctic and back each year. Some birds may fly non-stop for thousands of miles across great expanses of ocean, mountains, and deserts. Nesting is on the most northerly land masses in North America including northern Greenland and Canada's Arctic Archipelago. During the North American winter, they will be enjoying summer in the southern hemisphere as far south as Terra del Fuego on the southern tip of South America. Along the way these world travelers will sometimes stop for a brief rest somewhere in Ohio, usually along the shores of Lake Erie. Compared to many other Sandpiper species that travel through the state, the Red Knot is rather rare.

Size: 12 inches.

Presumed range in Ohio

Abundance: Rare in Ohio.

Migratory Status: Rare summer resident from mid-April though mid-September.

Variation: Fall and juvenile plumages slightly paler than breeding adults.

Habitat: An obligate of grasslands and prairies. Migrants will also use pastures and fields.

Breeding: Nest is a shallow scrape on the ground lined with grass. Four eggs.

Natural History: The bulk of the Upland Sandpiper's summer range is in the northern Great Plains. A few summer very sparsely east of the Mississippi River and into Ohio. Unlike most other members of the sandpiper family, the Upland Sandpiper avoids coastal areas in favor of prairies and grasslands well into the interior of the continent. Historically, these birds were much more numerous. Market hunting in the late 19th century saw countless numbers of dead Upland Sandpipers shipped by rail from their nesting grounds on the northern plains to markets in the east. At the same time they were being hunted mercilessly on their winter habitats in the Pampas of South America. Even more devastating to their populations was the conversion of the native American prairie to cropland. Amazingly, the species survives. They are rare and declining in Ohio and are regarded as an Endangered Species by ODNR.

Class—**Aves** (birds)

Order—**Chariidriformes** (shorebirds)

Family—**Scolopacidae** (sandpipers)

Greater Yellowlegs *Tringa melanoleuca*	**Lesser Yellowlegs** *Tringa flavipes*	**Solitary Sandpiper** *Tringa solitaria*

Summer

Summer

Winter

Size: 14 inches.

Size: 10.5 inches.

Presumed range in Ohio (both species)

Size: 8.5 inches.

Presumed range in Ohio

Abundance: Greater Yellowlegs is usually the less common of the two, but both species are fairly common during migration.

Migratory Status: Both species are transient spring and fall migrants but they can be seen in Ohio from March through October (except they are both absent through most of June). Peak spring migration is in late April and early May. Fall peak for Greater is August/September. Lesser begins fall migration as early as July.

Abundance: Fairly common.

Migratory Status: April and May. July to October. Peak fall migration is in August.

Variation: Speckled appearance is less prominent on winter adults and juveniles of both species.

Variation: Summer plumage has more distinct white spotting on the back.

Habitat: Both species are seen in a wide variety of wetland habitats during migration, including mudflats, flooded agricultural fields, and marshes.

Habitat: Pond margins, lake shores, and along creeks and rivers.

Breeding: Greater breeds in northern bogs, Lesser in drier, more upland habitats. Both species nest on the ground and three to four eggs is the typical clutch size for both.

Breeding: Nests in trees and uses old songbird nests. Three to five eggs, usually four.

Natural History: These two related species are frequently seen together. When seen together they are easily recognized by size. When not in found in mixed flocks they are best identified by the shape of the bill. Greater's bill is longer and ever so slightly upturned at the tip. The Greater Yellowlegs is the least social of the two, and although it is seen in small flocks it can also be seen singly. Both species were once heavily hunted and during the days of market hunting both species experienced steep population declines. Hunting still occurs in some areas of their migratory range, especially in the Caribbean. Both spend the summer in the boreal regions of Canada and Alaska and winter from the Gulf Coast of the southeastern United States southward into South America. Food items for the Greater include both aquatic and terrestrial invertebrates as well as some small aquatic vertebrates like small frogs or fish. Lesser's food items are mainly invertebrates, both aquatic and terrestrial, but some small fish are also eaten. Both feed mostly by wading in shallows, but the Lesser is a more active feeder, wading rapidly and picking food from both the surface and the water column. It will also feed in this manner in terrestrial habitats such as grassy shorelines or meadow areas. Greater feeds both diurnally and at night, when it employs a sweeping motion of the bill back and forth through the water, apparently catching food by feel. The major threat to both species today is probably loss of habitat, both on wintering grounds in South America (loss of wetlands) and on summer range in North America, i.e., logging in boreal forests (Greater), and loss of wetlands in Alaska (lesser).

Natural History: As implied by their name, the Solitary Sandpipers are nearly always seen alone during migration. In this respect they differ markedly from most other members of their family. They also differ in their nesting habits, as they are the only North American member of the Scolopacidae family that nests in trees. When feeding it wades in shallows and plucks its food from the surface or beneath the water. Rarely probes the mud with its bill. Food is mostly invertebrates, both aquatic and terrestrial. Insects make up the bulk of the terrestrial foods. They also take aquatic insects and their larvae, small, crustaceans, snails, and some vertebrate prey such as small minnows or tadpoles. Due to their solitary habits and the fact that they breed in trees in remote boreal forests, little is known about their population status, but it appears to be stable.

Class—**Aves** (birds)

Order—**Chariidriformes** (shorebirds)

Family—**Scolopacidae** (sandpipers)

Willet *Tringa semipalmata*	**Wilson's Phalarope** *Phalaropus tricolor*	**Short-billed Dowitcher** *Limnodromus griseus*

Size: 15 inches.	Presumed range in Ohio	**Size:** 9.5 inches.	Presumed range in Ohio	**Size:** 11 inches.	Presumed range in Ohio
Abundance: Rare in Ohio.		**Abundance:** Rare in Ohio.		**Abundance:** Fairly common.	
Migratory Status: Migrant. Seen in in spring in late summer / early fall.		**Migratory Status:** Has been observed in Ohio from from May to September.		**Migratory Status:** Migrant. Peaks in May. Also in July, August and Sept.	

Variation: No sexual dimorphism but does exhibit seasonal plumage variations. Winter plumage (not seen in Ohio) lacks brown speckling.

Habitat: In migration uses pond banks, mud flats, lake shores, riverbanks, and flooded fields.

Breeding: Lays four eggs in nest on the ground. Does not nest in Ohio. Migrants nest on the northern plains.

Natural History: The Willet is a true "shorebird" that is quite familiar to those who frequent America's seashores. Both coasts of America are home to Willets during the winter, and some will nest in coastal marshes. Others fly into the interior of North America and nest as far north as the central Canadian prairie. It is these migrants that can sometimes be seen in Ohio. Crustaceans, mollusks, insects, small fish, and polycheate worms are listed as food items. Feeds both day and night. In the 1800s they were hunted for food and for their eggs which were also eaten, resulting in a significant decrease in populations. Today these are fairly common shorebirds whose population appears stable at an estimate of about a quarter of a million birds. In Ohio the most likely place to see this rare migrant is along the Lake Erie shoreline.

Variation: Sexual, seasonal, and ontogenic variations. Non-breeding birds are gray above and all white beneath. Juveniles are mottled brown above.

Habitat: Uses marshes on breeding range, shallow water habitats along lake shores, ponds, etc. in migration.

Breeding: Breeds on inland marshes and wetlands in the west-central US and Canada. Always lays four eggs.

Natural History: Phalaropes are known for the unique role reversal of the sexes. In these birds the female is the most vividly colored while the male has drab plumage. Even more unusual, it is the male that incubates the eggs in the nest. These birds are salt lake specialists and during migration they congregate in large flocks around alkaline and highly saline lakes of the interior of North America. The winter habitat is similar saline lakes in the Andes Mountains of South America. Birds seen in Ohio are mostly rare wanderers, but there is evidence of rare nesting occurring in the state. They may range over a wider portion of Ohio than shown on the map above during migration. The slightly smaller (eight-inch) **Red-necked Phalarope** (*P. lobatus*) may also be seen in Ohio along the Lake Erie shoreline on rare occasions during migration periods.

Variation: Breeding birds are rich brown. Winter birds uniformly gray with whitish belly. Sexes are alike (see photos above).

Habitat: In inland migrations dowitchers use mud flats and lake shores. Many migrate along the coasts.

Breeding: Breeds in bog and muskeg habitats of northern Canada and Alaska. Both species lay four eggs.

Natural History: The nearly identical **Long-billed Dowitcher** (*Limnodromus scolopaceus*-not shown) can also be seen in Ohio during spring and fall migrations, though it is less common than the Short-billed Dowitcher. Distinguishing between the two in the field is difficult even for experts. The Long-billed is slightly larger at 11.5 inches. It migrates earlier in the spring and later in the fall than the Short-billed. In Ohio, the Long-billed is seen mostly in the far northern portion of the state. The Short-billed may be seen anywhere in the state. Like many shorebirds both species of dowitcher were heavily hunted during the days of market hunting. At that time, it was not known that the two similar dowitchers constituted two distinct species. The existence of two species was not finally confirmed until 1950.

Class—**Aves** (birds)

Order—**Chariidriformes** (shorebirds)

Family—**Scolopacidae** (sandpipers)

Woodcock *Scolapax minor*	Wilson's Snipe *Gallinago delicata*	Ruddy Turnstone *Arenaria interpres*

Size: 11 inches.	Presumed range in Ohio	**Size:** 10.5 inches.	Presumed range in Ohio	**Size:** 9.5 inches.	Presumed range in Ohio
Abundance: Fairly common.		**Abundance:** Fairly common.		**Abundance:** Uncommon.	
Migratory Status: Seen in Ohio from Feb. through mid-Nov. Most common in the spring.		**Migratory Status:** Can be seen Year-round in Ohio. More common in migration periods.		**Migratory Status:** Spring and fall migrant, seen in Ohio mostly late spring and early fall.	

Variation: No plumage variations. Females are significantly larger.	**Variation:** No significant sexual or seasonal plumage differences.	**Variation:** Seasonal plumage variations. Breeding plumage shown above.
Habitat: Swamps, regenerative woodlands, thickets, and weedy fields in bottomlands or uplands with moist soils.	**Habitat:** Mudflats, flooded grassy fields, marshes, river bars, water-filled ditches, temporary pools, and grassy pond banks.	**Habitat:** Winters on sandy beaches along both coasts. May use lake shores, mud flats, or river banks during inland migrations
Breeding: Nest is on the ground and not concealed. Lays four eggs as early as late February.	**Breeding:** A rare nester in wetlands in northernmost Ohio. Lays four eggs in nest on a hummock within marsh or swamp.	**Breeding:** Breeds in the arctic tundra and coastlines from Siberia and Alaska across Canada to Greenland.
Natural History: The Woodcock is unique among American sandpipers in that it is strictly an inland species. It is also the most common member of its family that breeds widely throughout the state. Woodcock are known for their elaborate courtship flights that consist of an upward twisting corkscrew accompanied by a twittering call. The long beak is used to probe moist soils for invertebrates. Among its unique features are a flexible upper bill that aids in extracting the favorite food, earthworms, and eyes which are situated far back on the head, allowing for backward vision while feeding. One of the most remarkably cryptic of the sandpipers, Woodcocks are nearly impossible to detect when motionless on the forest floor. Woodcock are classified as a game bird and hunted in many areas, including Ohio.	**Natural History:** As with other members of the sandpiper family, the beak of the Wilson's Snipe contains sensory pits near the tip which help to locate invertebrate prey hidden in the mud. It also shares the Woodcock's rearward positioned eyes for watching behind and above while feeding. This is another highly camouflaged species that is nearly invisible when immobile. It is one of the most common and widespread members of the sandpiper family that often relys on its cryptic coloration when approached. Sitting quietly until nearly trod upon it will burst from the grass with a twisting, erratic flight while emitting a raspy call. Like the Woodcock the Wilson's Snipe is regarded as a game bird, but few people hunt them. Their breeding populations in Ohio have been negatively impacted by loss of wetland habitats.	**Natural History:** Most Ruddy Turnstones travel up and down America's coastlines during migration, but a few migrate through inland regions of the continent. This is one of the most northerly ranging birds in America, traveling to the northernmost extreme of the continent to breed each summer. Its name comes from its habit of using its beak to overturn pebbles and stones on beaches in search of small invertebrate prey. It also feeds on ocean carrion found on beaches. On the breeding grounds the primary food source is mosquitoes and other dipteran insects. The unusual genus (*Arenaria*) contains only two species and their position in the phylogeny of the shorebirds is unclear. In Ohio they are most commonly seen in the northern part of the state, especially in the vicinity of Lake Erie. Migrants may rarely be seen statewide.

Class—**Aves** (birds)

Order—**Chariidriformes** (shorebirds)

Family—**Scolopacidae** (sandpipers)

Family—**Laridae** (gulls and terns)

Spotted Sandpiper *Actitis macularia*	Glaucus Gull *Larus hyperboreus*	Great Black-backed Gull *Larus marinus*

Size: 7.5 inches.

Abundance: Fairly common

Migratory Status: Summer resident. Arrives in April. Departs in late summer or early fall.

Presumed range in Ohio

Variation: Winter birds lack the spots on the breast and are grayer on the back. Most Spotted Sandpipers seen in Ohio will be in summer plumage.

Habitat: In migration uses edges of ponds, lake shores, stream courses, and river bars.

Breeding: Nests on the ground in grassy situations. Lays two to four eggs. Widespread nester in glaciated Ohio.

Natural History: Unlike most sandpipers that exhibit strong flocking tendencies, the Spotted Sandpiper is always seen singly or in very small groups. This is one of the most widespread sandpipers in America and one of the few that nests in the lower forty-eight. The distinctly spotted breast along with a habit of constantly bobbing up and down makes the Spotted Sandpiper one of the most recognizable members of the Scolopacidae family. Feeds on a wide variety of aquatic and terrestrial invertebrates, especially dipteran (fly) larvae. Also eats significant quantities of mayflies, crickets, grasshoppers, caterpillars, beetles, and mollusks, crustaceans, and worms. In Ohio this species is reportedly common along the major rivers of the state in summer, where it uses riverbanks and gravel bars.

Size: 27 inches.

Abundance: Uncommon in Ohio.

Migratory Status: Winter resident throughout Lake Erie and along the Lake Erie shoreline.

Presumed range in Ohio

Variation: Juveniles are dusky and have a pinkish bill with a distinct black tip. Adults are pure white on head, breast, and belly with pale gray wings.

Habitat: Northern coastlines of both coasts in winter. Arctic coasts in summer. Habitat in Ohio is Lake Erie.

Breeding: Nest is on the ground in open tundra. Often on ledges or atop steep cliffs. Usually lays three eggs.

Natural History: This is a northern gull that breeds far to the north on arctic coasts. Winters on northern coastlines, both Pacific and Atlantic and also throughout the Great Lakes region. They are rarely seen inland from Lake Erie in Ohio. As with most gull species they are opportunistic predators as well as unashamed scavengers. The list of food items includes most types of aquatic organisms that are small enough to be swallowed as well as terrestrial foods such as the eggs and chicks of other birds that may be nesting nearby. There are two other similar gull species that nest in the arctic and can be seen on Lake Erie in the winter. They are the **Thayer's Gull** (*Larus thayeri*), and the **Iceland Gull** (*Larus glaucoides*). Both are similar in habits and habitat to the more common Glaucus Gull.

Size: 30 inches.

Abundance: Fairly common.

Migratory Status: Winter resident along the Lake Erie shoreline and northernmost Ohio.

Presumed range in Ohio

Variation: Age-related plumage varition significant. Juveniles are mottled brown on the wings and the back. Adults have jet black wings and back.

Habitat: A gull of the Atlantic coastline from Nova Scotia to Florida. Winter habitat includes the Great Lakes.

Breeding: Nests in the far northeastern coastline of North America. Three eggs is typical. Nest is a scrape on the ground.

Natural History: At thirty inches in length and with a nearly five-and-a-half-foot wingspan, the Great Black-backed Gull is the largest and heaviest gull in America. By the early 1900s the Great Black-backed Gull had become a very rare bird in America due to egg collecting and feather hunting. Today the species is recovering and may be expanding its range. Like all gulls it is an oportunistic feeder and it may have benefited from utilizing human refuse as food source. Another very similar but smaller gull species, the **Lesser Black-backed Gull** (*Larus fuscus*) can also be seen in the Great Lakes region in winter, though it is much less common. The Lesser Black-backed Gull is a much smaller gull at 21 inches in length, but has the same color pattern as the Great Black-backed Gull.

Class—**Aves** (birds)

Order—**Chariidriformes** (shorebirds)

Family—**Laridae** (gulls and terns)

Ringed-billed Gull *Larus delawarensis*	Herring Gull *Larus argentatus*	Bonapartes Gull *Chroicocephalus philadelphia*
	  Juvenile / Adult	  Winter

Ringed-billed Gull

Size: 17.5 inches.

Presumed range in Ohio

Abundance: Very common.

Migratory Status: Year-round resident in north, winter resident or migrant statewide.

Variation: Juveniles are brownish gray, two-year-olds resemble adults but with greenish legs and bill.

Habitat: Primarily in the vicinity of lakes and rivers, but also in rural crop fields and in urban areas.

Breeding: Nest is usually on the ground on sandbars or rocky beaches. May nest on rooftops in urban areas. Lays two to four eggs.

Natural History: The Ring-billed Gull is one of the most common and widespread gull species in America. Most population estimates put their number in the millions, and they may be increasing. This is the gull commonly seen around inland lakes in summer and along coastal beaches in winter. They are also seen in urban parking lots or hanging around fast food restaurants ready to swoop in and grab a dropped french fry. They can be common in garbage dumps and may be seen foraging with starlings and other urban birds around dumpsters. These are highly gregarious birds that travel in flocks and nest in colonies. Food is almost anything, from carrion to insects, fish, rodents, earthworms, and human refuse. Nesting in Ohio occurs along Lake Erie and urban areas in glaciated Ohio.

Herring Gull

Size: 25 inches.

Presumed range in Ohio

Abundance: Common.

Migratory Status: Year-round resident in north, winter resident or migrant statewide.

Variation: Highly variable as juvenile. Younger birds are dark brownish gray with dark eyes ad get lighter with age.

Habitat: In Ohio these birds are most common along Lake Erie. But they do occur across much of glaciated Ohio.

Breeding: Nest is on the ground in a bowl-shaped scrape lined with vegetation. Also nest on rooftops in urban areas. Two to three eggs are laid.

Natural History: Like the smaller Ring-billed Gull, the Herring Gull is an opportunistic feeder that will eat almost anything, including human garbage. This fact may account in part for their population rebound in recent decades. Like other gull species, they are gregarious and they often nest in large colonies. Only about 50 percent of the young gulls hatched each year reach adulthood, but the species seems to be thriving. Their numbers were drastically reduced during the 1800s but they have recovered completely and may be more numerous now than in historic times. The presence of man-made garbage dumps that serve as a smorgasboard for these birds may explain their recent population expansion. They are widespread in their distribution and are common on both of America's coastlines.

Bonapartes Gull

Size: 13.5 inches.

Presumed range in Ohio

Abundance: Fairly common.

Migratory Status: Year-round but most common in fall and early winter. Moves south with freeze up.

Variation: Summer plumage adult shave a black head. Juveniles resemble winter adults.

Habitat: Frequents large rivers and larger lakes when in Ohio. Summer habitat is wetlands in boreal forests.

Breeding: The only gull that nests in trees, using conifers bordering remote lakes in Canada and Alaska. Typically lays three eggs.

Natural History: Many people tend to lump all gull species together and refer to them all as "seagulls." Most species however, including the Bonaparte's Gull, are often inland birds during the breeding season. Like other gulls, many Bonaparte's Gulls will spend the winter along America's coastlines and sometimes far out to sea. Small to moderately large flocks can be seen on inland rivers and lakes in throughout Ohio during migration and through early winter. America's smallest gull, they feed mostly on small fish such as shad and shiners, but like other gulls they are highly opportunistic feeders and will eat a wide variety of insects and other invertebrates. Unlike other gull species however, they are not typically seen around towns or dumps. They will gather in large flocks for migration.

Class—**Aves** (birds)

Order—**Chariidriformes** (shorebirds)

Family—**Laridae** (gulls and terns)

Franklin's Gull *Leucophaeus pipixcan*	**Little Gull** *Hydrocoloeus minutus*	**Forster's Tern** *Sterna fosteri*

Size: 14.5 inches.	Presumed range in Ohio 	**Size:** 11 inches.	Presumed range in Ohio 	**Size:** 14 inches.	Presumed range in Ohio 
Abundance: Rare in Ohio.		**Abundance:** Very rare.		**Abundance:** Uncommon.	
Migratory Status: Migrant. Most migrate through the great plains but a few wanderers may be seen in Ohio.		**Migratory Status:** Migrant and very rare winter resident. May be seen on Lake Erie from late August through April.		**Migratory Status:** Migrant. Most common in April/May and August/September. A few may be around all summer.	

Variation: Specimen shown above is an adult in breeding plumage. In winter and juvenile birds the black hood is replaced by a gray head with a white forehead and the bill is solid black.	**Variation:** Adult birds in breeding plumage have an all black head. Non-breeding adults and juveniles have black reduced to the top of the head and a prominent black blotch behind the eye.	**Variation:** Exhibits both seasonal and age-related plumage variations. Juveniles resemble winter adults (see photos above) but juveniles have more of a brownish coloration on the back.
Habitat: Migrants use lakes, rivers, marshes, flooded fields, and pastures.	**Habitat:** In Ohio this gull is seen only on Lake Erie.	**Habitat:** Marshes. Both fresh and salt. Also beaches and coastlines.
Breeding: Breeds in marshes in the great plains of Canada and north central US. Nest is on floating mats of vegetation amid marshland. Lays two to four eggs.	**Breeding:** There are only a few dozen records of this species breeding in America. Nest is in marsh on floating mats of vegetation. Lays three to four eggs.	**Breeding:** Breeds both along the gulf coast and on inland marshes in the center of the continent. One to four eggs in nest of matted vegetation within marsh.
Natural History: Adults in breeding plumage have a faint pinkish blush on the breast and belly feathers. A few of these breeding birds may pass through Ohio in spring, but most Franklin's Gulls seen in Ohio appear during southward migration in the fall. As with other gull species, the Franklin's Gull matures slowly and it takes three years to achieve the mature adult plumage shown in the photo above. Like other gulls the Franklin's is an opportunistic feeder that will eat both plant and animal matter. Most foods are invertebrates (insects, worms, crustaceans, etc.). Another gull with a black head that may rarely be seen in Ohio is the **Laughing Gull** (*L. atricilla*), although that species is "accidental" in Ohio.	**Natural History:** A native of the old world, the Little Gull apparently become established in North America as recently as a few decades ago. They are most common along the northeast coast of the US, but are rare even there. In Ohio this species is seen only on Lake Erie where it is extremely rare. Very few studies have been conducted into the natural history of this species in North America and less in known about it than any other gull in America. It usually occurs in small flocks or in the company of other gull species such as the Bonapartes Gull. At only 11 inches long it is the world's smallest gull species. It feeds on small fishes and insects and will also scavenge. Probably consumes aquatic invertebrates as well.	**Natural History:** This species is probably most common in Ohio in the vicinity of Lake Erie. They can be seen statewide during migration, usually frequenting the states major river systems and large impoundments or natural lakes. They are sometimes seen in the company of gulls and other tern species, especially in winter along the coastlines of America where gulls and terns are both extremely common. These medium-size terns feed almost exclusively on small fish that are captured by diving from above. When "fishing" they fly back and forth over water with the bill pointed downward and plunge headlong into the water. They are graceful fliers that sometimes hover when schools of fish are located.

Class—**Aves** (birds)

Order—**Chariidriformes** (shorebirds)

Family—**Laridae** (gulls and terns)

Common Tern *Sterna hirundo*	**Caspian Tern** *Hydroprogne caspia*	**Black Tern** *Chlidonias niger*

Common Tern — **Size:** 15 inches. **Abundance:** Common. **Migratory Status:** Spring, summer, and early fall resident. Most common near Lake Erie from July through October. *Presumed range in Ohio*

Variation: First-year juveniles and winter birds have white foreheads and all black bill. White on forehead reduced on second-year juvenile in summer colors.

Habitat: Migrating birds usually associate with major rivers and large lakes. Islands and beaches are frequently used.

Breeding: Nests mostly in Canada and along the Atlantic coastline. A few nest in Ohio on man-made platforms in Lake Erie marshes. Lays two to three eggs.

Natural History: The Common Tern is well known to conservationists. They are symbolic of the fight to save many of America's bird species from wanton slaughter. From the early European settlement of North America to the late 1800s, unregulated over-hunting of America's wildlife nearly wiped out many species. Millions of herons, egrets, waterfowl, and shorebirds were killed for food and for the millinery trade. At the same time America's large mammal species also suffered dramatic population declines. Today many wildlife species, including terns, have recovered dramatically, but tern populations are still below historical numbers nationwide and the Common Tern is an endangered species in Ohio.

Caspian Tern — **Size:** 21 inches. **Abundance:** Uncommon. **Migratory Status:** Migrant. Most common April and May and again in August/September. Rare in summer. *Presumed range in Ohio*

Variation: In winter birds the black cap becomes mottled with white. Juveniles are similar to winter adults. Sexes are alike.

Habitat: Mainly coastal birds in winter, they use rivers, large lakes, and marshes in migration.

Breeding: North American populations nest both on coasts and large bodies of water in the interior of the continent. Does not nest in Ohio. One to three eggs.

Natural History: The worlds largest tern and also the most widespread. Found all over the world, the Caspian Tern breeds on every continent except Antarctica. Despite its wide range it is not as common in North America as many other terns. Feeds almost entirely on fish. Feeds by hovering and diving. When diving often submerges completely. Food is mostly fish. This is the only large tern regularly seen inland. They are found along the southern coastlines as well and in winter stay along the coasts. They are also seen inland in winter throughout the Florida peninsula. Although they will nest in some of the great lakes farther to the north, they do not nest on Lake Erie. These large terns are known to live up to 26 years.

Black Tern — **Size:** 9.75 inches. **Abundance:** Rare in Ohio **Migratory Status:** Summer resident of western Lake Erie marshes. Rare migrant elsewhere in the state. *Presumed range in Ohio*

Variation: In winter and in juvenile birds the dramatic black color of the breast and belly is replaced by white. Transitional plumage shown above.

Habitat: Habitat in Ohio is the shallow, freshwater marshes along Lake Erie.

Breeding: Nest is built upon floating vegetation or muskrat platforms. Nests can be vulnerable to flooding. Two to three eggs is typical.

Natural History: Winters along coastlines from Central America to northern South America. There is a European subspecies that winters in Africa. Like most terns these birds are highly social and usually seen in flocks. Unlike other terns however they feed heavily on insects, especially in summer. This is the only tern seen in Ohio that has a dark breast and belly. Although the number of Black Terns today is estimated to be in the hundreds of thousands, this Figure is paltry compared to the size of the population that existed before modern agricultural practices destroyed much of their breeding habitat. Always rare in Ohio, they are regarded as an endangered species by ODNR.

Class—**Aves** (birds)

Order—**Gaviiformes** (loons)	Order—**Pelecaniformes** (pelicans)	Order—**Suliiformes** (tropical sea birds)
Family—**Gaviidea**	Family—**Pelecanidae**	Family—**Phalacrocoracidae** (cormorants)
Common Loon *Gavia immer*	**White Pelican** *Pelecanus erythrorhynchos*	**Double-crested Cormorant** *Phalacrocorax auritus*

Summer

Red-throated Loon—winter

Winter

Size: 32 inches.	**Size:** 62 inches.	**Size:** 33 inches.
Abundance: Uncommon in Ohio.	**Abundance:** Rare in Ohio.	**Abundance:** Common.
Migratory Status: Spring/fall migrant mostly. Rare resident in summer and early winter.	**Migratory Status:** Spring-fall migrant. Seen in Ohio March to June and again from Sept. to Nov.	**Migratory Status:** Spring through fall resident in north; rare year-round in southern Ohio.

Presumed range in Ohio (all three)

Variation: Sexes are alike but exhibits significant seasonal plumage changes. See photos above.

Variation: Juvenile birds are duskier and have a dusky gray bill. Breeding birds develop a projection on the bill.

Variation: Juveniles are much browner and have whitish throat and breast. Breeding plumage has white crest.

Habitat: Highly aquatic. In inland areas such as Ohio the Common Loon lives on lakes. They may also be seen along both coasts in winter.

Habitat: In Ohio restricted to larger lakes and rivers. Elsewhere commonly uses large marshlands, natural and man-made lakes, large rivers, and coastlines.

Habitat: Lakes, rivers, estuaries, and swamplands. In Ohio they are most common on the islands in Lake Erie. Increasing throughout Ohio.

Breeding: Nests is built on small islands in northern lakes. Usually lays two eggs. Chicks often ride on adults back.

Breeding: Nests in colonies in protected areas such as islands on large lakes. Does not nest in Ohio. Lays two eggs.

Breeding: Large colonies nest on islands in Lake Erie. Bulky nest of sticks and floating debris. Lays two to four eggs.

Natural History: On lakes and marshes in the far north the call of the Common Loon echoes through the wilderness. The sound is so distinctive and unique that it has inspired many poetic depictions. "Haunting," "ethereal," and "lonely" are words that are often used in conjunction with describing its yodeling cry that can carry for a great distance. They call both day and night on the breeding grounds in the northern half of the continent, but they are rarely heard calling on their winter range. Remarkable swimmers, they dive beneath the surface and propel themselves through the water with their powerful webbed feet. Fish caught in this manner are the main food item. Another loon species, the **Red-throated Loon** (*G. stellata*), is a very rare late fall migrant on Lake Erie (see inset photo).

Natural History: Although wandering flocks of White Pelicans may suddenly appear on almost any large body of water in Ohio, they are most commonly seen on the western Lake Erie. Unlike their cousin the Brown Pelican which feeds by plunging into the water, White Pelicans feed in a more placid manner. Flocks of feeding White Pelicans corral fish by swimming in a coordinated group and dipping the head beneath the surface in perfect unison. The appearance of a feeding flock is that of a perfectly choreographed ballet. Competition between baby White Pelicans in the nest is fierce, and the strongest nestling often kills its sibling. Thus, usually only one of the two young survive. Primarily a bird of the southern coasts in winter and the Great Plains region in summer. Increasingly seen in Ohio.

Natural History: Cormorants are rarely seen far from water. They are thoroughly aquatic birds that have webbed feet and frequently submerge and swim underwater in search of fish. Their exclusive diet of fish and their uncanny aquatic abilities have caused these birds to come into conflict with man. Occurring in large flocks, they will concentrate in areas where food is most readily available. Under natural conditions they catch a wide variety of fish species and thus do not impact significantly upon fisheries. However, around fish farms or hatcheries they can become quite a nuisance. In some regions (including in the Lake Erie region) they have become an ecological problem by crowding out other colonial nesting species such as herons and egrets.

Class—**Aves** (birds)

Order—**Podicipediformes** (grebes)

Family—**Podicipedidae**

Red-necked Grebe *Podiceps grisegena*	**Pied-billed Grebe** *Podilymbus podiceps*	**Horned Grebe** *Podiceps auritus*

Size: 18 inches.	**Size:** 13 inches.	**Size:** 14 inches.
Presumed range in Ohio	Presumed range in Ohio	Presumed range in Ohio
Abundance: Rare in Ohio.	**Abundance:** Fairly common.	**Abundance:** Uncommon.
Migratory Status: Spring and fall migrant. April/May and Nov/Dec.	**Migratory Status:** Year-round resident. Mostly in spring, fall, and summer.	**Migratory Status:** Can be seen in Ohio from early fall through late spring.
Variation: Winter plumage is gray and white (similar to Horned Grebe photo).	**Variation:** Winter birds are grayer and lack the prominent dark ring on bill.	**Variation:** Winter plumage (shown) is usually seen in Ohio.
Habitat: Summers on shallow lakes, marshes, and bays of large lakes across Canada and Alaska. Winters in marine habitats. Bays, esturaries, and offshore.	**Habitat:** Completely aquatic, the Pied-billed Grebe uses everything from large lakes to small farm ponds. Also open water areas of swamps and marshes.	**Habitat:** In Ohio this species uses the larger lakes as well as large marshes with open water. They are not usually seen on small ponds.
Breeding: Nesting is on northern lakes. Four to five eggs is typical (as many as nine).	**Breeding:** Nests on floating platform among emergent vegetation. Four to eight eggs.	**Breeding:** Nests on floating platform among emergent vegetation. Five to seven eggs.
Natural History: By mid-winter most of these grebes are along the coasts. Some will linger in the Great Lakes into winter. In Ohio these birds are mostly restricted to the immediate area of Lake Erie. But in severe winters when the great lakes freeze over, large numbers may irrupt southward and at these times they may be seen on open water anywhere in the state. They are circumpolar in distributiion in the northern hemisphere. The grebes are known for their elaborate courship displays and "dances." As many as a dozen different postures may be displayed during one of these courtship dances. The pair often engage in a mutually responsive movements that does give the appearance of two highly choreographed dancers. Feeding is done entirely in the water. Most feeding is in shallows but they are capable swimmers and divers and may feed in deep water. Food items include fish, crustaceans, and aquatic insects.	**Natural History:** A night-time migrator, this little grebe evades potential threats by submerging and they sometimes swim with just the head sticking out the water. They feed on a wide variety of small fish and other aquatic vertebrates as well as crustaceans and insects. This is the most widespread and common grebe in North America and they range from coast to coast. They are most common during summer in the "Prairie Pothole" habitats of the west-central US and Canada. In winter they move as far south as Central America. They can be seen all winter across the southern half of the US, but tend to concentrate along the gulf coast in winter. Most breed in more northerly regions of the continent, but there are a widespread records of Pied-billed Grebes breeding throughout the glaciated regions of Ohio. These little grebes are almost never seen in flight as they escape threats by diving and swimming.	**Natural History:** As is the case with other grebes (and loons), their adaptations for an aquatic lifestyle include the legs being positioned far back on the body. The legs can also be flared outward to a remarkable degree to facilitate underwater swimming maneuvers. As a result of this adaptation, these birds are very clumsy on land and walk with difficulty. Breeding on marshes and lakes in the northernmost portions of the continent, these birds are a transient migrant in much of Ohio. Breeding birds (seen in Ohio in spring) are handsomely marked with chestnut neck and flanks and golden brown head stripe that flares out to form "horns." Food is small fish, crustaceans, insects, etc. Their summer range is to the west and north of Ohio, while the winter range is well to south. Thus this grebe is a transient migrant that is seen rather briefly within Ohio.

Class—**Aves** (birds)

Order—**Anseriformes** (waterfowl)

Family—**Anatidae** (ducks, geese, and swans)

Mallard *Anas platyrhynchos*	**Black Duck** *Anas rubripes*	**Northern Pintail** *Anas acuta*

Size: 23 inches.	Presumed range in Ohio	**Size:** 23 inches.	Presumed range in Ohio	**Size:** Up to 25 inches.	Presumed range in Ohio
Abundance: Very common.		**Abundance:** Uncommon.		**Abundance:** Uncommon.	
Migratory Status: Both a year-round resident and a seasonal migrant.		**Migratory Status:** Year-round breeding resident but more common as migrant.		**Migratory Status:** Absent from Ohio from late May through late summer.	

Variation: Pronounced sexual plumage variation (see photos above).

Variation: Sexes are very similar, females have a darker bill than males.

Variation: Profound sexual dimorphism (see photos above). Male larger.

Habitat: Found in aquatic situations everywhere, from deserts to tundra to southern swamplands, ponds, lakes, etc.

Habitat: Fond of estuaries and coastal marshes. Inland will use other aquatic habitats (lake, marshes, swamps, etc.).

Habitat: Open country. In Ohio uses large flooded bottomland fields and marshes along river valleys.

Breeding: Nests on the ground in close proximity to water. Lays up to 13 eggs and will re-nest if nest is destroyed.

Breeding: For breeding favors coastal marshes and beaver ponds and bogs in boreal forests. Lays up to 14 eggs.

Breeding: Breeds in marshes, potholes, and tundra in the northern and western portions of the continent. Three to 12 eggs.

Natural History: By far the most familiar duck in America. The Mallards has been widely domesticated but it is also the most common wild duck in the United States. Many parks and public lakes around the country have semi-wild populations that are non-migratory. Highly adaptable, this is the most successful duck species in America, perhaps in the world. It is the source of all breeds of domestic duck except the Muscovey and they are thus an important food source for humans. They are also a highly regarded game bird and they are hunted throughout North America. They range throughout the northern half of the globe and their range in the western hemisphere closely coincides with the North American continent. Mallards are one of the most common breeding ducks in Ohio. Between wild ducks and semi-tame populations in urban parks, breeding has been recorded in every county.

Natural History: The Black Duck is very similar to the Mallard in size, shape, and voice, and the two species are known to hybridize. In appearance and other traits however they are quite different. This is one of the few puddle ducks that does not range throughout the continent, being restricted to the eastern half of America. Like many of America's duck species, the Black Duck has been impacted negatively by human-related changes to the landscape and environment in America. Drainage of wetlands, urbanization along northeastern coastlines, and deforestation have hit this species harder than most other ducks and the population has declined significantly in the last half-century. Interbreeding with the more adaptable Mallard may also be a threat to this uniquely American Duck. Though they may be seen throughout the state as a migrant or winter resident, as a breeding bird they are very rare in Ohio.

Natural History: Northern Pintail populations are in decline. Modern agricultural practices on the great plains of the US and Canada are the greatest threat. They are also highly susceptible to droughts in the prairie regions, which limit breeding habitat. Food is mostly plant material but some aquatic invertebrates are also eaten. On wintering grounds waste grain from farming operations has become an important food source. In recent decades the species has benefited from a number of conservation efforts by state and federal agencies as well as private organizations, most notably Ducks Unlimited, an organization funded by duck hunters. Conservation efforts that have recently benefited the species are reduced hunter harvest and changing agricultural practices in the in the prairie pothole region. Though large numbers may migrate through the state, the Pintail is very rare as a breeding duck in Ohio.

Class—**Aves** (birds)

Order—**Anseriformes** (waterfowl)

Family—**Anatidae** (ducks, geese, and swans)

Gadwall *Anas strepera*	American Wigeon *Anas americana*	Green-winged Teal *Anas crecca*

Size: 20 inches.

Abundance: Fairly common.

Migratory Status: Winter resident, seasonal migrant and rare year-round.

Presumed range in Ohio

Variation: Significant sexual dimorphism (see photos above).

Habitat: Marshes and potholes of the great plains in summer. Uses all aquatic habitats in winter.

Breeding: Nests among thick vegetation near water, often on islands in marshes or lakes. Lays seven to 12 eggs.

Natural History: Gadwalls breed and summer largely in the great plains region. In winter they are seen all across the southern half of America, with the greatest numbers wintering along the western gulf coast coastal plain. Populations of this duck can fluctuate significantly depending upon water levels in the prairies of Canada and the north-central US. Droughts and poor agricultural practices that eliminate habitat can cause populations to plummet. Conversely, good rainfall and good wildlife conservation practices by farmers have shown to be a real boon to this and many other duck species that depend on the marshes and potholes on the great plains for nesting habitat. Adult Gadwalls feed mostly on plant material. Ducklings rely heavily upon high protein invertebrates for growth and development. The Gadwall is a rare breeder in Ohio's western Lake Erie marshlands.

Size: 19 inches.

Abundance: Fairly common.

Migratory Status: Winter resident, seasonal migrant and rare year-round.

Presumed range in Ohio

Variation: Significant sexual variation. See photos above.

Habitat: Winter range includes all types of aquatic habitats in the state (swamps, marshes, lakes, ponds, etc.).

Breeding: Nests near shallow freshwater wetlands and potholes mostly in the North American prairie. Three to 12 eggs.

Natural History: The American Wigeon also goes by the name "Baldpate," a reference to the white crown of the male. This duck has a very similar old world counter part, the Eurasian Wigeon, which ranges throughout much of Europe and Asia. American birds feed mostly on plant material, but females when breeding opt for a higher protein diet of invertebrates. One of the more northerly ranging members of the "puddle duck" group, some individuals will summer as far north as the Arctic coastal plain of Alaska. These ducks may be seen in Ohio from September through April, but peak numbers occur in late fall or early spring. Some merely pass through the state during north-south migrations, but a some may reside in Ohio throughout the winter. A few will nest in the western Lake Erie marshes. As with other puddle ducks, this species is susceptible to population declines during droughts.

Size: 14 inches.

Abundance: Fairly common.

Migratory Status: Spring-fall migrant very rare breeder and rare winter resident.

Presumed range in Ohio

Variation: Significant sexual variation. See photos above.

Habitat: Winter range includes all types of aquatic habitats in the state (swamps, marshes, lakes, ponds, etc.).

Breeding: Nest is in dense vegetation in wetland habitats of the far north. Six to nine eggs are laid as early as May.

Natural History: This is the smallest of America's "puddle ducks," and also one of the more common. They range throughout the northern hemisphere, with a distinct subspecies being found in Eurasia. They are fast and agile fliers and flocks of Green-winged Teal move back and forth across the southern half of the continent all winter in response to weather patterns. Populations of this duck appear stable and may even be increasing. About 90 percent of the population breeds in Canada and Alaska where they favor river deltas and boreal wetlands over the typical "pothole" habitats used by many puddle ducks. Some nesting has occurred in northern Ohio. Their remote nesting habitats in the far north are largely undisturbed by man, which may account in part for this species' abundance. As with many species, the increasing daylight hours of spring triggers migration and breeding instincts.

Class—**Aves** (birds)

Order—**Anseriformes** (waterfowl)

Family—**Anatidae** (ducks, geese, and swans)

Blue-winged Teal *Anas discors*	**Shoveler** *Anas clypeata*	**Wood Duck** *Aix sponsa*
 Male  Female	 Male  Female	 Male  Female

Size: 15.5 inches.

Presumed range in Ohio

Abundance: Fairly common.

Migratory Status: Spring through fall resident. March to November.

Variation: Significant sexual dimorphism (see photos above).

Habitat: Marshes, beaver ponds, bays, and other shallow-water habitats.

Breeding: Nest is concealed in dense vegetation near water but above high water line. Lays six to 12 eggs.

Natural History: The food of this species is mostly plant material including algae and aquatic greenery. Many seeds and grains are also eaten, especially in winter when they converge on rice fields and other flooded agricultural areas in America's lower coastal plain. Breeding females will consume large amounts of invertebrates during the breeding season. These ducks are early fall migrators and one of the last to migrate back north in the spring. Many will winter as far south as South America, but substantial numbers can be seen along the lower coastal plain of North America all winter. Most breed and spend the summer on the central prairies of the US and Canada. But widespread breeding has been documented across Ohio. By far the most breeding in Ohio occurs in the western Lake Erie region. Young ducks are typically highly precocial, and babies will leave the nest within hours of hatching.

Size: 19 inches.

Presumed range in Ohio

Abundance: Fairly common.

Migratory Status: Mostly September through May. A few remain year-round.

Variation: Significant sexual dimorphism (see photos above).

Habitat: Prefers shallow habitats. Swamps, marshes, flooded fields, bays.

Breeding: Breeds in northern and western United States (including Alaska) and in Canada. Averages 10 to 12 eggs.

Natural History: The Shoveler's name is derived from the unique shape of its bill, which is a highly effective sieve for straining tiny organisms from water. They are often observed swimming along with the bill held under water or skimming the surface. Like several of America's duck species, the Shoveler is holarctic in distribution and breeds in Europe and Asia as well as North America. Eurasian birds winter southward to north Africa and the pacific region. All ground-nesting birds are vulnerable to mammalian predators and the Shoveler is no exception. Red Foxes and Mink are significant predators on the nesting females, while skunks are a major threat to the eggs. Ohio represents the southeastern limit of this species breeding range and breeding of Shovelers in Ohio is rare. The nationwide population of these ducks seems to be on the increase, but waterfowl populations tend to be subject to significant annual variations.

Size: 18.5 inches.

Presumed range in Ohio

Abundance: Common.

Migratory Status: Year-round resident. Becomes scarce in north during winter.

Variation: Significant sexual dimorphism (see photos above).

Habitat: Beaver ponds, swamps, flooded woodlands, and farm ponds.

Breeding: Nests in tree hollows and takes readily to artificial nest boxes. Lays about eight to 12 eggs typically.

Natural History: Male Wood Ducks are one of the most brilliantly colored birds in America. The bulk of the Wood Duck population in America occurs in the forested eastern half of the country. Populations plummeted during the latter half of the 19th century as America's forests were felled and swamplands drained. Populations began to recover by the 1950s and today the species is thriving. Most state wildlife agencies in America began placing Wood Duck nest boxes in suitable habitat many decades ago. The ducks responded favorably and a very high percentage of babies hatch in the man-made nests annually. Wood Ducks are widely hunted and make up a significant number of ducks killed by hunters annually. Although they are a small duck, they are considered by many as highly palatable. Along with the Mallard, the Wood Duck is the most common breeding duck in Ohio.

Class—**Aves** (birds)

Order—**Anseriformes** (waterfowl)

Family—**Anatidae** (ducks, geese, and swans)

Lesser Scaup *Athya affinis*	Ring-necked Duck *Athya collaris*	Redhead *Athya americana*

Size: 16.5 inches.	**Size:** 17 inches.	**Size:** 19 inches.
Abundance: Common.	**Abundance:** Uncommon.	**Abundance:** Fairly common.
Migratory Status: Winter resident and spring/fall migrant.	**Migratory Status:** Winter resident and spring/fall migrant.	**Migratory Status:** Winter resident and spring/fall migrant.
Presumed range in Ohio	Presumed range in Ohio	Presumed range in Ohio
Variation: Sexually dimorphic. See photos above.	**Variation:** Pronounced sexual dimorphism. See photos above.	**Variation:** Pronounced sexual dimorphism. See photos above.
Habitat: Likes larger bodies of water and deeper water than many other ducks. Regularly uses large lakes and rivers in the state as well as flooded river bottoms.	**Habitat:** Open water habitats including shallow bays and flooded river bottoms. Also uses open marshes and large rivers and lakes, where it tends to use mostly shallow-water areas.	**Habitat:** Primarily a marshland species that alternates between prairie potholes and gulf coastal marshes. In migration they will use a variety of wetland habitats, especially the bays of large lakes.
Breeding: Eight to 10 eggs is typical. Nests in west-central US, Canada, and Alaska.	**Breeding:** Nests in subarctic regions of Canada and the northern Rockies in the United States. Lays six to 14 eggs.	**Breeding:** Breeds almost entirely in the "prairie pothole" region. Females often lay their eggs in other ducks nests.
Natural History: These ducks are the most widespread and common of the "diving ducks." Diving ducks are capable of diving deeper and prefer deeper waters than the "puddle ducks." They are also more clumsy on land and need a running start on the water to get airborne. They thus favor larger lakes and rivers over small ponds and swamplands. These ducks often gather in large flocks on open water. These large flocks are called "rafts." Rafts of Lesser Scaup are a common sight on large lakes in Ohio in winter. A slightly larger version of the Lesser Scaup, known as the **Greater Scaup** (*Athya marila*) can also be seen in Ohio in winter. Both species like open water. The Greater Scaup tends to favor coastal areas and salt or brackish marshes, but it does migrate through much of the eastern US, including Ohio.	**Natural History:** Closely related to and very similar in appearance to the scaups, the Ring-necked Duck should be called the Ring-billed duck. Although there is a brownish ring around the neck of the male, it is only visible when the bird is in the hand. The broad white ring near the tip of the bill and the narrow white ring at the base of the bill are both readily discernible on birds in the field. Unlike its relatives, the scaups which will feed on crustaceans, insects, and other aquatic invertebrates, the diet of the Ring-necked Duck is mostly vegetarian. Unlike their similar relatives the scaups, Ring-necked Ducks favor small lakes, ponds, and swamps over large rivers and lakes. Like other North American ducks, their movements in winter are determined by weather. Freeze-ups of open water will instigate massive movements.	**Natural History:** An entirely North American species, the Redhead is mostly a vegetarian and feeds heavily on tubers and aquatic vegetation. Most Redheads congregate in winter on the western gulf coast of Louisiana, Texas, and northwest Mexico. In fact hundreds of thousands will concentrate in this region each winter. Here they feed mostly on the roots of shoalgrass. They will also eat some animal matter, mostly aquatic invertebrates. Redheads are easily decoyed and during the days of the market hunting their populations suffered dramatic declines. Recovery in the last few decades has been significant and in a good year the population may reach a million birds. The Redhead has been recently been confirmed to be a very rare breeding bird in the western Lake Erie region of Ohio. Regarded as a Species of Special Interest by ODNR.

Class—**Aves** (birds)

Order—**Anseriformes** (waterfowl)

Family—**Anatidae** (ducks, geese, and swans)

Canvasback *Athya valisineria*	**Bufflehead** *Bucephala albeola*	**Common Goldeneye** *Bucephala clangula*

Size: 21 inches.	Presumed range in Ohio	**Size:** 13.5 inches.	Presumed range in Ohio	**Size:** 18.5 inches.	Presumed range in Ohio
Abundance: Uncommon.		**Abundance:** Common.		**Abundance:** Uncommon.	
Migratory Status: Winter resident and spring/fall migrant.		**Migratory Status:** Winter resident and spring/fall migrant.		**Migratory Status:** Winter resident and spring/fall migrant.	

Variation: Strong sexual variation. See photos above.

Variation: Significant sexual variation. See photos above.

Variation: Significant sexual variation. See photos above. Juvenile like female.

Habitat: The primary breeding habitat for this species is known as "Aspen Parkland" habitat, which is found mostly in Canada. Winters mostly in marshes and bays along both coasts.

Habitat: Most winter in salt water habitats on the coast but a few overwinter on inland lakes and rivers in Ohio. In summer they use boreal forests and parklands in Canada.

Habitat: In winter this species uses large lakes and rivers in Ohio. They are also fairly common in winter in coastal regions. In summer they are a bird of the boreal forests.

Breeding: The large nest is built from grasses and hidden vegetation. Clutch size averages around seven or eight.

Breeding: Cavity nester. Nest is often an old woodpecker hole. Clutch size ranges from a few to over a dozen eggs.

Breeding: Cavity nester that will use artificial nest boxes. May nest over a mile from water. Seven to 12 eggs.

Natural History: One of the most adept of the diving ducks, Canvasbacks have been known to dive to a depth of 30 feet. Feeds mostly on plant material including roots and rhizomes, but will also eat mud-dwelling invertebrates. This is strictly a North American species and is one of the least common duck species in America. They are vulnerable to droughts, habitat loss (mostly from agriculture), and water pollution that can impact the abundance of aquatic food plants. The Canvasback population is closely monitored by the US Fish and Wildlife Service and in years of low numbers hunting of this species may be banned. Even in years when hunting is allowed, the bag limits are typically very low (one per day). At least one instance of Canvasbacks breeding in Ohio has been confirmed in recent years at Cedar Point National Wildlife Refuge in Lucas County.

Natural History: America's smallest of the diving ducks, the Bufflehead is one of the few duck species that will remain with the same mate year after year. Breeding pairs usually return to the same pond or marsh to breed each year as well. With the exception of some seeds, these ducks are mostly carnivorous, feeding on aquatic insects, crustaceans, and mollusks. Unlike the puddle ducks which often feed on the surface, the Bufflehead finds all its food by diving. Although they are often seen on deep-water lakes in Ohio, they feed in the shallows along the banks or in the backs of bays. Although rarely seen in large flocks, this is one of the few duck species that has actually increased in numbers in the last few decades. The ODNR website reports that in the late fall and early winter many thousands of Buffleheads congregate on Lake Erie in the vicinity of Kelleys Island.

Natural History: As with other diving ducks the Common Goldeneye is an excellent swimmer that feeds by diving beneath the surface. They propel through the water using only the feet, with the wings held tight against the body. They are mostly carnivorous but they do eat some plant material in the form of tubers and seeds. Aquatic invertebrates are the main food and include (in order of importance) crustaceans, insects, and mollusks. Fish constitute only a small portion of the diet. Male Common Goldeneyes engage in a complex courtship display to attract females or reinforce the pair bond. These ducks are holarctic in distribution, breeding in boreal forests throughout the northern hemisphere. They can be seen in Ohio from November through March, but may they leave the state in mid-winter if excessive cold causes the freeze up of open waters.

Class—**Aves** (birds)

Order—**Anseriformes** (waterfowl)

Family—**Anatidae** (ducks, geese, and swans)

Ruddy Duck *Oxyura jamaicensis*	**Long-tailed Duck** *Clangula hyemalis*	**Surf Scoter** *Melanita perspicillata*

Size: 15 inches.

Abundance: Fairly common.

Migratory Status: Winter resident and spring/fall migrant.

Presumed range in Ohio

Variation: Significant sexual variation. See photos above.

Habitat: Marshes, ponds, lakes, and to a lesser extent rivers. This is a true "Prairie Pothole" species and nearly 90 percent of nesting occurs in the prairie pothole habitats in the northern plains.

Breeding: Nest is usually built in cattails or other aquatic vegetation. Seven or eight eggs is average.

Natural History: Ruddy Ducks are primarliy western birds that range generally from the Great Plains to the west coast. Winter range includes most of the eastern US and a few individuals are regularly seen in Ohio in winter. Although they may rarely appear on impoundments in the Appalachian region, these ducks are more commonly seen in Ohio farther to the west or sometimes along the Ohio River. The larvae of aquatic insects of the order Diptera (flies, mosquitos, midges) are the primary food of these ducks. Although these are small ducks, their eggs are quite large and are in fact the largest eggs (relative to body size) of any North American duck. This species seems to be expanding its breeding range eastward into the Great Lakes region. A few Ruddy Ducks now nest in Ohio's western Lake Erie marshes.

Size: Up to 21 inches.

Abundance: Rare in Ohio.

Migratory Status: Winter resident and spring/fall migrant.

Presumed range in Ohio

Variation: Males have very long tails and are more strikingly colored.

Habitat: Summer habitat is arctic wetlands and seashores and deep-water lakes. Winter habitat mostly coastal marine environments, but also large freshwater lakes, especially the Great Lakes.

Breeding: Nests in the arctic region on islands and peninsulas of freshwater lakes or in wetland tundra. Six to eight eggs.

Natural History: Also known as "Oldsquaw" these are primarily northern ducks that often wander far south in winter. Although they have been recorded in a variety of localities around the state, in Ohio they are most likely to be seen around Lake Erie in the north or on the Ohio River in southern Ohio. These little ducks are great divers, and can dive to depths over 150 feet to reach marine invertebrate foods consisting mostly of benthic crustaceans. Also eats insects and their larvae and to a lesser extent fish and fish eggs. This is one of the most northerly breeding ducks in the world and they nest well into the arctic. There is some evidence that populations on the west coast are in decline. Status of eastern populations unknown but believed stable. Often roosts in large "rafts" well offshore along coastlines or in large inland lakes.

Size: 21 inches.

Abundance: Rare in Ohio.

Migratory Status: Winter resident and spring/fall migrant.

Presumed range in Ohio

Variation: Significant variation. Females and juveniles are brownish.

Habitat: In winter this species will use large lakes and rivers in northern Ohio. They are most common in winter in coastal regions. In summer they are a bird of the boreal forests.

Breeding: Nests near shallow inland lakes in the far north, often well into the Arctic Circle. Seven to 12 eggs.

Natural History: There are a total of three Scoter species in North America and all three have been seen in Ohio during winter months. They sometimes are seen on Lake Erie or major rivers and impoundments in northern Ohio during winter. But they usually associate with coastal waters and they are often collectively referred to as "Sea Ducks." They will summer inland in the far north of northern Canada and Alaska. Waterfowl of all species are well known for wandering widely and sometimes appearing in areas far from their normal habitats. Two other scoter ducks, the **Black Scoter** (*M. nigra*) and the **White-winged Scoter** (*M. fusca*), can also be seen in Ohio (note insets). All three are northern ducks that spend the summer in northern Canada. Of the three scoter species the Surf Scoter is the most commonly seen in Ohio.

Class—**Aves** (birds)

Order—**Anseriformes** (waterfowl)

Family—**Anatidae** (ducks, geese, and swans)

Common Merganser *Mergus merganser*	**Red-breasted Merganser** *Mergus serrator*	**Hooded Merganser** *Lophodytes cucullatus*
Non-breeding male	Male Female	Male Female

Size: 25 inches. **Abundance:** Uncommon. **Migratory Status:** Winter resident and spring/fall migrant. — Presumed range in Ohio	**Size:** 23 inches. **Abundance:** Fairly common. **Migratory Status:** Winter resident and spring/fall migrant. — Presumed range in Ohio	**Size:** 18 inches. **Abundance:** Fairly common. **Migratory Status:** Year-round resident and migrant. — Presumed range in Ohio
Variation: Exhibits pronounced sexual dimorphism in breeding plumage with males having dark greenish head and white breast. Winter plumages (seen in Ohio) are similar in both sexes.	**Variation:** Significant plumage variations between the sexes during the breeding season. Also exhibits seasonal variation with winter males (and juveniles) resembling females.	**Variation:** Shows strong sexual dimorphism. Males are strikingly marked, having black heads with white "hood" and black wings and back. Females are more subdued (see above).
Habitat: In winter uses large lakes and rivers and larger reservoirs.	**Habitat:** Uses larger lakes and rivers when migrating through Ohio.	**Habitat:** In winter uses swamps, shallow bays of lakes, and river floodplains.
Breeding: Nests in tree cavities or sometimes in root crevices on the ground. 10 or 12 eggs is average. Some nesting recorded in NW Ohio.	**Breeding:** Nests on the ground. Nest is well hidden beneath overhanging vegetation or in cavities. Five to 24 eggs. One nesting record for Ohio.	**Breeding:** Cavity nester. Most nesting in Ohio is in the western Lake Erie marshes, but widespread nesting occurs in Ohio. Lays 12 eggs maximum.
Natural History: Most Common Mergansers seen in Ohio will be in non-breeding plumage (shown above). A bird of northern climates and cold waters, the Common Merganser spends the summer on lakes in the boreal forests of Canada, Alaska, and in the cold water streams of the Rocky Mountains. They are also found throughout Eurasia. Fish is the primary food for this species. Their bill is serrated for holding slippery prey and they are excellent divers and underwater swimmers. They are excellent fishermen and can dive to a depth of tens of yards and have been known to stay submerged up to two minutes. They use their bill to probe in mud or gravel for aquatic insects, mollusks, crustaceans, and worms.	**Natural History:** During winter these birds show a preference for coastal regions where they use estuaries and salt water bays and salt / brackish water marshes. Like its larger relative the Common Merganser, the Red-breasted has a holarctic distribution and is found in Europe and Asia as well as North America. In summer this species ranges even farther north than its larger cousin, being found as far north as the Arctic Ocean and southern Greenland. Food is mostly small fish that are grasped with the serrated bill. Also eats aquatic invertebrates and amphibians. Feeds both in shallow water and in deep water up to at least 25 feet deep. Flocks may feed cooperatively, with all the birds diving together to corral schools of minnows.	**Natural History:** Unlike our other two merganser ducks, both of which are holarctic in distribution, the Hooded Merganser is strictly a North American duck. Another odd distributional trait is the fact that these birds are rare in the great plains region, where many North American duck species are most common. They have a more diverse diet than the larger mergansers, feeding less on fish and more on aquatic invertebrates that are located by means of well developed underwater vision capability. Winter waterfowl surveys indicate that over 50 percent of the population winters in the Mississippi flyway. Most birds winter to the south of Ohio, but this species can be seen year-round throughout the state.

Class—**Aves** (birds)

Order—**Anseriformes** (waterfowl)

Family—**Anatidae** (ducks, geese, and swans)

Snow Goose *Chen caerulescens*	Canada Goose *Branta canadensis*	Greater White-fronted Goose *Anser albifrons*
  White Morph / Blue Morph	 	 
Size: 30 inches.	**Size:** 36–45 inches.	**Size:** 28 inches.
Abundance: Uncommon in Ohio.	**Abundance:** Very common.	**Abundance:** Rare in Ohio.
Migratory Status: Winter migrant.	**Migratory Status:** Year-round resident and seasonal migrant.	**Migratory Status:** Winter migrant.
Variation: Two distinct color phases occur. Juveniles are uniformly gray.	**Variation:** No variation. Sexes and juveniles are all alike.	**Variation:** Juveniles lack black spots on belly. Sexes are alike.
Habitat: In Ohio these geese are mostly seen in the western part of the state where they use very large agricultural fields.	**Habitat:** In Ohio the habitat includes all types of aquatic situations, from urban parks to remote and inaccessible marshes, swamps, or beaver ponds.	**Habitat:** When migrating through Ohio they will use large agricultural fields for feeding and roost on open water or bays in large lakes.
Breeding: Nests only in the high Arctic Tundra of Canada and Alaska.	**Breeding:** Nests above the water line but near water. Four to eight eggs is typical.	**Breeding:** Breeds in the Arctic Coastal Plain. Average clutch size is four or five.
Natural History: Snow Goose populations have exploded in the last few decades, probably as a result of having so much habitat and food available throughout migration routes and on wintering grounds. The grain fields of Midwestern and southern United States provides more than an adequate food source. Mid-continent populations are expanding their migration routes eastward from their historical range west of the Mississippi River. Today they can be found every winter in parts of Ohio and they are sometimes seen as far east as the Appalachian Plateau. There is also an east coast population that winters along the Atlantic coast from New Jersey to the Carolinas. Snow Geese often occur in huge flocks that number hundreds or even thousands of birds. The **Ross's Goose** (*C. rossii*) is a smaller version of the Snow Goose that may rarely be seen in Ohio in the company of Snow Geese.	**Natural History:** This is the most recognized wild goose in America, due in large part to the fact that tame and semi-tame populations are found in parks and on rivers, ponds, and lakes in both urban and rural regions. Resident Canada Geese are numerous in Ohio, but their numbers are swelled dramatically during winter, as birds from farther north visit the state for either a brief stopover or a months-long stay. The characteristic "V formation" of Canada Geese in flight is a familiar sight and their musical, honking call is to many a symbol of wild America. They are heavily hunted throughout America both for sport and for food. Many tens of thousands are killed by hunters each year. They are long-lived birds and have been known to survive over forty years. There are several races of Canada Goose and they vary in size. An identical dwarf species of goose called the **Cackling Goose** (*B. hutchinsii*) is the size of a Mallard.	**Natural History:** Although they may migrate throughout the much of state west of the Appalachian Plateau, White-fronted Geese are found in their greatest numbers west of the Mississippi River. While they are holarctic in distribution, they are not as common in North America as the Canada Goose or Snow Goose. Most of the North American populations of these geese use the Mississippi and Central Flyways, but a smaller population occurs in the Pacific Flyway. Oddly, they are rarely seen in the Atlantic Flyway. Mississippi Flyway birds (some of whom may stray eastward into Ohio) will usually winter along the gulf coast from Louisiana and Texas to northeastern Mexico. During migration small flocks may be seen traveling with larger flocks of Canada or Snow Geese, but they tend to segregate themselves when resting or feeding. They may be expanding their migration routes eastward.

Presumed range in Ohio (shown for each species)

Class—**Aves** (birds)	
Order—**Anseriformes** (waterfowl)	
Family—**Anatidae** (ducks, geese, and swans)	
Mute Swan *Cygnus olor*	**Tundra Swan** *Cygnus columbianus*

Size: 56 inches.	Presumed range in Ohio 	**Size:** 53 inches.	Presumed range in Ohio
Abundance: Uncommon.		**Abundance:** Rare in Ohio.	
Migratory Status: Year-round resident.		**Migratory Status:** Winter migrant and rare winter resident.	

Variation: Some juveniles are brownish for the first year.	**Variation:** Juveniles are "dingy" white with orange bill.
Habitat: Ponds, lakes, marshes, and swamps in both urban and rural areas.	**Habitat:** Large lakes and large, open agricultural fields are used in migration.
Breeding: Nest is platform of grasses up to six feet wide. Near water but above floodplain. About six eggs per clutch.	**Breeding:** Breeds on the tundra of the Arctic Coastal Plain. Three to five eggs are laid.

Natural History: The Mute Swan is a Eurasian species that is common in parks, zoos, farms, and private preserves all across America. Many have become feral or semi-feral and the species seems to be increasing in the wild in America. The impact of this exotic species on native wildlife populations is unknown, but some state wildlife agencies regard them as a nuisance animal. Many state wildlife agencies have active removal programs. ODNR actively manages Mute Swans where they may be a threat to native species. In some other states they are protected. These large waterfowl are primarily vegetarians, but they will eat small amounts of animal matter. When threatened Mute Swans arch the wings over the back and pull the long neck back between the wings in a display known as "busking." They are graceful and elegant in flight or on the water, but rather clumsy on land due to the fact that the legs are located so far back on the body.

Natural History: Although the Tundra Swan is America's most common swan species, these large swans are rare in Ohio. But they do pass through the state during migration. Most winter along the Atlantic coast from the Chesapeake Bay south to North Carolina and on the Pacific Coast from Washington to central California. In winter they use coastal estuaries and will fly inland to forage on waste grain in agricultural fields. Young swans stay with the parents throughout the first year until returning to their arctic breeding grounds the following spring. Prior to the passage of the first migratory bird protection legislation in 1918, these birds had become quite rare. Today their numbers have recovered substantially and a few states now allow a limited harvest during waterfowl season. Migratory flights over Ohio may include flocks numbering hundreds of swans, but smaller groups of one or two dozen is more common.

CHAPTER 5
THE TURTLES OF OHIO

Table 6.

The Orders and Families of Ohio Turtles

Class—**Chelonia** (turtles)

Order—**Cryptodira** (straightneck turtles)

Family	**Chelydridae** (snapping turtles)
Family	**Kinosternidae** (mud and musk turtles)
Family	**Emydidae** (water and box turtles)
Family	**Trionychidae** (softshell turtles)

Class—**Chelonia** (turtles)

Order—**Cryptodira** (straightneck turtles)

Family—**Chelydridae** (snapping turtles)	Family—**Kinosternidae** (mud and musk turtles)

Common Snapping Turtle
Chelydra serpentina

Size: Maximum length 20 inches. Record weight 86 pounds. Maximum size for Ohio specimens about 35 pounds.

Abundance: Very common.

Variation: No variation occurs in Ohio specimens. Specimens found on the Florida peninsula differ slightly.

Presumed range in Ohio

Habitat: Found in virtually every aquatic environment in the state. Ponds, lakes, rivers, creeks, swamps, and marshes.

Breeding: Eggs are deposited in underground chambers excavated by the female turtle. A typical clutch contains 25 to 50 eggs. Hatchlings are about the size of a quarter. Hatchlings may overwinter in nest chamber and emerge the following spring. Excessive drought that hardens soil can trap baby turtles in the nest chamber and result in mortality.

Natural History: These common turtles can be found in any aquatic habitat in the state, including tiny farm ponds or tributaries narrow enough for a person to step across. They even can exist in waters that are heavily polluted with sewage. They will feed on some plant material but are mainly carnivorous and will eat virtually anything they can swallow. Fish, frogs, tadpoles, small mammals, baby ducks, crayfish, and carrion are all listed as food items. Hatchling turtles often must travel long distances to find a home in a pond or creek, and adults occasionally embark on long overland treks, presumably in search of a more productive habitat after depleting the food source in a small pond or creek. These long hikes overland usually occur in the spring. The ferociousness of a captured snapping turtle is legendary and their sharp, powerful jaws can inflict a serious wound. When cornered on land they will turn to face an enemy and extend the long neck in a lunging strike that is lighting fast and so energetic that it may cause the entire turtle to move forward several inches. By contrast when under water they almost never bite. Old adults tend to have a very smooth carapace, whereas younger turtles exhibit a rougher, more serrated upper shell.

Common Musk Turtle
Sternotherus oderatus

Size: About 4 inches in length as an adult. Record length is 5.875 inches. Hatchlings are tiny, just under an inch in length.

Abundance: Fairly common.

Variation: Males have larger, thicker tails than females. Females tend to be slightly larger, otherwise there is little variation.

Presumed range in Ohio

Habitat: Primarily a stream dweller, but can be found in a variety of aquatic habitats including swamps, marshes, lakes.

Breeding: Female lays two to five eggs under leaf litter or sometimes merely on top of the ground. Unlike many aquatic turtles that make long excursions into upland areas to lay their eggs, the Common Musk Turtle deposits its eggs in the vicinity of water. The eggs hatch into tiny turtles that are less than inch in length.

Natural History: Nocturnal and crepuscular and completely aquatic in habits. Unlike most aquatic turtles in Ohio, the Common Musk Turtle rarely basks, but when it does it may climb several feet up into branches that overhang the water. When disturbed while basking they will launch themselves clumsily into the safety of the water. Since they seldom leave the water, the carapace is often covered with a thick growth of algae. Their name comes from the presence of musk-producing glands that emit an unpleasant odor when the turtles are handled. This musk also accounts for their other common name, "Stinkpot." The Common Musk Turtle is widespread throughout the eastern United States, being found from the gulf coast north to the great lakes, but they are absent from most of the higher elevations of the Appalachian Plateau. They are an omnivorous species that feeds on a variety of aquatic plant and animal matter. Like many turtle species, the Eastern Musk Turtle is a long lived species and one captive zoo specimen lived for 55 years. They reach their highest densities in waters with abundant aquatic vegetation. They are easily identified by the two distinct white or yellowish stripes on the side of the face and neck.

Class—**Chelonia** (turtles)

Order—**Cryptodira** (straightneck turtles)

Family—**Emydidae** (water and box turtles)

Red-eared Slider *Trachemys scripta*	**Spotted Turtle** *Clemmys guttata*	**Painted Turtle** *Chrysemys picta*

Red-eared Slider

Size: 6–8 inches.

Abundance: Fairly common.

Variation: Males are smaller and have longer claws on the front feet.

 Presumed range in Ohio

Habitat: Most common in large bodies of water but can be found in any aquatic habitat in the state except for very small streams.

Breeding: Females leave the safety of the water and crawl hundreds of yards to upland areas to deposit their eggs in an underground nest chamber dug with the hind legs. Large females may lay 20 eggs, younger females lay fewer.

Natural History: Highly aquatic but sometimes seen far from water. Omnivorous. Eats a variety of water plants as well as mollusks, minnows, dead fish, aquatic insects, crustaceans, etc. Young are more carnivorous, while mature turtles will consume more plants. Old specimens tend to darken with age and very old specimens can be nearly all black (see inset). These are hardy turtles that will emerge from the mud to bask on logs on warm, sunny days throughout the winter. There are three subspecies of slider turtles in America, one of which, the **Red-eared Slider** (subspecies *elegans*), is found in Ohio. For decades baby Red-eared Sliders were sold in pet stores across America. As a result, they have been introduced into many areas outside their original range and today they are one of America's most widespread turtles.

Spotted Turtle

Size: Up to 4.5 inches

Abundance: Uncommon.

Variation: Yellow spots fade with age. Very old individuals may be solid black.

Presumed range in Ohio

Habitat: Prefers sluggish waters. In Ohio inhabits lakes, marshes, swamps, and slow-moving rivers. Sometimes found in wet meadows or wet woods.

Breeding: Mating takes place in early spring through early summer with eggs being laid from May to July. Female digs a flask-shaped hole and deposits from one to eight eggs. Two clutches per year is not uncommon.

Natural History: These handsome little turtles range throughout the Atlantic slope of the eastern United States from southern Maine to northern Florida. A disjunct population is found throughout the Great Lakes region, and it is to this population that the Ohio Spotted Turtle belongs. The Great Lakes population is in decline and this species is regarded as threatened in Ohio. They were probably once much more widespread in glaciated Ohio prior to the draining of wetlands that began with settlement and the advent of modern agricultural practices. The Spotted Turtle is both an omnivore and a scavenger. Aquatic grasses and algea make up the vegetarian diet with insects, crustaceans, snails, amphibian larvae, and fish listed as food items. Opportunistic feeding on carrrion is also reported. They are shy and docile and rarely attempt to bite when captured.

Painted Turtle

Size: 4–6 inches.

Abundance: Very common.

Variation: There are four subspecies. Only one occurs in Ohio. See below.

 Presumed range in Ohio

Habitat: Avoids fast-flowing streams in favor of still or slow-moving waters. Common in swamps, marshes, ponds, and lakes throughout its range.

Breeding: Females lay 10–15 eggs within a flask-shaped underground nest chamber dug with the turtles hind legs. Egg laying occurs from late May to early July. Eggs hatch in about 10 weeks. Hatchlings are the size of a quarter.

Natural History: The Painted Turtles are among the most common and widespread of the Emydidae turtles in America. There are three subspecies recognized in North America and they range from the Atlantic coast well into the Great Plains. The race that is native to Ohio is the Midland Painted Turtle (*C. p. marginata*). This is probably the most common aquatic turtle in Ohio. Like other members of their family they spend a great deal of time basking on floating logs and they are quick to slide into the water if approached too closely. They are omnivorous turtles that eat a very wide array of plant and animal foods as well as carrion such as fish heads and entrails discarded by fishermen. Hatchlings grow rapidly and can double in size their first year. Growth slows with size and age. Longevity in the wild may be as much as 40 years.

Class—**Chelonia** (turtles)

Order—**Cryptodira** (straightneck turtles)

Family—**Emydidae** (water and box turtles)

Blanding's Turtle *Emydoidea blandingii*	**Common Map Turtle** *Graptemys geographica*	**Ouachita Map Turtle** *Graptemys ouachitensis*
	 Female	Male top, female bottom 

Size: Maximum of 11.125 inches. Ohio turtles 5–7 inches.

Presumed range in Ohio

Size: Males to 6.5 inches. Females reach 11 inches.

Presumed range in Ohio

Size: Males to 5 inches. Females to 10 inches.

Presumed range in Ohio

Abundance: Generally uncommon in Ohio. May be locally common in northwest Ohio.

Abundance: Probably fairly common statewide but unverified from many counties.

Abundance: Very rare in Ohio. Occurs in several disjunct localites in southern Ohio.

Variation: Amount of light, irregular spots and lines on carapace is variable. Some individual have spots significantly faded or no spots at all.

Variation: In mature adults, females are larger and have larger heads. Hatchlings are miniature replicas of the adult but more vivid in color and pattern.

Variation: Males are smaller than females and have longer front claws. Young resemble adults but have prominent markings on the plastron.

Habitat: In Ohio the habitat is marshes and wetlands along the margins of Lake Erie. Also uses wet meadows and is commonly seen on land.

Habitat: Primarily found in larger rivers and lakes, but also found in smaller tributaries near their confluence with larger streams.

Habitat: Primarily lives in rivers and river impoundments. They can also be found in the oxbows and swamps associated with major rivers.

Breeding: Ten to 15 eggs are laid by the female in an underground nest chamber that she digs at night. Only one clutch per year is produced.

Breeding: Breeds in early spring and eggs are laid in June. Most egg laying occurs in the morning. The average clutch size is about 10 eggs.

Breeding: Breeds in spring and fall. Eggs are laid in early summer and average about 10 per clutch. May lay two clutches per year.

Natural History: The oldest known wild specimen of Blanding's Turtle was calculated to be 77 years old. Crayfish are reported to be the favorite food item. Among aquatic foods listed are insects, fish, fish eggs, and frogs are along with algae. On land they will eat earthworms, slugs, insect larvae, leaves, grasses, and berries. It is thought that the Blanding's Turtle is closely related to the more terrestrial Box Turtle. Like the Box Turtle the Blanding's does posses a hinged plastron. Like their cousin the Box Turtle, the greatest threat to adult Blanding's Turtles is the automobile. Their nests are raided by a variety of predators including foxes, Oppossums, Raccoon and especially Striped Skunks.

Natural History: Diurnal and crepuscular in activity. These turtles are fond of basking on logs but are very wary and will disappear into the water if approached. Food items include crustaceans, fish, insects, and aquatic plants. They also eat mollusks and the thick, crushing surface of the jaws suggests that small mussels may be an important element in the diet. The Common Map Turtle is one of the more widely distributed of the map turtles and can be found from the great lakes southward into Arkansas and Alabama. They also range widely throughout Ohio and are probably found statewide, although they have not been documented from every county in the state. They have a lifespan in the wild of at least 20 years.

Natural History: Food includes insects, dead fish, aquatic invertebrates, and plant material, especially algae. The carapace (top shell) of this species has a rough, serrated appearance that is more pronounced in younger turtles. They are good climbers and will bask on steep trunks or limbs overhanging water. This turtle's name is derived from the Ouachita Mountains of Arkansas, where the first specimen described to science was found. This species is widespread to the west of Ohio but occurs only sporadically in our state. The map above is at best an approximation, as the exact range of this species in the state may not be fully known. It is regarded as a Species of Special Concern by the ODNR.

Class—**Chelonia** (turtles)
Order—**Cryptodira** (straightneck turtles)
Family—**Emydidae** (water and box turtles)

Eastern Box Turtle
Terrapene carolina

Female laying eggs

Presumed range in Ohio

Size: Averages 4 to 6 inches in length. The record length is just under 8 inches.

Abundance: Very common.

Variation: There are four subspecies of this common land turtle. Only the eastern race occurs in Ohio. It is a highly variable subspecies. In fact, no two specimens look exactly alike (see photos above). The color and pattern on each specimen is as individual as a fingerprint. Sexes can be differentiated by examination of the bottom part of the shell (plastron). Males have a concave plastron and females a flat plastron. In adult turtles, males tend to be slightly larger than females.

Habitat: Occupies a wide variety of habitats from open fields and pastures to deep woods. Can be found in both upland areas and lowlands, but is most common in damp woods, edge areas near creeks and streams, and wooded bottom lands.

Breeding: Breeding takes place in late April and May with egg deposition in late June or early July. Up to six eggs may be laid but two to three is more common. Young hatch in late fall and some may overwinter in their underground nest chamber before emerging the following spring. Newly hatched baby Box Turtles do not possess the hinged plastron and are thus unable to tightly close themselves within their shell.

Natural History: These familiar turtles often go by the name "Terrapin." They are primarily diurnal and are most active in the morning and the late afternoon. They sometimes burrow into the mud during hot weather, and overwinter by burrowing themselves into loose soil or deep leaf litter. The hibernation burrow is quite shallow, only a few inches deep. Studies have shown that they are tolerant of some freezing, a trait that enables survival of such a shallow hibernator. Still, hibernation is a significant source of mortality among adults. Their diet is omnivorous and they consume berries, fruits, and mushrooms as well as a wide variety of insect prey and other invertebrates. Earthworms and snails are a favorite animal food and blackberries and mulberries are among the favorite plant foods. Box Turtles are known for their longevity and reports of their living up to a century are common but difficult to verify. Some researchers report a life span of 80 years, while others say 30 to 40 years is probably the average in the wild. When threatened they will retract the head and feet into the shell which can then close tightly by means of hinges on the front and back of the plastron. The muscles that close the shell are remarkably strong and efforts to pry open the shell of a frightened Box Turtle are futile. They are tough little turtles that can sometimes survive serious injury such as the shell being cracked open by a glancing blow from an automobile tire. Turtles with badly deformed but completely healed shells are sometimes found. In regions where wildfires are common many are seen with shells that are completely scarred by fire. There is some Concern among conservationists that commercial collecting of these turtles for foreign markets may be threat to their long term survival. Habitat degradation is a much more imminent threat, and automobiles take a fearful toll on these endearing animals on highways throughout their range each summer.

Class—**Chelonia** (turtles)

Order—**Cryptodira** (straightneck turtles)

Family—**Trionychidae** (softshell turtles)

Smooth Softshell Turtle *Apalone mutica*	**Spiny Softshell Turtle** *Apalone spinifera*

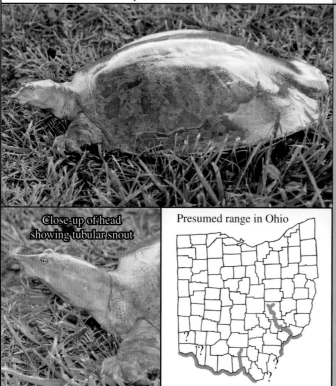

Underwater

Close-up of head showing tubular snout

Presumed range in Ohio

Sunning on streambank

Presumed range in Ohio

Size: 12 to 14 inches.

Abundance: Rare in Ohio.

Variation: No significant species variation in Ohio. There are two other Smooth Softshell species found in parts of the southeast. Females attain a much larger size than males.

Habitat: Essentially an inhabitant of streams, both large rivers and small creeks. Flowing water is a requirement for this species, but it is found in large river impoundments.

Breeding: Eggs are laid in excavated chambers on exposed sandbars in late spring or early summer. About a dozen eggs is typical.

Natural History: The Smooth Softshell is found mostly in flowing streams with fine gravel or sand bottoms. They are capable of great speed in the water and will actively forage for fish and other small aquatic animals. They are also ambush predators that burrow into the soft substrate of streams and extend their long necks with blinding speed to grab passing fish. Insects are also an important food item, along with various small aquatic animals and some plant material such as seeds and berries. Because of their permeable skin and requirement of clear streams and rivers these turtles may be under significant threat from water pollution. Damming of major rivers can also impede their natural movements and dispersal. All species of softshell turtles have elongated, snorkel-like snouts which they will use to breath when buried in sand or mud at the waters edge.

Size: Maximum of 18 inches.

Abundance: Fairly common.

Variation: No subspecific variation among Ohio specimens, but there are a total of five subspecies in America. Adult females may be twice the size of males.

Habitat: Occurs in both large and small steams and in impoundments. May also be found in farm ponds in some areas. Shows a preference for habitats with sandy substrates.

Breeding: A dozen or more eggs are laid between May and August (most in June or July). Nests are often on sandbars of creeks or rivers.

Natural History: Crayfish, fish, and insects are the primary food items, but dead fish and other carrion can be an important food item, especially in lakes where fishing is common. Spiny Softshells are active from April to October in Ohio. They hunt both by ambush and by active pursuit. When immobile they can remain under water or several hours. Because of the soft, permeable shells and skin, softshells are more susceptible to dehydration than other turtle species and thus they seldom stray far from water. These turtles are harvested as food in many parts of their range, and much of this harvest is to date unregulated. Some believe this practice may pose a long term threat to the species. Like all softshell turtles the Spiny has a long and flexible neck, which makes handling these turtles without being bitten difficult. Wild adults may bite savagely if handled.

CHAPTER 6
THE REPTILES OF OHIO

Table 7.

The Orders and Families of Ohio Reptiles

Class—**Reptilia** (reptiles)

Order—**Squamata** (snakes and lizards)

Suborder—**Lacertilia** (lizards)

Family	**Phrynosomatidae** (spiny lizards)
Family	**Scincidae** (skinks)

Suborder—**Serpentes** (snakes)

Family	**Colubridae** (harmless egg laying snakes)
Family	**Dipsadidae** (small rear-fanged snakes)
Family	**Natricidae** (harmless live-bearing snakes)
Family	**Crotalidae** (pit vipers)

THE REPTILES OF OHIO

PART 1: LIZARDS

Class—**Reptilia** (reptiles)
Order—**Squamata** (snakes and lizards)
Suborder—**Lacertilia** (lizards)

Family—**Phrynosomatidae** (spiny lizards)	Family—**Scincidae** (skinks)
Eastern Spiny Lizard *Sceloperus undulatus*	**Ground Skink** *Scincella lateralis*

Ground Skink column:

Size: 3 to 5 inches.

Abundance: Rare in Ohio.

Variation: Color may vary from reddish brown to golden brown or chocolate brown. Often with a metallic quality. Some have small dark flecks on the back.

Presumed range in Ohio

Habitat: Dry upland woods and pine woodlands. Micro-habitat consists of leaf litter and detritus on the forest floor.

Breeding: Small clutches of three to five eggs is typical. May lay two clutches per year. Unlike other Ohio skinks, the female Ground Skink does not remain with the eggs until hatching. Hatchlings are tiny, measuring less than two inches in length.

Natural History: These tiny ground dwellers dive quickly beneath leaf litter when approached and they are easily overlooked. Often, their presence is revealed by the rustling sound made as they forage through the dry leaves. Despite being rarely observed, they can be quite common in many areas. Foods are tiny insects and other small invertebrates living among the leaf litter on the forest floor. They also go by the name "Little Brown Skink." They are widespread throughout the southeastern half of America and are most common in the deep south. In Ohio they are have a restricted range and are generally quite rare. This is the smallest lizard found in Ohio and in fact they are one of the smallest lizards in America. Perhaps the most interesting anatomical feature of the Ground Skink is the fact that the lower eyelid is equipped with a transparent "window" that allows this lizard to see with its eyes closed.

Eastern Spiny Lizard column:

Size: Maximum of 7.25 inches.

Abundance: Very common.

Variation: Exhibits some sexual dimorphism with males having bright blue patches on the throat and on each side of the belly. There is no age-related variation. Babies resemble adults and no significant species variation occurs.

Presumed range in Ohio

Habitat: Dry, upland woods. Found in both pure deciduous woods and in pine dominated woodlands.

Breeding: Egg layer. Deposits six to 15 eggs in rotted logs, stumps, etc. Two clutches per year are common.

Natural History: A woodland species, the eastern Fence Lizard spends much of its time on tree trunks and fallen logs. Its color and pattern perfectly matches the bark of most trees within its range. This is a very common lizards in the unglaciated Allegheny Plateau in southeastern Ohio. They can also be common in the Bluegrass Section of the Interior Low Plateau Province in extreme southeastern Ohio. They are quite arboreal in habits an will regularly climb trees to great heights. Feeds on insects, spiders, etc. Both sexes are often seen perched on rocks, logs, or stumps in wooded areas. Breeding males are especially conspicuous as they attempt to attract females by sitting atop rocks or stumps and methodically raising and lowering their body to show off the bright blue patches on the undersides. This is the only representative of its family in the midwest, but the spiny lizard family is a large and diverse group in the deserts and grasslands of America's arid southwest.

Class—**Reptilia** (reptiles)
Order—**Squamata** (snakes and lizards)
Suborder—**Lacertilia** (lizards)
Family—**Scincidae** (skinks)

Five-lined Skink *Plestiodon fasciatus*	Broad-headed Skink *Plestiodon laticeps*

Size: Maximum of about 8 inches.

Abundance: Common.

Habitat: Most common in damp woodlands but also found in swamps and in drier upland areas. The presence of rocks and logs is important for micro-habitat, and patches of sunlit areas for basking is also important.

Presumed range in Ohio

Variation: Young are the most brightly colored with distinct pale yellow stripes and bright blue tails. Adult females resemble the young but with age become faded with indistinct stripes less blue in the tail. Adult males are plain brown above with reddish cheek patches that become very vivid during the breeding season.

Breeding: Eggs (six to 12) are laid in May or early June in rotted logs, stumps, sawdust, mulch, or other moisture retaining material. Females may remain with eggs until they hatch in late July or early August.

Natural History: The young of this species are strikingly colored with bright blue tails and they sometimes go by the name "Blue-tailed Skink." These common and well known lizards are fond of sunning on decks, porches, sidewalks, and patios of homes in rural areas. They feed on a wide variety of insects, spiders, and arthropods and they are a useful species in controlling invertebrate pests around the home. Unfortunately they are highly vulnerable to pesticides and are easily killed by exterminators who commonly spray around the foundation of houses. Like their larger cousin they are sometimes regarded and venomous and referred to as "Scorpion Lizards." In truth there are no venomous lizards found in the eastern United States. The only venomous lizard in the United States is the Gila Monster of the desert southwest region of America.

Size: Maximum of 13 inches.

Abundance: Rare in Ohio.

Habitat: Mesic woodlands, wetland areas, and also dry upland woods with moist micro-habitat. These lizards are restricted to the southern Ohio and occur in widely disjunct locales in the state.

Presumed range in Ohio

Variation: Young have blue tails and yellow stripes and resemble Five-lined Skinks. In the adults the females have faded, indistinct lines and the males are uniformly brown with bright red cheeks. During breeding the red intensifies and may encompass the entire head.

Breeding: Females will vigorously defend their eggs that are usually laid on the ground in a hollowed out depression beneath sheltering log or inside a hollow stump.

Natural History: These very large skinks are quite arboreal and often den in tree hollows many feet above the ground. These arboreal dens are used only during summer and hibernation takes place underground. In much of the southeast they are known as "Scorpion Lizards" and some believe the myth that they are dangerously venomous. Although they will bite if handled, they are totally harmless to humans. This is Ohio's largest lizard species and the largest individuals can barely exceed a foot in length. Insects are the main food but they will also eat small mammals such as baby mice. Like most reptiles they are vulnerable to pesticides and are easily killed by exterminators who commonly spray around the foundation of houses. The lizards do a much safer job of controlling insects and spiders around the outside of the home and spraying outside foundations and yards should be discouraged.

THE REPTILES OF OHIO

PART 2: SNAKES

Class—**Reptilia** (reptiles)

Order—**Squamata** (snakes and lizards)

Suborder—**Serpentes** (snakes)

Family—**Colubridae** (harmless egg-laying snakes)

Racer	Midland Rat Snake	Eastern Fox Snake
Coluber constrictor	*Pantherophis spiloides*	*Pantherophis vulpinus*

Northern Black Racer

Hatchling

Blue Racer

Hatchling

Size: Average 4 to 5 feet. Maximim of 6 feet.

Abundance: Very common statewide. Blue race in north, black in south.

Presumed range in Ohio

Size: Average 5 to 6 feet. Maximum 8 feet 4 inches.

Abundance: Very common. One of the most common large snakes in Ohio.

Presumed range in Ohio

Size: Average 4 or 5 feet. Record 5 feet 10 inches.

Abundance: Rare in Ohio. Restricted to western Lake Erie region.

Presumed range in Ohio

Variation: Nine subspecies are found across North America. Two occur in Ohio, the Northern Black Racer (subspecies *constrictor*) and the Blue Racer (subspecies *foxii*). Blue Racer has a more bluish color. Young racers have a pattern of distinctive saddles (see inset).

Habitat: Racers are habitat generalists that may be found in most natural habitats within the state. They favor dry upland woods and overgrown fields. They are most common in ecotone areas.

Breeding: Females lay about a dozen (from five to 20) eggs in rotted logs, humus, etc. Eggs are laid in early summer and hatch in about two months. Like most egg layers, the Racer reproduces annually (some live bearing snakes breed only every other year).

Natural History: Racers are alert, active snakes that relentlessly prowl in search of almost any type of animal prey that can be swallowed. They will eat insects, amphibians, lizards, other snakes, nestling birds, eggs, and small mammals. Quite speedy for a snake, they can reach a blazing 12 to 15 mph. Due to their feeding habits and habitat adaptability, the racers are among the most successful and widely distributed snakes in America.

Variation: These snakes exhibit some variation in the dorsal pattern of adults. Most show a blotched pattern on the back, but in some individuals this pattern is obscured by an overall dark coloration. Young are light gray with charcoal blotches. See inset photo.

Habitat: Found in virtually all habitats within the state. They are least common in areas of intensive agriculture or urbanized areas, but they can persists in urban regions if there is some cover.

Breeding: An egg layer that lays up to 20 (average about a dozen) eggs. Eggs are laid in old woodpecker holes or hollow limbs above ground or in rotted stumps, beneath logs, or anywhere some form of humus is present to prevent dessication. Breeds annually.

Natural History: This is the most arboreal snake species in America and adults spend a great deal of time in trees. They often choose a regular den site in old woodpecker holes or hollows of trees and may be seen sunning with the forepart of the body emerged from a hole. They will climb to great heights in search of bird nests. They are also at home on the ground and in addition to birds and eggs they will also eat mice, squirrels, and other small mammals.

Variation: Shows little variation. Ground color varies somewhat, light brown to reddish. Juveniles are lighter.

Habitat: Inhabits woodlands, marshes, and prairies. Found in both mesic and xeric soils. In Ohio range is restricted to the western Lake Erie region where it is found in all types of habitats.

Breeding: Breeding occurs in spring or early summer with egg deposition following fertilzation by about a month. Clutch size is about a dozen eggs, though it can be twice that amount.

Natural History: The bulk of this species range is in northern Illinois, most of Wisconsin, and the western half of Michigan's Upper Peninsula. The population of eastern Fox Snakes that exists around the western end of Lake Erie is disjunct by many miles from the main population farther to the west. This probably represents a "relict" population that was cut off from the rest of this snakes contiguous range by habitat changes at some time in the geological / climatological history of the region. The food of this species is primarily endothermic vertebrates, mostly hatchling birds, bird eggs, and small mammal such as mice and voles.

Class—**Reptilia** (reptiles)

Order—**Squamata** (snakes and lizards)

Suborder—**Serpentes** (snakes)

Family—**Colubridae** (harmless egg-laying snakes)

Black Kingsnake *Lampropeltis getulus*	Eastern Milksnake *Lampropeltis triangulum*	Rough Green Snake *Opheodrys aestivus*

Size: Average about 4 feet. Maximum 6 ft. 2 inches.	**Size:** Record is 4 feet 4 inches. Most adults are about 3 ft.	**Size:** Average 2–3 feet. Record 3 feet 11 inches.

Presumed range in Ohio

Presumed range in Ohio

Presumed range in Ohio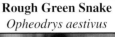

Abundance: Uncommon. Found only in a few counties in southeast Ohio.

Abundance: Common and widespread throughout the state.

Abundance: Probably fairly common. Found only in southernmost Ohio.

Variation: Can show some variation in the amount of light speckling present. Younger snakes usually show a chain-like pattern of light speckles. Older adults can be nearly solid black dorsally.

Variation: There is little variation among Ohio specimens. Juveniles tend to be a little brighter in color between the dark saddles. Young have reddish saddles that turn brown with age.

Variation: This species is remarkably uniform in appearance throughout its wide range. A very rare blue morph can occur with a genetic abnormality that omits yellow pigments.

Habitat: Mature woodlands, successional areas, weedy fields, and edge habitats in uplands, bottom lands, swamps, and marshes.

Habitat: Eastern Milk Snakes are habitat generalists. They may be found in swamps, marshes, and bogs as well as in drier habitats like rocky hillsides.

Habitat: Open fields, pastures, and edges of woods and fields. Often common in wetlands where there are low bushes and shrubs overhanging water.

Breeding: An annual breeder that lays eight to 12 eggs in early summer. Eggs are laid in moisture-retaining medium, often inside rotted stumps or logs. Eggs hatch in about 60 days.

Breeding: Egg layer. Eggs are deposited in rotten logs, stumps, or beneath a flat rock. Lays from six to 24 eggs. Hatchlings are about eight or nine inches in length and resemble bright adults.

Breeding: Three to 12 eggs are laid in late spring or early summer. The babies are slender, miniature replicas of the adult. The tiny babies are so small and cryptic that they are almost never seen.

Natural History: Common Kingsnakes are best known for their habit of killing and eating other snakes, including venomous species. These powerful constrictors are immune to the venom of pit vipers and will kill and eat any snake that is small enough to be swallowed whole. They also eat rodents, birds, lizards, and baby turtles. They are mainly terrestrial in habits but have been found inside of standing dead trees several feet off the ground. They may be active both day and night are but mostly crepuscular and during hotter months tend to become more nocturnal. Their range in Ohio is restricted to a few counties in the Unglaciated Allegheny Plateau.

Natural History: The name comes from the habit these snakes have of entering stock barns in search of mice. Early settlers erroneously thought the snakes were there to suckle from the milk cow (that every pioneer family kept on the farm). These snakes eat many lizards and will also consume other, smaller snakes. Reptile eggs may be eaten along with amphibians and small mammals like mice. Milk Snakes enjoy a resistance to snake venom and baby copperheads, cottonmouths, or rattlesnakes may be eaten by large adults. Although they are presumed to occur statewide, documentation is missing from many counties across Ohio.

Natural History: Rough Green Snakes live in dense bushes and shrubs where their bright green color renders them invisible. Arthropods of many varieties are their prey. Food includes spiders, caterpillars, crickets, and grasshoppers to name a few of their favorites. These snakes are sometimes called "grass snakes" in reference to their bright green coloration. There is a widespread belief that they have become extremely rare and endangered. In fact their populations are probably fairly stable, although they are certainly vulnerable to habitat destruction wrought by modern agricultural practices as well as the widespread use of insecticides.

Class—**Reptilia** (reptiles)

Order—**Squamata** (snakes and lizards)

Suborder—**Serpentes** (snakes)

Family—**Colubridae** (harmless egg-laying snakes)	Family—**Dipsadidae** (rear-fanged snakes)

Smooyh Green Snake	**Eastern Hognose Snake**
Opheodrys vernalis	*Heterodon platyrhinos*

Black Morph

Black and Yellow Morph

Black and Orange Morph

Hooding

Size: Average about 18 inches. Record 31 inches.

Presumed range in Ohio

Abundance: Uncommon. Sparsly distributed in Ohio.

Presumed range in Ohio

Variation: None.

Variation: Higly variable. See photos above for common color morphs.

Habitat: Open fields, pastures, meadows, and edges of lakes, ponds, or marshes. Generally a snake of open habitats but may be found in open woods.

Habitat: Hognose Snakes are most common in habitats with sandy soils which facilitate easy burrowing. They tend to be more common in sandy creek bottoms and river valleys. They prefer areas with moist soils but can also be found in upland woods and fields.

Breeding: Clutch size is relatively small and may be as few as three or four eggs or as high as a dozen. Egg laying has been reported from June to August.

Breeding: Hognose snake breed in early spring and lay up to two dozen eggs. Nests are probably in an underground chamber in sandy soil. Young snakes are about 8 inches in length and always have a spotted pattern. Babies are grayish brown with well defined dark gray or black blotches.

Natural History: Like the similar Rough Green Snake (preceding account) the Smooth Green Snake often goes by the common name "Grass Snake" or "Green Grass Snake." These small snakes eat a variety of invertebrate prey including slugs, spiders, millipedes, crickets, grasshoppers, and caterpillars, to name a few. This diet makes them exceptionally vulnerable to insecticides and widespread applications of chemicals on agricultural fields may pose a serious threat to this handsome little snake. Unlike the larger Rough Green Snake that climbs into bushes and small trees, the Smooth Green Snake tends to stay close to the ground. Except for a small area of southwestern Ohio, the two Green Snakes are not found together. Where they do occur together they are easily identified by the presence (or absence) of keeled scales.

Natural History: The Eastern Hognose Snake is famous for the elaborate performance it puts on when threatened. First, they will spread the neck like a cobra (hence the nickname "Spreading Adder"), and with the mouth wide open they will strike repeatedly. They always intentionally miss with the strike and never bite even when picked up and handled. The initial "cobra display" is always accompanied by loud hissing. When their complicated bluff fails to deter the threat they will roll onto their back, stick out their tongue, and give a convincing impression of being dead. Their primary food is frogs and toads. They possess enlarged teeth in the back of the upper jaw that are used to puncture the bodies of toads that have gulped air and inflated themselves in an attempt to become to large to be swallowed. The saliva of these snakes is mildly toxic, but is not considered to be a threat to humans. The food of these snake is almost entirely toads and frogs, making them one of the more specialized feeders among Ohio's snakes. Salamanders are reported to have been found in the stomachs of a few individuals as well. Anecdotal evidence suggests theses snakes may be declining. Their habit of feeding on toads and frogs almost exclusively may make them vulnerable to insecticides, as frog and toads are primarily insect eaters. To the uninformed or "snake phobic" persons, an Eastern Hognose Snake performing its "cobra" mimicry can be a frigthening sight. To early pioneers this snake must have seemed a real threat. The extent to which it has been misunderstood is evidenced in the array of ominous nicknames which Ohions have assigned this species. In addition to the afore mention "Spreading Adder" are names such as "Hissing Viper," "Hognose Viper," and "Puff Adder."

Class—**Reptilia** (reptiles)
Order—**Squamata** (snakes and lizards)
Suborder—**Serpentes** (snakes)
Family—**Dipsadidae** (rear-fanged snakes)

Ringneck Snake *Diadophis punctatus*	**Wormsnake** *Carphophis ameonus*

Size: Average about 14 inches. Maximum 2 feet.	Presumed range in Ohio	**Size:** 8 to 11 inches. Record length 13.4375 inches.	Presumed range in Ohio
Abundance: Very common.		**Abundance:** Common.	
Variation: A highly variable species with twelve subspecies nationwide. Only the Northern Ringneck Snake (*D. p. edwardsii*) occurs in Ohio.		**Variation:** There are two subspecies of this snake. Specimens from Ohio are difficult to assign to either subspecies and considered "intergrades."	

Habitat: A woodland species that lives in rotted logs, stumps, and beneath rocks and leaf litter on the forest floor.

Habitat: Found in a variety of habitats, but mostly in woodlands. Like other small terrestrial snakes its micro-habitat is beneath the leaf litter, logs, rocks, etc.

Breeding: Lays up to a dozen eggs, usually fewer in rotted logs or other moisture retaining places. Young are about five inches long at hatching.

Breeding: From one to 12 eggs are laid in late June or July and hatch in two to three months. Hatchlings are only about three inches in length.

Natural History: With its uniformly charcoal gray body and bright yellow ring around the neck, the Ringneck Snake is one of the most recognizable snakes in Ohio. In some areas it is also one of the most abundant snake species in the state. Especially in the Appalachian Plateau Province. These small snakes are often uncovered by humans beneath boards, stones, leaves, or other debris. The distinctive yellow or cream-colored collar around the neck readily identifies them, and even those unfamiliar with reptiles have no trouble recognizing this species. They feed mostly on soft-bodied insects and other invertebrates. Earthworms are a favorite food. When threatened they will often hold aloft the tightly curled-up tip of the underside of their bright yellow tail to distract a predator. This defense mechanism is probably designed to direct an attackers attention away from the vulnerable head to the less vulnerable tail. Despite having enlarged grooved teeth in the rear of the jaw for envenoming small prey, they are harmless to man.

Natural History: A confirmed burrower that lives under leaf litter, logs, rocks, and even man-made debris such as old boards, discarded shingles, etc. Feeds on tiny soft-bodied invertebrates such as insect larvae, termites, and earthworms. The aptly named worm snakes do in fact resemble earthworms. Their tiny, conical head and smooth glossy scales help to facilitate burrowing through tiny tunnels created by earthworms, termites, or insect larvae. These snakes are often turned up in back yards by people gardening, raking leaves, or doing other types of yard work. Like the ringneck snakes, worm snakes possess tiny grooved teeth in the rear of the jaw that serve to introduce a mild venom into the bodies of prey. These tiny teeth are too small to penetrate human skin and these snakes are thus completely harmless to man. Their range in Ohio is restricted to the southern portions of the Appalachian Plateaus province in the southeastern corner of the state. However, there are apparently isolated populations in a few counties in southwestern Ohio (see map above).

Class—**Reptilia** (reptiles)
Order—**Squamata** (snakes and lizards)
Suborder—**Serpentes** (snakes)
Family—**Natricidae** (harmless live-bearing snakes)

Northern Water Snake—*Nerodia sipedon*		**Plainbelly Water Snake** *Nerodia erythrogaster*
Northern Water Snake *N. s. sipedon*	**Lake Erie Water Snake** *N. s. insularum*	

Young

Size: Average about 3.5 feet. Record is 59 inches.

Size: Average 4 feet. Record 59 inches.

Abundance: Both subspecies are very common within their respective ranges.

Abundance: Very rare in Ohio.

Variation: There are four subspecies and two can be can be found in Ohio. Both Ohio subspecies vary somewhat in color. The Northern race ranges from brown, tan, or reddish brown to gray-brown. Northern Water Snakes almost always will always exhibit a pattern of darker bands across the back that contrasts with the lighter color between the bands. A few snakes from northern Ohio may have the dorsal pattern greatly reduced, a character that is common in the Lake Erie Water Snake.

Presumed range in Ohio. Lake Erie Water Snake is in dark gray.

Variation: There are four color morphs of Plainbelly Water Snake in America. Each was once regarded as a distinct subspecies. The Northern Copperbelly Water Snake is the morph that occurs in Ohio. Juveniles show a distinctive blotched pattern. See inset above.

Habitat: These snakes are aquatic animals but they do sometimes wander away from water in search of a mate or as a result of natural dispersal. They are very fond of small farm ponds or small streams as habitat, but they can also be found in large lakes and in swamps and marshes. The Lake Erie subspecies is restricted to the region of Lake Erie known as the "West Basin Islands" region.

Habitat: Although primarily aquatic, this water snake is less tied to water than any of its kin and they will often wander far from permanent water. They are found in creeks, rivers, lakes, ponds, and wetlands throughout their range. They may also occur in seasonal marshes and wet meadows and they may be found in dry habitats on occasions.

Breeding: Females may mate with several males in the spring. Birthing occurs in late summer to early fall. Live born young can number two or three dozen, but the largest females may produce nearly 100 babies. Young females may have as few as six or eight.

Breeding: Large females can produce litters numbering over 40 babies. Breeds in early spring and babies are born in late summer.

Presumed range in Ohio

Natural History: Northern Water Snakes adapt well to man-made environments like large lake impoundments where they can thrive in the rip-rap of dams and levees. Frogs and fish are the two favorite food items for these snakes. Around man-made impoundments or on Lake Erie they can become very numerous near boat docks and fishing areas where they scavenge on dead or dying fish and fish heads left behind by fishermen. Like most other water snake species, they are fond of basking in the sun atop debris and limbs overhanging water. As with other water snakes they are commonly confused with the venomous Cottonmouth, even in areas of the country where the Cottonmouth does not occur (like Ohio). Their dorsal pattern of dark brownish bands on a lighter brown background also causes them to be mistaken for another venomous species, the Copperhead, which does occur in much of southern Ohio. Although fairly common within its limited range, the Lake Erie Water Snake (subspecies *insularum*) is regarded as an endangered species by the Ohio Department of Natural Resources. Animals that have very restricted distribution are always more vulnerable than those that have much broader ranges.

Natural History: This snake is found in Ohio only in Williams County. The Northern Copperbelly morph of the Plainbelly Water Snake was once considered a distinct subspecies. As a rare subspecies it was being considered for federal endangered status. Some biologist question the validity and motive for abandoning the subspecies concept for snakes like the Northern Copperbelly.

Class—**Reptilia** (reptiles)

Order—**Squamata** (snakes and lizards)

Suborder—**Serpentes** (snakes)

Family—**Natricidae** (harmless live-bearing snakes)

Queen Snake *Regina septemvittata*	Smooth Earth Snake *Virginia valeriae*

Size: Average 2 feet. The record lenght of this species is right at 3 feet.

Presumed range in Ohio

Size: Usually around 10 inches in length. The record is 15 inches.

Presumed range in Ohio

Abundance: Common.

Abundance: Uncommon.

Variation: There are no subspecies of the Queen snake and there is very little variation among specimens in Ohio. Dorsal stripes are less evident on snakes preparing to shed.

Variation: There are three subspecies nationwide. The eastern race (*V. v. valeria*) is the one that occurs in Ohio. Color may vary slightly from brown to grayish or reddish.

Habitat: Found mostly in limestone creeks but also in natural lakes and impoundments. Also uses large rivers. Most common in creeks with flat stones for hiding beneath.

Habitat: Smooth Earth Snakes are basically a forest species. Though they live mostly in upland habitats, their micro-habitat is moist soils beneath leaf litter, logs, stones, etc.

Breeding: The Queen Snake is a live-bearer that will produce up to a dozen young per litter, a relatively small number for an aquatic snake. Young are typically born in late summer or early fall. Babies are quite small, about 7 inches in length and very slender.

Breeding: These snakes are live bearers that give birth to from four to 12 young. The young snakes resemble the adults and measure about three to three and half inches in length. They are about the girth of a pencil lead and may be mistaken for an earthworm.

Natural History: The Queen Snake is a specialized feeder that preys almost exclusively on recently molted, soft-bodied crayfish. As a result their distribution is limited to areas where this common crustacean is abundant. They are often found hiding beneath flat stones in limestone creeks throughout their range . Like other water snakes they may be seen basking from limbs and branches overhanging water. A habit which has lead to the nickname "Willow Snake" in parts of Ohio. This species occurs nearly statewide, but they are absent from a few areas of the state (see map). In ideal habitats (limestone creeks with abundant crayfish), this can be a very common snake.

Natural History: The Smooth Earth Snake is a tiny, docile snake that could not manage to bite a human even if they were so inclined, which they are not. Their food consists of small insects, snails, and mostly, earthworms. These are secretive little serpents that sometimes emerge to prowl about on the surface after summer rains. Otherwise they are easily overlooked except by herpetologists who know where to find them beneath logs, stones, or amid accumulated humis on the forest floor. As with other small snakes that burrow beneath detritus on the floor of woodlands, these little snakes are occasionally turned up by rural residents as they rake mulch from flower beds in the spring.

Class—**Reptilia** (reptiles)

Order—**Squamata** (snakes and lizards)

Suborder—**Serpentes** (snakes)

Family—**Natricidae** (harmless live-bearing snakes)

Butlers Garter Snake	Eastern Ribbon Snake	Eastern Garter Snake
Thamnophis butleri	*Thamnophis sauritus*	*Thamnophis sirtalis*

Size: About 18 inches. Record 29.

Abundance: Uncommon in Ohio.

Variation: There are no subspecies of this snake and there appears to be little variation among Ohio specimens. The stripes may vary from yellow to buff.

Presumed range in Ohio

Habitat: Most often found in proximity to water. Stream sides, lake shores, wet meadows, and marshes. In Ohio most common near western Lake Erie.

Breeding: Breeds soon after emerging from hibernation in April. Eight or 10 young are born in July or August.

Natural History: This is a small garter snake with an exceptionally small head. It is similar in many ways to two other very rare garter snakes that occur in Ohio. They are the **Plains Garter Snake** (*Thamnophis radix)* and the **Short-headed Garter Snake** (*Thamnophis brachystoma*); both are very rare garter snakes that *each occur in a single county* in Ohio. The Great Plains Garter is found in Wyandote County and the Short-headed Garter in Mahoning County. Both these species are common and widespread in other regions of the country. Their presence in Ohio represents highly localized, disjunct populations that are probably "relict populations." Remnants of a once more wide ranging population that was decimated by climatic or habitat changes.

Size: 18 to 28 inches. Record 38.

Abundance: Fairly common.

Variation: A total of three subspecies are found in the eastern United States. Two, the Eastern Ribbon Snake and the Northern Ribbon Snake occur in Ohio.

Presumed range in Ohio

Habitat: Occupies aquatic and semi-aquatic habitats from swamps and marshes to streams, stream edges, and mesic bottom-land woodlands.

Breeding: 10 to 20 young is typical. Birthing occurs in late summer following breeding in the early spring.

Natural History: Eastern Ribbon Snakes are both diurnal and nocturnal in habits. They often climb into low shrubs and vines. They are alert snakes that hunt by both smell and with their excellent eyesight that is attuned to quick movements of fleeing prey. Food items include insects, frogs, and minnows, crayfish, and tadpoles. Although these snakes are nearly always found near water, they tend to live near the edges of wetlands rather than within them. In many ways the ribbon snakes occupy a niche that is halfway between an aquatic and a terrestrial species. The Common Ribbon Snake (subspecies *sauritus*) is found in southern Ohio while the Northern Ribbon Snake (subspecies *septentrionalis*) can be found in northern Ohio.

Size: Average 2 feet. Max 51 inches.

Abundance: Very common.

Variation: There are nine subspecies of this widespread snake in the United States. The eastern subspecies (*T. s. sirtalis*) is the only one in Ohio.

Presumed range in Ohio

Habitat: A habitat generalist that favors pastures, fields, and rural yards. Can be seen almost anywhere, including vacant lots in urban areas.

Breeding: Garter Snakes are live-bearers that give birth to enormous litters of up to 60 babies.

Natural History: The Eastern Garter Snake is the one snake that everyone knows. They are one of the most common snakes in the eastern US. They are non-specialized feeders that will eat insects, earthworms, frogs, toads, salamanders, fish, and rarely small mammals such as baby mice or voles. Their name is derived from their resemblance to the old fashioned "garters" that were used to hold up men's socks. The name has been widely familiarized to "Garden Snake" in many places. Still appropriate as they are often encountered in peoples gardens. They are a ubiquitous species that may be found in both wilderness or urban regions. They are most common in edge habitats. Melanistic specimens are known to be fairly common along the shores of Lake Erie.

Class—**Reptilia** (reptiles)

Order—**Squamata** (snakes and lizards)

Suborder—**Serpentes** (snakes)

Family—**Natricidae** (harmless live-bearing snakes)

Kirtland's Snake *Clonophis kirtlandii*	Redbelly Snake *Storeria occipitomaculata*	Brown Snake *Storeria dekayi*

Size: Record length is 24 inches.	 Presumed range in Ohio	**Size:** 10 to 12 inches, record 16.	 Presumed range in Ohio	**Size:** Average 12 inches, record 19.	 Presumed range in Ohio
Abundance: Rare. Threatened in Ohio.		**Abundance:** Uncommon.		**Abundance:** Common.	
Variation: No significant variation in Ohio.		**Variation:** No siginificant variation in Ohio.		**Variation:** No significant variation in Ohio.	

Habitat: Usually associates with moist environments both in woodlands and open areas. Also inhabits swamps and marshes. Wet meadows are favored.	**Habitat:** Mostly found in wooded areas, in both lowland and uplands. They can also be found in fields around the edges of woods.	**Habitat:** Woodlands, grassy fields, and wetlands. May sometimes be found even in urban areas, especially vacant lots littered with old boards or scrap tin.
Breeding: Live-bearer. Litters may be as small as three or four or as many as 10 or 15. Young are born in late summer to early fall.	**Breeding:** Live-bearer. Litters number from five to 15. Newborn babies are only about three inches in length and no bigger around than a matchstick.	**Breeding:** Gives birth to five to 20 young (rarely more, as many as 40). Baby snakes are about three inches long with the girth of a toothpick.
Natural History: The Kirtland's Snake is an enigmatic species. It was once thought to be related to the water snakes, but is now considered to be closer to garter snakes in its phylogeny. Though its original range probably included most of glaciated Ohio, its requirement for wet meadow and marshes means that it is found only where these uncommon habitats remain. In Ohio it is most common in the vicinity of western Lake Erie and in the Cincinnati area. Earthworms and slugs are listed as its primary prey. It is mostly a nocturnal hunter and hides by day beneath boards, stones, or other structures. When threatened these snakes will flatten the body to such an extreme as to create a ribbon-like appearance to the snake. Like many obscure snake species, the Kirtland's Snake is named for an early naturalist.	**Natural History:** Redbelly Snakes usually remain hidden by day beneath rocks, logs, etc., and emerge at night to hunt insects and small soft-bodied invertebrates such as earthworms, slugs, beetle larvae, isopods, etc. These snakes sometimes exhibit a peculiar behavior when threatened. If voiding of feces and musk fails to discourage a handler, they will curl their upper lip in an strange expression of apparent ferocity. It is a purely fallacious display however as their tiny teeth could never penetrate human skin. There are three subspecies of Redbelly Snake in America. Ohio's is the Northern Redbelly Snake (subspecies *occipitomaculata*). The Redbelly Snake is rarely seen by Ohions due to both its relative scarcity in the state and to its secretive habits. They are sometimes uncovered by people doing yard work in regions where they are found.	**Natural History:** This diminutive snake is often found in vacant lots of large cities and towns, where it hides beneath boards, trash, even small pieces of cardboard. It feeds primarily on earthworms and slugs, but also reportedly eats insects, amphibians eggs, and tiny fishes. Brown Snakes are known to hibernate communally, an odd behavior for a tiny snake that should have no trouble finding adequate crevices in which to spend the colder months. These snakes are sometimes called "Dekay's Snake," in honor of an early American naturalist. Brown Snakes can be very common snakes in some areas of Ohio, while they are completely absent in other areas. They have probably fared better than most other Ohio snakes in adapting to the changes man has brought to the original habitats of the state.

Class—**Reptilia** (reptiles)

Order—**Squamata** (snakes and lizards)

Suborder—**Serpentes** (snakes)

Family—**Crotalidae** (pit vipers)

Copperhead *Agkistrodon contortrix*	Timber Rattlesnake *Crotalus horridus*	Massassauga Rattlesnake *Sistrurus catenantus*

Light morph

Dark morph

Size: Average 2.5 to 3 feet. The record is 58 inches.	Presumed range in Ohio	**Size:** Averages about 4 feet. Record is 6 feet 2 inches.	Presumed range in Ohio	**Size:** Average about 2 feet. Record 39.5 inches.	Presumed range in Ohio
Abundance: Fairly common.		**Abundance:** Rare.		**Abundance:** Very rare.	
Variation: Colors vary from tan to reddish brown.		**Variation:** Quite variable. See photos above.		**Variation:** No significant variation in Ohio.	

Habitat: Copperheads are primarily woodland animals, but they do wander into overgrown fields and thickets where rodent prey is abundant. Edge areas and small woodland openings chocked with briers, saplings, and weeds are prime habitat.

Habitat: As their name implies Timber Rattlesnakes are forest animals. Within their woodland habitats they are most common in upland areas with rocky outcrops and talus slopes. They inhabit both mature forests and second growth woodlands, as well as forest edges.

Habitat: Wetlands primarily. Inhabits swamps, marshes, wooded floodplains. Once ranged across much of glaciated Ohio but has been extirpated from many areas of the state. It is absent from much of the area shown on the map above, which may not be accurate.

Breeding: Breeds in spring or in the fall. From four to 12 young are born in late August through September. The resources required to produce a litter by a live-bearing snake are considerable and can be quite stressful on the female. Thus many copperheads likely produce litters only ever other year.

Breeding: Timber Rattlesnakes typically breed in August and the females delay implantation of embryos until the following spring. The young snakes are then born in late summer or early fall, about a year after breeding. Females will produce young only every other year. Average litter is six to 12.

Breeding: Young are born in late July, August, or September. Five or six babies is common but can be as many as 14. Baby snakes are eight to 10 inches in length and are miniature replicas of the adults except for possessing the bright yellow tail tip seen on some other baby crotalid snakes like the Copperhead.

Natural History: Like most pit vipers copperheads are primarily nocturnal, especially during hotter months. In early spring and fall they may be seen abroad during the day. Young snakes eat some invertebrates and small vertebrates such as young frogs, lizards, and small snakes. Larger snakes prey on small mammals (mice and voles), and the young of ground nesting birds. Insects are also taken. In areas of undisturbed habitat these can be common snakes but they are secretive and discreet. They account for more snakebites than any other venomous snake in Ohio.

Natural History: This is one of the largest rattlesnake species in America and their bite is quite capable of killing a human. Fortunately they are peace loving animals that only strike as a last resort. Timber Rattlesnake populations have declined significantly in many areas of their range, including in Ohio. Today they are absent from vast areas of their former range shown on the map above and they are an endangered animal in Ohio. These large snakes feed mostly on mammals, with squirrels and chipmunks being a favorite food, along with mice, voles, and young rabbits.

Natural History: The name Massassauga comes from the Chippewa Indian name for a marshy area at the mouth of a river. Which is one of this snakes primary natural habitats. During summer months they may leave the sanctity of the swamp or marsh and venture into nearby fields or uplands. Food items include rodents, amphibians, birds, crayfish, and insects. In some regions they are known to hibernate in crayfish burrows. Today this is one of the rarest rattlesnakes in America and their remaining populations are highly fragmented and isolated from one another.

CHAPTER 7

THE AMPHIBIANS OF OHIO

Table 8.

The Orders and Families of Ohio Amphibians

Class—**Amphibia** (amphibians)

Order—**Anura** (frogs and toads)

Family	**Ranidae** (true frogs)
Family	**Scaphiopodidae** (spadefoots)
Family	**Hylidae** (treefrogs)
Family	**Bufonidae** (true toads)

Order—**Caudata** (salamanders)

Family	**Ambysotmatidae** (mole salamanders)
Family	**Salamandridae** (newts)
Family	**Plethodontidae** (lungless salamanders)
Family	**Proteidae** (mudpuppies and waterdogs)
Family	**Cryptobranchidae** (giant salamanders)

THE AMPHIBIANS OF OHIO

PART 1: FROGS AND TOADS

Class—**Amphibia** (amphibians)

Order—**Anura** (frogs and toads)

Family—**Ranidae** (true frogs)

Wood Frog *Lithobates sylvatica*	**Northern Leopard Frog** *Lithobates pipiens*	**Green Frog** *Lithobates clamitans*

Wood Frog		Northern Leopard Frog		Green Frog	
Size: 2 to 3 inches. **Abundance:** Fairly common. **Variation:** Little variation in Ohio. May vary from light tan to dark brown.	Presumed range in Ohio 	**Size:** 3 to 4 inches. **Abundance:** Fairly common. **Variation:** The skin between the spots varies from greenish to brown or tan.	Presumed range in Ohio 	**Size:** 2 to 4 inches. **Abundance:** Very common. **Variation:** Ground color varies from brownish to greenish.	Presumed range in Ohio 
Habitat: This is a forest species that is most common in Kentucky in the Appalachian Mountains region. It prefers mesic woods near streams.		**Habitat:** Wet meadows, vegetated fields, wetland, and stream edges. This species wanders extensively into grassy fields in bottom lands.		**Habitat:** Found in virtually every aquatic habitat within the state, from small ponds and large lakes to streams and wetlands.	
Breeding: Breeds in winter. This is the earliest breeding frog in Kentucky and they may breed as early as January. Eggs are laid in ephemeral pools and small fishless bodies of water.		**Breeding:** Breeding occurs in the early spring in ponds, marshes, and swamps. Females will lay two to five thousand eggs. Tadpoles grow from less than an inch to nearly four inches before transforming.		**Breeding:** Breeding can begin as early as May and continue until August. Up to 4,000 eggs may be deposited. Two clutches per year can occur. Eggs hatch in as little as a week.	
Natural History: Despite the fact that this is the most widespread frog species in America, there are no subspecies and it shows little variation. Wood frogs from Canada and Alaska are identical to those found northern Alabama or northern Georgia. This is the most cold tolerant frog species in Ohio and it ranges farther to the north than any of its kin. They can be frozen solid and recover without harm when thawed. Food is a variety of small invertebrates. Like many frogs, Wood Frogs migrate overland during periods of heavy rainfall. They can be commonly seen on roadways at night during the breeding season. In Ohio they are most common in the Appalachian Plateau Province but they have been extirpated from much of the Till Plains Section of the Interior Lowlands Province. They are still found in the Huron-Lake Erie Plains Section.		**Natural History:** Insects and spiders are the mainstay of this frog's diet. It is not uncommon for these frogs to be seen far from water during the summer months. But they retun to ponds and wetlands in the late fall to hibernate in the mud underwater. These are familiar animals to anyone who has dissected frogs in a biology class. In recent years their numbers in the wild have experienced an unexplained decline. In many regions specimens are being found with deformities to limbs. Some possible causes include chemical pollutants, acid rain, a pathogenic fungus that attacks frogs, or a combination of these and other, as yet unknown factors. In Ohio the number one threat is habitat destruction, most notably the draining of beaver ponds, swamps, and marshes. In more recent times agricultural practices that result in the draining of farm ponds has depleted habitats even more.		**Natural History:** A drive through a wetland on a rainy night in late summer when the tadpoles of *Lithobates clamitans* are emerging onto land will reveal astounding numbers of small frogs crossing the roadway as they disperse into new territories. Adult frogs feed on insects primarily but other arthropods including small crayfish are frequently eaten. Minnows and other small aquatic vertebrates are also potential prey. These frogs are easily confused with the much larger Bullfrog, but are distinguished by the presence of a fold of skin (known as a dorso-lateral fold) that runs along each side of the back. These frogs require smaller bodies of water than the larger Bullfrog and they can be found in almost any moist environment, including temporary puddles. Like other aquatic frogs they sometimes wander away from water on rainy nights to forage for insects in grassy areas.	

Class—**Amphibia** (amphibians)

Order—**Anura** (frogs and toads)

Family—**Ranidae** (true frogs)		Family—**Scaphiopodidae** (spadefoots)

Bullfrog
Lithobates catesbeianus

Pickerel Frog
Lithobates palustris

Eastern Spadefoot
Scaphiopus holbrookii

Size: 4 to 8 inches.

Abundance: Common.

Variation: Females grow larger. Males have a larger tympanum and have a yellow throat.

Presumed range in Ohio

Size: 3 inches.

Abundance: Uncommon.

Variation: Ground color (skin color between the spots) varies from tan to brown.

Presumed range in Ohio

Size: 2 to 3 inches.

Abundance: Uncommon.

Variation: Ground color varies from brown or olive through gray to black.

Presumed range in Ohio

Habitat: Ponds, lakes, and streams as well as swamps and marshes. May travel overland between ponds or wetland areas during rainy weather.

Habitat: Prefers spring fed streams and clear, cool waters in woodland areas. Also found in swamps and marshes. May occur in fields near streams.

Habitat: Requires loose, sandy soil that facilitates easy burrowing. In Ohio restricted to large river valleys in the Unglaciated Allegheny Plateau region.

Breeding: Breeding and egg laying occurs from late spring through mid-summer. Several thousand eggs can be laid and two clutches per year is not uncommon.

Breeding: Breeds in ponds, ditches, or permanent streams. Beaver Ponds are reported as a favorite breeding site. Lays 2,000 to 4,000 eggs. Tadpoles transform in about three months.

Breeding: Breeds explosively during periods of heavy rainfall from late spring throughout the summer. Up to 5,000 eggs hatch within a few days. Tadpoles grow and transform rapidly.

Natural History: These are the largest frogs in Ohio (and in fact in the U.S). Their hind legs are considered to be a delicacy by many. They are regarded as a game animal and are hunted for food during the annual "frog season." In some places they are raised commercially for food and for research or teaching laboratories. They may venture far from water and will travel from pond to pond during rainy weather. Bullfrogs hunt mostly by utilizing a "sit and wait" ambush strategy. Food is almost any animal small enough to be swallowed, including other frogs. There is even a record of a large Bullfrog eating a baby rattlesnake! Bullfrog tadpoles can take up to two or rarely three years to transform into froglets. Populations in the north have shorter growing seasons and thus take longer to mature into frogs.

Natural History: Pickerel Frogs are distinguished from Leopard Frogs by their square rather than round spots. These frogs secrete a toxin from the skin that protects them from many predators and is strong enough to kill other frogs kept with them in a small container. Among the predators that are able to eat them however is another frog species, the Bullfrog. These are hardy frogs that may be active from March through October in Ohio. Northern populations of Pickerel Frogs show a preference for clean water and seem to be suceptible to pollution. In this respect the Pickerel Frog may be an indicator species that can provide an early warning regarding environmental threats like water pollution. The status of Ohio populations appears stable but is unknown for certain.

Natural History: The name "Spadefoot" comes from a sickle-shaped horny structure on the hind feet that is used for digging into the ground. They spend much of their lives in burrows only a few inches deep and emerge only on rainy nights. During dry weather they may spend weeks in the burrow without feeding. They secrete a toxic substance which is an irritant to mucus membranes, thus making these anurans unpalatable to many potential predators. Touching the face or other sensitive skin after handling a Spadefoot will result in an uncomfortable burning sensation. Although widespread and quite common farther to the south, in Ohio the Spadefoot is sporadically distributed. When handled they will usually assume a "hunkered down" position with the head and hind feet tucked under the belly.

Class—**Amphibia** (amphibians)

Order—**Anura** (frogs and toads)

Family—**Hylidae** (treefrogs)

Cope's Gray Treefrog and Gray Tree Frog	Blanchard's Cricket Frog
Hyla chrysoscelis and Hyla versicolor	*Acris blanchardi*

Size: Averages about 2 inches. Max of just under 2.5 inches.

Presumed range in Ohio

Abundance: Taken together, the two Gray Treefrog species are fairly common animals in Ohio.

Variation: There are actually two identical species in the Gray Treefrog complex. They can only be reliably differentiated by the sound of their call or by laboratory examination. Both species have the ability to change color from gray to green. Shade of gray can range from a dark sooty gray to a light smoky gray.

Habitat: Habitat is chiefly woodlands. These treefrogs are more adapted to dry uplands than most members of their genus and they can be found far from water in dry upland woods. They are also common in wetland areas and mesic woodlands.

Breeding: Breeds from late spring through summer in small bodies of water ranging from small ponds to roadside ditches. Up to 2,000 eggs are laid.

Natural History: These highly arboreal treefrogs are rarely seen on the ground and they often climb high into treetops to forage for insects. They are mainly nocturnal but they may be active by day on cloudy or rainy days or in cooler weather. They shelter by day in small hollows in tree trunks or limbs and have been known to take up residence in small bird nest boxes such as a wren box or bluebird box. They will also live in the rain gutters of house roofs. They can sometimes be seen sitting in the opening of their hiding place with the head and front feet exposed. They possess remarkable camouflage abilities and the gray, lichen-like pattern of their skin will perfectly match the bark of the tree they occupy. They can produce a natural anti-freeze in the blood which allows them to hibernate in tree hollows above the ground, or in leaf litter on the forest floor. Most members of the genus *Hyla* are southern animals, but these frogs range far into the northern states and even into parts of southern Canada. Food items are small insects and arthropods. The identical species known as the Gray Treefrog (*Hyla versicolor*) occurs sympatrically with the Cope's Gray Treefrog (*Hyla chrysoscelis)* in parts of Ohio. The two species were originally seperated based on the sound of their calls. It was then learned that the Gray Treefrog (*H. versicolor*) possessed double the normal number of chromosones (tetraploid), while the Cope's Gray Treefrog (*H. chrysoscelis)* has the normal (diplioid) complement of chromosones. More recent laboratory analysis shows differences in the red blood cells of these two cryptic species. The two are so similar in appearance that even experienced herpetologist cannot differentiate between the two based on appearance alone. Very experienced herpetologist can identify them by their calls, but even this can be difficult unless both are calling at the same time. The calls of both species can change with temperature changes, creating an overlap of respective sounds produced, which makes identification of a single calling frog difficult.

Size: 1.5 inches.

Abundance: Very common.

Variation: Brown, reddish brown, tan, or gray green. Often with X-shaped marking on back.

Habitat: Shorelines of ponds, along creeks, temporary pools, marshes, swamps, wet meadows, and uplands.

Breeding: Breeds from spring through late summer. Up to 400 eggs per clutch.

Natural History: These tiny frogs are most commonly seen along the receding shorelines of ponds and lakes in late summer or early fall. When startled they will often jump into the water and then immediately swim back to shore. This may be an "out of the frying pan into the fire" behavior intended to keep them from the jaws of hungry fish. They are often seen far from water in fields and woodlands, but are always more common in wetland habitats and permanently damp areas. Their name comes from their call which resembles that of a cricket, but a group of Cricket Frogs calling in chorus is more accurately described as sounding like the sound of many small stones being rapidly clicked together. There are three morphologically indistinguishable Cricket Frog species found in the eastern United States. The Blanchard's Cricket Frog is regarded as a distinct species based on laboratory analysis of DNA. South of the Ohio River it is replaced by the identical Eastern Cricket Frog.

Presumed range in Ohio

Class—**Amphibia** (amphibians)

Order—**Anura** (frogs and toads)

Family—**Hylidae** (treefrogs)

Midland Chorus Frog *Pseudacris triseriata*	**Mountain Chorus Frog** *Pseudacris brachyphona*	**Spring Peeper** *Pseudacris crucifer*

Size: Up to 1.25 inches.  Presumed range in Ohio	**Size:** Max 1.5 inches.  Presumed range in Ohio	**Size:** About 1 inch.  Presumed range in Ohio
Abundance: Common.	**Abundance:** Fairly common.	**Abundance:** Common.
Variation: Ground color varies from brown to grayish. Dorsal pattern can be stripes or spots.	**Variation:** From brown to olive green. Dorsal pattern also varies from prominent to absent.	**Variation:** Ground color varies. Usually tan or brown. Sometimes grayish or reddish.
Habitat: Low wet fields, bottomland woods, swamps, marshes, ponds, or bogs. Also found in uplands that are in close proximity to bottomlands, creeks, or other permanent water.	**Habitat:** Mountain forests in the central and southern Appalachians. An upland adapted species that associates with mesic micro-habitats. Can be found on upland ridges far from water.	**Habitat:** Woodlands and thickets, usually near water. Most common in lowlands (swamps, marshes, etc.), but also found in upland areas adjacent to creek bottoms or wetlands.
Breeding: Very early breeders that may begin breeding as early as February. Breeding is in ephemeral pools in flooded fields, roadside ditches, etc.	**Breeding:** Breeds early (February and March). Utilizes woodland ponds, ephemeral pools, and even water-filled ruts in old logging roads.	**Breeding:** Spring Peepers begin breeding activity as early as late winter and continue into early spring. Several hundred eggs are laid in shallow water.
Natural History: At the first signs of spring these frogs appear and gather in large numbers to breed. Breeding may be interrupted several times by cold snaps and freezing weather. The name comes from their "chorus" of breeding calls that carries over quite a long distance. Standing water in flooded bottomlands and shallow, water-filled depressions in croplands are favorite breeding sites for this frog. Though amazingly common during the brief breeding season, most of the rest of the year they seem to disappear. Although they can be found statewide, they are more common in the glaciated regions of the state. This is one of the earliest breeding frogs in Ohio and breeding can begin as early as late January in the southern half of the state. Breeding may be interrupted by cold fronts.	**Natural History:** This tiny frog is a mountain forest adapted species that can be found at high elevations. They are a shy species that is rarely observed except during the breeding season. The rest of the year they are scattered throughout the forest and are easily overlooked amid leaf litter and woodland debris. Mountain Chorus Frogs range throughout the central and southern Appalachians from Pennslyvania to northern Alabama and extreme northeast Mississippi. In Ohio their range is restricted to the Unglaciated Allegheny Plateaus region. Despite their wide range the biology of this secretive little frog is not well understood. Mountain Chorus frogs are true to their name and are only found in upland regions, whereas other chorus frogs will frequent lowlands.	**Natural History:** Another dimunitive frog that is heard more often than seen. The name comes from the sound made when breeding frogs are calling. The call is a rapidly repeated "peep, peep, peep." Despite their small size, a chorus of calling spring peepers can be heard for a distance of up to a mile. Although members of the treefrog family they live mostly on the ground. The species name *crucifer* is latin for "cross bearer" and refers to the x-shaped mark that is always present on this frogs back. These little frogs, along with their cousins the Chorus Frogs, are a true harbinger of spring throughout much of the eastern United States. They may breed in the same flooded field pools with Chorus Frogs or even in the same pool. They feed on tiny insects and arthropods.

Class—**Amphibia** (reptiles)

Order—**Anura** (frogs and toads)

Family—**Bufonidae** (true toads)

American Toad *Bufo americanus*	Fowler's Toad *Bufo fowleri*

Size: 2 to 4 inches.	Presumed range in Ohio	**Size:** Average of 2 to 3 inches.	Presumed range in Ohio
Abundance: Very common.		**Abundance:** Common.	
Variation: Varies from light tan to very dark brown, olive brown, reddish, or grayish.		**Variation:** Varies in color from dark brown to reddish brown, tan, or grayish brown.	
Habitat: Virtually anywhere. Inhabits dry uplands and moist lowlands from remote wilderness to urban lawns.		**Habitat:** All habitats within the state but shows a preference for sandy, loose soils in bottomlands.	

Breeding: Breeding in Ohio usually begins in April. Eggs are laid in long strings of clear gelationous material. Breeding sites are small ponds, water-filled ditches, or temporary pools in seasonally flooded lowlands. Eggs hatch in about one week into tiny black tadpoles that metamorph into quarter-inch toadlets in mid-summer.

Breeding: Breeding begins shortly after emerging from hibernation. In Ohio most breeding is about a month later than with the American Toad, usually begining in early May. Shallow ponds, ditches, creeks, flooded fields, etc. are all used as breeding sites but this species is also likely to breed in streams. From 5,000 to 10,000 eggs are laid.

Natural History: American Toads eat a wide variety of insects and other small arthropods. They are adept burrowers and like other toads possess hardened spade-like structures on the hind feet that are used for digging. These toads can be told from the similar and sympatrically occuring Fowler's Toad by the their larger warts and the fact that the dark spots on the back never have more than two warts per spot. The similar Fowler's Toad may have up to six warts per dark spot. Although they are sometimes active by day, these toads are primarily nocturnal in habits. They usually spend the day at least partially buried in loose soil or beneath leaf litter or other debris. When attacked by a predator they will inflate their bodies by gulping air. This behavior sometimes works if the predator is an animal like a snake that must swallow its food whole. The common eastern Garter Snake along with the eastern Hognose Snake are two of their major predators. Like most other toads the American Toad likes loose soils that facilitate easy burrowing.

Natural History: The natural history of the Fowler's Toad is similar to that of the American Toad. Fowler's Toads emerge from hibernation later in the spring and breed later in the spring. Young toadlets do not emerge from the tadpole stage until late summer. Fowler's Toads like open habitats and sandy soils. They often take up residence in gardens that are kept well tilled and thus maintain loose soils that facilitate easy burrowing. Encouraging toads in the garden provides an all natural and benign form of pest control. Placing a half buried water dish in the center of the garden that is kept filled during the dry summer months will make life more pleasant for garden toads. Fowler's Toads avoid the deep woods and are probably more common in Ohio in the western half of the state. Like many toads (and many treefrogs) the Fowler's Toad secretes a toxic substance from the skin when threatened. While this toxin can cause irritation to sensitive areas and membranes, the old wives' tale that toads cause warts is a fallacy.

THE AMPHIBIANS OF OHIO

PART 2: SALAMANDERS

Class—**Amphibia** (amphibians)

Order—**Caudata** (salamanders)

Family—**Ambystomatidae** (mole salamanders)

Tiger Salamander *Ambystoma tigrinum*	**Spotted Salamander** *Ambystoma maculatum*	**Marbled Salamander** *Ambystoma opacum*

Size: Average about 8 inches. Max 14 inches.  Presumed range in Ohio	**Size:** Average 6 inches. Maximum 9 inches.  Presumed range in Ohio	**Size:** 3 to 4 inches. Record 5.3125 inches.  Presumed range in Ohio
Abundance: Generally uncommon. Found in glaciated Ohio only.	**Abundance:** Common. Found thoughout Ohio except northwest.	**Abundance:** Fairly common in southeastern Ohio. Rare along the lake.

Variation: The light markings can appear as irregular spots, blotches, or stripes. The color of the light pigments can vary as well and may be yellow, orange, or greenish. Spotted Salamander, has spots that are more rounded.

Habitat: Woodlands and fields, in both upland an lowland areas. This species seems avoids the Appalachian Plateaus Province in Ohio. It is widespread however in the western half of the state.

Breeding: Breeds in small, fishless bodies of water like stock ponds, vernal pools, and "borrow pits." Breeding occurs in mid-winter with a few hundred to several thousand eggs produced by the female. Males and females migrate to breeding ponds where breeding takes place. Eggs are encased in a ball of jelly-like material and hatch in about a month.

Natural History: The large size of the Tiger Salamander allows it to feed on much larger prey than most salamander species. Although invertebrates such as earthworms and insect larvae are the major foods, small vertebrates may also eaten and captive specimens will eat baby mice. Despite their large size, Tiger Salamanders are rarely seen except during the late winter breeding season when they travel to breeding ponds.

Variation: The polka dot spots on the Spotted Salamander may be yellow or orange. The number of spots varies widely, and a few individuals may lack spots altogether. Tiger Salamander's spots are more irregular, less round.

Habitat: Primarily woodland areas, but also found in overgrown fields and edges bordering agricultural lands. They are rare in northwest Ohio and possibly extirpated in much of that region.

Breeding: Breeds in the same types of aquatic habitats as the Tiger Salamander (ponds, ditches, etc.). Migration to breeding sites occurs during periods of heavy rainfall in late winter. Eggs are deposited in large gelatinous masses in ponds or wetland pools. Eggs hatch in a few weeks and larvae transform into minature adults in two to four months. Young adults are about two to three inches long.

Natural History: Primarily subterranean in habits. Lives in underground burrows and beneath rocks, logs, or leaf litter on the forest floor. During periods of hot dry weather retreats deeper underground or stays in the vicinity perennially wet areas. Feeds on a wide variety of insects and invertebrates as well as a few small vertebrates. In the late winter they may be observed on rural roads at night during rainy weather.

Variation: Sexually dimorphic when breeding. Light colors are gray or silver in the female and white in the male.

Habitat: Most fond of bottomlands and stream floodplains (especially during breeding) but they can also common in upland woods adjacent to lowlands.

Breeding: Breeds in the fall during rainy weather. Overland migration is common. Eggs are laid on land under rocks, logs, etc. in low lying areas subject to flooding. Hatching is delayed until eggs are flooded by fall rains.

Natural History: This is one of the few salamanders to exhibit sexual dimorphism. The light markings are wider and whiter on the male and narrower and more silver or grayish on the female. These sexual differences manifest during breeding. Like other members of the "mole salamander" family, Marbled Salamanders are fossorial in habits. In fact, this species may be even more secretive than many of its kin. Thus, though they are fairly common they are not readily observed. They can reportedly produce a noxious secretion from the tail which may help to ward off some predators. Adults probably feed on most any small animal they can swallow. Larvae have been known to eat the eggs of small frogs.

Class—**Amphibia** (amphibians)
Order—**Caudata** (salamanders)
Family—**Ambystomatidae** (mole salamanders)

Small-mouthed Salamander *Ambystoma texanum*	**Streamside Salamander** *Ambystoma barbouri*	**Jefferson Salamander** *Ambystoma jeffersonianum*

Size: 4 to 5 inches.

Presumed range in Ohio

Abundance: Fairly common in most of glaciated Ohio. Very rare or absent in the Appalachian Plateau.

Variation: Varies in color from uniform dark gray to blue-gray with varying amounts of silver or light gray flecking

Habitat: Found in a variety of habitats from woodlands to grassy meadows. Most common in lowlands and stream bottoms but also in upland areas.

Breeding: Breeds in late winter or very early spring. May lay up to several hundred eggs in large clumps. Ponds, wetland pools, or flooded roadside ditches may be used for egg deposition. Larvae transform into adults in about six to eight weeks, sooner in warmer weather.

Natural History: Like other members of its genus the Smallmouth Salamander spends most of its time in underground burrows or beneath rocks, logs, or leaf litter. They will emerge on rainy nights to forage above ground. Feeds on a wide variety of soft-bodied invertebrate prey such as earthworms, slugs, and grubs. The Smallmouth Salamander is very similar in appearance to the Streamside Salamander and the best clue to identification between the two species is to refer to their respective range maps. Geography is the best guide to differentiating the two in Ohio. Ohio's "unisexual salamanders" are often hybirdized with this species.

Size: 4 to 5 inches.

Presumed range in Ohio

Abundance: Fairly common within its rather restricted range in southern and southeastern Ohio.

Variation: Varies in color from uniform dark gray to light gray or blue gray. The amount of silver or whitish flecking also varies, and may be absent.

Habitat: Found mostly in woodlands within close proximity to streams. Thus creek bottoms and river valleys are more frequently inhabited.

Breeding: Breeds in limestone-bottomed streams in late fall to early winter. This is the only *Ambystoma* salamander that breeds strictly in streams. It also lays fewer eggs than others and its eggs are deposited singly rather than in large clumps.

Natural History: In most respects other than breeding habits the natural history of the Streamside Salamander is similar to that of the very similar-looking Smallmouth Salamander. The two species are very difficult to distinguish based on appearance alone. In fact, they were once regarded as being members of the same species. Soft-bodied invertebrates are probably the main food item for the adults and the larvae are known to eat small crustaceans (isopods, etc.) as well as worms and other benthic organisms. Can best be told from the very similar Small-mouthed Salamander by geography (see range maps). Even herpetologists find the two confusing.

Size: Up to 8 inches.

Presumed range in Ohio

Abundance: Fairly common in southeastern Ohio. Uncommon and sporadic in northern Ohio.

Variation: There is some variation in the amount of light blue spots that are present. Older adults tend to lose their spots and become darker.

Habitat: An upland forest species mostly. This is primarily a northern species that reaches the southernmost limits of its range in Kentucky.

Breeding: Breeding occurs in late winter or early spring, with eggs being deposited in woodland ponds. As with all *Ambystoma* salamanders, the eggs hatch into larvae that spend up to a year as thoroughly aquatic, gilled salamanders before transforming into adults.

Natural History: Although primarily nocturnal, Jefferson's Salamanders are sometimes seen abroad on rainy, heavily overcast days. These salamanders have an unnamed "sister species" that represents an enigma for biologists. Throughout much of northern and western Ohio exists a unique population of salamanders known as "unisexual salamanders." They are similar in appearance to the Jeffersons Salamander but they are a hybrid population that incorporates genetic material from two or more (up to five) different *Ambystoma* species. These unisexual populations are probably most closely related to the Streamside Salamander (previous).

Class—**Amphibia** (amphibians)

Order—**Caudata** (salamanders)

Family—**Salamandridae** (newts)	Family—**Plethodontidae** (lungless salamanders)	
Eastern Newt *Notophthalmus viridescens*	**Allegheny Mt. Dusky Salamander** *Desmognathus ochrophaeus*	**Northern Dusky Salamander** *Desmognathus fuscus*

Size: Adults to 5 inches. Efts 3 inches.

Presumed range in Ohio

Abundance: Common in the Appalachian Plateau Province. Uncommon elsewhere.

Variation: No significant geographic variation. Significant ontogenic variation (see Natural History section).

Habitat: Adults are found in ponds, swamps, or other permanent water. Eft stage is a terrestrial animal of woods.

Breeding: Breeds in spring. Males deposit packages of sperm which are taken up by the female into the cloaca where fertilization occurs internally before eggs are then laid. Hatchlings metamorph into efts in four to five months.

Natural History: Newts are unique among Ohio salamanders in having an extra stage in their life cycle. Following hatching the young spend the summer as gill breathing larvae then undergo a transformation to an air breathing semi-adult that lives on land for up to three years. Newts in this terrestrial stage are call "efts." After one to three years the eft returns to the water and undergoes another metmorphosis into a totally aquatic adult. After returning to the water the coarse skin of the eft becomes smooth and the round tail flattens vertically to become fin-like. Their life span can be up to 15 years. Newts produce a neurotoxin in their skin that protects them from many predators.

Size: Average 3 to 4 inches. Record length 4.375 inches.

Presumed range in Ohio

Abundance: Very common where found in the state. Restricted to northeastern corner.

Variation: Many show a broad, light stripe dorsally. Others may be uniformly very dark brown.

Habitat: A forest species found in mesic woodlands. Favors hemlock ravines or the vicinity of streams and seeps.

Breeding: Breeding may occur both in spring and fall. Gravid females lay up one to two dozen eggs in seepage areas where there is a constant moisture little temparture variation. Female stays with the eggs until they hatch.

Natural History: Several studies suggest that within ideal habitat these small salamanders can be so numerous as to outnumber all other vertebrate life forms in the area. When a species is this common, it usually means that it is a highly valuable member of the local ecosystem. It is known that salamanders are food for a very wide array of predators, including snakes, shrews, probably every type carnivore in the area, and a wide array of bird species (including some songbirds). Being prey for so many predators, these little salamanders are remarkable quick and agile. When uncovered from beneath a flat rock of log on the forest floor tthey can dissappear with surprising speed.

Size: Average 3 to 4 inches. Record length 5.5625 inches.

Presumed range in Ohio

Abundance: Very common within its range. Absent from much of the Interior Lowlands.

Variation: Color varies from gray through many shades of brown. May show yellowish spots on the dorsum.

Habitat: Springs, seeps, and spring-fed brooks in wooded areas. Beneath rocks, detritus, or in the muck of forest streams.

Breeding: Eggs are laid under rocks in the vicinity of streams. The eggs (average 15–30) are laid in clusters of individual eggs that are not contained in a gelatinous mass like the mole salamanders.

Natural History: The Northern Dusky and its kin are salamanders that are often well known to rural folk. Many a youngster has amused themselves on a hot summer day by rolling stones and logs in mountain streams to try and catch these slippery and quick moving salamanders. They are often collected for fish bait in many areas within their range and sometimes go by the name "Spring Lizards." They are frequently sold in bait stores in the Appalachian region. Although this practice probably has no significant impact on this common species, accidental "by catch" of some rarer species may have an negative impact on those less common species. Mainly nocturnal, they will emerge at night to forage.

Class—**Amphibia** (amphibians)

Order—**Caudata** (salamanders)

Family—**Plethodontidae** (lungless salamanders)

Eastern Redback Salamander *Plethodon cinereus*	Northern Slimy Salamander *Plethodon glutinosus*	Northern Ravine Salamander *Plethodon electromorphus*

Size: 3–4 inches. Maximum 5 inches.

Presumed range in Ohio

Abundance: Very common. Can exceed one salamander per square yard in ideal habitats.

Variation: Considerable variation in the dorsal pattern. Some Redback Salamanders are not red on the back at all, but uniformly gray. This color morph is known as the "lead-backed phase."

Habitat: Chiefly woodlands. This is another terrestrial but retiring species that hides beneath leaf litter, logs, etc.

Breeding: Female lays about 10 eggs on land and guards them until they hatch. Babies hatch fully formed.

Natural History: Much of this salamanders range is to the north and east of Ohio. In fact this is one of the most northerly ranging salamanders in eastern North America and can be found as far north as the Canadian provinces of Quebec, Nova Scotia, and New Brunswick. In the heart of its range this is not only the most common salamander species, but one of the most common vertebrate species. In ideal habitats it seems that every rock or log will have one of these small salamanders hiding beneath it. Savvy environmental educators around the state often use this salamander to introduce children to the wonders of nature. Watching a group of kids hunt for salamanders in a nearby park or preserve is a testament to the fact that human beings are inherently interested in the natural world.

Size:Size: Maximum 8.25 inches.

Presumed range in Ohio

Abundance: Can be very common in ideal habitat. Not as common as the Redback Salamander.

Variation: The ground color is consistanly black or very dark gray. Does vary considerably in the amount of light flecking. Coloration of the light flecks ranges from white, silvery, or golden.

Habitat: Another woodland species. More common in upland woods and hillsides than in bottomlands.

Breeding: 12 to 15 eggs seems to be the average. As with other *Plethodon* Salamanders, young hatch fully formed.

Natural History: The name is derived from the fact that slimy salamanders exude a thick, sticky mucus from the skin when handled. This material is difficult to wash off and once dried becomes black and crusty. Herpetologists capturing slimy salamanders sometimes wear the residue of salamander mucus on their hands for days before it finally wears off. The food of these woodland species is undoubtedly a wide variety of soft-bodied insects, insect larvae, annelids, small crustaceans, and other tiny invertebrate life found among the leaf litter on the forest floor. Until the advent of DNA technology there was only one ubiquitous species of Slimy Salamander that ranged across most of the eastern United States. There are now over dozen individual species. Only one species (Northern) occurs in Ohio.

Size: About 4 inches. Maximum 5.75.

Presumed range in Ohio

Abundance: Can be very common in ideal habitat. Not as common as the Redback Salamander.

Variation: Some variation in background color. The color of the widespread metallic-like flecking can vary from silverish to gold. The amount of this flecking can also vary, or be absent.

Habitat: As its name implies this species prefers the steep slopes of deep, forested ravines in rugged terrain.

Breeding: As with other *Plethodon* salamanders there is no larval stage and the young appear like miniature adults.

Natural History: Of the several species of small salamanders depicted in this book the Ravine Salamander is noteworthy because of its tiny legs and its predilection for living along the slopes of steep valleys and ravines. Like other woodland salamanders this species is easily overlooked hiding beneath rocks, logs, bark, and humus beneath our feet. Like many other small amphibians they disappear underground during hot, dry weather, re-emerging during rains or in cooler seasons. They are most active in the spring and fall and may be active during warm weather even in the dead of winter. This species is widespread across much of Ohio but is absent from the Huron-Lake Erie Plains, the northwestern portions of the Till Plains, and the northeastern Unglaciated Allegheny Plateau.

Class—**Amphibia** (amphibians)

Order—**Caudata** (salamanders)

Family—**Plethodontidae** (lungless salamanders)

Four-toed Salamander *Hemidactylium scutatum*	**Green Salamander** *Aneides aeneus*	**Southern Two-lined Salamander** *Eurycea cirrigera*

Size: Average 2–3 inches. Record 4.

Abundance: Uncommon to rare.

Variation: Dorsal ground color varies from brown to gray or orange.

Presumed range in Ohio

Size: Maximum about 5.5 inches.

Abundance: Rare in Ohio.

Variation: Slight variation in the amount of dorsal markings.

Presumed range in Ohio

Size: Max 4 inches, average about 2–3.

Abundance: Common.

Variation: Ground color varies slightly from bright yellow to dingy brownish.

Presumed range in Ohio

Habitat: Mature woodlands, usually near woodland bogs, springs and seeps, or small woodland ponds.

Habitat: Wet cliff faces and rocky outcrops with seeping water. Most common in areas of sandstone substrates.

Habitat: Streams, wetlands, and seeps. Mostly a lowland animal but also found in mesic upland environments.

Breeding: Eggs are laid in winter at the edge of streams, ponds, etc. Females remain with the eggs until hatching in about four weeks.

Breeding: Lays its eggs in moist rock crevices. Up to 30 eggs are attached to the ceiling of a rock crevice. There is no larvae and hatchlings resemble adults.

Breeding: Several dozen eggs are attached to the underside of rocks and brooks. Eggs hatch into aquatic larvae that transform in one or two years.

Natural History: The name comes from the fact that they have only four toes on the hind foot (other terrestrial salamanders in Ohio have five). There is also an obvious constriction at the base of the tail that is unique to this species. It is at this constricted location that the tail will be broken off as a defensive manuever. The most readily identifiable characteristic of this species is its white belly with black spots. No other salamander in Ohio is similarly colored and patterned. This salamander has a greater geographic range than any other in America. It is found from Nova Scotia, Canada to the gulf coast and west to Minnesota and Arkansas. But like many amphibians this species is threatened by habitat destruction and has been in decline for decades. The disappearance of vernal pools, bogs, and streamside habitat to agriculture and urban development is probably the most significant threat.

Natural History: This is a salamander that is easily recognizable by its green, lichen-like markings on a black ground color. It is the only truly green salamander in Ohio. This is a cliff dwelling animal that lives in cracks and crevices of rock faces. Damp sandstone cliffs with seeping water are its primary habitat. In Ohio this species is found only in three counties in the southernmost part of the state. Its head and body are dorso-ventrally flattened, an adaptation that enables it to squeeze through narrow cracks in the rocks. Some experts report that Green Salamanders have been found within crevices in the bark of trees. One well known biologist from the University of Kentucky (the late Dr. Roger Barbour) suggested that the now extinct American Chestnut tree with its deeply furrowed bark may have once been an important habitat for the species. Few Ohioans will ever see this secretive little salamander.

Natural History: The members of this genus (*Eurycea*) are often called "Brook Salamanders," in reference to their propensity to inhabit small, clear streams. Other habitats are also utilized and the Southern Two-lined Salamander is often found in swamps or bottomland woodlands in the vicinity of seeps. Springs and seeps that emerge from ridges and upland areas that border bottomlands and swamps are good places to find this small and secretive salamander. Brook Salamanders differ from their family relatives the "Woodland Salamanders" (genus *Plethodon*) in that they have a strong affinity to aquatic stream habitats as adults. They are also different in another important respect. Brook Salamanders must undergo an aquatic larval stage in their life cycle while "Woodland Salamanders" hatch into fully formed, tiny replicas of the adults. This is one of two nearly identical species of Two-lined Salamanders found in Ohio.

Class—**Amphibia** (amphibians)

Order—**Caudata** (salamanders)

Family—**Plethodontidae** (lungless salamanders)

Northern Two-lined Salamander	Long-tailed Salamander	Cave Salamander
Eurycea bislineata	*Eurycea longicauda*	*Eurycea lucifuga*

Size: Max 4 inches, average about 2–3.	**Size:** Record 7.75 inches.	**Size:** Record 7.125 inches.
Presumed range in Ohio 	Presumed range in Ohio 	Presumed range in Ohio 
Abundance: Common.	**Abundance:** Fairly common.	**Abundance:** Rare in Ohio.
Variation: Ground color varies slightly from bright yellow to dingy brownish.	**Variation:** Ground color varies from yellow to orange or rarely, reddish.	**Variation:** Ground color varies from bright red to reddish brown or orange.

Habitat: Streams, wetlands, and seeps. Mostly a lowland animal but also found in mesic upland environments.

Habitat: Spring runs, small clear creeks, in the vicinity of seeps, and near cave openings.

Habitat: Although frequently found in caves, this salamander also lives in upland woods beneath rocks, logs, etc.

Breeding: Several dozen eggs are attached to the underside of rocks and brooks. Eggs hatch into aquatic larvae that transform in one or two years.

Breeding: Breeds in late winter or early spring. Eggs are deposited in streams and springs or often in caves. Larvae metamorphose in about a year.

Breeding: Several dozen eggs are attached to the underneath side of rocks underwater; in springs or waterways, and both inside and outside of caves.

Natural History: In appearance and in almost every other regard this species is indistinguishable from the Southern Two-lined Salamander. Their natural history (habitat requirments, food, breeding, etc.) are essentially the same. The easiest way to tell them apart is by geography. There are some subtle morphological differences however that herpetologists use to differentiate the two species. For instance the Northern species has 15 or 16 costal grooves, while the Southern Two-lined has only 13 or 14. Costal grooves are shallow, vertically oriented grooves that are present on the sides of most salamanders. If the salamander is in hand these grooves are readily visible to the naked eye and their number is often an important morphological character used to identify salamander species.

Natural History: These salamanders can often be found beneath rocks within small clear streams. They also live in mesic woodland environments, usually in the vicinity of a permanent stream. Here they may be found hiding beneath or within rotted logs or stumps. On rainy nights they can be encountered on roads as they roam around in search of tiny invertebrate prey. Although they can reach an impressive length of over seven inches, they are a slim-bodied animal and over half their length is tail. In Ohio these are animals of the Allegheny Plateau and Interior Low Plateau provinces and they are absent from the Huron-Lake Erie Plains and from the northern and central Till Plains, though they are found in some areas in the southernmost Till Plains of Ohio.

Natural History: The distribution of this species reaches its northenmost extension in southeastern Ohio. They are thus absent from most of the state. Adults of this species have prehensile tails and they are good climbers. They are sometimes seen clinging to the walls of caves. Despite their name these salamanders are not true troglodytes (cave dwellers). They inhabit mostly the twilight zone of caves as well as more typical terrestrial habitats in mesic upland woods. They can be found beneath rocks, logs, etc. and can be common near springs and seeps in upland areas. Like many other salamanders, the tail may break off if grasped. This defensive "escape mechanism" is widespread among salamander (and also lizards). It is technically known by the name "caudal autotomy."

Class—**Amphibia** (amphibians)

Order—**Caudata** (salamanders)

Family—**Plethodontidae** (lungless salamanders)

Spring Salamander *Gyrinophilus porphyriticus*	**Red Salamander** *Pseudotriton ruber*	**Mud Salamander** *Pseudotriton montanus*

Spring Salamander
Gyrinophilus porphyriticus

Red Salamander
Pseudotriton ruber

Mud Salamander
Pseudotriton montanus

Size: Up to 9 inches.

Presumed range in Ohio

Abundance: Uncommon in Ohio.

Variation: Dorsal ground color varies from pinkish or light red to reddish brown or purplish. Four subspecies.

Size: Up to 7 inches.

Presumed range in Ohio

Abundance: Fairly common.

Variation: Tends to darken with age, a condition known as "ontogenic melanism." Four subspecies, one in Ohio.

Size: Up to 8 inches.

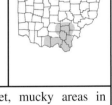
Presumed range in Ohio

Abundance: Rare in Ohio.

Variation: There are four subspecies. Only the Midland Mud Salamander (*P. m. diasticus*) is found in Ohio.

Habitat: Springs, seeps, and spring-fed streams as well as caves. Also on the forest floor near water. Range includes the entire Appalachian Plateau.

Breeding: Eggs are laid in water (stream or spring) during summer and hatch in the fall. The aquatic larval stage can be exceedingly long, lasting on average four to five years. Rarely up to 10 years in cave dwelling populations.

Natural History: This is one of the more diurnal salamander species, and adults have been observed prowling on the forest floor during daylight hours. In some areas of their range they are reportedly very common in cave habitats. These are large salamanders and they are fierce predators of a wide variety of small animal life, including other salamanders. There are four very similar subspecies, two of which range into Ohio. They are the Kentucky Spring Salamander (*G. p. duryi*), found in a few counties in south central Ohio, and the Northern Spring Salamander (*G. p. porphyriticus*), ranging throughout the rest of the Unglaciated Allegheny Plateau.

Habitat: Found within and in the vicinity of springs and spring-fed brooks. Found both in the water and under moss, logs, etc., in the vicinity of water.

Breeding: Several dozen eggs are laid in the water in spring fed streams during late summer/fall. Females will guard the eggs until they hatch in the winter. Totally aquatic larvae can take 1.5 to 3 years to transform into adults.

Natural History: Adult Red Salamanders will wander away from water and may be found in moist environments a good distance from springs or streams. Young adults are bright, fire-engine red with scattered black specks throughout the body. As they age they tend to become darker on the back and very old individuals may be uniformly dark gray or deep purple dorsally. There are four subspecies. Only the northern subspecies (*P. r. ruber*) occurs in Ohio. It is widespread in throughout the Allegheny Plateau and is a fairly common salamander. They are easily observed on rural roads in the southern Appalachians on rainy nights in early spring.

Habitat: Mud. Wet, mucky areas in close proximity to seeps and spring runs. Also found beneath leaf litter an accumulated detritus within streams.

Breeding: Eggs are laid in fall and winter in spring runs or bogs. About one to two dozen eggs are laid. Larvae are less than 3/4 inch at hatching. They reach up to three inches before transforming into adults after 1.5 to 2.5 years.

Natural History: In both appearance and life history the Mud Salamanders are similar to the Red Salamanders. The easiest way to distinguish between the two is to note the size and concentration of the black spots. Mud Salamanders have larger, more widely spaced spots and the spots are more perfectly rounded, resulting in something akin to a "polka dot" pattern. Most experts agree that Mud Salamanders are more closely tied to water than the similar Red Salamander. They are also are more secretive and less commonly seen than the more terrestrially oriented Red Salamander.

Class—**Amphibia** (amphibians)
Order—**Caudata** (salamanders)
Family—**Proteidae** (mudpuppies and waterdogs)
Mudpuppy—*Necturus maculosus*

Size: Average 12 inches. Record 19.5.

Abundance: Can be locally common.

Variation: None.

Presumed range in Ohio

Breeding: Breeding and egg laying occurs in the fall. Female Mudpuppies hollow out a nest beneath a sunken log or rock where they will lay from a few score to over a hundred eggs. The eggs are attached to the underside of a rock or log where the nest has been excavated. The female remains with eggs during incubation.

Natural History: Mudpuppies have extensive external gills that resemble downy feathers. Some think the gills are reminiscent of the ears of a dog, thus the name "Mudpuppy." These are totally aquatic salamanders that never lose the gills of the larvae. This condition of permanent larval characteristics is known scientifically as "neotony" and is a phenomena that is not rare in salamanders of several species. Mudpuppies prey on fish eggs, insects, mollusks small crustaceans, and annelids.

Family—**Cryptobranchidae** (giant salamanders)
Hellbender—*Cryptobranchus allegheniensis*

Size: Up to 30 inches in length and very heavy bodied.

Abundance: Rare. Declining throughout America.

Variation: Some variation in ground color. Reddish, brown, tan, or chocolate. A very similar but distinct species occurs in the Ozarks region.

Habitat: Clear pure streams. Once found throughout the Appalachians and much of the Interior Plateau. Populations now restricted to remote, unpolluted streams. Large underwater rocks are used as a refuge.

Breeding: Fertilization is external and eggs are laid in a nest guarded by the male. Lays over 400 eggs.

Presumed range in Ohio

Natural History: These huge, totally aquatic salamanders have deep folds and wrinkles in the skin. They have very large, dorso-ventrally flattened heads and laterally flattened, fin-like tails. They are completely aquatic and feed on crustaceans, minnows, and invertebrates with crayfish reported as a primary prey. They require clean, unpolluted flowing waters and they are in decline throughout their range due to stream degradation, impoundments, and chemical pollutants. This is one of America's largest salamander species, but it is dwarfed by its larger relative from Japan. The world's largest salamander, the Pacific Giant Salamander, is native to pristine streams in the mountains of Japan, where it can reach five feet in length. The range map above may not be an accurate depiction of the Hellbenders range in the state today. Many streams throughout Ohio lack their original water quality and can no longer support this bizarre and interesting creature. Photo supplied by John R. MacGregor.

CHAPTER 8
THE RIVERS AND STREAMS OF OHIO

As a preface to the next chapter (Chapter 9, The Fishes of Ohio), this short chapter is intended to provide a brief introduction into the waterways of Ohio, which are home to the state's fish species. The state of Ohio boasts over 25,000 miles of named rivers and streams. The largest of which, the Ohio River, makes up the southern and southeastern border of the state for a distance of just over 450 miles. In addition to the state's rivers and streams, numerous natural lakes and impoundments provide habitat for the state's fish species. The most significant of these of course is Lake Erie, whose shoreline provides the northern border for much of the state (actually the state line extends well out into the lake and thus many islands in the sourtheastern portion of the lake are part Ohio).

Most of Ohio's rivers and streams drain into the Ohio River, which is in turn a part of the much larger Mississippi River drainage. Approximately two-thirds of the land area of Ohio is contained in the Ohio River watershed. The northernmost portion of the state however drains into Lake Erie, which is a part of the Great Lakes / St. Lawrence River watershed. The map below and those on the next page show these various watersheds and how they affect the state of Ohio.

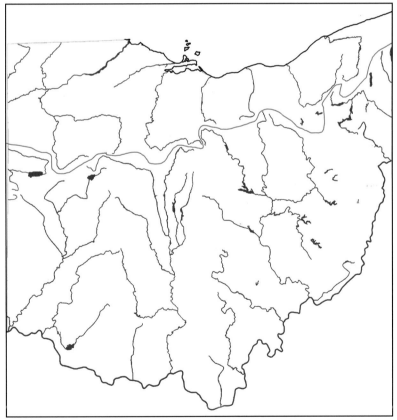

Figure 8. The map above shows the major rivers and streams of Ohio. The red line indicates the division between the Ohio River watershed and the Great Lakes/St. Lawrence River watershed.

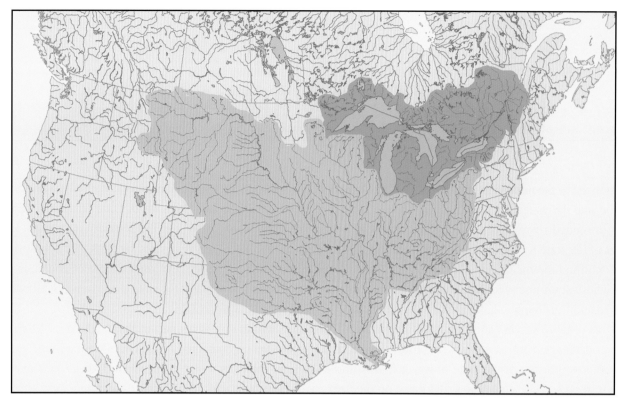

Figure 9. The map above shows the major rivers and lakes of North America and the two major watersheds that affect Ohio. The region drained by the Mississippi River watershed is shaded in gray. The Great Lakes / St. Lawrence watershed is shaded in green. The Mississippi River watershed can be divided into several smaller watersheds, one of which is the Ohio River watershed. Figure 10 below shows the Ohio River watershed in orange.

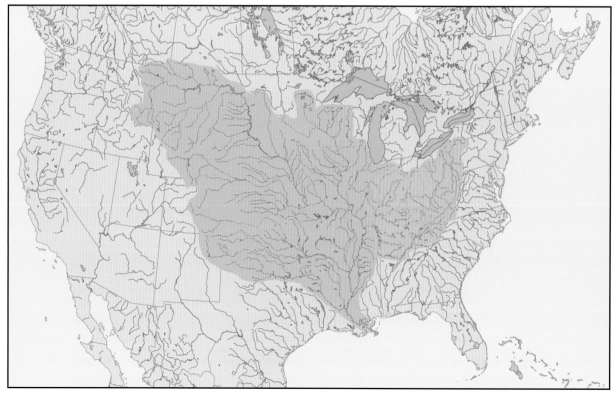

Figure 10. The Ohio River watershed in orange is a part of the Mississippi River drainage system. The two maps shown above are derived from maps created by the Commission for Environmental Cooperation.

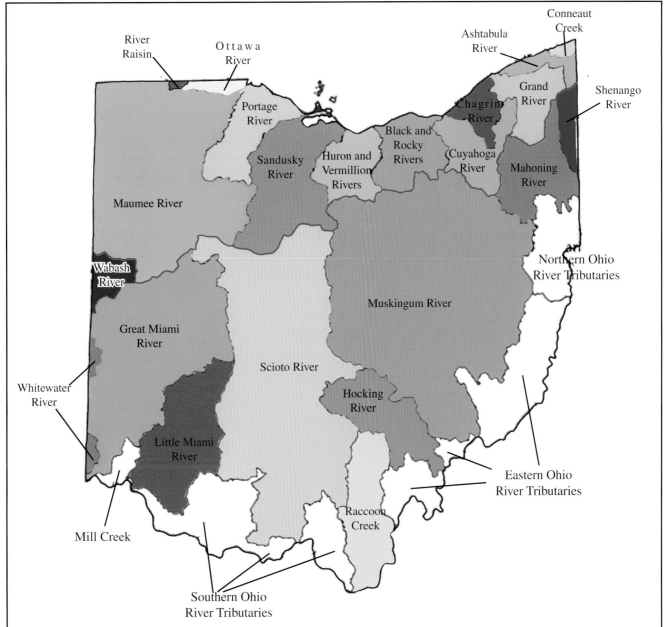

Figure 11. This map shows how the two major watersheds in Ohio are divided into smaller drainages. The areas in white are regions of the state that drain directly into the Ohio River via smaller creeks. The red line denotes the division between the Ohio River drainages and the Great Lakes/St. Lawrence River drainages. Map above is derived from original produced by Ohio EPA.

Both the Ohio River watershed and the Great Lakes / St. Lawrence River watershed consist of increasingly smaller tributaries, each of which constitutes its own drainage area. The map below shows how the large watersheds in the state are comprised of smaller drainage basins (watersheds).

Some appreciation of the above drainage basins (or watersheds) can provide insight into the distribution of Ohio's fish species. More importantly, conservation organizations can monitor these various watersheds for pollution and other factors that may impact upon the health of fish populations contained within them.

According to the Ohio EPA, "barely over one-half of Ohio's streams and rivers harbor good or exceptional quality fish and/or aquatic invertebrate assemblages." Like all other habitat types within the eastern United States, the waterways of Ohio have been highly altered by man. In addition to numerous dams and impoundments, the waterways of Ohio have suffered severe insults from both pollution and siltation.

Direct pollution from industry and resource extraction is an important source of stream degradation throughout America. But of equal importance is indirect contamination from agriculture. Agricultural related pollution and stream degradation can come in the form of chemical runoff or the destruction of vegetated buffer zones by farmers needing to maximize the production area of their land. Erosion and siltation from row cropping operations impact nearly every stream in the western half of the state. To a lesser extent, livestock operations statewide can also have negative impacts as cattle destroy creek banks and stir up silt from stream bottoms. Today nearly 50 percent of the state's streams no longer support the high diversity of fish and other aquatic species that once were abundant within their banks. A total of 33 of Ohio's fish species are now regarded by the Ohio Department of Natural Resources as threatened or endangered. Nine more are considered to be species of Concern and 10 species that occured in the state at the time of European settlement are now gone. The future for many of Ohio's fish species is, frankly, quite grim. If we regard this fact as a warning sign relating to the health of our aquatic ecosystems, and surely they are just that, then all Ohioans should be acutely concerned about the future of Ohio's waterways. We often hear reasonable people argue against stringent protections of our environment. But few things are more important than these protections. Humans can survive for a maximum of four minutes without air and maximum of four days without water. It follows then that our paramount priorities should be to ensure that we all always have clean air to breath and pure water to drink!

The series of maps shown on the previous two pages gives a good representation of how smaller streams and their watersheds are integrated into larger streams and larger watersheds. What also becomes apparent from these maps is that when it comes water, everything (and everyone) downstream is affected by the quality of the water and the overall environmental health of the waters upstream. The environmental quality of that tiny creek in your backyard or on your farm affects not only the life of organisms living within that stream, but also organisms within the larger aquatic ecosystems into which it flows. And ultimately, the aquatic wildlife living in Lake Erie and the North Atlantic, or in the Mississippi River, Louisiana's coastal marshes, the depths of the Gulf of Mexico, and the magnificent coral ecosystems of the great reefs of the Caribbean.

The following chapter is an introduction to the 176 fish species that call the state of Ohio home. Some are familiar, many others are largely unknown to most Ohioans. All are important members of Ohio's wild fauna and each plays a role in an ecological scheme so complex that we have just begun to understand it.

It should be noted here that the range maps for Ohio's fishes that appear in the following chapter may not always accurately depict that species range within the state. While a number of reliable sources were referenced in the creation of the maps, in some cases the sources reviewed reflected some disparities. Although most of the maps are believed to be fairly accurate, the reader should keep in mind that creating range maps is always problematic and some range maps may represent "presumptions" of a particular species range within Ohio.

CHAPTER 9
THE FISHES OF OHIO

Table 9.
The Orders and Families of Ohio Fishes

Class—**Actinopterygii** (ray-finned fishes)

Order—**Perciformes** (typical fishes)

Family	**Centrarchidae** (sunfishes)
Family	**Moronidae** (true basses)
Family	**Scianidae** (drums)
Family	**Percidae** (perches and darters)
Family	**Gobiidae** (gobies)

Order—**Salmoniformes**

Family	**Esocidae** (pikes)
Family	**Salmonidae** (trout and salmon)
Family	**Osmeridae** (smelts)
Family	**Umbridae** (mudminnows)

Order—**Anguilliformes** (eels)

Family	**Anguillidae** (freshwater eels)

Order—**Amiiformes** (bowfin)

Family	**Amiidae** (bowfin)

Order—**Gadiformes**

Family	**Gadidae** (codfish)

Order—**Clupeiformes** (sardines, herrings, and shads)

Family	**Clupeidae** (herring and shad)

Order—**Siluriformes** (catfishes)

Family	**Ictaluridae** (american catfishes)

Order—**Acipenseriformes** (primitive fishes)

Family	**Acipenseridae** (sturgeons)
Family	**Polyodontidae** (paddlefish)

Order—**Lepisosteiformes** (gar)

Family	**Lepisosteidae** (gars)

The Orders and Families of Ohio Fishes—continued

Order—**Cypriniformes** (minnows and suckers)

Family	**Catastomidae** (suckers)
Family	**Cyprinidae** (minnows)

Order—**Cyprinodontiformes** (topminnows and livebearers)

Family	**Fundulidae** (topminnows)
Family	**Poecilidae** (livebearers)

Order—**Gasterosteiformes** (mostly small marine fishes)

Family	**Gasterosteidae** (sticklebacks)

Order—**Osteoglossiformes** (bonytongues)

Family	**Hiodontidae** (mooneyes)

Order—**Percopsiformes** (pirate perch and cavefish)

Family	**Aphredoderidae** (pirate perch)
Family	**Percopsidae** (trout perch)

Order—**Atheriniformes**

Family	**Atherinidae** (silversides)

Order—**Scorpaeniformes**

Family	**Cottidae** (sculpins)

Class—**Actinopterygii** (ray-finned fishes)

Order—**Perciformes** (typical fishes)

Family—**Centrarchidae** (sunfishes)

Largemouth Bass *Micropterus salmoides*	**Smallmouth Bass** *Micropterus dolomieui*	**Spotted Bass** *Micropterus punctulatus*

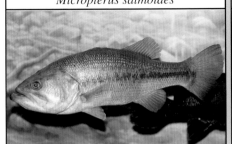  

Size: May reach 38 inches and 22 pounds. Ohio record size is just over 13 pounds and 22 inches.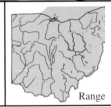

Size: Maximum of up to 11 pounds. Ohio record size is 9.5 pounds and 23.5 inches.

Size: Maximum of 8 pounds Average adult is about 3 to 4 pounds Ohio record size is 5.5 pounds and 21 inches.

Abundance: Very common.

Abundance: Common.

Abundance: Fairly common.

Natural History: This is probably America's most popular freshwater game fish, pursued by anglers throughout the country. Indeed an entire sporting industry has evolved around the pursuit of this fish. Found in virtually any large body of water in the state. Also in smaller streams and small farm ponds. Produced in captivity for stocking.

Natural History: Prefers clearer, cooler, more highly oxygenated waters than the Largemouth Bass. Crayfish are a preferred prey, especially for stream dwelling Smallmouth Bass. Like its cousin the Largemouth Bass, this is an important game species. It is renowned among sport fishermen for its tenacious fighting abilities when hooked.

Natural History: Intermediate between the two previous species in both the size of the mouth and in its habitat preferences. Primarily a fish of flowing waters but can tolerate warmer conditions than the Smallmouth. Avoids the still waters favored by the Largemouth. Tongue feels rough to the touch, smooth on the other two *Micropterus* bass.

Bluegill *Lepomis macrochirus*	**Longear Sunfish** *Lepomis megalotis*	**Warmouth** *Lepomis gulosus*

Size: Record of 4 pounds, 12 ounces. Ohio record is 3.28 pounds and 12.75 inches. Most are under 0.5 pound.

Size: World record size is 1 pound 12 ounces. Ohio record .41 pounds and 8 inches.

Size: Record of 2 pounds 7 ounces. Ohio record 1.32 pounds and 10.75 inches. Most are about 6–7 inches.

Abundance: Very common.

Abundance: Very common.

Abundance: Uncommon in Ohio.

Natural History: The Bluegill is Ohio's best known sunfish. This is the first fish caught on hook and line by many a young angler. It is an important game fish throughout the state. They are regularly stocked in new impoundments and are found in virtually every significant body of water in Ohio, including most farm ponds.

Natural History: Breeding males are one of the most brilliantly colored of the sunfishes. Clear streams with gravelly or sandy substrates are the primary habitat. There are two very similar species in Ohio. The smaller **Northern Sunfish** (*L. peltastes*) is found in the Lake Erie drainages, while the Longear Sunfish is in the Ohio drainage. Both look alike.

Natural History: A fish of lowland creeks and swamps, the Warmouth is most common in the southern United States. Although it occurs statewide it is sporadically distributed and may be absent from many areas. It prefers waters with thick growths of aquatic plants. The name comes from a patch of teeth that are present on the tongue.

Class—**Actinopterygii** (ray-finned fishes)

Order—**Perciformes** (typical fishes)

Family—**Centrarchidae** (sunfishes)

Redear Sunfish *Lepomis microlophus*	**Pumkinseed** *Lepomis gibbosus*	**Green Sunfish** *Lepomis cyanellus*

Size: Record 4 pounds 13 ounces. Ohio record 3.58 pounds and 15 inches. Averages about 8–10 inches.  Range	**Size:** Ohio record 1.1 pounds and 10.5 inches. The maximum length for this species is 16 inches.  Range	**Size:** Maximum recorded size is 2 pounds 2 ounces. and 12 inches in length. Ohio record is 1 lb. and 10.625 inches.  Range
Abundance: Uncommon. Introduced.	**Abundance:** Common.	**Abundance:** Very common.
Natural History: These fish also go by the name "Shellcracker," a reference to their habit of eating small freshwater mollusks such clams and snails. The natural distribution of this fish was originally the southeastern United States. Today it has been widely introduced throughout much of the eastern US, including the southern half of Ohio.	**Natural History:** Found mainly in the northern United States and along the eastern seaboard. Inhabits still or slow-moving waters. Snails and bivalves are a major food source. In this sense the Pumkinseed is similar to the Redear Sunfish. It also resembles the Redear Sunfish and could be considered the northern counterpart of that species.	**Natural History:** This is a fairly common fish throughout the state. It may be found in ponds and lakes, but its natural habitat is quite pools of slow-moving streams. It is known to hybridize readily with other *Lepomis* sunfishes, especially the Bluegill. Tolerates warm, low oxygen, muddy waters better than most other sunfishes.

Orange-spotted Sunfish *Lepomis humilis*	**Rock Bass** *Ambloplites rupestris*	**White Croppie** and **Black Croppie** *Pomoxis annularus* and *Pomoxis nigromaculatus*

Male

Female

Size: Average adult size is only 2 to 3 inches. Maximum reported length is about 4 inches.  Range	**Size:** Record size 3 pounds, 10 ounces and 13.25 inches in length Ohio record is just under 2 pounds.  Range	**Size:** Record for White 5 pounds 3 oz. Record for Black 6 pounds Ohio record is 4.5 pounds for Black. White 3 pounds 14 oz.  Range
Abundance: Uncommon, increasing.	**Abundance:** Fairly common.	**Abundance:** Common.
Natural History: Inhabits creeks and rivers where it favors quiet water pools with cover in the form of brush. When it occurs in lakes and impoundments it is found in shallow bays. Nests in gravel. Eats mainly small aquatic insect larvae and small crustaceans. Female is less colorful than the male (see photos above).	**Natural History:** Also known as the "Goggle Eye," the Rock Bass is a fish of clear, cool waters. They are primarily a stream fish that is found in clear streams and lakes with good water quality throughout the state. The natural distribution is from the Great Lakes region west to the Dakotas and south into northern Alabama, including all of Ohio.	**Natural History:** The Black Croppie likes clearer waters than the White Croppie, though both are often found in the same waters. Popular game fishes, both species have been widely introduced across America. Positive ID can be made by counting the stiff spines on the dorsal fin. White Croppie has only six, Black has seven or eight.

Class—**Actinopterygii** (ray-finned fishes)

Order—**Perciformes** (typical fishes)

Family—**Moronidae** (true basses)

White Perch *Morone americana*	**White Bass** *Morone chrysops*	**Striped Bass** *Morone saxatilis*

Size: Ohio record size is 1.75 pounds and 14.125 inches. Maximum size attained is about 22 inches. 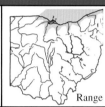 Range	**Size:** World record 5 pounds 9 ounces. Averages 10–14 inches and about a pound. Ohio record 4 pounds  Range	**Size:** World record of 78.5 pounds is from salt water. Ohio record is 37 pounds and 41 inches in length.  Range
Abundance: Generally uncommon.	**Abundance:** Generally uncommon.	**Abundance:** Uncommon.
Natural History: The White Perch is native to streams and brackish waters east of the Appalachian Plateau. They have been introduced into Lake Erie and now also occur in the lower portions of some rivers that drain into the lake. Introduction into a few other inland lakes in Ohio has occurred as well.	**Natural History:** These important game fish are famous for forcing schools of bait fish to the surface then attacking them in a feeding frenzy. Bait fish leaping from the water create a visible indicator of the presence of feeding bass. Savvy fishermen look for these eruptions of bait fish known as "jumps."	**Natural History:** Striped Bass were originally anadromous fish that lived in salt water but migrated into freshwater rivers to spawn. They are widely stocked in lakes by wildlife agencies (including in nearby Kentucky), where they have now adapted to a freshwater. In Ohio they occur in the Ohio River.

Family—**Sciaenidae** (drums)

Freshwater Drum
Aplodinotus grunniens

 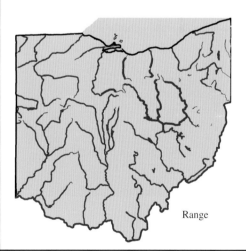

Range

Size: Record size is 54 pounds. Ohio record is 23.5 pounds and 37 inches in length. About 10 pounds is average.

Abundance: Generally common. They can become very common in some lake environments.

Natural History: This is the only member of the drum family that lives in freshwater. Most are salt water fishes and several are important food and sport fishes. By contrast the Freshwater Drum is not highly regarded by sport anglers despite the fact that they obtain an impressive size and will sometimes strike artificial lures meant for bass, trout, or other "game fishes." The flesh of the Freswater Drum is edible, but not very palatable. In Ohio they often go by the name "Sheephead." They are also sometimes called "grunt" or "croaker' in reference to the fact that they are capable of emitting grunting sounds from the air bladder.

Class—**Actinopterygii** (ray-finned fishes)

Order—**Perciformes** (typical fishes)

Family—**Percidae** (perch and darters)

Yellow Perch *Perca flavescens*	**Walleye** *Sander vitreus*	**Sauger** *Sander canadensis*

Size: World record 4 pounds 3 ounces. Ohio record 2 pounds and 14 ounces. Averages less than a pound.  Range	**Size:** World record is 25 pounds. Average is 2 to 4 pounds. Ohio record is 16 pounds 3 ounces.  Range	**Size:** World record 8 pounds 12 ounces. Average about a pound. Ohio record is 7 pounds, 5 ounces.  Range
Abundance: Common	**Abundance:** Fairly common.	**Abundance:** Fairly common.
Natural History: Native to the northern and eastern United States, Yellow Perch have recently expanded their range into more southerly regions. They are a popular pan fish in the north. In Ohio they are found in both man-made and natural lakes throughout the state, and are common in Lake Erie.	**Natural History:** Walleye live in larger rivers, impoundments, and natural lakes where deep water provides the cool temperatures these fish require. They are regarded as one of the most palatable of the game fishes. Found statewide but most common in Lake Erie and the lower portions of rivers that drain into it.	**Natural History:** Found throughout the Midwest and northward to Canada, the Sauger is a smaller relative of the Walleye that is more adapted to turbid waters. Hybridization between the Walleye and the Sauger results in a fish known as the "Saugeye," which can attain a much larger size than the Sauger.

Eastern Sand Darter
Ammocrypta pellucida

Size: A tiny fish, the Eastern Sand Darter can reach a maximum of 3.25 inches. The average size is usually just under 3 inches. Photo is nearly three times life-size.

Abundance: Probably uncommon today. Siltation of streams is a major threat. A species of Concern in Ohio.

Natural History: The aptly named Sand Darter is associated with sandy substrates of medium to large streams. When not swimming about in search of food or a mate they stay buried in the sand except for the top of head. Their translucent colored bodies render them effectively invisible under these conditions. They require relatively clean waters with clean sandy bottoms. Unfortunately, due to siltation, these are conditions that no longer exist in vast stretches of many rivers and streams. These unusual little fish are virtually unknown to most Ohioans.

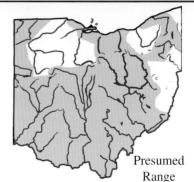

Presumed Range

Class—**Actinopterygii** (ray-finned fishes)		
Order—**Perciformes** (typical fishes)		
Family—**Percidae** (perch and darters)		
The Logperch Darters—genus *Percina*—7 species in Ohio (6 shown below)		

Logperch *Percina caprodes*	**Dusky Darter** *Percina sciera*	**Gilt Darter** *Percina evides*

Size: Average 3 to 5 inches. Maximum of 7. **Abundance:** Fairly common. 	**Size:** Average 3 to 4 inches. Maximum of 5. **Abundance:** Uncommon but rebounding. 	**Size:** Average 2.5 inches. Maximum 3.5 inches. **Abundance:** Very rare. Endangered in Ohio. 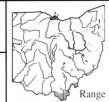

Blackside Darter *Percina maculata*	**Channel Darter** *Percina copelandi*	**Slenderhead Darter** *Percina phoxocephala*

Size: 2–3 inches. Maximum length 4.5 inches. **Abundance:** Uncommon. 	**Size:** 1.5 to 2 inches. Maximum 2.5 inches. **Abundance:** Rare. Threatened in Ohio. 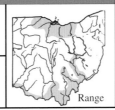	**Size:** 2.5 to 3 inches. Maximum 4 inches. **Abundance:** Uncommon but rebounding. 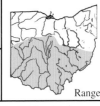

Natural History: The darters of the genus *Percina* were originally represented by a total of eight species in Ohio. Today one (Longhead Darter-*P. macrocephala*) is apparently extirpated, leaving a total of seven extant species in the state. Several of these are uncommon or rare, and only the Blackside Darter and the Logperch can be regarded as fairly common fish in Ohio. There as many as 40 *Percina* species in the US and collectively they range throughout much of the eastern United States. All occur east of the Rocky Mountains and most are found east of the Great Plains. The infamous Snail Darter, which was the subject of a great environmental controversy that arose over the construction of the Tellico Dam in Tennese, is a member of this genus. Most of these fishes tend to inhabit the larger creeks (or even rivers), but some can be found in small (even tiny) creeks. A few species have adapted to lake life in reservoirs that have inundated their former riverine habitats, but all must return to streams to lay their eggs in flowing waters. Their habitats range from deep pools to shallow riffle areas, and all species spawn in the shallow gravel rifles of small or medium-size creeks. The dependance upon clean, unaltered streams for breeding means these fishes face serious threats in America. In Ohio the invasive Round Goby is threat to species around Lake Erie. Along with their smaller relatives the *Etheostoma* darters (next several pages), these are some of Ohio's most interesting and colorful fishes. Both groups have become popular with aquarists, and in fact the darters have helped usher in a new style of fish keeping that focuses on native freshwater fishes of North America. Many aquarists, once introduced to the darters, will abandon the keeping of exotic tropical fishes for these beautiful "home grown" aquarium fishes. The diet of these fishes consists mostly of tiny aquatic insects and their larvae, which makes keeping them in captivity quite challenging for the aquarist. For those interested in keeping these fascinating fish in captivity the book *American Aquarium Fishes* from Texas AandM University Press is a handy reference. Longevity in the wild is probably no more than a few years. Generally the darters of this genus are larger than their relatives in the *Etheostoma* genus which begin on the next page. The two groups can be told apart by the presence of a row of enlarged scales on the belly of the *Percina* group. Six representative examples of Ohio's *Percina* are shown above. In addition the those species shown above, there is one other *Percina* darter that is found in Ohio. That species is the River Darter (*P. shumardi*). It is a threatened species that occurs in the Ohio River and its immediate tributaries.

Class—**Actinopterygii** (ray-finned fishes)

Order—**Perciformes** (typical fishes)

Family—**Percidae** (perch and darters)

The True Darters—genus *Etheostoma*—12 species in Ohio (9 shown below and 3 on next page)

Rainbow Darter	Johnny Darter	Greenside Darter
Etheostoma caeruleum	*Etheostoma nigrum*	*Etheostoma blennoides*

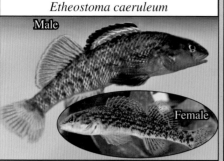

Size: Maximum length is just over 3 inches.

Abundance: Common in smaller streams.

Size: Average 2 to 2.75 inches. Max of 3 inches.

Abundance: Ohio's most common darter species.

Size: Largest of the *Etheostoma*. Reaches 6.5 in.

Abundance: Fairly common in larger streams.

Variegate Darter	Banded Darter	Least Darter
Etheostoma variatum	*Etheostoma zonatum*	*Etheostoma microperca*

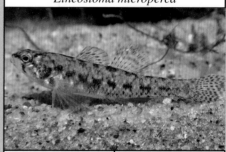
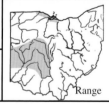

Size: Reaches a maximum size of 4.5 inches.

Abundance: Fairly common in unpolluted streams.

Size: Maximum total length recorded is 3.2 inches.

Abundance: One of Ohio's more common darters.

Size: One of America's smallest fish. Max 1.75 in.

Abundance: Uncommon. Species of Concern.

Orangethroat Darter	Bluebreast Darter	Fantail Darter
Etheostoma spectabile	*Etheostoma camurum*	*Etheostoma flabellare*

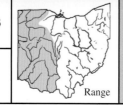

Size: Maximum length just under 3 inches.

Abundance: Fairly common in western Ohio.

Size: Maximum length of 3.5 inches.

Abundance: Uncommon but rebounding.

Size: Maximum length of 3.3 inches.

Abundance: Fairly common.

Class—**Actinopterygii** (ray-finned fishes)

Order—**Perciformes** (typical fishes)

Family—**Percidae** (perch and darters)

Iowa Darter *Etheostoma exile*	**Spotted Darter** *Etheostoma maculatum*	**Tippecanoe Darter** *Etheostoma tippecanoe*
 Male	 Male	 Female

Size: Very small. Maximum length 2.75 inches.	**Size:** Can reach a maximum length of 3.5 inches.	**Size:** Very small. Averages 1.5 inches. Max 1.7.
Abundance: Rare in Ohio. Endangered in Ohio.  Range	**Abundance:** Rare in Ohio. Endangered in Ohio.  Range	**Abundance:** Rare in Ohio. Threatened in Ohio.  Range

Natural History: With at least 148 species distributed across North America, the genus *Etheostoma* boasts more species than any other genus of freshwater fish in the United States. Among them are some of America's rarest fish and some of our most common. In coloration they range from a camouflaging mottled brown to remarkably colorful. Sexual dimorphism is common and is especially pronounced during the breeding season. In many species the breeding males rival the most colorful of tropical aquarium fishes. Most species are strongly sexually dimorphic, with the females being more subdued in color and sometimes outright drab. The stunning breeding color of the male is usually temporary and replaced by a much more faded appearance through the rest of the year following spring breeding. The females of these fishes are often so similar that even expert ichthyologists can have difficulty identifying them. New species have been recently described and there are most likely new species yet to be discovered. Unlike most fishes, they lack air bladders for flotation and they are mostly bottom dwellers that hug the sand and gravel bottoms of flowing streams. When startled they will move in quick, short dashes, hence the common name "darter." Ohio is home to 12 species of *Etheostoma*. Ohio's neighbor to the south (Kentucky) boasts nearly 50 species! Tennessee has the most of any state, at least 70 species! Collectively their habitats in Ohio include probably every drainage within the state and they are found in waterways ranging from Lake Erie to swamps, large rivers, and small creeks. Most species associate with flowing streams and many favor places with robust current. In these riffle areas they hug the substrate in water that may be only a couple of inches deep. Deep pools are used by other types of darters, and all may retreat to deeper pools in winter. A few species have a very restrictive distribution, being confined to a small area of drainage. Many species require pristine water conditions and these little fish can be a barometer to help determine the quality of Ohio's waterways. Like "the canary in the coal mine" they are often the first fishes to suffer from the effects of water pollution, siltation, and other forms of stream degradation. Before the passage of the Clean Water Act and other enviornmental legislation in the 1970s, many of Ohio's darters had dissappeared from vast stretches of the state's waterways. Efforts to restore Ohio's river and streams to more natural conditions in recent years has paid off with a resurgence in the state's fish populations, including many of the darters. However, several Ohio species are still regarded as threatened or endangered. The very small size of these fishes restricts their diet to micro-invertebrates such as small aquatic insects and their larvae, tiny crustaceans, and other very small aquatic life.

Family—**Gobiidae** (gobies)

Round Goby (*Neogobius melanostomus*) and **Tubnose Goby** (*Proterorhinus semilunaris*)

Size: Averages about 5–6 inches but can reach a maximum length of 10 inches.	 Round Goby	 Range
Abundance: They are quite common in Lake Erie and within the lower portions of its tributaries.		

Natural History: The gobies are exotic invasive species native to Eurasia that appeared in the Great Lakes sometime around 1990 and were first discovered in Lake Erie in 1995. As is often the case with exotic species, these fish have not been good for the great lakes. Though relatively small, they are voracious predators of the fry and eggs of game fish as well as smaller fish species such as darters and minnows. They are prolific reproducers that breed several times per year and they are blamed for the depletion of many native species throughout the great lakes region, especially the native darters and sculpins. It is believed they arrived in the great lakes in the ballast water of the many container ships that ply the waters of the great lakes.

Class—**Actinopterygii** (ray-finned fishes)

Order—**Salmoniformes**

Family—**Esocidae** (pikes)

Northern Pike *Esox lucius*	**Grass Pickerel** *Esox americanus*	**Muskellunge** *Esox masquinongy*

 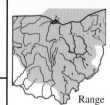 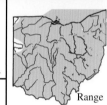

Northern Pike
Esox lucius

Size: Record size of 62.5 pounds is from Europe. North American record is 46 pounds

Abundance: Uncommon.

Range

Natural History: The Northern Pike is a fish of clear waters with abundant aquatic vegetation. Like all members of the pike family it is a highly carnivorous ambush predator with a very large mouth. The shape of the jaws is like a duck bill, and the jaws are equipped with rows of sharp, barracuda-like teeth.

Grass Pickerel
Esox americanus

Size: Average 8 to 10 inches. Maximum about 15 inches and 1.5 pounds.

Abundance: Fairly common.

Range

Natural History: Inhabits swamps and streams. In smaller creeks it usually is found in quiet pools. This fish likes clear waters and avoids muddy streams. This is the smallest of the pike family and thus feeds on smaller prey. Minnows and other small fish are the principal prey.

Muskellunge
Esox masquinongy

Size: Record size 69 pounds, 11 ounces. Ohio record 55 pounds and just over 4 feet.

Abundance: Uncommon.

Range

Natural History: Known as the "Muskie" by fishermen, this largest of the pikes is a prized game fish and one of the most difficult fishes to catch. They live in both man-made lakes and clear water rivers where they favor the deep pools containing boulders, logs, and other types of hiding places.

Family—**Salmonidae** (trout and salmon)

Rainbow Trout *Onchorhynchus mykiss*	**Pink Salmon** *Onchorhynchus gorbuscha*	**Brown Trout** *Salmo trutta*

 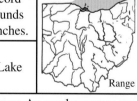 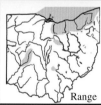

Rainbow Trout
Onchorhynchus mykiss

Size: World record 42 pounds 2 ozs. Ohio record 21 pounds

Abundance: Uncommon. Stocked by ODNR.

Range

Natural History: The Rainbow Trout was originally native to pacific drainages of the northwest. Today they have been widely introduced across much of America. They require cold, clear waters and thus are limited in distribution in Ohio. Several streams in Ohio along with Lake Erie are regularly stocked by the ODNR.

Pink Salmon
Onchorhynchus gorbuscha

Size: Ohio record just over 3 pounds and 20.125 inches.

Abundance: Uncommon. Lake Erie mostly.

Range

Natural History: An anadromoous species native to the pacific northwest of America. Has been introduced into the Great Lakes. First seen in Lake Erie in 1979 and has now adapted to a freshwater existance. Adults move out of the lake and into the lower reaches of some eastern Lake Erie drainages to spawn. Sometimes called "Humpback Salmon."

Brown Trout
Salmo trutta

Size: World record 40 pounds 4 ounces.

Abundance: Uncommon. Stocked by ODNR.

Range

Natural History: Like the Rainbow Trout this species has been introduced into Ohio where cool, clear waters allow for its survival. In the most ideal waters, some natural reproduction may occur, but most of the Brown Trout caught by anglers in Ohio were hatched in fish hatcheries and stocked by the ODNR.

Class—**Actinopterygii** (ray-finned fishes)

Order—**Salmoniformes**

Family—**Salmonidae** (trout and salmon)

Brook Trout *Salvelinus fontanalis*	**Lake Trout** *Salvelinus namaycush*	**Lake Whitefish** *Coregonus clupeaformis*

Size: World record 14.5 pounds.

Abundance: Rare. Occurs in two small streams.

 Range

Natural History: The Brook Trout is the only trout native to the eastern United States. This fish requires cooler water temperatures than our other trouts, and is less tolerant of changes in stream conditions. It is native to a few streams in northwestern Ohio, but has been eradicated from most of its former range in the state.

Size: Ohio record 20.5 pounds and 34 inches.

Abundance: Uncommon. In Lake Erie only.

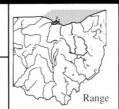 Range

Natural History: The Lake Trout is a northern species that reaches its southern limits in Lake Erie. Historically they were more common but they have suffered from parasitism by the Sea Lamprey and from degradation of the lakes water quality. These are fish of deep, cold waters and they are usually found well offshore.

Size: Can reach a maximum of 15 pounds and 30 inches.

Abundance: Fairy common. In Lake Erie only.

 Range

Natural History: Another northern species that reaches its southern distribution limits in Lake Erie. Inhabits deep, cold waters with high dissolved oxygen content. In summer this species retreats to depths of more than 40 feet. Although not rare, they are much less common than in historical times before the impact of human activities.

Cisco *Coregonus artedi*	Family—**Osmeridae** (smelts)	Family—**Umbridae** (mudminnows)
	Rainbow Smelt *Osmerus mordax*	**Central Mudminnow** *Umbra limi*

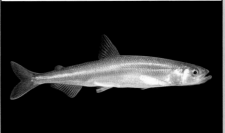

Size: Maximum length of 20 inches and up to 3 pounds

Abundance: Rare and endangered in Ohio.

 Range

Natural History: These fish were once so common that a single fisherman might catch over a hundred in a day's fishing on Lake Erie. Now endangered in Ohio waters. A northern species that reaches the southernmost limits of its range in Lake Erie. Inhabits deep, cold waters of natural lakes from the arctic to the Great Lakes region. Sometimes goes by the name "Lake Herring."

Size: Adults average 8 to 10 inches with a max of 14.

Abundance: Common in Lake Erie.

Natural History: Although they are a small fish the Rainbow Smelt is an important food fish in the great lakes region, where they are usually served fried with the bones intact. Many people along the Lake Erie coastline would be surprised to learn that this is not a native species. Rainbow Smelt were introduced into Lake Erie and other Great Lakes in early 1900s.

Size: Maximum length of 5.25 inches. Average about 2–3 inches.

Abundance: Fairy common.

 Range

Natural History: The Central Mudminnow is the only Ohio representative of a very small family of fishes found in both North America and in Europe. They live in swamps and still waters of oxbows or slow-flowing lowland creeks. Prefers areas with mucky bottom and can tolerate waters with low oxygen by using the air bladder like a lung. Able to survive in drought prone backwaters.

Class—**Actinopterygii** (ray-finned fishes)

Order—**Anguilliformes** (eels)	Order—**Amiiformes**	Order—**Gadiformes**
Family—**Anguillidae** (freshwater eels)	Family—**Amiidae** (bowfin)	Family—**Gadidae** (codfish)

American Eel *Anguilla rostrata*	**Bowfin** *Amia calva*	**Burbot** *Lota lota*

Size: Can reach 4 feet in length.

Abundance: Fairly common in large to moderate undammed rivers.

Range

Natural History: Eels have one of the most remarkable life cycles of any fish. After hatching far out in the Atlantic Ocean tiny larvae migrate to the coast and swim hundreds of miles upstream in inland rivers. After as many as 15 years adults return to the sea to spawn and die. Dams can hinder dispersal and the occurrence of eels today is sporadic.

Size: Record size 21.5 pounds.

Abundance: Fairly common. Most common in western Lake Erie.

Range

Natural History: This is the only surviving species of an ancient family of primitive fishes that dates back to the age of the dinosaurs. Found in swamps, lakes, and oxbows. In some places they go by the nickname "Grinnel." These fish are capable of gulping air into the swim bladder to breath and burrowing into the mud to survive during droughts.

Size: Record size 18.5 pounds.

Abundance: Generally uncommon in Ohio. A species of Concern.

Range

Natural History: A relative of the salt water cod, haddock, and pollock, all of which are important food fishes. The Burbot is the single freshwater species of the entire order. They are cold water fish that inhabit large rivers, including the Ohio. They are primarily nocturnal and usually confined to deep waters. Also found in Europe and Asia.

Order—**Clupeiformes** (sardines, herrings, and shad)

Family—**Clupeidae** (herring and shad)

Skipjack Herring *Alosa chrysochloris*	**Alewife** *Alosa pseudoharengus*	**Gizzard Shad** *Dorosoma cepedianum*

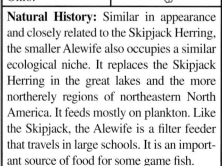

Size: Up to 21 inches and 3.75 pounds.

Abundance: Fairly common.

Range

Natural History: Originally an anadromous species that is now mostly land-locked due to the presence of dams on most major rivers. Although they are sometimes caught by fishermen they are not regarded as good table fare. Their range is restricted mostly to larger rivers and their impoundments. Skipjack Herring are related to the next species (Alewife), which occupies the same niche in the Lake Erie drainages.

Size: Typically 8–10 inches but can reach 15.

Abundance: Uncommon in Ohio.

Range

Natural History: Similar in appearance and closely related to the Skipjack Herring, the smaller Alewife also occupies a similar ecological niche. It replaces the Skipjack Herring in the great lakes and the more northerely regions of northeastern North America. It feeds mostly on plankton. Like the Skipjack, the Alewife is a filter feeder that travels in large schools. It is an important source of food for some game fish.

Size: Can reach 20 inches and 3.5 pounds.

Abundance: Common.

Range

Natural History: Gizzard Shad are plankton feeders that filter tiny organisms from the water through specialized gill rakers. These fish occur in major rivers and their large impoundments throughout the eastern United States, including all the larger rivers in Ohio. The young and immatures are an important forage species for many other fish, including many game species. Even adults are prey for larger fish.

Class—**Actinopterygii** (ray-finned fishes)

Order—**Siluriformes** (catfishes)

Family—**Ictaluridae** (american catfishes)

Yellow Bullhead *Ameiurus natalis*	**Black Bullhead** *Ameiurus melas*	**Brown Bullhead** *Ameiurus nebulosus*

Size: Maximum of 19 inches. Record weight 3 pounds 10 ounces.

Range

Abundance: Common.

Natural History: Widespread, common, and easily caught on hook and line the Yellow Bullhead is a familiar fish to many Ohions. They are often known by the nickname "Mudcat." Ranges from the central Great Plains eastward, including all of Ohio. Told from other bullheads by yellow colored chin barbels.

Size: Record weight is 8 pounds but few will ever exceed 3 pounds.

Range

Abundance: Fairly common.

Natural History: Black Bullheads are mainly nocturnal fishes that do not feed during the day. They live in still water pools in streams or in natural lakes and man-made impoundments. They can be distinguished from the Yellow Bullhead by their dark chin barbels. From the Brown Bullhead by the lighter color of the caudal fin.

Size: Maximum length 21 inches. May rarely reach 6–8 pounds.

Range

Abundance: Uncommon.

Natural History: Very similar to the Black Bullhead. The least common of the Ohio's *Ameiurus* catfishes. As with other bullheads, the parent fish stay with the eggs until hatching and the newly hatched young swim in schools near the surface with the mother bullhead in attendance. Found in ponds, lakes, sloughs, creeks, and small rivers.

Channel Catfish *Ictalurus punctatus*	**Blue Catfish** *Ictalurus furcatus*	**Flathead Catfish** *Plylodictus olivaris*

Size: Maximum of about 65 pounds. Ohio record 37.5 pounds and 31.5 inches.

Range

Abundance: Common.

Natural History: Perhaps our best known catfish and a popular game species. Grown commercially as a food fish on fish farms in the south and sold in groceries and restaurants. Specimens in clear water are uniformly dark (as in photo above). Individuals from turbid waters are light gray with black spots. Often stocked in farm ponds in Ohio.

Size: Maximum size 150 pounds and 5 ft. Ohio record 96.5 pounds and 54.5 inches.

Range

Abundance: Uncommon.

Natural History: This is America's largest catfish and old reports of specimens in excess of 300 pounds exist, though their reliability is questioned. This is an important game fish and also important commercially. Most common in Ohio in the Ohio River and the lower reaches of its major tributaries. Listed by ODNR as a Species of Concern.

Size: Maximum of about 100 pounds. Ohio record 76.5 pounds and 58.625 inches.

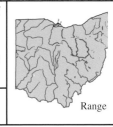

Range

Abundance: Fairly common.

Natural History: Second in size only to the Blue Catfish. Found mostly in rivers and in impoundments of larger rivers. Adults are mainly nocturnal and spend the day hidden among submerged structure such as logs or rocks. In river environments uses deep pools. Often hides in caves in river banks. More predaceous than our other large catfish.

Class—**Actinopterygii** (ray-finned fishes)

Order—**Siluriformes** (catfishes)

Family—**Ictaluridae** (american catfishes)

Madtoms—genus *Noturus* (5 species in Ohio)

Northern Madtom *Noturus stigmosus*	Brindled Madtom *Noturus miurus*	Mountain Madtom *Noturus eleutherus*

Size: Maximum length 5.25 inches. Average 2–4 inches.

Abundance: Rare. Endangered in Ohio.

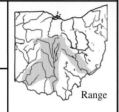 Range

Size: Maximum length 5.25 inches. Average 3 inches.

Abundance: Fairly common in medium streams.

 Range

Size: Maximum length 5 inches. 2-3 inches average.

Abundance: Uncommon. ODNR threatened.

 Range

Tadpole Madtom *Noturus gyrinus*	Stonecat *Noturus flavus*
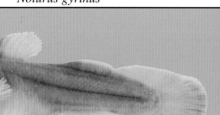	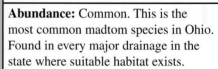

Size: Average around 3 inches. Maximum 5 inches.

Abundance: Fairly common. Most common in northwestern Ohio in lentic waters and slower streams, especially where there is aquatic vegetation.

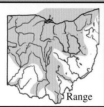 Range

Size: 12 inches. Average around 7–8 inches.

Abundance: Common. This is the most common madtom species in Ohio. Found in every major drainage in the state where suitable habitat exists.

 Range

Natural History: These are small catfishes. The largest example of the genus is the widespread Stonecat (*N. flavus*) which can reach a length of 12 inches. Most are much smaller, averageing only a few inches in length. There are 26 species total in this genus. A total of six species historically occurred in Ohio but one species has not been found for many decades and is presumed extirpated (Scioto Madtom, *N. trautmani*). One species in Ohio is endangered and another is regarded as a threatened species. All Madtoms are secretive and nocturnal, and are thus relatively unknown to the general public. Most Madtom species occur in the eastern portion of America, but a few species range well into the Great Plains and the Stonecat can be found as far west as Wyoming and Montana. Like other American catfishes the Madtoms have spiny dorsal and pectoral fins that produce a mild venom. A puncture from one of these spines can result in a significant amount of pain and swelling, but it is not life threatening. Like all catfishes, madtoms have a fleshy fin between the dorsal fin and the tail known as an "adipose fin." In most madtoms this fin connects to the caudal (tail) fin, a character that immediately separates madtoms from the rest of the catfish family. These are predaceous fish that feed on a wide variety of aquatic life consisting of both invertebrates and very small fishes. They feed and are active mostly at night, and spend the days hidden beneath overhanging root wads or burrowed into detritus of deep pools. Human refuse is also used as a refugia, with old tires and even beer cans reportedly used as daytime hiding places. Most madtoms are stream fishes that inhabit creeks and small to medium-sized rivers. The Mountain Madtom, Stonecat, and Northern Madtom can also be found in large rivers.

Class—**Actinopterygii** (ray-finned fishes)

Order—**Acipenseriformes** (primitive fishes)

Family—**Acipenseridae** (sturgeons)

Shovelnose Sturgeon *Scaphirynchus platorynchus*	**Lake Sturgeon** *Acipenser fulvescens*

Size: Maximum of 33 inches and 10 pounds. Average adult size is about 2 feet.

Range

Abundance: Very rare in Ohio. Still found in small numbers in the Ohio River. Listed as endangered by the ODNR.

Natural History: The Shovelnose Sturgeon lives in the deep channels of the Mississippi, Ohio, Missouri, Tennessee, Arkansas, and Red Rivers. They were also once found in the Rio Grande, but are extirpated there. The numerous dams that now exist on America's rivers have negatively impacted many fish species, especially the sturgeons. Shovelnose Sturgeon are fish of flowing rivers, thus they cannot live in lakes or river impoundments.

Size: Record 310 pounds. Maximum length 8 feet. Averages 4 to 6 feet and 50 to 100 pounds as an adult.

Range

Abundance: Very rare in Ohio. Still found in small numbers in Lake Erie. Extirpated from the Ohio portion of the Ohio River.

Natural History: Now highly endangered, the Lake Sturgeon inhabits the deep channels of the large rivers draining the middle of America as well as the great lakes. Their range includes all the great lakes and the Mississippi (except near the mouth), the Missouri, the Ohio, the Cumberland, the Arkansas, and the Tennessee rivers. They may live for up to 150 years. Large females will lay up to three million eggs. Females attain a greater size than males.

Family—**Polydontidae** (paddlefish)

Paddlefish
Polyodon spathula

Size: Can reach at least 180 pounds and over 7 feet. Ohio record 5 feet 184 pounds.

Abundance: Uncommon in Ohio. Restricted to the Ohio River and its lower triburaries.

Range

Natural History: Paddlefish often go by the name "Spoonbill Catfish," but in fact they are not related to the catfishes. They are a member of a very small, primitive order of fishes that have skeletons that are mostly cartilage. The Polydontidae family contains only two species (the other is a giant found in China that can reach lengths of over 20 feet). America's Paddlefish lives in larger rivers with turbid waters. Their flesh is edible and is commercially valuable. In recent years they have been harvested for their roe which serves as a substitute for the caviar that was once provided by the now rare sturgeons. They feed by filtering plankton and small invertebrates from gently flowing waters. Like the other fish on this page they have been impacted by dams which prohibit movement. They can survive in lakes and river impoundments and they may have once occurred in Lake Erie. Although they are harvested for both their flesh and their eggs in other regions of the country they are protected in Ohio where they are now regarded as a Threatened Species.

Class—**Actinopterygii** (ray-finned fishes)

Order—**Lepisosteiformes** (gar)

Family—**Lepisosteidae**

Shortnose Gar	Spotted Gar
Lepisosteus platostomus	*Lepisosteus oculatus*

Size: Maximum of about 5 lbs and 33 inches. No information is available on the maximum size attained by Ohio specimens.

Range

Size: Maximum size about 3.5 feet. No information is available on the maximum size attained by Ohio specimens.

Range

Abundance: Uncommon to rare. This is an endangered species in Ohio. Restricted to the Ohio River and its major tributaries.

Abundance: Very rare in Ohio and an endangered species. Range in Ohio is restricted to Lake Erie.

Natural History: An inhabitant of quite pools and floodplains of rivers and large creeks. Also found in swamps and oxbows and can tolerate waters with high turbidity. During periods of severe drought can survive for days in the mud of drying pools. In addition to fish also eats insects and crayfish. Successful reproduction is dependent upon floodplain backwaters and loss of these habitats through stream channelization has impacted negatively on this fish in Ohio.

Natural History: Habitat is swamps, sloughs, oxbows, natural lakes, and slow-moving creeks. This gar prefers clearer waters with less siltation than the similar Shortnose Gar. Heavily vegetated waters are preferred. Told from the Longnose Gar by short snout and from the Shortnose Gar by the presence of spots on the snout and on the pectoral and pelvic fins. Longnose and Shortnose Gar lack spots on the pectoral and pelvic fins. Food is mostly fishes.

Longnose Gar
Lepisosteus osseus

Range

Size: Record 50 pounds (6 feet in length). Ohio bowfishing record 19 pounds and 53 inches. Most are about 3–4 feet as adults.

Abundance: Ohio's most common gar. Found statewide in suitable habitats but absent from many areas shown on the range map.

Natural History: Ohio's most widespread gar species, the Longnose Gar can be found in both large and medium-size rivers as well as large creeks. Also common in natural lakes and oxbows and in man-made impoundments. Utilizes quite pools, backwaters, shallow bays, oxbow lakes, and swamps. Females average larger than males and can live over 20 years. Highly piscivorous, feeding mostly on shad and other forage fishes. All gar species have the ability to obtain oxygen directly from the air via the air bladder. This ability allows gar to survive droughts conditions that are fatal to most other fish species. Gar have been seen squirming in pools of mud where backwaters have dried out almost completely. As long as the mud remains moist enough to prevent dessication these amazing fishes can survive. The flesh of all gar species is edible but the roe is poisonous. Native Americans roasted gar whole in campfires and then peeled off the hard, bony skin. They also made arrow points from the triangular ossifications in the skin of very large specimens. In addition to the species shown on this page, one other gar, the giant Alligator Gar (maximum 10 feet and 300 pounds) once occurred in the Ohio River in the vicinity of Cincinnati.

Class—**Actinopterygii** (ray-finned fishes)
Order—**Cypriniformes** (minnows and suckers)
Family—**Catstomidae** (suckers)

Largemouth Buffalo
Ictiobus cyprinellus

Size: Can reach a maximum of 80 pounds.

Abundance: Fairly common.

Range

Natural History: Largemouth Buffalo are important commercial food fishes. Found in large rivers and their backwaters and in impoundments. This species is more accepting of silt laden waters than others of its genus. Breeds during spring in flooded fields and backwaters. May be negatively impacted in flood controlled rivers and streams.

Smallmouth Buffalo
Ictiobus bulbalus

Size: Maximum probably about 30 pounds.

Abundance: Fairly common.

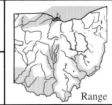
Range

Natural History: A river fish that also thrives in lakes and impounds. Less likely to be found in turbid water than the Largemouth Buffalo and also is more fond of waters with some current. Feeds on bottom-dwelling invertebrates and plants. Like all three of the *Ictiobus* (buffalo fishes), this fish is harvested commercially for human consumption.

Black Buffalo
Ictiobus niger

Size: Up to at least 30 pounds, probably more.

Abundance: Uncommon in Ohio.

Range

Natural History: Least common of the Buffalo fishes and listed as a species of Concern in some states. Morphologically somewhat intermediate between the two previous species. In habits, feeding, etc., most similar to the Smallmouth Buffalo. Found in large and medium-size rivers throughout much of the Mississippi drainage system.

Blue Sucker
Cycleptus elongatus

Size: Can reach 20 pounds. Maximum length 40 in.

Abundance: Uncommon. Threatened in Ohio.

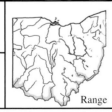
Range

Natural History: A unique member of the sucker family, the Blue Sucker is the only species of its genus. Although its range includes all of the Mississippi, Ohio, Missouri, and western gulf coastal rivers, this is today a rare fish throughout most of its range. It prefers fast-flowing channels over hard bottom. Dams and siltation impact both.

White Sucker
Catastomus commersonii

Size: Maximum 25 inches and 7 pounds.

Abundance: The most common sucker in Ohio.

Range

Natural History: Inhabits a wide variety of small rivers and creeks as well as natural and man-made lakes, and are more common in the eastern two-thirds of the state. Although bony, their flesh is quite palatable and they are sought for food and sport in some regions. A similar species, the **Longnose Sucker** (*C. catastomas*) lives in Lake Erie.

Spotted Sucker
Minytrema melanops

Size: Maximum of about 18 inches.

Abundance: Fairly common.

Range

Natural History: Lives in pools and slow-moving waters of large and small rivers, as well as larger creeks. Moves into smaller creeks in spring to spawn over gravel or rocks. Feeds on small aquatic invertebrates. Although fairly widespread, this is not a common fish and it may be decreasing in much of its range as water quality declines.

Class—**Actinopterygii** (ray-finned fishes)
Order—**Cypriniformes** (minnows and suckers)
Family—**Catastomidae** (suckers)

Quillback
Carpoides cyprinus

Size: Maximum about 2 feet and 12 pounds.

Abundance: Common in most drainages.

Range

Natural History: Found statewide the Quillback most common in slow-moving streams. Food is benthic invertebrates sucked from the substrate. Occurs both in rivers and impoundments but may be less tolerant of turbid conditions than its larger cousin the River Carpsucker. Like the River Carpsucker this is a commercial food fish.

Highfin Carpsucker
Carpoides velifer

Size: Maximum about 15 inches and 2 pounds.

Abundance: Least common of the carpsuckers.

Range

Natural History: This is the smallest of the Carpsuckers and is therefore not highly valued by commercial fishermen. This species inhabits medium to large rivers and favors clearer waters with some gravel substrates. Highfin Carpsukers are less common than our other two species. Siltation and lake impoundments may be limiting factors.

River Carpsucker
Carpoides carpio

Size: Maximum 25 inches and 10 pounds.

Abundance: Fairly common in larger rivers.

Range

Natural History: Found in the larger rivers and their reservoirs. Distribution in Ohio is restricted to the Ohio River and the lower portions of its major tributaries. Food is tiny invertebrates sucked from mud of the bottom of a river or lake. Known to live at least 10 years. Valued as a commercial food fish.

Lake Chubsucker
Erimyzon sucetta

Size: Maximum about 15 inches.

Abundance: Rare. Listed as a Threatened Species in Ohio.

Range

Natural History: The Lake Chubsucker as its name implies inhabits natural lakes and slow-moving streams that connect with wetlands. They are also found in a few man-made impoundment lakes in the state. They are very similar to and difficult to distinguish from the Western Creek Chubsucker, which is found mostly in clear, gravel, or sand bottomed streams.

Western Creek Chubsucker
Erimyzon claviformis

Size: Maximum about 15 inches.

Abundance: Fairly common but has declined in recent decades.

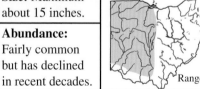
Range

Natural History: The Creek Chubsucker is widespread throughout the western, glaciated portion of Ohio. It is fairly common in small and large creeks in areas with sand or gravel substrate. They eat tiny crustaceans, insects, and algae. Very similar in appearance to the Lake Chubsucker, which has 11 or 12 dorsal fin rays as opposed to nine or 10 in the Creek Chubsucker.

Northern Hogsucker
Hypentelium nigricans

Size: Maximum size 22.5 inches.

Abundance: Fairly common in clear streams with silt-free bottoms.

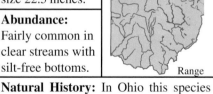
Range

Natural History: In Ohio this species is found mostly in large, clear creeks with rocky substrates. This is a bottom dweller that hugs the substrate and sucks small aquatic invertebrates from sand or gravel. The name "Hogsucker" comes from their method of feeding that entails "rooting" in the substrate like a hog. They are very cryptically patterned and blend in well with gravel bottoms.

Class—**Actinopterygii** (ray-finned fishes)
Order—**Cypriniformes** (minnows and suckers)
Family—**Catastomidae** (suckers)
Redhorse Suckers—genus *Moxostoma* (7 species in Ohio, 5 shown)

Golden Redhorse *Moxostoma erythrurum*	Black Redhorse *Moxostoma duquesnii*	Shorthead Redhorse *Moxostoma macrolepidotum*

| **Size:** Maximum of about 26 inches and 4.5 pounds. | 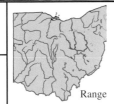 | **Size:** Record size 26 inches and 7 pounds. |  | **Size:** Can reach 19 inches and 3 pounds. | 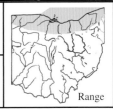 |
| **Abundance:** The most common redhorse in Ohio. | Range | **Abundance:** Fairly common in upolluted streams. | Range | **Abundance:** Fairly common in larger rivers. | Range |

River Redhorse—*Moxostoma carinatum*	Silver Redhorse—*Moxostoma anisurum*
 	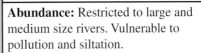

| **Size:** The largest of the redhorse suckers reach at least 29 inches and 10.5 pounds. | 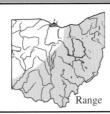 | **Size:** Official record 25 inches and 8.25 pounds. Unconfirmed reports of up to 10 pounds. |  |
| **Abundance:** Uncommon. Restricted to larger rivers. Listed as a Species of Concern by ODNR. | Range | **Abundance:** Restricted to large and medium size rivers. Vulnerable to pollution and siltation. | Range |

Natural History: The Redhorse Suckers are the most diverse group within the sucker family, with 20 species found in North America. The genus ranges across much of the eastern United States and their are seven species that range into Ohio. All are similar in appearance and can be difficult to properly identify. Collectively, they range throughout the state and probably every major drainage in Ohio has at least one species. Their flesh is described as good but bony, and they are sometimes pursued by anglers both for food and sport. In some regions of their range there are "gigging seasons" for these species, and they are hunted at night with lights and gigs from specialized boats. This practice is fairly common in the clear rivers of the Ozark Plateau in Missouri. Some anglers will use bow-fishing techniques for these species as well. Although they will persist in reservoirs they always spawn in small to medium-size streams with gravel substrates. These are stream fishes that are typically found in clear waters. Pictured above are five of Ohio's *Moxostoma* species. The other species (not shown) are the **Greater Redhorse** (*M. valenciennesi*), and the **Smallmouth Redhorse** (*M. breviceps*). The Greater Redhorse is a northern fish that occurs in Ohio only in the northwestern corner of the state . The Smallmouth Redhorse is very similar to the Shorthead Redhorse (shown above). The Shorthead Redhorse is found only in the Lake Erie-St. Lawrence drainage, while the Smallmouth Redhorse replaces it in the Ohio River watershed. These fishes are often mistaken for Carp. Unlike the Carp, which is a non-native species from the old world that can live in waters of poor quality, the Redhorse Suckers require unpolluted waters. In this manner their presence is an indicator of the overall health of a stream.

Class—**Actinopterygii** (ray-finned fishes)
Order—**Cypriniformes** (minnows and suckers)
Family—**Cyprinidae** (minnows)

Grass Carp *Ctenopharyngodon idella*	**Silver Carp** *Hypophthalmichthys molitrix*	**Bighead Carp** *Hypophthalmichthys nobilis*

Size: 4 feet and 100 pounds (in Asia).

Abundance: Generally uncommon but widely distributed in Ohio.

Size: Can reach 60 pounds.

Abundance: Currently restricted to the Ohio River but spreading rapidly.

Size: Up to 3 feet and 90 pounds.

Abundance: Currently restricted to the Ohio River but spreading rapidly.

Natural History: Inhabits pools and backwaters of large rivers and both man-made and natural lakes. Introduced into the United States from Asia to control aquatic plant growth in commercial minnow ponds. As with most alien species, the Grass Carp probably does more harm than good to the environments where it has become established.

Natural History: Native to China, the Silver Carp has become established in the larger rivers of the eastern United States. These fish consume tiny zooplankton and algae that is filtered from the flowing water of large river channels. Originally imported into Arkansas along with the Bighead Carp to control algae blooms in fish ponds.

Natural History: Like the previous species this fish is native to China. Now widespread in the major rivers of the eastern US, this is a filter feeder that inhabits the flowing waters of large river channels. Though both species of *Hypophthalmichthys* were intentionally introduced, they are now regarded as environmentally harmful aliens.

Common Carp *Cyprinus carpio*	**Goldfish** *Carassius auratus*	**Golden Shiner** *Notemigonus crysoleucas*

Size: Angling record is 55 pounds.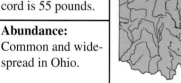

Abundance: Common and widespread in Ohio.

Size: Maximum 20 inches and 5 pounds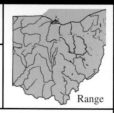

Abundance: Uncommon but widely distributed.

Size: Maximum size 14.5 inches.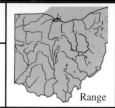

Abundance: Common and widespread.

Natural History: Many people are surprised to learn that the Common Carp is an invasive species in America. Native to Eurasia, they were first brought to the US in the early 1800s. They are now widespread and common in most aquatic habitats in America. A benthic feeder that "roots" like a hog in muddy bottoms and increases water turbidity.

Natural History: Native to Asia, the Goldfish is now widely established across most of North America. The gaudy colors commonly seen in fish ponds and pet stores rarely survive in wild populations. Found in most rivers and lakes and can survive in tiny ponds. More tolerant of pollution and siltation than many native species.

Natural History: This minnow is well known among fishermen and is sold as a bait fish in many regions of the US. In their natural habitat they are fish of still water pools of streams and backwaters of rivers. They will also thrive in impoundments and small farm ponds. Millions are raised commercially each year to be sold in bait stores.

Class—**Actinopterygii** (ray-finned fishes)
Order—**Cypriniformes** (minnows and suckers)
Family—**Cyprinidae** (minnows)

Redside Daces—genus *Clinostomus*	**Striped Shiners**—genus *Luxilus*	**Longnose Dace**—genus *Rhinichthys*
Rosyside Dace—*C. funduloides* **Redside Dace**—*C. elongatus*	**Striped Shiner**—*L. chrysocephalus* **Common Shiner**—*L. cornutus*	**Blacknose Dace**—*R. atratulus* **Longnose Dace**—*R. cataractae*

Rosyside Dace (breeding color)

Common Shiner / Striped Shiner

Longnose Dace / Blacknose Dace

Size: Both species can reach 4.5 inches.	 Redside-light gray / Rosyside-dark gray	**Size:** Both species can reach 8 inches.	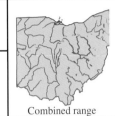 Combined range	**Size:** Longnose can reach 5 inches, Blacknose 4.	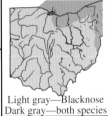 Light gray—Blacknose Dark gray—both species
Abundance: Redside is common. Rosyside is rare.		**Abundance:** Striped is common, Common is uncommon!		**Abundance:** Blacknose common. Longnose rare in Ohio.	

Natural History: There are two nearly identical *Clinostomus* Daces in Ohio. Rosyside Dace occurs only in a few small streams in south-central Ohio. Redside is more widespread. Both live in clear water creeks or small, clear rivers with gravel, sand, or rock substrates.	**Natural History:** Two very similar species that often hybridize where their range overlaps. Both are stream fishes that live in small to medium-size creeks with clear water and sand or gravel substrates. Common Shiner is found in northern Ohio only.	**Natural History:** Longnose Dace inhabits both fast-flowing streams and the Lake Erie shoreline. Blacknose Dace is found in clear streams and is more widespread in Ohio. Both require sand or gravel substrates and clear waters, but Blacknose tolerates some turbidity.

Southern Redbelly Dace *Chrosomus erythrogaster*	**Central Stoneroller** *Campostoma anomalum*	**Creek Chub** *Semotilus atromaculatus*

Size: Maximum of 4.5 inches.	 Range	**Size:** Maximum of about 11 inches.	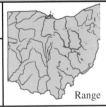 Range	**Size:** Maximum of 12 inches.	 Range
Abundance: Common in small, clear, flowing streams.		**Abundance:** One of the most common stream fish in Ohio.		**Abundance:** Very common. Found in probably every creek in Ohio.	

Natural History: Can be found in very small streams only a few feet across. Requires clean, unpolluted waters with moderate to fast current and abundant riffles and pools. Often very common in small streams in forested regions, especially those that are fed by springs or seeps. This species is an indicator of good water quality. The breeding males are one of the most colorful minnows in America. Food is mostly insects, some caught by leaping into the air.	**Natural History:** Nearly every stream within their range capable of supporting fish life will have a population of Stonerollers. Their name comes from their habit of aggressive bottom feeding in gravelly stream beds, moving small stones in the process. Male Stonerollers will also move pebbles with their mouths in the construction of the spawning bed. They use their lower mandibles to scrape algea and tiny organisms from gravel, stones, submerged logs, etc.	**Natural History:** One of the most widespread and common creek fishes in America, the Creek Chub probably inhabits nearly every stream in Ohio that is capable of supporting fish life. Like many minnows, breeding males develop tubercles on the head and snout, leading to the common nickname "Hornyhead" (see inset photo above). Creek Chubs are often found in very small creeks where they may be the top fish predator.

Class—**Actinopterygii** (ray-finned fishes)
Order—**Cypriniformes** (minnows and suckers)
Family—**Cyprinidae** (minnows)

River Chub
Nocomis micropogon

Juvenile

Size: Maximum length 12.5 inches. Along with the Creek Chub this is the of the largest of Ohio's native minnows.

Abundance: Fairy common. This species is found state-wide. It is reportedly very common in some locales.

Range

Natural History: The River Chub inhabits medium to large rivers in areas of swift currents. Like the many other chubs breeding males have grossly enlarged heads with horny tubercles. During the breeding season the male's head also turns pupleish or pink. Males gather pebbles with their mouths and stack them to create large spawning mounds that may be several inches high and two feet across. These large minnows are sometimes caught by fishermen using worms as bait.

Hornyhead Chub
Nocomis biguttatus

Size: Smaller than the River Chub but can reach a maximum of just over 10 inches. About 6 inches is average.

Abundance: Fairly common but generally a much less common species in Ohio than the River Chub.

Range

Natural History: Similar to the preceding species but much less common in Ohio and found in smaller streams with less current. The name comes from the hard tubercles that form on the head of the male during breeding season. These fish will gather pebbles into a large mound where the female lays her eggs. Males guard these nest mounds from predators, making them an attractive site for other small minnows to deposit their eggs as well.

Silver Chub
Macryobopsis storeiana

Size: From 3 to 9 inches as an adult.

Abundance: Uncommon. This species is good example of the fact that many of the state's fishes are completly unknown to most Ohio residents.

Range

Natural History: This species inhabits the deep waters of the Ohio River and the lower portions of its major tributaries. It is also found in Lake Erie. It is an important forage species for many larger game fish.

Streamlined Chub—*Erimystax dissimilis*
Gravel Chub—*Erimystax x-punctatus*

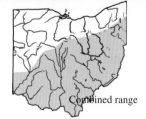

Streamlined Chub

Gravel Chub

Size: Streamlined Chub can reach 5.5 inches. Gravel Chub is a little smaller, reaching only about 4.5.

Abundance: The Gravel Chub is the most widespread in Ohio but neither is common.

Combined range

Natural History: These small minnows live in medium and large rivers. They favor flowing water over gravel bottoms and are intolerant of siltation. Their presence in a waterway is an indicator of a healthy stream.

Class—**Actinopterygii** (ray-finned fishes)

Order—**Cypriniformes** (minnows and suckers)

Family—**Cyprinidae** (minnows)

Bigeye Chub	Pugnose Minnow	Mississippi Silvery Minnow
Hybopsis amblops	*Opsopoeodus emiliae*	*Hybognathus nuchalis*

Size: May reach 4 inches.

Abundance: Uncommon to rare. Exirpated from much of Ohio.

Range

Size: Max of about 2.5 inches.

Abundance: Rare in Ohio. Regarded as endangered by ODNR.

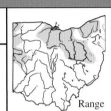
Range

Size: May reach 6 inches maximum.

Abundance: Very rare in Ohio. May no longer be found in the state.

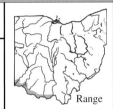
Range

Natural History: A fish of small rivers and large creeks. Declining over much of its range, due mainly to siltation. Once found statewide, this species has dissappeared from much of Ohio. The fact that it is vulnerable to poor water quality makes it an "indicator species," warning of poor stream health.

Natural History: This tiny minnow is widespread across the southeast from South Carolina to eastern Texas. It also ranges northward up the Mississippi and Ohio drainages as far as the southern Great Lakes. Habitat is backwaters and pools of low gradient streams with clear water and abundant aquatic vegetation. These conditions are now rare in Ohio.

Natural History: An inhabitant of larger river systems where it lives mostly in the sloughs and backwaters. These fish are bottom feeders that ingest tiny algae and detritus from silt. They are found throughout much of the Mississippi River drainage as well as in the lower portions of the Ohio River drainage. Possibly extirpated in Ohio.

Redfin Shiner	Scarlet Shiner
Lythrurus umbratilis	*Lythrurus fasciolaris*

Breeding Male (below)
Non-breeding (inset)

Size: A rather small minnow. Maximum length of only about 3.5 inches.

Abundance: Fairly common and widespread in much of Ohio except the southeast. Most common in the northwestern portion of the state.

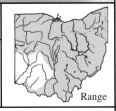
Range

Size: Another small minnow. Maximum length of only about 3.5 inches.

Abundance: Restriced to southwestern corner of Ohio where it replaces the closely related Redfin Shiner. It is a fairly common species within this range.

Range

Natural History: The Redfin Shiner is mostly a fish of small to medium creeks. They are more tolerant of poor water quailify than many other stream fishes and are thus thriving and in some places out-competing other minnow species. The breeding males are among our most colorful minnows, but they will lose their dramatic colors following breeding. They are known for the habit of laying their eggs in the spawning beds of other species such as sunfish.

Natural History: Like the closely related previous species, the Scarlet Shiner can be found in smaller creeks and medium-size rivers but is also fairly common in larger rivers. Though tolerant of turbid, silt-laden waters it also lives in clear streams. Food for both *Lythrurus* species is small aquatic insect larvae such as mayfly and midge nymphs supplemented by filamentous algeas. The ranges of these two similar species are mutually exclusive in Ohio (see range maps).

Class—**Actinopterygii** (ray-finned fishes)

Order—**Cypriniformes** (minnows and suckers)

Family—**Cyprinidae** (minnows)

Fathead Minnows—genus *Pimephales* (3 species in Ohio)

Bluntnose Minnow *Pimephales notatus*	**Bullhead Minnow** *Pimephales vigilax*	**Fathead Minnow** *Pimephales promelas*

Size: Males can reach 4.25 inches. Females smaller.		**Size:** Males can reach 3.5 inches. Females smaller.		**Size:** Males can reach 4 inches. Females smaller.	
Abundance: The most common fish in Ohio probably.	Range	**Abundance:** Fairly common in the Ohio drainage.	Range	**Abundance:** Common. Widely introduced.	Range

Natural History: These are very common minnows that may be found in rivers, creeks, reservoirs, and even ponds occasionally. They are tough little fishes that can survive warm, low-oxygen waters and waters with high turbidity. Breeding males of all three species have very dark, nearly black heads and tubercles on the snout. Their resilience, rapid reproductive capacity, and ease in rearing in captivity has led to the Bluntnose Minnow and the Fathead Minnow being widely used as a bait minnows, where they are often sold under the nickname "Tuffy." A reddish colored strain of the Fathead Minnow known as "Rosy Red" has also been bred for sale in bait stores. Because of their prolific use for bait, these minnows have become widely established across the United States and Canada and they are today perhaps the most common fish species in North America. These minnows are mostly bottom feeders that eat a variety of tiny invertebrates as well as algae.

Western Tonguetied Minnow *Exoglossum laurae*	**Suckermouth Minnow** *Phenacobius mirabilis*	**Silverjaw Minnow** *Ericymba buccata*

Size: Maximum length 6.25 inches.		**Size:** Maximum length 4.75 inches.	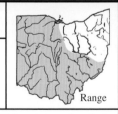	**Size:** Maximum length 3.75 inches.	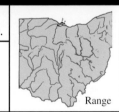
Abundance: Rare in Ohio. Regarded as Threatened by ODNR.	Range	**Abundance:** Fairly common and probably expanding in Ohio.	Range	**Abundance:** Very common in suitable habitats within the state.	Range

Natural History: This unusual minnow has always had a rather restricted range in Ohio. Found historically in the upper reaches of the Great and Little Miami Rivers, it has declined significantly and today is restricted to the Mad River drainage. The population that occurs in Ohio is isolated and disjunct by hundreds of miles from other populations in Pennslyvania and West Virginia.	**Natural History:** This minnow is a habitat non-specialist that occurs in both small creeks and large rivers. It is tolerant of a wide variety of conditions from clear flowing waters to still waters with some turbidity. The common name "Suckermouth" is derived from the sub-terminal position of the mouth which is typical of the sucker family (Catastomidae).	**Natural History:** The Silverjaw Minnow is unique among Ohio minnows in having a series of visible cavities within the upper jaw below the eye. The function of these cavities may be tactile or sensory. Habitat is clear streams with sand or rock substrates. Some ichthyologists place this species in the genus *Notropis,* others argue that the unique jaw cavities warrant its own genus.

Class—**Actinopterygii** (ray-finned fishes)
Order—**Cypriniformes** (minnows and suckers)
Family—**Cyprinidae** (minnows)
True Minnows—genus *Notropis* (12 species in Ohio, pictured below and on next page)

Silver Shiner *Notropis photogenis*	**Bigeye Shiner** *Notropis boops*	**Emerald Shiner** *Notropis atherinoides*

Size: Maximum length about 5.5 inches.

Abundance: Most common in the Ohio R. drainage.

Range

Size: Maximum length about 3.5 inches.

Abundance: Very rare in Ohio. Threatened.

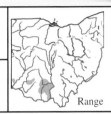
Range

Size: Maximum length about 5 inches.

Abundance: Common, especially in Lake Erie.

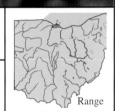
Range

Rosyface Shiner *Notropis rubellus*	**Sand Shiner** *Notropis stramineus*	**Mimic Shiner** *Notropis volucellus*

Size: Maximum length about 3.5 inches.

Abundance: Fairly common except in northwest Ohio.

Range

Size: Maximum length about 3.5 inches.

Abundance: Fairly common in streams with sand bottoms.

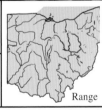
Range

Size: Maximum length about 3 inches.

Abundance: Uncommon and declining in Ohio.

Range

River Shiner *Notropis blennius*	**Channel Shiner** *Notropis wickliffi*	**Bigmouth Shiner** *Notropis dorsalis*

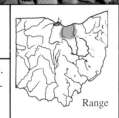

Size: Can reach a total length of 5 inches.

Abundance: Common in the Ohio River.

Range

Size: Maximum of only about 3 inches.

Abundance: Common in the Ohio River.

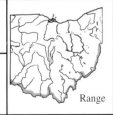
Range

Size: Maximum of only about 3 inches.

Abundance: Rare. A Threatened Species in Ohio.

Range

Class—**Actinopterygii** (ray-finned fishes)

Order—**Cypriniformes** (minnows and suckers)

Family—**Cyprinidae** (minnows)

True Minnows—genus *Notropis* (continued from previous page)

Popeye Shiner *Notropis ariommus*	Spottail Shiner *Notropis hudsonius*	Ghost Shiner *Notropis buchanani*
		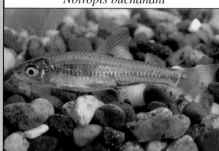
Size: Can reach a maximum length of 3.5 inches. 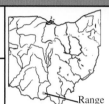	**Size:** Can reach a maximum of 5.75 inches. 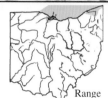	**Size:** Very small, usually under 2 inches. Max. 2.5. 
Abundance: Very rare in Ohio. Once thought extirpated.	**Abundance:** Common in Lake Erie.	**Abundance:** Uncommon in Ohio.

Natural History: *Notropis* is largest genus of minnows in North America with as many as 83 species across the continent. In fact, this is the second largest generic group of fishes in North America, surpassed only by the darters of the *Etheostoma* genus. The exact status of some species included in this genus is problematic and taxonomic changes occur frequently within the group, with occasional species being re-assigned to another genus and some being added from other genera. Their distribution is generally east of the Rocky Mountain Continental Divide, and most species occur within the Gulf of Mexico Drainage Basin. At least 12 species are extant in Ohio but three have been extirpated (the Pugnose Shiner, Blackchin Shiner, and Blacknose Shiner). Many others are common, but one, the Popeye Shiner (*N. ariommus),* is presently endangered in the state. Two others, the Bigeye Shiner (*N. boops*) and the Bigmouth Shiner (*N. dorsalis*), are threatened. Collectively, the Shiner Minnows are found in virtually all aquatic habitats within the state and their combined ranges encompass all of Ohio. The breeding males of many *Notropis* species are quite colorful. Even those species that don't acquire significant color on the body will typically acquire yellow, orange, or red color in the fins of nuptial males. At least one species, the Emerald Shiner (*N. atherinoides*) is widely used as a bait minnow.

Carp Minnows—genus *Cyprinella* (2 species in Ohio)

Spotfin Shiner *Cyprinella spiloptera*	Steelcolor Shiner *Cyprinella whipplei*

Size: Averages about 3 or 4 inches but can reach nearly 5 inches. 	**Size:** Averages 3 to 4 inches. Maximum 5.5 inches. 
Abundance: Very common. In fact, this is one of the most common and widespread minnows in Ohio.	**Abundance:** Uncommon. Restricted mostly to the Ohio River and the Hocking River. Introduced elswhere.
Natural History: Unlike some stream fishes that require flowing waters, the adaptable Spotfin Shiner can thrive in man-made watersheds. Food is tiny invertebrates and algae.	**Natural History:** Found in medium to large rivers. Food is a variety of tiny invertebrates. Both of Ohio's *Cyprinella* minnows were once included in the genus *Notropis*.

Class—**Actinopterygii** (ray-finned fishes)

Order—**Cyprinodontiformes** (topminnows and livebearers)

Family—**Fundulidae** (topminnows)

Blackstriped Topminnow *Fundulus notatus*	**Northern Studfish** *Fundulus catenatus*	**Banded Killifish** *Fundulus diaphanus*

Size: Maximum of about 3 inches. **Abundance:** Common in in sluggish streams in western Ohio.	 Range	**Size:** Can reach 7 inches in length. **Abundance:** Still rare in Ohio, but possibly increasing.	 Range	**Size:** Maximum of about 5 inches. **Abundance:** Uncommon to rare. May be resurging along Lake Erie.	 Range

Natural History: The topminnows get their name from the fact that they are always seen right at the water's surface. They feed on both emerging aquatic insects and tiny terrestrial insects that fall or fly onto the water. The characteristic white spot on the top of the head of many species is easily visible as they suspend at the surface. Most species are found in the Mississippi River Basin, but in Ohio they occur in both the Ohio and the St. Lawrence drainages. The Blackstripe Topminnow is the most widely distributed *Fundulus* species in Ohio, being found throughout the western half of the state. Meanwhile the Banded Killifish is restricted to the Ohio River and the immediate vicinity of Lake Erie. The Northern Studfish is not native to Ohio but has been introduced into a few streams.

Family—**Poeciliidae** (livebearers)

Western Mosquitofish—*Gambusia affinis*

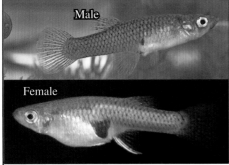

Size: Females 2.5 inches, males 1.25 inches.

Natural History: True to their name, these tiny fish eat large numbers of mosquito larvae. Uniquely among Ohio fishes, they give birth to fully formed young. They live in the shallows of swamps and backwaters, where they will forage in water less than an inch deep. Mosquito fish are a southern fish that is not native to Ohio, but have been widely introduced and occur sporadically across the state. These diminutive fish may look familiar to many aquarists in Ohio, as they are a close relative of the aquarium Guppy.

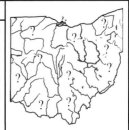

Range-Widely introduced across the state but range undetermined.

Order—**Gasterosteiformes** (mostly small marine fishes)

Family—**Gasterosteidae** (sticklebacks)

Brook Stickleback—*Culaea inconstans*

Size: Average about 2.5 inches, maximum of 3.5 inches.

Abundance: Fairly common around Lake Erie.

Natural History: Sticklebacks are unsual fishes that are distantly related to the seahorses. In fact, most members of their order (Gasterosteiformes) are marine and include such strange fishes as the pipefish, tubenoses, and trumpetfishes to name a few. The stickleback family is represented in the United States by a total of only four species, one of which occurs in Ohio. The males of this species are well known for constructing elaborate nests from plant materials and fiercely guarding the eggs.

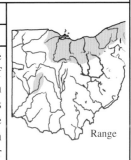

Range

Class—**Actinopterygii** (ray-finned fishes)

Order—**Osteoglossiformes** (bonytongues)

Family—**Hiodontidae** (mooneyes)

Mooneye *Hiodon tergisus*	**Goldeye** *Hiodon alosoides*

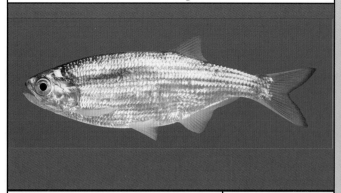

Size: Average adult size is about 12 to 15 inches. Maximum of 17 inches and 2.5 pounds.

Abundance: Decimated by pollution and siltation, this species is generally uncommon in Ohio. Though it has been rebounding in recent years.

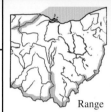
Range

Natural History: The Mooneye is one of only two species in the family Hiodontidae, which is endemic to North America. Their appearance is very similar to their distant relatives the shads and herrings. They live in large rivers and lakes and feed on a wide variety of invertebrate and small vertebrate prey.

Size: Average 15 to 17 inches and about 2 pounds, but can reach 20 inches and 3 pounds.

Abundance: Rare and endangered in Ohio. Once common but has declined significantly in Ohio in the last several decades.

Range

Natural History: Similar to the Mooneye but found in rivers with higher turbidity. Unlike the Mooneye, this species does not thrive in impoundments, but does exist in natural lakes and backwaters of large rivers. It is a food fish in parts of Canada, where it is eaten smoked. Succeptible to chemicals and negatively impacted by water pollution.

Order—**Percopsiformes**

Family—**Aphredoderidae** (pirate perch) / Family—**Percopsidae** (trout perch)

Pirate Perch *Aphredoderus sayanus*	**Trout Perch** *Percopsis omiscomaycus*

Size: Maximum 5.5 inches. Average adult is around 3 to 4 inches.

Abundance: Very rare and endangered in Ohio. Pirate Perch were recently re-introduced into the state by ODNR after having been extirpated.

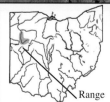
Range

Natural History: The Pirate Perch is endemic to North America. It lives in swamps and spring-fed wetlands among heavy aquatic vegetation. May also be found in backwaters of large creeks and small rivers. Although they are small fishes, they have rather large mouths and they are quite predaceous on insects, crustaceans, and small fishes.

Size: Adults average about 3 or 4 inches. Maximum length 6 inches.

Abundance: Fairly common in Ohio. Most common in Lake Erie and its lower tributaries but also found in most other river systems in the state.

Range

Natural History: The Trout Perch lives in lakes and quiet pools of larger streams. It feeds on insects, crustaceans, and small fish. Mainly nocturnal, it spends the day in deep water and moves into the shallows at night to feed. This is a species of high latitudes that approaches the southernmost limits of its range in Ohio.

Class—**Actinopterygii** (ray-finned fishes)

Order—**Atheriniformes**	Order—**Scorpaeniformes** (scorpion fish)
Family—**Atherinidae** (silversides)	Family—**Cottidae** (sculpins)
Brook Silverside *Labidesthes sicculus*	**Mottled Sculpin** *Cottus bairdi*

Size: About 3 to 4 inches is average. Can reach 5 inches.		**Size:** Can reach a maximum of 6 inches in length.	
Abundance: Fairly common. In Ohio inhabits both streams and natural lakes, including shallows and bays in Lake Erie.	Range	**Abundance:** Rare in northwestern Ohio. Fairly common in clear, cool streams in much of the rest of the state.	

Natural History: The silversides are related to the famous marine species the Grunnion, a Pacific Ocean fish that spawns in unfathomable numbers on west coast beaches. Silversides travel in large schools near the surface of lakes and rivers and are important prey for larger fish species, including many game fish. They require clear water with abundant aquatic vegetation.

Natural History: Typically a fish of upland streams and spring-fed runs where they inhabit the fast-flowing regions with gravel or rocky substrates. Also found in Lake Erie. All Sculpins have large mouths that enable them to take larger prey than would be suspected for such a small fish. They are highly cryptic and nearly impossible to see when motionless on the gravel of stream beds.

REFERENCES

Chapters 1, 2, and 10

Print

Bailey, Robert G. 2009. *Ecosystem Geography, From Ecoregions to Sites.* Springer Science and Business Media, New York, NY.

Hunt, Charles B. 1974. *Natural Regions of the United States and Canada.* W.H. Freeman and Company, San Francisco, CA.

Ricketts, Taylor, H., Eric Dinerstein, David M. Olson, and Colby J. Loucks, et al. 1999. *Terrestrial Ecoregions of North America.* World Wildlife Fund and Island Press. Washington, DC.

US Forest Service Research Bulletin NRS 36. 2009. *Ohio Forests.* US Forest Service. Newtown Square, PA.

Internet

ODNR Division of Natural Areas and Preserves—www.naturepreserves.ohiodnr.gov

Ohio Environmental Protection Agency—www.epa.state.oh.us

US Enviornmental Protection Agency / Ecoregions of North America—www.epa.gov/wed/pages/ecoregions.htm

The Encyclopedia of Earth—www.eoearth.org

United States Geological Survey-www.usgs/science/geology/regions

Commission for Environmental Cooperation—www.cec.org

Mammal References

Print

Barbour, Roger W. and Wayne Davis 1974. *Mammals of Kentucky.* University Press of Kentucky. Lexington, KY.

Bowers, Nora, Rick Bowers, and Kenn Kafuman. 2004. *Mammals of North America.* Houghton Mifflin Company. NY, NY.

Campbell, Joshua W., Micheal T. Mengak, Steven B. Castleberry, and Jason D. Mejia. 2010. *Distribution and Status of Uncommon Mammals in the Southern Appalachian Mountains.* Southeastern Naturalist 9(2) 275–302.

Donofrio, Joana. 2009. *Demographics of Ohio's River Otter Population.* The Ohio State University College of Food, Agriculture, and Environmental Science.

Gottschang, Jack L. 1981. *A Guide to the Mammals of Ohio.* The Ohio State University Press.

Hall, E.R. 1951. *American Weasels.* University of Kansas Museum of Natural History. Vol.4: 1–466.

Hine, James S. 1912. *Ohio Moles and Shrews.* Ohio Journal of Science. Vol. 12 n5. 494–496.

Kays, Roland W. and Don. E. Wilson. 2009. *Mammals of North America.* Princeton University Press. Princeton, NJ.

McDonald, Kenneth P. and Denis S. Case. 1990. *The Status of the Ermine (Mustela erminea) In Ohio.* The Ohio Journal of Science, Vol. 90: 46–47.

Rybak, Edward J., Elaine J Neufarth, and Stephen H. Vessey. 1975. *Distribution of the Jumping Mouse Zapus hud-*

sonius in Ohio. Ohio Journal of Science, Vol. 75 n4 184–187.

Trani, Margaret K., Mark Ford, and Brian R. Chapman. 2007. *The Land Manager's Guide to Mammals of the South.* The Nature Conservancy, Southeast Region. Durham, NC.

Walker, E.P. 1983. *Walkers Mammals of the World.* The John's Hopkins University Press. Baltimore, MD.

Whitaker, John O. Jr. and W. J. Hamilton Jr. 1998. *Mammals of the Eastern United States.* Cornell University Press. Ithaca, NY.

Wilson, Don E. and Sue Ruff. 1999. *North American Mammals.* Smithsonian Institution.

Internet

Kentucky Department of Fish and Wildlife Resources—www.kdfwr.state.ky.us

Kentucky Bat Working Group—www.biology.eku.edu/bats

International Union of Concerned Naturalists—www.iucnredlist.org

Nature Serve Explorer—www.natureserve.org

Ohio Department of Natural Resources—www.wildlife.ohiodnr.gov

Smithsonian National Museum of Natural History—www.mnh.si.edu

Mammalian Species, American Society of Mammologists species accounts—www.science.smith.edu

Bird References

Print

Clark, William S. and Brian K. Wheeler. 1987. *A Field Guide to Hawks-North America.* Peterson Field Guides, Houghton Mifflin Co. Boston, MA.

Dunn, John L., Kimball Garret, Thomas Shultz, and Cindy House. *A Field Guide to Warblers of North America.* Peterson Field Guides, Houghton Mifflin Co. Boston, MA.

Farrand, John, Jr. 1998. *An Audubon Handbook, Eastern Birds.* McGraw Hill Book Co. New York, NY.

Floyd, Ted. 2008. *Smithsonian Field Guide to the Birds of North America.* Harper Collins Publishers. New York, NY.

Harlan, Robert N., Joseph W. Hammond, David C. Dister, Bernard F. Master, and Bill Whan. 2008. *Annotated Checklist of the Birds of Ohio.* Ohio Birds Records Committee, North Bend, OH.

Johnsgard, Paul A. 1988. *North American Owls, Biology and Natural History.* Smithsonian Institution Press, Washington, DC.

Kaufman, Ken. 2000. *The Birds of North America.* Houghton Mifflin Co., New York, NY.

Mengel, Robert M. 1965. *The Birds of Kentucky.* American Ornithologist's Union Monogram, no. 3. The Allen Press, Lawrence, KS.

Palmer-Ball, Brainard. 1996. *The Kentucky Breeding Bird Atlas.* The University Press of Kentucky, Lexington, KY.

Peterson, Roger T. 1980. *A Field Guide to the Birds, Eastern Birds.* Houghton Mifflin Co., Boston, MA.

Rodewald, Paul G. Matthew B. Shumar, Aaron T. Boone, David L. Slager, and Jim McCormac (Editors). 2016. *The Second Atlas of Breeding Birds in Ohio.* The Pennsylvania State University Press, University Park, PA.

Vanner, Micheal. 2003. *The Encyclopedia of North American Birds.* Parragon Publishing, Bath, UK.

Internet

Cornell University Lab of Ornithology-Birds of North America Online—http://birds.bna.cornell.edu.bna/species

Ohio Department of Natural Resources—www.wildlife.ohiodnr.gov

Ohio Ornithological Society—www.ohiobirds.org
McGill Bird Observatory—www.migrationresearch.org
Environment Canada—www.ec.gc.ca
Ebird—www.ebird.org
Waterfowl Hunting Management in North America—www.flyways.us
NatureServe Explorer—www.natureserve.org

Turtle References

Print

Buhlmann, Kurt, Tracey Tuberville, and Whit Gibbons. 2008. *Turtles of the Southeast.* The University of Georgia Press, Athens, GA.

Collins, Joseph T. and Travis W. Taggart. 2009. *Standard Common and Scientific Names for North American Amphibians, Turtles, Reptiles and Crocodilians.* The Center for North American Herpetology, Hays, KS.

Conant, Roger and Joseph T. Collins. 1998. *Reptiles and Amphibians of Eastern/Central North America.* Houghton Mifflin Co., Boston-New York.

Ernst, Carl H., Jeffrey E. Lovich, and Roger W. Barbour. 1994. *Turtles of the United States and Canada.* Smithsonian Institution Press, Washington and London.

Niemiller, Matthew L., R. Graham Reynolds, and Brian T. Miller. 2013. *The Reptiles of Tennessee.* The University of Tennessee Press, Knoxville, TN.

Trauth, Stanley E., Henry W. Robison, and Michael V. Plummer. 2004. *The Amphibians and Reptiles of Arkansas.* The University of Arkansas Press, Fayetteville, AR.

Internet

Ohio Department of Natural Resources—www.wildlife.ohiodnr.gov
NatureServe Explorer—www.natureserve.org

Reptile References

Print

Collins, Joseph T. and Travis W. Taggart. 2009. *Standard Common and Scientific Names for North American Amphibians, Turtles, Reptiles and Crocodilians.* The Center for North American Herpetology, Hays, KS.

Conant, Roger and Joseph T. Collins. 1998. *Reptiles and Amphibians of Eastern/Central North America.* Houghton Mifflin Co., Boston-New York.

Meade, Les. 2005. *Kentucky Snakes. Their Identification, Variation, and Distribution.* Kentucky State Nature Preserves Commission.

Niemiller, Matthew L., R. Graham Reynolds, and Brian T. Miller. 2013. *The Reptiles of Tennessee.* The University of Tennessee Press, Knoxville, TN.

Wynn, Douglas E. and Scott M. Moody. 2006. *Ohio Turtle, Lizard, and Snake Atlas.* Ohio Biological Survey., Columbus, OH.

Wright, Albert Hazen and Anna Allen Wright. 1957. *Handbook of Snakes of the United States and Canada.* Comstock Publishing, Ithaca, NY.

Shupe, Scott. 2005. *US Guide to Venomous Snakes and Their Mimics.* Skyhorse Publishing, New York, NY.

Trauth, Stanley E., Henry W. Robison, and Michael V. Plummer. 2004. *The Amphibians and Reptiles of Arkansas.* The University of Arkansas Press, Fayetteville, AR.

Ohio Department of Natural Resources—www.wildlife.ohiodnr.gov

The Center for North American Herpetology—www.naherpetology.org

NatureServe Explorer—www.natureserve.org

Amphibian References

Print

Collins, Joseph T. and Travis W. Taggart. 2009. *Standard Common and Scientific Names for North American Amphibians, Turtles, Reptiles and Crocodilians.* The Center for North American Herpetology, Hays, KS.

Conant, Roger and Joseph T. Collins. 1998. *Reptiles and Amphibians of Eastern/Central North America.* Houghton Mifflin Co., Boston-New York.

Niemiller, Matthew L. and R. Graham Reynolds. 2011. *The Amphibians of Tennessee.* University of Tennessee Press, Knoxville, TN.

Trauth, Stanley E., Henry W. Robison, and Michael V. Plummer. 2004. *The Amphibians and Reptiles of Arkansas.* The University of Arkansas Press, Fayetteville, AR.

Dodd, C. Kenneth. 2013. *Frogs of the United States and Canada.* Johns Hopkins University Press, Baltimore, MD.

Pfingsten, R.A., J. G. Davis, T.O. Matson, G.J. Lipps, Jr., D. Wynn, and B.J. Armitage (Editors), 2013. *The Amphibians of Ohio.* Ohio Biological Survey Bulletin New Series. Volume 17 Number 1. .xiv + 899 p.

Internet

Ohio Department of Natural Resources—www.wildlife.ohiodnr.gov

The Center for North American Herpetology—www.naherpetology.org

International Union of Concerned Naturalists—www.iucnredlist.org

NatureServe Explorer—www.natureserve.org

Fish References

Print

Burr, Brooks M. and Melvin L. Warren, Jr. 1986. *A Distributional Atlas of Kentucky Fishes.* Kentucky Nature Preserves Commission.

Clay, William M. 1974. *The Fishes of Kentucky.* Kentucky Department of Fish and Wildlife Resources, Frankfort, KY.

Eddy, Samuel. 1969. *How to Know the Freshwater Fishes.* Wm. C. Brown Company Publishers, Dubuque, IA.

Etnier, David A. and Wayne C. Starnes. 1993. *The Fishes of Tennessee.* The University of Tennessee Press, Knoxville, TN.

Goldstein, Robert J. with Rodney Harper and Ridchard Edwards. 2000. *American Aquarium Fishes.* Texas AandM University Press, College Station, TX.

Miller, Rudolph J. 2004. *The Fishes of Oklahoma.* The University of Oklahoma Press, Norman, OK.

Page, Lawrence M. and Brooks M. Burr. 2011. *Peterson Field Guide to Freshwater Fishes of North America North of Mexico.* Houghton Mifflin Harcourt, Boston—New York.

Pflieger, William L. 1975. *The Fishes of Missouri.* Missouri Department of Conservation, Springfield, MO.

Rice, Daniel L. and Gary Meszaros. 2014. *The Native Fishes of Ohio.* The Kent State University Press. Kent, OH.

Internet

FishBase—www.fishbase.org

North American Native Fish Association—www.nanfa.org

National Fish Habitat Action Plan—www.fishhabitat.org

NatureServe Explorer—www.natureserve.org

Ohio Department of Natural Resources—www.wildlife.ohiodnr.gov

USGS Fact Sheets—www.search.usgs.gov

International Union of Concerned Naturalists—www.iucnredlist.org

Kentucky Department of Fish and Wildlife Resources—www.kdfwr.state.ky.us

Encyclopedia of Life—www.eol.org

GLOSSARY

Aestivate / Aestivation—Dormant state of inactivity usually brought on by hot, dry conditions. The opposite of hibernation, which is a winter-time dormancy.

Amphipod—A Crustacean of the order Amphipoda. Includes the freshwater shrimps.

Anadromous—Ascending into freshwater rivers to spawn.

Annelid / Annalida—A class of invertebrate organisms commonly known as worms.

Anuran—A member of the amphibian order Anura (the frogs and toads).

Arboreal—Pertaining to trees.

Arthropod—A member of the invertebrate phylum Arthropoda.

Aspen Parkland—An open or semi-open area (usually grassland) that is intermingled with groves of Aspen.

Barbel—A long "whisker-like" appendage orginating near the mouth of fishes, often sensory.

Barrens—Open areas within normally forested or brushy habitats.

Benthic—Pertaining to the bottom of a stream or lake.

Bivalve—An organism of the phylum Molluska (mollusks) or Branchiopoda having a shell consisting of two halves.

Boreal—Northern.

Borrow Pit—Shallow ditches and ponds created by road construction when earth is "borrowed" from a nearby area to build up road beds.

Buteo—A hawk belonging to the genus Buteo. Also known as the "Broad-winged Hawks."

Cache—The act of storing or hiding food for future use.

Carapace—The top half of the shell of a turtle.

Carnivore—A meat eater.

Caudal—Pertaining to the tail.

Chromosone—Long strand of proteins and DNA found within the nucleus of a cell.

Circumpolar—Literally, around the poles. Usually used in reference to the geographic range of an organism that is found throughout the northern hemisphere.

Cloaca—A common opening for reproductive and excretory functions in an organism. Typical for all animals except mammals.

Congeneric—Belonging to the same genus.

Conspecific—Belonging to the same species.

Contiguous—In contact with or adjoining.

Copepod—A group of tiny crustaceans belonging to the suborder Copapoda. Many are microscopic and aquatic and are important food for tiny fishes and other small aquatic organisms.

CRP—Conservation Reserve Program.

Crustacean—A member of the class Crustacea. A class of Arthropod organisms that includes the crayfish, lobsters, crabs, shrimps, barnacles, copepods, and water fleas.

Cryptic—Pertaining to concealment.

Dipteran—An insect of the order Diptera. Includes flies, mosquitos, gnats, and midges.

Disjunct—Not attached to or not adjoining.

Dessicate / Dissication—Dry out.

Diurnal—Pertaining to day. Being active by day.

Dorsal—The top or back of an organism.

Dorso-ventral—The region between the side and the belly of an organism, or along the lower side adjacent to the belly.

Echolocate / Echolocation—The use of sound waves to navigate or move about, as in bats.

Ecoregion—A large unit of land or water containing a geographically distinct assemblage of species, natural communities, and environmental conditions.

Ecotone—The region where one or more habitats converge.

Embryo—A young animal that is developing from a fertilized egg. Embryonic stage ends at birth or hatching.

Endemic—Native to a particular area.

Endotherm / Endothermic—A organism that regulates its body tempaerature internally. Warm blooded.

Ephemeral—Fleeting. Temporary.

Extirpated—No longer found within a given area.

Extant—Still present. Opposite of extirpated.

Fecund / Fecundity—Capable of producing abundant offspring.

Fin Rays—The bony structures that support the membranes of a fishes fin.

Fossorial—Burrowing or living in underground burrows.

Gastropod—A class of the animal phylum Molluska. Includes snails and slugs.

Herbaceous—A type of flowering plant which does not develop woody tissue.

Holarctic—The circumpolar region that includes North America, Europe, and Asia.

Homogeneous—Of the same kind.

Insectivorus—Insect eating.

Invertivorous—Feeding on invertebrates.

Intergrade—An organism which possesses morphological characteristics that are intermediate between two distinctly different forms.

Irruptive—The sudden movement of animals from one portion of their range to another, often very distant portion of their range. As in when Snowy Owls occasionally move down from the Arctic region into the southern half of North America.

Isopod—An order of Crustaceans that includes the familiar pillbugs.

Kames—Hills or ridges formed by the deposition of sand and gravels from glaciers.

KDFWR—Kentucky Department of Fish and Wildlife Resources.

Keeled Scales—The presence of a small ridge down the middle of the dorsal scales on snakes.

Lentic—Non-flowing bodies of water, lakes, swamps, ponds, etc.

Mandible—The lower jaw of an animal or the bill of a bird.

Marine—Pertaining to living in a salt water environment.

Mast—Seeds produced by plants in a deciduous forest. Usually means the cumulative production of acorns, nuts, berries, seeds, etc., which are widely utilized by wildlife as food.

Melanistic—A predominance of the dark pigment known as melanin. The opposite of Albinistic.

Mesic—Damp or moist.

Metabolic / Metabolism—The sum of the chemical activity that occurs within a living organism. Usually relates to the digestion of food and utilization of food compounds within the body.

Metamorphose—Change of the body. Usually refers to the change from an immature stage to a more mature stage (as in a tadpole to a frog).

Metamorphosis—Abrupt physical change of body form.

Millinery Trade—The sale of bird feathers.

Molt—The shedding of and renewal (replacement) of skin, hair, or feathers.

Moraine—Large mass of earth, sand, gravels, and rock bulldozed by glacial movement. Moraines usually accumulate along the sides and in the front of glaciers.

Morphology—The study of the body form, shape, and structure of organisms, including colors or patterns.

Muskeg—A Sphagnum bog occuring the boreal (northern) regions of North America.

Neotropical—Pertaining to the tropical regions of the western hemisphere.

Nuptial—Pertaining to breeding.

Obligate—In biology, occuring within a restricted environment.

ODNR—Ohio Department of Natural Resources.

Omnivore—Eats both plant and animal matter.

Ontogenetic—Related to the development or age of an organism.

Opercle flap—The bony structure on the side of a fish's head that covers the gills. Also sometimes called gill cover.

Organism—A living thing.

Orthopteran—A member of the insect order Orthoptera. Includes such well known insects as crickets and grasshoppers.

Ossification—The formation of bone.

Palearctic—The geographic region that includes Europe and northern Asia.

Parthenogenesis—The development of an ovum (egg) without fertilization.

Passage Migrant—Refers to birds that merely migrate

through an area without staying any appreciable amount of time.

Pectoral—Pertaining to or located in the chest area.

Pelage—Fur.

Pelvic—Pertaing to or located in the region of the pelvis (hips).

Phylogeny—The evolutionary relationships and/or evolutionary history of organisms.

Physiography—Refers to the natural features of a landscape, e.g., mountians, rivers, plains, etc.

Piscivorous—Fish eating.

Plastron—The ventral (bottom) portion of a turtles shell.

Plumage—The feathers of a bird.

Polychaete worms—Annelid worms (Phylum Annelida) belonging to the class Polychaeta. Mostly marine but some are freshwater.

Precocious—Having adult (or highly developed) characteristics in the young.

Precocial—being highly precocious.

Predaceous—Feeding on other animals, being a predator.

Piscivorous—Fish eating.

Puddle Duck—Ducks belonging to the genus *Anas*.

Prehensile—Grasping. As in a prehensile tail that is able to wrap around and grasp a tree limb.

"Reclamation"—the act of restoring some semblance of natural habitat onto land ravaged by activites such as strip mining.

Reclamation usually involves sowing wild grasses and planting of tree seedlings.

Regenerative—Refers to the ability to repair or replace damage or destroyed tissues or structures.

Riparian—Pertaining to the bank of a stream or river.

Sexual Dimorphism—Morphological differences between the sexes.

Species of Concern—A species or subspecies which might become threatened in Ohio under continued or increased stress.

Species of Special Interest—A species that occurs periodically and is capable of breeding in Ohio.

Successional Woodlands / Areas—Landscape areas (usually woodlands) that are undergoing change from an early stage of development to an older stage. As in woodlands regenerating following logging operations.

Sympatric / Sympatrically—A condition where more than one species occurs in the same or overlapping area or habitat.

Taiga—A type of forest occuring in the far north. Usually dominated by dwarfed spruces.

Topography—The configuration of the land surface. Literally, "the lay of the land."

Troglodyte—Cave dwelling. Usually refers to organisms that live in caves.

Turbid—Water that is opaque due to the high amount of suspended silt particles.

Tympanum—The circular ear structure on the side of the head of frogs and toads.

USFandWS—Acronym for the United States Fish and Wildlife Service.

Ventral—Pertaining to the belly or bottom side of an organism.

Vernal—Pertaining to spring. Also frequently used to describe temporary ponds and pools that hold water only during the wet season.

Vestigial—A rudimentary structure. Usually a remnant, degenerative structure that was once (in the evolutionary history of the organism) a fully functioning structure.

Xeric—Dry.

Zygote—A fertilized egg that has not yet begun to divide.

INDEX OF COMMON NAMES

PHOTO CREDITS

John R. MacGregor
Least Weasel, Allegheny Woodrat, Southern Bog Lemming, Meadow Jumping Mouse, Masked Shrew, Silver-haired Bat, Eastern Red Bat, Hoary Bat, Eastern Small-footed Bat, Northern Bat, Northern Redback Salamander, Four-toed Salamander, Green Salamander, Hellbender.

Matthew R. Thomas
Eastern Sand Darter, Blackside Darter, Channel Darter, Slenderhead Darter, Variegate Darter, Banded Darter, Fantail Darter (MandF), Skipjack Herring, Northern Madtom, Tadpole Madtom, Stonecat, Spotted Sucker, Quillback, River Redhorse, Streamlined Chub, Silver Chub, Pugnose Minnow, Mississippi Silvery Minnow, Bullhead Minnow, Silver Shiner, Rosyface Shiner, Mimic Shiner.

David Speiser www.lilibirds.com
Sedge Wren, Wilson's Warbler (M), Mourning Warbler, Connecticut Warbler, Golden-winged Warbler (M), Alder Flycatcher, Yellow-bellied Flycatcher, Snow Bunting, Northern Shrike, Surf Scoters, Long-tailed Duck (MandF), Black Scoters, Northern Shrike.

Don Martin Bird Photograpy
Olive-sided Flycatcher, Willow Flycatcher, Least Flycatcher, Ruby-crowned Kinglet (M), Kirtland's Warbler, Clay-colored Sparrow, Henslow's Sparrow, Snowy Owl (F), Virginia Rail, Western Sandpiper, Baird's Sandpiper.

Konrad Schmidt
Iowa Darter, Least Darter, Silver Redhorse, Common Shiner, River Shiner, Blackchin Shiner, Bigmouth Shiner, Spottail Shiner, Ghost Shiner, Trout Perch, Rainbow Smelt.

Brian Zimmerman
Spotted Darter (M), Tippecanoe Darter (F), Lake Chubsucker, Highfin Carpsucker, Popeye Shiner, Channel Shiner, Banded Killifish.
Brook Stickleback
Western Tongue-tied Minnow

James Kiser
Evening Bat, Northern Short-tailed Shrew, Bluebreast Darter.

Phil Myers
Meadow Vole, Smokey Shrew.

Uland Thomas
Mooneye

Cheryl Tanner
Eastern Harvest Mouse

Jeffrey Offermann
Long-tailed Weasel

Sterling Daniels
Hairy-tailed Mole

Don Brockmeir
Blue Grosbeak (F)

Dave Frymire
Brook Silverside

T. Travis Brown
Mottled Sculpin

Phil Myers, IV
Badger

Jeff Poklen
Glaucus Gull, Little Gull

Nate Tessler
Pink Salmon, White Perch

Wayne T. Helfrich
Star-nosed Mole

James H. Harding
Butler's Garter Snake

Tom Murray
Goshawk

*all other photographs are by Scott Shupe.

ABOUT THE AUTHOR

Naturalist Scott Shupe began his professional career in 1971 at the famed Ross Allen Reptile Institute and Venom Laboratory in Silver Springs, FL. He later worked at the St. Augustine Alligator Farm in St. Augustine, FL and with Reptile Gardens in Rapid City, SD. From 1992 to 2002 he enjoyed an association with the Knight and Hale Game Call company in Cadiz, KY where he served as director of The Woods and Wetlands Wildlife Center, a private zoo/nature center. He is the founder and original owner of the Natural History Educational Company, an organization of professional naturalists that provided live-animal wildlife education programs to thousands of schools throughout the United States.

He has served as a host and narrator for wildlife-related television programming (In the Wild-Outdoor Channel), produced educational life science videos, and has appeared as a guest naturalist on a number of public television programs and satellite networks. He has been recognized for his contributions to conservation education by the US Fish and Wildlife Service, named naturalist of the year by the Kentucky Society of Naturalists, awarded the Jesse Stuart Media Award for his educational video productions, and received the Environmental Stewardship Award from the Kentucky Environmental Quality Commission. Since 1987 he has contracted annually with the Kentucky Department of Parks to provide naturalist programming in state parks across Kentucky. Since 2005, he has enjoyed an association with the Kentucky Reptile Zoo and Venom Laboratory, acting as an outreach ambassador for educational programming.

He has written for outdoor and nature periodicals and scientific journals and his wildlife photographs have appeared in dozens of nature magazines and books. This is his fourth book on nature and wildlife and his third book for Skyhorse Publishing. He also authored *US Guide to Venomous Snakes and their Mimics*, *Venomous Snakes of the World*, *A Handbook for Use by US Amphibious Forces*, and *Life List of North American Birds*. A professional naturalist with nearly forty years experience in a wide array of nature interpretation, wildlife tourism, education, writing, and wildlife photography and videography, he currently lives on a ninety-acre private wildlife refuge Graves County, Kentucky just outside his hometown of Farmington.

Contact Scott Shupe at kscottshupe@gmail.com.